D1451796

The Wild and Free Cookbook

by Tom Squier

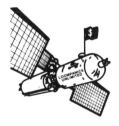

Loompanics Unlimited
Port Townsend, Washington

The Wild And Free Cookbook

© 1996 by Tom Squier

Published by:
Loompanics Unlimited
PO Box 1197
Port Townsend, WA 98368
Loompanics Unlimited is a division of Loompanics Enterprises, Inc.

Cover design by Shaun Hayes-Holgate
Cover Color by Jim and Mary Woodring with Justin Hampton
Illustrations by Michael Killman
and John Megahan/The Technical Sketch

ISBN 1-55950-128-6
Library of Congress Card Catalog 95-79302

Contents

Dedication

This book is dedicated to the memory of Martha Raye with love and affection. I had the honor of being one of her honorary pallbearers when we laid her to rest. God bless you, Maggie. We'll all miss you!

Thomas K. "Tom" Squier is a retired U.S. Army Special Forces Master Sergeant who taught classes in military subjects and survival skills at the John F. Kennedy Special Warfare Center and School in Fort Bragg, North Carolina, the Jungle Warfare School in Panama, and many other places around the world. Squier holds an M.S. in herbology and a doctorate in naturopathic medicine. He has appeared on numerous radio AND TV talk shows, and is one of North America's most highly respected citizen environmentalists.

"Every Special Forces soldier and outdoorsman should have this book!"

Col Pete Stenhard

Acknowledgements

I really have to thank my wife, Frances, for all her help and support throughout the writing of this book. There were times, I admit, I almost felt like calling her what Newt called Hillary. But when I was sick, or in pain, she encouraged me and when I was feeling good she called from her office to ask if I was working on my book. I want to thank her and Jessica and Mandy for trying my recipes and giving me some of theirs to share with you. Thanks, ladies. Thanks to Tom, Jr. for his support and for being the person I tried to set an example for.

I have to thank my agent Victoria Sanders, of the Victoria Sanders Literary Agency in New York, for all the hours she has put in on my behalf and the support and encouragement she has offered all along, and for doing the leg work so I could write.

I want to thank especially my grandparents for helping raise me with a love for the environment. Even though they are gone, I feel their guiding hands constantly. I hope that they are proud of the man I have become.

And I want to thank all my friends who contributed recipes, poems and quotes for their time and support. Thank you all.

I also owe a special debt of gratitude to Janet Robertson. She is the manager of Aberdeen Florist and Garden Center and has saved me a couple of times when I was out of town and called to have just the right flowers sent to Frances for special occasions I couldn't be there for. She is also the computer guru who saved me on more than one occasion when my keyboard was holding me hostage. Thanks, Janet!

Frances Squier

And I am indebted to Frances for keeping up the yard when I was no longer able to do it and allowing me time to cook, study and write. I planted a lot of plants in our gardens over the years and she cares for them now and keeps the limbs, pinecones and needles policed up, grass mowed and the place looking great enough to draw plenty of compliments. I would be afraid to guess how many miles and hours she has logged on that mower seat. In the summertime when it doesn't get dark until 10 o'clock, working in the yard and gardens is like a second job with her.

I cannot ignore all the hours my daughter Amanda spent typing recipes for me. Thanks, I know you're busy.

Author's Introduction

I wrote this second edition of my wild foods cookbook because the first one sold out after all the road kill publicity, and because I had more things to say and more recipes to share. As I stated in the first edition, I wanted to share some of my favorite recipes with my friends, new and old. I wanted to share my concern for the environment and love for the earth with everybody, and I wanted to write a cookbook that would be interesting enough to get the whole family reading it.

I am sure that there are some things that will have certain family members going, "Oh Yuck!" but I believe that everybody can find some new recipe they like, even if they substitute chicken, beef or pork for the game meats.

I hunt and fish to eat, and because I do, I believe that it is right to do this, but I do it with a respect for the Earth I live on and the other life I share it with.

Foreword

When the nation reawakened to the joys of nature more than two decades ago, Tom Squier did not reawaken. Thomas K. Squier was born with the awareness of nature, what it has to offer as food, medicine and other uses that have enriched his life.

He learned from his people in the mountains of North Carolina; he took that knowledge with him and learned more in service in the U.S. Army. In every post, in the states and overseas, he added to his own survival techniques and offered them in courses taught to those who might be lost one day in a hostile land.

In his book, Tom shares many ideas and stories that make him a unique teacher, lecturer and newspaper columnist.

No true survivalist, or wild food enthusiast, can ever have too many reference books. In *The Wild and Free Cookbook*, Tom has his own special approach. I like his special way of relaying his experiences, his attention to details and his love for what his native land has to offer.

Edelene C. Wood, President
National Wild Foods Association
Parkersburg, WV 26104

Wild Foods Are Good Foods!

A lot of American dollars are wasted each year — no, each day! — on megadoses of vitamins. One of the most popular vitamins for us to spend our hard-earned bucks on is ascorbic acid, better known to most of us as vitamin C. It has definitely been proven that vitamin C will prevent scurvy which manifests itself in the form of skin lesions, hemorrhage of the mucous membranes and generally poor health. It has also been suggested that ingesting large amounts of this vitamin will help prevent colds, promote healing and fight cancer. However, I say that many of us waste money on too much vitamin C because the body can only use so much and the rest is excreted. Megadoses of unused vitamin C result in brightly colored urine. Because vitamin C is also known to fight infection, it is therefore a good idea to meet the government's minimum required daily amount of 70 milligrams. Smokers need more.

We seem to set our standards by orange juice. 100 grams ($3^1/_2$ ounces) of orange juice contain approximately 50 milligrams of vitamin C in the form of ascorbic acid. An equal amount of the raw leaves of one of our commonest weeds, dock, or its cousin, sheep sorrel, contains 119 milligrams. The same amount of raw black currants contains 200 milligrams. One of the most popular Southern greens, poke sallet, contains 136 milligrams in its raw form, but can't be eaten raw. Even cooked, poke beats orange juice with 82 milligrams of vitamin C.

Strawberry leaf tea contains so much vitamin C that Johns Hopkins University at first accused Euell Gibbons of faking his test results. Other very high sources are cayenne peppers, wild mustard and amaranth greens.

We have always been taught to eat carrots to keep our vision in tip-top shape, and the source we have been taught to seek out is carrots. We measure vitamin A, or retinol, in international units (IU), and our daily requirement is said to be around 5,000 IU. To be technically specific, many plants contain large amounts of beta-carotene, which is called pro-vitamin A, and which readily converts in metabolism to vitamin A. Fortunately, vitamin A is fat-soluble, so for most Americans the excess amounts are stored in the body's insulating layer and we shouldn't need extra retinol in the diet. The highly touted carrots contain 40,920 IUs per 100 grams. This is obviously much more than we need, so even though some wild foods don't compare, they are more than adequate. Raw black or red cherries contain 4,170 IUs per 100 grams. 1,360 IUs are found in 100 milligrams of cranberries, dandelion greens in 100 milligram servings contain a whopping 63,500 IUs, and cress or "creasey greens" contain 29,960 IUs. Even better for us than spinach, lamb's quarters contain 52,620 IUs of vitamin A per $3^1/_2$-ounce serving when eaten raw. Other very high sources are wild mustard, raw plums, purslane and swamp cabbage from the palm tree.

Many of us add another vitamin — E — to our diet because of the benefits it supposedly has for our hair, muscles and overall health. Also known as tocopherol, vitamin E draws attention most when there is a deficiency such as atrophied muscles, weakness, and vascular abnormalities. Vitamin E is also fat-soluble, so it stores in the body and is readily available in most of our diets in the form of vegetable oils, grains and cereals. Commercially, tocopherols are used to prevent rancification of fats, particularly vegetable oils and their products. The toasted seeds of plantain and especially the oils of walnuts and other nuts are high in vitamin E, as are the grains of various wild grasses.

The B vitamins are used to aid metabolic processes in the body and keep the body running efficiently. Thiamine, or vitamin B1, functions in the enzyme system to help the body convert carbohydrates into energy. The recommended daily intake is at least 1 milligram for women and up to 1.4 milligrams for men. Raw peanuts or "goober peas" meet this demand, but there aren't many wild peanut patches around. However, another nut that isn't a nut — the pine nut — contains 1.28 milligrams per 100 grams. Wild rice with its bran intact contains 2.26 milligrams per 100 grams or more — or nearly twice our required daily need. Sunflower seeds are also high in B1 at 1.96 milligrams per 100 grams.

What we all want in our diet in this country it seems, is protein — that's why there are so many hamburger joints around! We need protein in our diet; we just usually get too much of it, and that could be a contributing factor to America's high cancer rates. Some people object to eating red meat for humane reasons — they want no animal flesh in their diet. Others, like myself, don't want to take in all those growth hormones, steroids and antibiotics along with God knows what else is force-fed to market meat animals. I don't, however, want all my protein to come from nuts and tofu, so I thank the Creator for the many tasty critters that populate the earth.

The USDA Handbook Number 8, *Handbook of Foods*, rates 100 grams of "regular ground" beef as containing 17.9 grams of protein. Terrapin turtle meat contains a little more protein at 18.6 grams, while mature soybeans contain twice as much at 34.1 grams per 100 grams. Other wilder sources of protein, though, are 19.4 grams per 100 grams for beechnuts, 12.6 for hazelnuts, 13.2 for hickory nuts, 31.1 for pine nuts and 20.5 for walnuts. Of course, nearly all dried nuts and beans are high in protein, but the best and more preferred sources seem to be wild meats. 100 grams of venison provides 21 grams of protein, but more easily obtained possum rates higher at 30.2, raccoon at 29.2 and frog legs at 16.4.

Wild foods, particularly properly gathered plant foods, are often more nutritious for us than store-bought vegetables because they frequently provide us with trace elements and minerals not available from commercially grown crops, particularly the hydroponically grown lettuce and tomatoes in the winter markets. Reports reveal that some "fresh" produce has been in cold storage for a year or more! Wild meats tend to be less cholesterol-dense, except for squabs and other baby birds who are fed a "milk" that the parents regurgitate.

Both wild plants and game meats lack the chemical additives and insecticides necessary to make raising crops and animals economically feasible. An extra benefit is the good we do our cardiovascular and respiratory systems by going out and gathering these wild foods. *THE KEY TO THE SAFE USE OF WILD PLANTS FOR FOOD OR MEDICINE IS POSITIVE AND ACCURATE IDENTIFICATION.* Always keep that in mind and you'll be safe gathering your own wild foods!

Karen Sherwood's Spiced Cattail Cakes

1 cup cattail pollen
1 tsp. wild ginger root, grated
1 tsp. dried spice bush leaves or berries
2 eggs, beaten
2 tbsps. oil
1 cup cattail root or other flour
1¼ cups spice bush tea or water
¼ cup maple syrup
additional oil for griddle

Mix all ingredients until well blended. Pour the batter onto a hot, oiled griddle or skillet. Cook until golden, flipping just once like a pancake. These are great with a little bit of warmed wild blueberries or maple syrup.

Remember when you gather cattails that they are bad about absorbing toxins from the waters they are growing in, particularly heavy metals, and that all water plants should be cooked or disinfected nowadays to prevent the forager from becoming a host to the parasite *Giardia lamblia*.

My friend Ron Hardt was a Ranger in the Army and taught survival, only to practice a survival lifestyle when he couldn't take any more of the Army's politics. He and his wife Heather eat a lot of wild foods, but don't think it is necessary to practice being miserable. That will come naturally when the time is right! Heather told me this next recipe "is an old standby." Cattail pollen is gathered by placing a paper or plastic bag over the male flower head when the time is right and shaking the golden dust or flour into the sack.

Heather Hardt's Cattail Muffins

$^1/_2$ tsp. salt	1 cup whole wheat flour
1 egg, beaten	1 cup cattail pollen
$^1/_4$ cup oil	$^1/_2$ cup maple syrup or honey
$1^1/_4$ cups milk	2 tsps. baking soda

Combine dry ingredients. Combine wet ingredients. Mix them together. Pour into greased muffin tins or paper cups. Bake 20 minutes at 400 degrees.

Karen Sherwood's Cattail Shoot Salad

4 cups young cattail shoots	$^1/_2$ cup pine nuts or walnuts
4 wild garlic bulbs	$^1/_2$ cup mayonnaise or vinaigrette
1 cup wild leeks or onions	$^1/_2$ cup dried wild carrot seed
$^1/_2$ cup watercress	

Combine all ingredients and toss well. Add dressing of your choice and mix well. Let sit in fridge one hour to let flavors mingle before serving.

I like this recipe, but I suggest adding daylily shoots or tubers, evening primrose roots or Jerusalem artichoke roots as the season permits.

To make a good dressing, Karen suggests the addition of 4 wild onion or garlic bulbs and 4 hot chile peppers to a quart of apple cider vinegar and letting it age long enough ahead of time — about two weeks — so that the flavors will merge.

Use Up Last Season's Game Harvest Now!

If we had to have a subtitle for this chapter, I guess it would be "waste not, want not!" or something like that, because as people start looking for freezer space for the fresh vegetables of the season, or fish, or whatever new game animal is in season, they begin in many cases by throwing out last season's game. It is a shame how much meat is wasted in this manner or because that special cut of meat had been saved for "just the right occasion" and then discarded because it was freezer burned, or to make room for something fresher.

There are several ways to use the long-stored meat that don't entail converting it to dog food or crab bait. First, let me go back and with 20/20 hindsight tell you how to solve the problem of freezer burned meat in many cases. Use the old Boy Scout motto, "Be Prepared," and if you are a hunter, or have friends who hunt, or are related to a hunter, and are likely to be putting some game in the freezer, be ready for it before you get it.

As hunting season approaches, have plenty of freezer paper, aluminum foil and Ziplock bags on hand. Meat that is properly wrapped will keep a lot better than meat that is just thrown in an empty bread bag and frozen because that's all there is on hand. I will have to say that I have also successfully tried a short term storage method that many (wives) may not like. I have frozen whole squirrels, rabbits and other small animals, especially roadkilled ones, intact with their fur on. This is quick, and prevents freezer burn if they are used in a short time. This is not totally out in left field as far as ideas go, because anglers often freeze fish whole in containers of water (like a milk carton) to prevent freezer burn and flavor loss.

Use some labeling method that tells you what the meat is and when it was frozen, so you can use it in a timely manner. Use freezer burned meat in recipes with lots of gravy or sauce, in chopped meat dishes, in highly flavored dishes like curries, and in soups and stews. Depending on how you intend to cook the freezer burned meat finally, sometimes it helps to soak it in milk, tomato juice or wine. Because freezer-burned meat tends to be tough, it often helps to go to the health food store and get some papaya juice to soak it in for a little while. This works well for tough meat cuts or old animals in general because of chemicals in the papaya that are used in commercial meat tenderizers. It provides some flavor and will tenderize even the toughest meat. Don't leave meat too long in the papaya juice, though, or it will rival Gerber's strained baby food for tenderness!

Basically any type of game meat can be used in spaghetti sauces, burgers and sausage, pot-pies and dumpling dishes, or in cold salads. You can cut the meat off the bone before cooking it, but it is usually easier to boil the meat and then de-bone it. That way, you can also use the water as "stock" for soup or other recipes or in cooking rice. You can also cut the meat off the bone to use it in highly spiced dishes such as chili, barbecue, quiche, Mexican dishes, Oriental stir-frys, in homemade ravioli or in omelets in the mornings. Just don't waste it!

Game In A Garden

2 cups cooked game meat	lettuce or other greens
hard-boiled eggs	tomato wedges
vinegar	olive oil
herbs	

I don't specify which herbs to use because you can pick your favorites — basil, mint, rosemary or mixed herbs — and combine them with equal quantities of oil and vinegar or with just vinegar alone.

Heat and then set aside to allow the flavors to build. Make a bed of chopped lettuce, add tomato wedges, chopped hard-boiled egg and sprinkle with chopped, cooked venison, dove or quail, rabbit or squirrel or whatever game meat you have on hand — even fish. I like to marinate the already cooked meat sometimes and broil it ever-so-slightly before putting it on the salad. Then sprinkle liberally with the herbed vinegar and oil while it is still hot.

Game Burgers Francais

1 pound ground or chopped game meat	**$^1/_2$ cup seasoned French or Italian bread crumbs**
1 egg, beaten	**salt and pepper to taste**
3 tbsp. tomato sauce	**1 tsp. Dijon mustard**
2 cloves garlic, minced	**$^1/_4$ tsp. each thyme, mint, chervil, parsley, basil**

Combine all ingredients and form into burgers. Grill or broil them until done the way you like them. Serve on French bread which has been rubbed with garlic and butter and grilled slightly.

The herbs don't have to be exact. In fact, you can change the flavor of the burgers by changing the herbs you use, and by leaving out the French mustard. For Mexican-style burgers use chili powder, cumin and cilantro; use a five-spice blend or star anise, fennel, cinnamon, ginger and black pepper for Oriental burgers; and for Italian burgers add more tomato sauce, oregano, marjoram, and savory. Leave out the mint and chervil which are more French-style herbs. Use garlic and imagination liberally in all your burgers (and other dishes).

Western-Style Game Omelet

1 cup chopped, cooked game meat	**8 eggs, beaten**
$^1/_2$ cup milk	**$^1/_4$ cup butter**
$^1/_4$ tsp. smoke flavored salt	**salt and pepper to taste**
$^1/_4$ cup bell pepper, chopped	**$^1/_4$ cup onion, chopped**
	1 cup cheese, shredded

Combine eggs, milk, salt and pepper, mixing well. Sauté bell pepper and onion in butter and remove. For each omelet, melt butter to cover bottom of pan. Pour in $^1/_4$ of the egg mixture when a drop of water will sizzle in the butter. Tilt pan back and forth to allow mixture to cook evenly. Add $^1/_4$ of each of the ingredients — bell pepper and onions, meat and cheese — and finish cooking to taste.

There is just no limit to what you can do with leftover game meat. If you enjoy quiches, you know the flavor combinations are limitless. Combine shredded game meat of any type with cooked rice or noodles and tomato sauce and herbs, and stuff bell peppers or large tomatoes with the mixture. Top with cheese and bake until done to your liking. Make game barbecue by cooking the meat, shredding it either by hand or in a food processor, adding your favorite homemade or commercial barbecue sauce and marinating a day in the refrigerator before serving.

Clean out that old game meat from the freezer and use it now rather than throwing it away later. Fix "beef bourguignon" or some other exotic dish and invite friends or relatives without revealing the source of the "beef."

Here is one more idea for what you can do with all the leftover game meat in your freezer. Give it to a volunteer fire department so they can make a big Brunswick stew and sell it by the plate as a fund-raiser. These guys (and gals) need all the help they can get, along with pats on the back so they can do the best job possible. These unpaid professionals just don't get enough credit for the job they do and the sacrifices they make. Not to mention having to go back to school so they can learn to risk their lives for us!

Wild Greens "In Season" In Spring

Many people look forward to the emergence of the wild greens that signal an end to winter and beginning of spring. In the past, these wild greens provided a welcome change from the winter's diet and acted as a tonic for the body, bringing a flood of cleansing agents and much needed vitamins and minerals.

Poke, *Phytolacca americana*, is one of those early spring wild greens that first "pokes" its head out of the ground on the slopes with an Eastern exposure. Look for poke by locating the large, ghostly white skeletons of last year's growth. The large perennial roots will provide about six weeks' worth of shoots once they begin growth, if they are kept cut. After that, they should be permitted to continue normal growth to sustain the plant for the future. Poke should not be eaten raw because it contains chemicals that create an intense gastric disturbance — it makes people very sick to the stomach.

Country people know this and they boil it in three changes of water to avoid problems. The novice weed-eater is sometimes fooled by the name "poke salad," which is really a corruption of the Old English word "sallet," which translates as "cooked greens." Euell Gibbons said that poke "is probably the best known and most widely used vegetable in America." But you have to know how to gather and prepare it properly for it to be safe.

When gathering any wild plant for food, be sure to forage and collect away from busy roadsides where it might be contaminated by automotive exhaust emissions which are filled with heavy metals and other chemicals readily absorbed by plants. Avoid areas where pesticides and other chemicals have been sprayed. This rules out golf courses for the most part for the forager. Look for early poke shoots and collect those that are six to eight inches tall. Don't use any plants already showing red in the stem or leaves, and cut off the pink end near the roots when you break off shoots. This is a danger signal with poke!

The folk uses of poke include making tinctures from the roots for arthritis and rheumatism, dye from the berries and drying the berries, as arthritis "pills." This is not a recommended practice! The roots are extremely toxic, and the Herb Trade Association in an effort to eliminate potential poisonings has stated: "Poke root is toxic and should not be sold as an herbal beverage or food, or in any other form which could threaten the health of the uninformed consumer." In 1989, three of my students at the Army's survival school who didn't pay attention in class had to be medivaced by helicopter to Womack Army Hospital after eating these roots. They were lucky that nausea and vomiting with severe diarrhea and cramping were their only problems! Other less fortunate weed-eaters have died.

The young shoots, though, according to some people, are better than asparagus and can be prepared in a variety of ways. However you fix them, be sure to cook them in at least two changes of water. With experience, people learn their own tolerance for poke, but it should always be parboiled to be on the safe side. One good way to fix poke is to cook the young shoots and then add them to a cream sauce which is served over toast. Or they can be just buttered and eaten. I like the barely opened leaves prepared Indian style. Boil them, change the water, and boil them again. Add a little bacon drippings (if desired), a post-Columbian seasoning, and 2 or 3 minced cloves of wild garlic, readily available at the same time. Then add a tablespoon or so to taste of cedar or hickory ashes and simmer until tender. Drain and pour a little vinegar over them and just a little butter. To be authentic, use butter whipped from walnut oil or other nut oils. When you use vinegar, always stick with the apple cider vinegar, not white distilled vinegar. Apple cider vinegar contains malic acid which provides many nutrients not available in distilled vinegar. Some nutritionists even say that white vinegar is capable of destroying red blood cells, leading to anemia in extreme situations.

Also in abundance in the spring is the little ground-covering chickweed, *Stellaria* species, in several forms. There are evergreen and tender chickweeds, and their flavor varies. You can find "Stellaria" listed as an ingredient in many weight loss formulas because it is believed to help dissolve fat in the body as it is high in organic nitrates. Whether it works or not, it is filled with nutrients. Chickweed is eaten raw or steamed, added to salads, soups and fritters. Fresh chickweed salad is delicious when gathered, rinsed and dressed with your favorite dressing. Let it marinate in the refrigerator a while before serving.

A nice dressing is made by combining 3 teaspoons of honey with half a cup of apple cider vinegar (or cider, if you like it sweeter), a tablespoon of sunflower oil and two tablespoons of finely chopped sunflower seeds or pine nuts.

The "fiddleheads" of bracken and other ferns will be drawing many foragers into the woods, too. The bracken fern, *Pteridium aquilinum*, becomes inedible as it matures and develops a toxin. Only the tightly curled and unopened fronds, the "fiddleheads," can be eaten. They, too, should be cooked in a change of water if eaten boiled or sautéed in butter. They are also good as ingredients in soups, stir-frys and quiches. Other ferns are eaten in other parts of the country, but again only the "fiddleheads" are consumed. There is a small industry in Vermont pickling the fiddleheads and marketing them commercially.

We have to mention dandelions, *Taraxacum officinale*, because they are really growing well by spring thaw and the best greens are harvested before blooms appear. As the plant matures, it develops a high latex content, seen in the form of the milky sap. The Spanish word for dandelion is *amargon* which means "bitter," while one French name, *pis-en-lit*, means "pee the bed." The scientific name, of course, translates as "official cure for disorders," referring to its wide use throughout history as a medicine.

Dandelion has long been a favorite cleansing and tonic spring green, and is known among herbalists as a liver tonic and blood cleanser. It is also a diuretic. The greens are high in vitamins A and C as well as calcium and other minerals. The flowers are used as they appear, to make dandelion wine, but the leaves are eaten raw in salads, cooked as a green or brewed into a tea. According to the *Lawrence Review of Natural Products*, this tea causes drowsiness in some individuals. It might be just the thing for bedtime, then, except for the warning contained in the French name. It has also been shown to help restore liver tone and function in heavy drinkers who quit or severely cut back on their alcohol intake. The roots of dandelion are washed, roasted until dry and crisp and then ground into a coffee substitute which is caffeine free and naturally sweet.

Chickweed Salad

1 gallon chickweed, chopped
1 cup wild onion tops and bulb, chopped
$^1/_2$ cup wild mustard flowers
1 cup wild mushrooms, chopped
$^1/_4$ cup honey
$^1/_4$ cup sunflower oil
$^1/_4$ cup apple cider vinegar

Combine chickweed with onion, mushrooms and mustard flowers. Shake oil, vinegar and honey together and drizzle over salad.

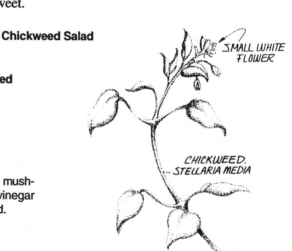

SMALL WHITE FLOWER

CHICKWEED.
STELLARIA MEDIA

Fiddlehead Cream Soup

2 cups fiddleheads
2 cups chicken stock or water
1 tbsp. walnut oil
4 tbsps. butter
1 cup heavy cream
2 tbsps. white wine (optional)

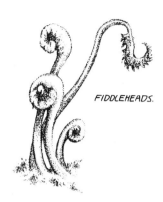

FIDDLEHEADS.

Sauté fiddleheads in butter and nut oil for 10 minutes over medium-low heat and add the chicken stock. Bring to a boil, cover and reduce heat, and simmer 20 minutes more. Add cream and simmer 10 more minutes, adding wine (if desired) at this time.

River Lady's Grannie's Poke Recipe

2 quarts poke leaves and stems
salt to taste
1 tsp. brown sugar

½ cup bacon drippin's
3 hard-boiled eggs

Cut up stalks and leaves. Bring to a boil and cook 10 minutes, rinse in cool water. Repeat. Bring to a boil again and rinse again. Boil until tender and drain. Pour into a large frying pan and add salt to taste and bacon drippin's. Add brown sugar and fry until dry, being careful not to burn. Cut up and serve with the top covered with sliced hard-boiled eggs.

Poke stalks can be parboiled and then either made into a delicious pickle with your favorite spices, or a mock rhubarb pie, or they can be rolled in corn meal and fried like okra out of season.

Iris Smith's Poke and Wild Onions

1 gallon poke leaves
drippin's
1 cup wild or green onions, chopped
2-4 ounces salt pork, cubed
salt to taste

Parboil chopped poke leaves in two changes of water. Fry salt pork until browned and sauté onions in pan grease. Add drippin's to taste, salt pork, onions and salt to taste to poke with enough water to cover and simmer 15 minutes more.

My neighbor gave me this recipe above and she modifies it to fix some of the best collards around without the parboiling required for poke greens. Of course, at home, you always serve greens with cornbread and vinegar with hot peppers in it.

Iris Smith
"You better eat your greens"

Reba McEntire's Poke Salad Delight

3 pounds poke greens
1 medium onion, diced
4 tbsps. butter
1 pound ground beef
6 beaten eggs
salt and pepper to taste

Parboil greens in enough water to cover for about 10 minutes, repeating twice. Drain. Brown onions in skillet with 2 tablespoons butter. Add seasoned ground beef and brown over medium heat. Drain off fat. In separate skillet, melt the rest of the butter and scramble the eggs lightly. Fold in poke greens, beef, and mix thoroughly.

There is no doubt that Reba really eats poke salad. She confessed to Ralph Emery in a nationally televised interview that she used to eat mountain oysters by the bucketful as a child. It

Reba McEntire

must be good for you. Look how she turned out!

I like poke greens or stems chopped and added to the chipped beef gravy known as SOS in the service and elsewhere. You can make some mighty tasty meals out of weeds. In the Army survival school, I always taught my students to make soup whenever possible because less of the nutrients were lost compared to other cooking methods, provided the juice was drunk. In Bertha Reppert's book, *A Heritage of Herbs*, we find this tasty recipe:

Weed Soup

2 quarts weeds (Good King Henry,
    lamb's quarters, sorrel, nettles,
    plantain, etc.)
3 onions, minced
1 cup salt pork

5 cups water
2 cups potatoes, diced
2 egg yolks
salt and pepper to taste
herbs to taste

Wash the weeds (one or all in combination) thoroughly and boil twice (except for garden sorrel if used); drain, then throw away the first cooking waters. Crisp the salt pork with the onions in a large pan; add the chopped parboiled weeds, the potatoes, and the 5 cups water. Season with salt and pepper and any herbs your family enjoys (a pinch each of thyme, parsley, rosemary and tarragon is good); simmer until the potatoes are soft. Add the 2 lightly beaten egg yolks slowly at the end of cooking. Serve hot.

As for dandelion recipes, I know of no better source than Dr. Peter Gail, referred to as "The Dandelion Man" in a magazine profile. As tenacious as the dandelions he loves and writes about, he has touted them in many articles and at least two books, *On the Trail of the Yellow-Flowered Earth Nail* and *The Dandelion Celebration*, from which these next recipes come:

Steamed Dandelion with Garlic and Chili Peppers

4-5 quarts fresh dandelion greens
garlic
chili pepper flakes

1 cup water
$^1/_2$ cup extra virgin olive oil
salt and pepper to taste

Clean and finely chop the dandelion greens. Put a maximum of 1 cup water in the bottom of a 6-quart saucepan, insert a steamer rack, and place the dandelion greens on top. Cover the greens with $^1/_2$ cup of 100% pure extra virgin olive oil, 1-2 cloves of garlic, salt, pepper, and chili pepper. Cover and steam until tender. Tip: You don't want too much water because you don't want it to mix with the oil.

Fried Dandelion Blossoms With Honey

fully opened dandelion blossoms
1 cup flour
1 egg, beaten
$^1/_2$ tsp. baking powder

1 cup milk
$^1/_2$ tsp. salt
honey to taste

Choose only the fully opened blossoms, being sure to remove all of the bitter stem (and the green part at the back of the flower). Next, thoroughly combine the milk, egg, flour, baking powder, salt and honey in a bowl. Dip the blooms into batter and drop into hot oil over a medium heat. Fry until golden brown. Remove and drain on absorbent paper. Serve hot or cold.

Peter Gail says, "The beauty of dandelions, however, is that you don't have to buy them, or their products! Dandelions are all around us, all year long, and they are free. So we might as well try them, right? There is no way they can hurt us and all kinds of ways that they can do us good, so we have everything to gain and nothing to lose!"

I have to tell you about another friend of mine, who has been kind enough to let me share with you some of the poems from his books. Jeff Eberbaugh wrote a couple of books titled *Gourmet Style Road Kill Cooking* and *Road Kill Cooking Redneck Style*, but they are really spoofs of eating road-killed animals and are not intended to be taken seriously. He says, "The road kill recipes in this book are written purely in fun. We in no way encourage anyone to try and run down wild animals on the road. But I do hope you will enjoy the humor in my road kill tails." It makes me mad to see anyone intentionally run over an animal, but I have found that you can eat road kills if you go about it in a sensible manner. I'll get to that at the end of the book, but in the meantime, when you see some of Jeff's poems, remember that he is just kiddin'!

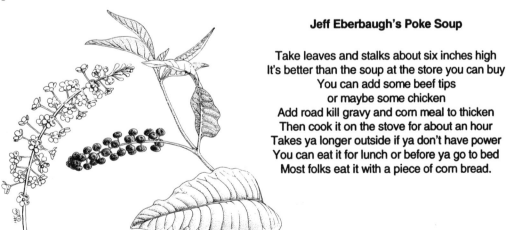

Jeff Eberbaugh's Poke Soup

Take leaves and stalks about six inches high
It's better than the soup at the store you can buy
You can add some beef tips
or maybe some chicken
Add road kill gravy and corn meal to thicken
Then cook it on the stove for about an hour
Takes ya longer outside if ya don't have power
You can eat it for lunch or before ya go to bed
Most folks eat it with a piece of corn bread.

Poke Sallet

Breams Brim With Good Taste and Nicknames

I get lots of requests for recipes for one of our most common freshwater fishes, which we normally refer to as a panfish. Everyone who grew up or has lived in the North Carolina Sandhills region or just about anywhere in the South knows that the name "bream" is pronounced like "brim," but our Yankee squatters always seem to have to say "breeeem" for some reason.

In the reference book, *Fishes of the Southeastern United States*, the author, Charles Manooch III, refers to it as the pumpkinseed or speckled perch, or *Lepomis gibbosus* and *L. microlophus* for biologists. Actually, the bream is in the group of fish we generally refer to as sunfish. Other members of this family, all of which are also called bream, go by such names as bluegills, warmouths, stump knockers, crappies, fliers, longear and redears. One type is even called "robin" because of the very red breast it sports during the mating and breeding seasons. These sunfish or bream are to fishing what the white-tailed deer is to hunting — one of the most popularly taken species, if not the all-time favorite!

Bream, sun perch or sunfish are found in virtually all of the country. They spawn from around April to September, and their bowl-shaped nests are easily seen around the edges of our lakes and ponds.

The females lay from 2,000 to 63,000 eggs which hatch in only 30 to 35 hours, explaining why there are so many being caught. Three pounds is a big one, but they can put up a fight for their size. Bream are caught on worms and crickets, spinners and poppers, hand-tied flies, and artificial lures resembling slimy purple worms. These generally round fish come in various color combinations of brown, green, orange and even pink with a wide variety of stripes, spots, and of course red or blue gill covers which lead to some of the common names.

Bream can be caught on any type of equipment from a cane pole to a $200 rod and reel combination, but if you are in a survival situation or just find yourself out at the lake without your tackle, you can always make a fishing outfit from stuff at hand. You can always carve hooks out of bone or wood, or make one from a safety pin, but why bother? As trashy as so many Americans are, you only have to look around a lake for some fishing string with hooks, sinkers and bobbers attached. You don't need a cumbersome pole, either. Tie one end of the string to the flip top on one of the many beer cans on shore and then wrap the line around the can. When you have it baited hold the can in one hand with the running end of the line pointing at the water. Get about three feet of line in your other hand and begin twirling the hook, line and sinker like David and his sling. Let go and it will cast perfectly. Watch your bobber. When you leave, roll up your rig and take it with you, or cache it if you know you will be coming back.

There are many ways to fix these bony little fishes, but usually they are deep-fried after rolling in corn meal, flour or pancake batter, or a combination of these. Manooch says, "Bream can be filleted, but those who do so discard the sweetest meat."

Cleaning is easily accomplished by scraping the scales off with either a dull knife or fish scraper. A fish scraper is simple to make by nailing soda or beer bottle caps upside down on a handle of wood. It is easy to replace if lost, and cheap, too. After scaling, the head is removed, the belly slit to the vent, and the innards removed. The air bladder and stomach may be used for bait, and if you find any egg sacs or roe, be sure to save them for frying.

Pan Fried Pan Fish

a mess of bream   salt and pepper to taste
flour or corn meal   oil

This is the simplest and most common way to eat sunfish. Clean them, roll in flour with salt and pepper to taste, and fry in hot oil until brown and crispy, about 4 minutes per side. Serve with cole slaw and hush puppies if you have them.

Bertha Reppert offers this old-time but simple and tasty recipe in *A Heritage of Herbs:*

Herbed Hush Puppies

2 cups cornmeal   1 cup water
1 tsp. salt   3 tbsps. fresh parsley, thyme and chives

Mix all ingredients and deep fry in hot fat. If dried herbs are used, substitute about $1\frac{1}{2}$ tablespoons.

Deboned Bream

a mess of bream   salted water

Drop cleaned, scaled bream into boiling salted water and simmer 5 minutes. Remove, cool and flake the meat away from the bones. This white meat can be used in salads, croquettes and soups. Deboned bream meat, with or without cheese, makes a really tasty omelet. Marinate the meat in soy sauce and ginger for use in stir-fry recipes.

Bream Loaf

3 cups flaked, cooked bream $1\frac{1}{2}$ sticks butter
1 tbsp. parsley   1 cup bread crumbs
2 eggs, beaten   salt and pepper to taste

Combine all ingredients and pour into a buttered loaf pan or baking dish with 1 inch of hot water. During cooking, this will keep the loaf moist and will steam away, preventing sticking and burning. Bake at 375 degrees for an hour and serve hot out of the oven with cheese, or tomato sauce, or lemon juice and parsley.

Frances' Fancy Baked Bream

cleaned bream   paprika
butter   onion slices
orange juice concentrate

Coat the surface of a broiling pan with butter. Lay in the fish and sprinkle with paprika. Add onion slices and drizzle with orange juice concentrate. Bake at 400 degrees about 20 minutes for large fish, less for smaller ones.

All of those people who think a bream's only purpose in life is to make a bass grow up big and strong don't know what they are missing! They are bony fish, but worth the trouble. Here is a little tip I'd like to share. Most people cut off the head and throw it away. Indians used to plant fish heads and innards with their corn and pumpkins because of their high organic nutrient content. My wife puts them in the bottom of large pots of soil in which grow some monster zucchini, tomatoes and cucumbers by the bucketful.

The top of the bream's head (and other fish as well) above the eyes has a narrow bone in it, but on either side of the bone are two quarter-sized or larger boneless chunks of meat. I like to save these in a bag as I clean the fish and freeze them. When there are small children at the table this meat can be fixed as fish nuggets and you don't have to worry about them choking on bones. These little chunks can also be used in omelets, stir-frys, fajitas and many other recipes.

I watched my sister-in-law, Betty Jo Crisp, patiently spend an hour picking the meat off the bones from a plate of smoked bream in order to make a special dip to drag potato chips through. When somebody else does the work, it is easy to say, "it was worth the trouble!," but I tell you it sure turned out good.

Betty Jo's Smoked Bream Dip

4 cups sour cream   **2 cups smoked bream flakes**
2 tbsps. chives, chopped

After you get the meat off the bones, fold the bream and the chives into the sour cream and put it back into the refrigerator for an hour or two to let the flavor develop. Serve with broccoli, carrots or other fresh veggies, or potato chips, or crackers.

This next recipe ain't really a bream recipe, but it would work well with bream. I'm adding it here for Doug Vermillion, my trout fishing friend, for the good job he did operating on me after my parachute accident.

My wife made up this recipe as part of her training when she had to clean and cook her own fish at Tom Brown's Survival, Tracking and Nature Awareness school.

Frances' Campfire Trout

trout   **dock leaves**
wild onions or garlic   **sheep sorrel**
wild mint   **butter if ya got it**

Clean the fish. For a trout this is easy because you don't have to scale them. You are only required to slit them open, remove the guts and rinse well. Cutting off the head and tail is optional. Stuff with wild onions, garlic, mint and sheep sorrel in any combination. Add a little butter. Wrap the fish in dock leaves and then foil. Bake in the coals of a campfire 15-20 minutes depending on size.

Strawberry Pickin' Time Is a Happy Time of Year

As far as wild fruits go, one of my favorite times of year is when the little wild strawberries are ripe and out there waiting to be picked. Many quarts of strawberries will be picked at those U-Pick-Em farms, and many more quarts will be eaten, but those farm-grown strawberries just can't compete with the wild ones for flavor!

It is really amazing how big strawberries can be grown now and how long the growing season can be extended with the everbearing varieties, but they can't begin to match the flavor of the little thumbnail-sized strawberries in the country. I know people agree with me, because I have seen whole families out picking these little red jewels. All sorts of animals like them — birds, mice and squirrels, insects of many species, even deer and box turtles. Apparently the judges at the county fair liked them, too, because they gave me a Blue Ribbon for my wild strawberry jam when I entered it in the "Women's Canned and Baked Goods" division.

There are several species of wild strawberries found around the world, but our commonest ones are known to botanists as *Fragaria virginiana*. If you have never tasted them and don't know how delicious they are, you are missing out on a real treat! Wild strawberries can give us a lot of pleasure all year round. They spread by runners, and a few plants will soon fill an open, sunny space, making an excellent groundcover. In the winter, the leaves may turn brilliant red, but the plants remain alive and green all through the cold season, even under the snow. The leaves can be brewed into a healthful tea rich in vitamin C. Herbalists have recommended it for scurvy, gum disease and other problems caused by lack of vitamin C. The delicious little fruits can be turned into jelly, frozen, or dried for making pemmican or for other later uses.

My favorite way of eating them, however, is to pick them fully ripe and float them in fresh whole milk. I hear they are pretty good with whipped cream, too. We had strawberries and real cream when I was a child, but my parents never bought Redi-Whip and Cool Whip, because they weren't invented. My cousins David and Russel and I would go to the dairy section of the A & P and when the manager wasn't looking we would take turns standing guard while the others squirted the whipped cream into our mouths and then put the cans back. Don't do that today, kids, and don't tell my mother, either. She'd still probably blister my butt after sending *me* to get the switch! "And leave a few leaves on the end, too, boy!"

Award Winning Strawberry Jam

4 cups wild strawberries	**4 cups sugar**
4 tbsps. lemon juice	**1 package pectin**

Mash half the berries, just enough to get a little juice and bring to a boil. If worse comes to worst, add $^{1}/_{4}$-$^{1}/_{2}$ cup of water, but be sparing with it. Quickly stir in sugar, lemon juice and pectin, then return to a full rolling boil. Simmer approximately 5 minutes, stirring constantly to avoid burning and sticking, or until juice will sheet from a spoon. (That means the whole spoonful slides off at once, rather than dribbling off like cough syrup when the spoon is tilted to one side.) Pour into sterilized, hot half-pint jars and seal with lids or paraffin. If you want to enter them in the fair, you will have to process them in a boiling water bath as described in the Ball canning book.

If you can hide the jam from your mother, it makes excellent Mother's Day and birthday presents. It probably won't last until Christmas without being eaten.

Wild Strawberry Leaf Tea

2 cups strawberry leaves   honey to taste

Wash leaves and drop into a quart of boiling water. Remove from heat and steep covered for 10 minutes. Strain, sweeten with honey and enjoy!

Easy Strawberry Pudding

2 cups strawberries, mashed   2 egg whites
$\frac{1}{2}$ cup confectioner's sugar $\frac{1}{2}$ cup strawberry jam
1 handful fresh strawberries   whipped cream

Whip together sugar, egg whites and strawberry pulp, beating about 15 minutes or until stiff. Spoon into dessert cups and chill in refrigerator. Just before serving, top with a dollop of whipped cream and a spoonful of jam, and a fresh berry or two.

Mom's Strawberry Shortcake

2 cups all-purpose flour   2 tbsps. honey
1 tbsp. baking powder   4 tbsps. vegetable oil
1 egg, beaten   1 cup milk
4 tbsps. powdered milk $\frac{1}{2}$ tsp. salt

Stir dry ingredients together with a fork. Combine egg, milk, honey and oil and fold into dry ingredients. Spoon into a large greased baking sheet in several lumps and smooth out. Bake at 400 degrees about 15 minutes or until a broom straw comes out clean.

2 quarts strawberries   1 cup honey
$1\frac{1}{2}$ cups whipping cream

While the shortcake is baking, whip cream and honey and fold in strawberries. Cool shortcake and split in half. Spoon on a layer of strawberries on one half, add the top, and spoon on the rest of the strawberries and whipped cream mixture.

To make an excellent dip, fresh strawberries can be folded into softened cream cheese, alone or with chopped nuts and/or finely minced pineapple. Spread on crackers, or on celery stalks. You can also combine strawberries with milk and ice cream in the blender to make a smoothie or a shake. Make your own topping for ice cream or pancakes by boiling equal amounts of strawberries and sugar, or honey, until it's as thick as you like it. Trailing strawberry plants are very attractive in a planter, indoors or out.

Strawberry Muffins

1 cup wild strawberries $\frac{1}{2}$ cup sugar
1 egg, well beaten   2 cups flour
4 tbsps. vegetable oil   1 cup milk
3 tbsps. baking powder $\frac{1}{2}$ tsp. salt

Mix strawberries and sugar. Set aside while preparing muffin mixture. Sift remaining dry ingredients together and stir in egg, milk and oil. Mix only until mixture is thoroughly dampened. Do not beat. Fold in strawberries. Pour into greased muffin cups, filling $\frac{2}{3}$ full. Bake in preheated oven at 350 degrees for 20 minutes or until done. Makes one dozen.

Wild Strawberry Pork Chops

2 pork chops per person   1 cup red wine
2 tbsps. cooking oil   1 cup honey
2 cups strawberries, mashed   salt and pepper to taste

Brown pork chops in skillet with oil, seasoning with salt and pepper to taste. Drain off excess grease, saving for seasoning, of course. Combine wine and honey and pour over chops. Cover and simmer 45 minutes. Add strawberries, stirring well, cover and simmer another 15 minutes.

The above recipe also works with venison, elk (which some consider venison), or other game meats, including birds such as quail and dove, rabbit, and surprisingly, some fish. Chicken is also good this way, if you like those nasty yardbirds! How many chickens does it take to digest a kernel of corn? You don't want to know!

Strawberry Cordial

alcohol
strawberries

Use rum if you like sweeter cordials, vodka or gin if you like them a little stiffer. Use white lightning if you can get it. Drain about $1/2$ of the bottle of liquor. You know what to do with it. Drop in strawberries until the bottle won't hold anymore or it starts to overflow. Replace the top and shake well. Put it away in a dark place where you won't see it for about six weeks and then check it. You can do the same thing with vinegar instead of liquor and use it for salads or greens.

Occasionally, I have the very special experience of hearing some of the stories of my youth told again by someone who has been telling them a long time. When I went to the Black Mountain Herbfest, one of the speakers was Mary Ulmer Chiltoskey, a celebrated author and historian from the Cherokee Reservation. She came there from her home in Alabama many years ago, and after 20 years married Going Back (G.B.) Chiltoskey. She studied and served for many years, writing in English and in the Cherokee language to help keep the history and lore of the past alive. After fifty years of loving efforts, she was made an honorary member of the Eastern Band of the Cherokee.

Now 89 years young, "Aunt Mary," as she has come to be known by all "the People," as the Cherokees call themselves, is still sought after to tell the stories that many have nearly forgotten. One of those stories is appropriate for the lesson it teaches. You can often hear someone say, "Aunt Mary... tell me the strawberry story again."

The Legend of the Strawberries

The young man and his wife seemed to be a perfect couple as they planned their new home and searched for food. Things went well as their routine continued each morning, he working on his arrow points and she cleaning the house and preparing meals. Then one day, like a storm, she burst from the house in anger, not even shutting the door behind her.

The man let her stay outside to cool off, but after a time called to her for something to eat. When she did not answer ,he stepped outside just in time to see her cresting a hill far off in the distance.

In confusion, he started toward the far-off mountain, intending to bring her back where she belonged. In his own anger at her leaving and his confusion as to why, he kept losing his footing and could not concentrate on the path. Finally he sat on a rock and called to the Great One for help. "What is the problem?" asked the Creator.

Upset and not knowing what had happened, the man said that his wife was getting away from him and he didn't know why. The Great One asked if the man had done something wrong or perhaps had neglected to do something important for her. The man was mad because the Great One was supposed to know everything and the man himself did not understand what had really happened. He was puzzled and afraid he might lose his wife.

"First, you must get some rest," said the Great One, "and while you are sleeping to get your strength and your thoughts back,I will put some things in her path to slow her down until you can catch up to your wife."

Right in the determined woman's path the Great One put a beautiful sarvis bush with its fluffy white blossoms, but she was so mad she didn't even appreciate its sweet smell as she brushed right through it. She never even saw the red June berries hanging for her to enjoy. The man was rested now and following her.

Next the Great One put in her path some huckleberry bushes loaded with fruit. Nobody can pass these fruits when they are ripe without eating a handful or so, even if the bushes belong to someone else. The man was getting closer as she was slowing down, but the Great One slowed her even more.

In her path the Great One put some blackberries, with big black fruit and stickers on their branches that caught at her dress as she passed through and slowed her even more. But the Great One thought about what motivates a woman more than anything but love — curiosity.

Among the leaves in the pathway he placed a bright red heart-shaped berry, and when she slipped as her heel crushed one, it smelled so sweet. She stopped to eat one or two and they were so good, she immediately thought of her husband and how much he would enjoy these strawberries. There were little berries and big berries and the biggest berries the Great One placed so that as she picked them she was heading home. Finally her husband burst into the clearing where she was picking strawberries and she burst into his arms, plopping a sweet strawberry into his mouth, saying not a word. They gathered berries in the afternoon sun together, the anger and confusion disappearing and forgotten.

While she gathered some leaves to make a little basket to carry the berries home for their supper, he collected a few of the plants — one here and another there, until he had enough to start a little patch of his own outside their door.

As he was carrying in the strawberry plants, she thought as she crossed the doorway, "Why in the world would I give up my home and all I have worked so hard for?" and vowed to herself, "I will never let anger carry me away again." The Great One smiled. She noticed how fragile the berries were, and to preserve a few for later she put them in a jar of honey. Even today, every good Cherokee wife keeps a jar of preserved strawberries on the shelf to remind her of the fragile nature of her home and the power of anger.

That story is typical of the kind of lessons that young Cherokees were taught when they didn't even know they were learning. Mary Chiltoskey says, "A story is an accounting of something that happened. When it is told over and over — I like to say multiple times — it becomes a legend, but it was based on a real event. If the event is about the Creator, or has to do with creation, it is called a myth."

Bring Wild Mushrooms Into the Kitchen (CAREFULLY!)

These days of changing weather patterns make it hard to resist bringing some of those wild mushrooms that are cropping up everywhere into the kitchen. This certainly can be economical. Some of the varieties that grow wild can also be found in the produce sections of our grocery stores, either dried or fresh, but pretty expensive in either case.

Picking wild mushrooms can be expensive, too! You can die if you aren't careful. That is why with mushrooms, more than any other wild food a forager can gather, positive identification is of the utmost importance. No, it's not just important — it's critical! You see, there are basically two types of mushroom poisons.

Some poisonous mushrooms act on the gastrointestinal system and they work fairly rapidly, too. Cramps, nausea and vomiting tell you that you got the wrong mushroom. There's a good chance you'll have some severe diarrhea as well. You might even mess in your pants before you can get to the toilet or behind the closest big tree. Even though you might wish you would die, you'll recover just about as quickly as you got sick once the mushrooms and toxins are out of your system.

The other poisonous mushrooms, the potential killers, work on the central nervous system, and you may have no symptoms at all for two or three days, or even longer. Then, all of a sudden, you get symptoms much like a heart attack — tightness in your chest with severe pains, irregular heartbeats and difficulty breathing. By this time it is often too late to do anything for you. Even if you are lucky enough to be diagnosed properly and able to be revived at the emergency room, you still might need a liver transplant.

One other mushroom toxification worth mentioning comes from a very delicious and normally benign little jewel known as *Coprinus atramentarius*, one of the little inky cap mushrooms. Its common name, Alcohol Inkycap, is a little misleading. It doesn't contain alcohol, but rather a substance similar to the drug Antabuse which makes you throw up violently when you drink alcohol. Don't use this one in your spaghetti sauce when you are planning to serve wine with the meal!

The inky caps are called that because when they are overripe, they "deliquesce," or turn into black, inky mush. Another inky cap that is referred to as a "choice edible" in many guides is the shaggy mane, *Coprinus comatus*. The skin on the top of the cap peels off in little fringed plates, with an appearance much like the shagbark hickory, hence the name.

Baked Shaggy Manes

1-2 dozen Shaggy Mane caps	$^1/_2$ cup half-and-half
salt and pepper to taste	2 tbsps. butter
1 tsp. cognac or sherry (optional)	

Wipe the mushroom caps with a paper towel and lay in a single layer in a casserole or baking dish. Dust lightly with salt and pepper, then drizzle with melted butter. Bake covered at 350 degrees for 20-25 minutes. During the last 5-8 minutes of cooking add the half-and-half and the cognac or sherry, if you desire it. Serve over rice or toast squares.

When you cook with wine, remember what Justin Wilson says: "If it ain't fit to drink, it ain't fit to cook with!"

One of the mushrooms my wife, Frances, gathers most frequently is the oyster mushroom, *Pleurotus ostreatus*. These large grayish-white mushrooms are just about the only gilled mushrooms you will find growing on dead trees and stumps. I hate to say "always," "never," or "the only," but the majority of mushrooms you find growing on dead trees have pores rather than gills. Some people say they look and taste like oysters. I prefer them oiled, dipped in an Italian herb blend and grilled over charcoal about five minutes per side, but there are other ways to fix them, too.

I also like them, and puffballs as well, rolled in a little flour, dusted with a Creole spice blend like Tony Chachere's, and deep-fried into chips.

Sliced puffballs can also be substituted for noodles in lasagna recipes because of their firm texture. The important thing about puffballs is to be sure you really have puffballs and not the "button stage" of an amanita, and that the flesh is still firm and white, not yellowing. When puffballs die, they turn into "Devil's snuff boxes," and are filled with spores which come out as a cloud of dust when stomped. A survivalist can use this "dust" either as a styptic to stop bleeding or in improvised explosives.

Tee Pee Cookery, Gwen Fisher's book of Native American recipes and life, says that "Beans, onions, and mushrooms were favorite and staple foods of many Indian

Tom Squier with oyster mushrooms.

tribes." One reason that mushrooms continue to be a favorite food is that they can be stored a long time after drying. Freshly picked mushrooms, except the inky caps, can be dried using a dehydrator or in the sun. These dehydrated mushrooms can be reconstituted for use at a later time by soaking them in wine, milk or water for a few minutes or can be added to soups and stews. Mushrooms contain a lot of water and a pound of fresh ones might dry down to a couple of ounces.

Oyster Mushroom Casserole

4 cups oyster mushrooms, sliced
1 cup buttermilk
1 stick butter
salt and pepper to taste

1 egg
$^1/_2$ cup Parmesan cheese, grated
1 cup herb-seasoned bread crumbs

Alternate layers of mushrooms and breadcrumbs in a casserole and dot each layer with butter. Beat the egg and buttermilk together and cover the mushrooms and breadcrumbs. Sprinkle with grated Parmesan and bake 20-30 minutes at 350 degrees or until a knife blade comes out clean when inserted in the middle.

Another tree-grower is the sulphur shelf mushroom, *Laetiporius sulphureus*. It looks like a bright orange shelf growing from the side of a tree or stump, and many vegetarians who used to be meat eaters like the consistency of this one. It is often substituted for chicken in recipes which call for meat, and can be baked, fried or boiled.

One of the more expensive mushrooms found in stores is the bolete, *Boletus edulis,* and other related species. In the store, it may be called a "cepe" or "porcini," depending on which company markets it. Learn to identify this one because they are delicious and versatile. Boletes have pores underneath, rather than gills, and they are generally removed before cooking, probably for appearance's sake. One rule of safety — pinch the flesh of your wild boletes. If it bruises blue, then get rid of it. There are some blue-staining boletes that will make you toss your cookies, and it's better to miss a good one than get a bad one! Boletes come in shades of brown and tan, yellow and white.

Healthy Bolete and Grain Soup

2 cups bolete caps, diced
$^1\!/_2$ cup barley and/or wild rice
1$^1\!/_2$ quarts water
salt and pepper to taste

1 pound venison or beef chunks
1 large onion, diced
1 beef bouillon cube

Bring water, meat, onion and grain to a boil and simmer, covered, until meat is tender. Add mushrooms, bouillon and salt and pepper, then simmer another 20-30 minutes, adding water if necessary.

In the Army, you could find signs in people's offices that said, "I must be a mushroom because they keep me in the dark and feed me bullshit!" Excuse me if that offends you. Only one type of mushroom — the white ones found in the stores — are grown that way, and they aren't as good for you as wild ones. The farmers who grow them warn how dangerous eating wild mushrooms can be, while selling their own bug-spray-laced products. They are sprayed intensely with insecticide to kill the beetle larvae that hide in the manure. The government says this is okay, because the spray disappears in 24 hours in full sunlight. Problem is, these mushrooms never see the sun unless you use them on a shish kebab cooked on the backyard grill. Like the song says, "There must be two sides to every story... and I'll tell you mine!" Wild mushroom hunting can be fun and rewarding, but remember what I said about only eating those you can positively identify!

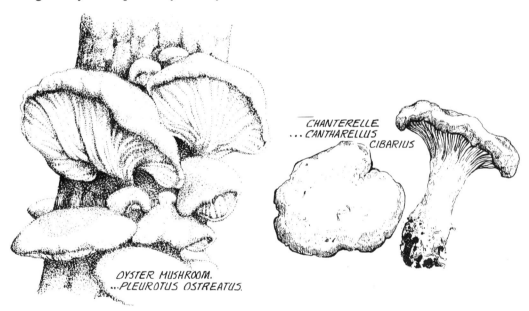

CHANTERELLE.
...CANTHARELLUS
CIBARIUS

OYSTER MUSHROOM.
...PLEUROTUS OSTREATUS.

In many parts of the world, mushroom foraging is a family hobby. In Germany, for example, families will pack the picnic basket and go out for the day, coming home from the woods and fields with a fresh load of fungi to dry, fry and pickle. In this country, people who were born in other parts of the world occasionally get into trouble eating mushrooms that look like the ones they harvested at home. The other people who get into trouble picking mushrooms are the ones who use them for "trippin'" or getting high. In North Carolina, my own state, possession of hallucinogenic mushrooms is a crime and is dealt with like any other "drug offense."

People who use mushrooms as a recreational drug here can get into trouble in a couple of ways. It is a felony to possess or to grow psychedelic mushrooms, and many arrests are made in the eastern counties when "hippies" collect psilocybin mushrooms off cow patties after a hot rainy spell. In one instance, New Hanover County deputies ran a story in the paper about the "hippies" collecting the hallucinogenic mushrooms, telling which road to take, where to turn, and where to find them. Then, as you would expect, they were there for the next several days arresting whoever followed the directions in the paper!

The other danger from hallucinogenic mushrooms comes from not being able to tell how much of the chemical is in each one and overdosing. Another dangerous favorite is the fly agaric, *Amanita muscaria*. In mild amounts, it is capable of making changes in the mind and body which some people find pleasurable. However, some guides caution that this mushroom can be dangerous or even deadly in sufficient quantities. Mushroom expert Dr. Andrew Weil states that "all psychedelics are intoxicants — that is, poisons." An even greater danger exists when seekers of this mushroom mistakenly gather some of its definitely deadly relatives. Our most poisonous mushrooms, and they are often prolific here, are amanitas. The destroying angel or death cup, *Amanita phalloides*, is well deserving of those names. It has taken many lives and is a prime argument for *not* casually taking mushrooms found in the wild. Fly agarics got their name, by the way, because they were once placed in bowls of milk as a fly bait and poison.

The best way to learn to identify mushrooms is to go in the field with an expert who can show you the subtleties of recognition on the spot and answer your questions as they come to mind. Another good way is to look at properly identified specimens side by side and compare them for yourself. I don't know where you can collect real mushrooms already identified like this, but in the mountains of western North Carolina there is an excellent alternative. The Nature Museum at Grandfather Mountain just off the Blue Ridge Parkway near Linville, North Carolina, offers the opportunity to study hand-carved mushrooms as close to real as any you will find in nature. The life-sized models are actually nicer than some you can find in the woods, and they have little skulls next to the deadly ones to remind you which are poisonous. Some mushroom enthusiasts and teachers have gone there just to make slides of these "textbook" examples.

The puffballs, *Calvatia* species, are among my favorites because they are so versatile, but I like the flavor of chanterelles, *Cantharus cibarius*, best, I think. The first time I tried to get my son, Tom, Jr., and my wife to eat them, both were a little apprehensive. I sautéed them in butter and really hated to share them, they were so good! Tommy balked at eating his and Frances was still waiting to take her first bite. She said something to the boy about trying them along with her and she ate one — little nibbles at first and then it was gone! Tommy still hadn't made any indication he was ready, so I urged him on verbally and Frances, with a sudden change of heart, told me it wasn't good to force him to eat something he didn't want to. Then, concerned for him, she grabbed his chanterelles and ate them before I could say a word.

Chanterelles and Chicken Livers

1 pound chanterelles	1/2 cup butter
1/4 cup olive oil	1 teaspoon white wine (optional)
1 pound chicken livers, halved	1 shallot or 2 wild onions, minced
1/4 teaspoon sage or rosemary	salt and pepper to taste

Clean and wipe dry the mushrooms. Sauté the shallot or onion in butter until transparent and add the mushrooms. Cook slowly until the mushrooms give up their liquid and the pan dries, but doesn't burn. Set aside mushrooms and onion. In the skillet, heat the olive oil and herbs. When oil is hot, add the livers and sauté until browned, but not fully cooked. Add chanterelles and wine and toss. Finish cooking for a couple of more minutes until done, but don't overcook.

A German legend tells of the Devil finding a wrinkled old lady in his path whom he promptly cut into pieces, scattering them about the woods. Every place a piece fell, a morel grew. In the German language, "morchel" is the name for both this mushroom and for wrinkled old ladies. Morels, *Morchella esculenta*, have a smoky flavor that some find to be enhanced by drying and rehydrating. Their hollow, pitted shape makes them look something like a giant peanut shell. Sara Ann Friedman, in her book, *Celebrating The Wild Mushroom*, says: "Even where it is plentiful, mushroom hunters will lie, cheat and steal for a mouthful — or a ton! Generous to a fault about revealing their sites for other kinds of mushrooms, morel hunters threaten to shoot on sight any person caught poaching on their territory."

Baked Stuffed Morels

morels	chopped garlic cloves
bread crumbs	white wine
butter	Parmesan cheese
chopped chives or wild onions	

Wash the morels quickly to remove dirt from pits or wipe with a damp cloth. Boil 2 minutes and drain. Remove and chop the stems, adding chopped garlic cloves to taste, (but not overpowering the mushrooms), a tablespoon of chives, and salt and pepper to taste. Some people like to add a little sausage to this stuffing mixture. Add the white wine, a little at a time, and simmer to mix the flavors just a little. Add bread crumbs and grated Parmesan cheese and mix thoroughly. Fill each morel's cavity with stuffing and bake at 350 degrees in a covered dish after drizzling with butter for 18-20 minutes, maybe a little longer if you use sausage in the stuffing.

One of the great things about mushrooms is that if you have a good edible one, you can use them interchangeably in most other mushroom recipes. One more note on puffballs. Cut them open long-wise, and if you see the silhouette of a mushroom, discard it because you have the button stage of another mushroom — likely a deadly amanita.

Stewed Mushrooms

2 tbsps. butter	2 cups mushrooms, diced
2 cups tomato sauce	1 tbsp. parsley, chopped
salt and pepper to taste	

Sauté mushrooms in butter and combine with other ingredients. Simmer on medium for 15 minutes. Serve over pasta, vegetables or meats.

Stuffed Cepes

8-10 bolete caps	$^1/_2$ pound sausage
1 large onion, diced	1 tbsp. butter
salt and pepper to taste	2 oz. herbed bread crumbs
1 garlic clove, minced	1 tbsp. parsley, chopped
$^1/_4$ cup milk	1 egg, beaten

Sauté onion and garlic in butter and add milk and bread crumbs. Combine egg with other ingredients and spoon into mushroom caps, after removing pores. Bake at 425 degrees for 15 minutes.

Breakfast Mushrooms Over Biscuits

2 tbsps. butter	1 cup puffball cubes, diced
1 teaspoon parsley, chopped	$^1/_2$ cup heavy cream
salt and pepper to taste	

Sauté puffball cubes in butter until tender — about 10 minutes. Add cream, parsley and salt and pepper, then simmer to thicken. Some folks add a little flour to help thicken it up, but I'd rather simmer it a little longer while the biscuits are baking. This recipe is also good with some chipped or dried beef added to it. Depending on when you served in the military, you may know chipped or dried beef in gravy as either "S.O.S. — shit on a shingle" (also made with ground beef) or "foreskins and toast." Enjoy! At the country club, they fix mushrooms in cream sauce over toast. Save the white bread to feed the ducks at the graveyard pond and stick to biscuits and corn bread!

Boletes and Eggs

2 eggs per person
chopped onion
1 tbsp. parsley, chopped
salt and pepper

$^1/_4$ cup diced boletes per egg
2 tbsps. milk per 2 eggs
butter

Remove the pores and the beetle babies from the boletes. Sauté mushroom and onion in butter. Whip eggs and milk with parsley and salt and pepper. Scramble eggs with mushroom and onion and serve with hot biscuits and grits and your choice of sausage, venison steaks or ham.

If you want to know more about mushroom societies in your own state, contact the North American Mycological Association, NAMA, at 3556 Oakwood, Ann Arbor, MI 48104-5213.

Groundhogs Are More Than Weather Forecasters

Jeff Eberbaugh's Groundhog Hoagies

Roadside Groundhog feet in the air
The meat's real tough but we don't care
Steel belted radial across his face
Don't worry 'bout the meat it won't hurt the taste
Pressure cook the pig for an hour real hard
Add two dill pickles and a handful of lard
Put in crushed red peppers ground real fine
Let it set for a month in salt water brine
Take it out and slice it and put it on some bread
Eat a groundhog hoagie before you go to bed.

I warned you before not to pay any mind to Jeff's recipes. Just have a laugh, but keep him out of the kitchen. Groundhogs can be good, *real* good, if fixed right. I remember as a child visiting some of the relatives on my father's side of the family. They weren't Native Americans — not with a name like Kalinauskis — but when I went to Uncle Bill and Aunt Mildred's to stay a few days, I got to shoot all the groundhogs I wanted. They hung out in the rock fences along the hillsides. Later I would think of that place when I was in Korea where they pile up rocks when the weather is good and stay in the house making up hard-to-say words when it ain't.

Every February 2nd we celebrate the "holiday" known as Groundhog's Day. Actually, very few people get this day off anymore unless it happens to fall on a weekend. Most young people would have forgotten the day long ago were it not for the electronic media — and Bill Murray's movie. Many calendars don't even bother to mark it any more, but when I was a child it always seemed like a big deal.

GROUND HOG DAY - Today (Feb. 2) is Ground Hog Day and Artist Glen Rounds of Southern Pines continues his and The Pilot's observance of the day. Shown above is Rounds report: "Ground Hog poses for his annual Portrait," but there's no weather report.

Courtesy of author & illustrator, Glenn Rounds.

Some folks believe that the weather in the near future depends on what happens on this historic day. Legend has it that if the groundhog sees his shadow as he comes out of his burrow, there will be six more weeks of bad weather; and if he doesn't, then Old Man Winter is on his way out for the year.

Like many of our customs, this one is rooted deep in our British heritage. It stems from a day called Candelmas in England, which is also celebrated on February 2nd. There, though, they depend on bears or badgers to cast a shadow. A little verse goes like this:

> If Candelmas be fair and bright,
> Come, winter, have another flight.
> If Candelmas brings clouds and rain,
> Go, winter, and come not again.

So, the explanation is that if it is cloudy and overcast the groundhog can't see his shadow and the clouds and rain are a sure sign that spring is on its way.

A little town in Pennsylvania helps keep the tradition alive by holding the official weather forecaster in a cage so that journalists can come each spring to report on his activities. "Punxsutawney Phil," as he is known to the media and the public is known to scientists as *Marmota monax*. He's been known to me many times as "supper!" Many people call him a whistle pig because of his habit of giving a shrill whistle when alarmed just before he dives into his burrow. He is also the woodchuck of "how much wood could a woodchuck chuck?" fame. Gardeners often call these rodents by names which aren't suitable for printing. For cooking purposes, the groundhog's cousins can be substituted, whether you call them marmots or rock chucks, or whatever.

In most places they can be hunted year 'round as varmints or simply as nongame animals. Many young farm boys have learned marksmanship with a .22 rifle hunting 'chucks in the rockpiles and fence lines. It's a lot less challenging than shooting rats at a dump, but the meat is better! Many varmint hunters shoot woodchucks exclusively, but don't eat them, and this is a shame because they are really good eating when properly prepared.

Chicken Fried Groundhog

1 or 2 groundhogs	³/₄ cup milk
1 tsp. salt	vegetable oil
1 egg, beaten	1 cup flour
1 tsp. pepper	

Cut groundhog into serving-sized pieces. Older ones may need to soak for 8 hours in salted water (1 tablespoon to 1 quart). Be sure to rinse them well before cooking or take the salt into consideration and don't add any more. Parboil 20 minutes. Drain and wipe dry. Combine egg with milk, flour, salt and pepper to make a smooth batter. Dip meat in batter and cook in hot oil until browned on all sides. Add a little water to skillet, cover and simmer over reduced heat until tender and thoroughly done.

I always tell my survival students and my family not to think of them as rodents, but as cave-dwelling cows with short, squatty legs and big teeth! Depending on where you live, groundhogs generally hibernate until mid-March, well after Groundhog Day. Their body temperature will drop from around 97 degrees down to around 40 degrees, and they may breathe only once every six minutes or so. Once they do wake up, however, it seems like all they do is eat, eat, eat! A single groundhog can destroy a pea patch or other garden overnight.

Brown Bag Groundhog

1 young groundhog
6 apples, cored & sliced

1 can apricots or pineapple crush
salt and pepper to taste

Thoroughly clean the groundhog and parboil whole until it starts to become tender. Drain and fill with apple slices. Salt and pepper the outside to taste. Pin down the apricots with toothpicks or cover with pineapple crush. Place in a brown paper bag, fold closed and bake at 350 degrees until well done. Remove from bag and bake 10-15 more minutes to brown. If you don't like the fruit taste, you can stuff it with your favorite rice or cornbread stuffing, sprinkle with your favorite herbs, and serve it like a small turkey with four drumsticks!

Several times my friend Nettie Gothard has asked me to either print some groundhog recipes in my newspaper column or send them in the mail because her son Kevin hunts them all the time and wants to know the best way to prepare them. The important thing to remember in cleaning a groundhog is to remove all the little white glands or nodules found under the front legs and in the small of the back. Some people like to soak the meat in salt water or vinegar water overnight, but that is generally not necessary. Like all fur-bearing animals, whether you shoot them or cook the FORD variety (Found On the Road Dead), you should try to keep the hair from touching the meat as much as possible. The US Department of Agriculture permits a certain amount of rat hair and even fecal matter to be included in flour, beans and other foodstuffs, but a hair on a piece of meat can discourage a non-hunter from trying some really good food!

Oven Barbecued Groundhog

1 young groundhog
stuffing mix

barbecue sauce

Stuff the groundhog if you desire, cover with barbecue sauce and roast in a pan at 350 degrees until done and tender, about 2 hours, depending on size. Baste as needed to keep covered with sauce. It can also be cooked over a good bed of coals or on a grill.

I heat my house with wood in a Black Bart stove insert in my fireplace. A thermostat controls the temperature by blowing the heat out through two fans. It works good, sometimes too good. I have discovered that on many days, the house will be warm enough and there will be such a bed of glowing red embers in the firebox that I can cook supper in there with grates. This energy-saving cooking method produces some really tasty meat if you add a few wet wood chips to make smoke — hickory, pecan or sassafras.

Old, tough chucks may need to be tenderized by parboiling before frying or roasting, but this is true of most other forms of old meat animals as well. You can also tenderize tough meat by soaking or baking it in milk or by coating it with puréed papaya or papaya juice.

Baked Groundhog in Sour Cream and Mustard

1 medium groundhog
spiced mustard
1 cup mushrooms, sliced
1 cup sour cream
5 tbsps. butter
1/2 cup carrots, sliced
1 tsp. Kitchen Bouquet

salt and pepper
1 onion, diced
1 tbsp. rosemary, chopped
flour
4 slices smoked bacon
3 tbsps. parsley, chopped
1/2 cup sweet cream

Cut groundhog into pieces and roll in flour seasoned with salt and pepper. Brown in butter on all sides. Spread spiced mustard on both sides and cover with bacon slices in a shallow baking dish. Sauté onion, carrots and mushrooms in the butter and add the herbs and Kitchen Bouquet. Salt and pepper to taste. Over low heat, stir in the sour cream and sweet cream, mixing well. Pour over the meat in the baking dish and bake at 350 degrees or until tender. You may need to add a little more cream or water to keep moist while cooking.

I suggest that you forget about using the groundhog to predict the weather, because as the *Encyclopedia Britannica* says, "Convincing statistical evidence does not support this tradition." I do predict, though, that if you try some of these recipes you will have a delicious meal. I prepared the next recipe for the Air Force's John Mitchell while we were in West Virginia teaching evasion techniques to soldiers in an exercise known as "Ridgerunner." John said it tasted like "cheap roast beef." I'll accept that. The groundhog lacks something a lot of supermarket beef supplies, though — steroids, antibiotics and growth hormones!

Groundhog Facil

1 groundhog, cut up	**2 large onions, diced**
salt and pepper to taste	**1 tbsp. juniper berries**

Cut up and rinse groundhog. Be sure to remove the "kernels" under the arms and in the back. Parboil in two changes of water for a total of 30 minutes. Arrange pieces in a baking dish and surround with diced onions and season with salt and pepper and juniper berries. Bake at 350 degrees for about 1 hour or until tender. In case you're wondering what kind of a spice "facil" is, it isn't a spice at all. It is the Spanish word for "easy," because this recipe is so easy to prepare.

Anytime you find any fat on a groundhog or any other game animal, cut it off before cooking. Game fat tends not to taste good. In game animals, some bitter vitamins and other chemicals store in fat as winter comes on. Many times with game there is no fat — that's why it's high in protein and lower in cholesterol for the most part.

I'm sorry! I keep forgetting that some people have these food aversions and prejudices that keep them from eating some really healthy food while they load themselves down with fat and cholesterol-filled meat from the store and all sorts of junk-food snacks. If you don't think you could eat one of these four-legged vegetarians, but find some of the recipes interesting, then try using chicken instead. But, let me add this. As long as you are happy with your grocery store chicken, don't ever follow the chickens around the yard at Farmer Carpenter's and watch them eat! It takes about three or four chickens to digest a kernel of corn, if you catch my drift.

Save those old groundhog hides. They make some extremely tough leather.

"Gourmet" Is a State of Mind, Not What You Eat!

There is a lot of interest in "gourmet" cooking and foods these days. Some restaurants and stores even use the word in their ads and names. Generally, we think of "gourmet" as a synonym for "expensive," but it doesn't have to be that way!

According to the Random House *College Dictionary*, "gourmet" is a French word that means "a connoisseur in the delicacies of the table." It doesn't say a word about having to be expensive, just a delicacy. Society has changed this noun into an adjective which is used to describe food that these people known as gourmets eat. When I was in New York a couple of years ago, gourmets were paying around $7.50 for a bowl of cream of sorrel soup. Sorrel is grown in European gardens, but is represented here by sheep sorrel, *Rumex acetosella*, which is generally considered a weed. It is easily recognized by its arrowhead-shaped leaves and lemony taste. Euell Gibbons said this tang makes it good with seafood. Sheep sorrel can be used in salads and soups, and in the summer can be puréed to make a refreshing and healthful wild beverage that tastes like lemon-lime Kool-Aid.

We live in an area that is home to many hunters of small game and big game and to fishermen who seek out both game fish and panfish. These spoils of the hunt and the fishing trip can be used to create some really special "gourmet" dishes. It isn't what you cook, it is how!

Creamed Sheep Sorrel

2 tbsps. butter	1 gallon sheep sorrel leaves
2 tbsps. flour	$^1/_2$ tsp. salt
1 pinch nutmeg, grated	1 cup cream or half-and-half
$^1/_2$ cup herbed croutons	1 hard-boiled egg, sliced thin

Clean the sheep sorrel, drain well, and chop very fine. Melt the butter in a saucepan, stir in the flour, and cook this "roux" until it turns a golden brown over medium heat. Stir in the sheep sorrel and cook slowly a few minutes to dry the water from the leaves. Season with salt and nutmeg. Stir in cream and bring the mixture to a boil. Reduce heat and simmer 5-10 minutes. Serve hot, garnished with the hard-boiled egg slices and croutons.

That recipe also works well with young dandelion leaves or even better with young poke leaves and shoots, provided they have been parboiled in two changes of water before proceeding with the recipe above. Many people like to add a couple of teaspoons of white wine to the creamed greens to make it even more "gourmet."

A good way to rid wild (or tame) greens of sand is to hold the bunch by the base and dip repeatedly into a sink full of water, swishing occasionally. The sand falls to the bottom and any unwanted protein floats to the side of the sink.

Soufflé de Pis-en-Lit au Jambon

2 quarts dandelion greens	2 tbsps. butter
$1^1/_2$ tbsps. flour	salt and pepper to taste
pinch grated nutmeg	$^1/_2$ cup hot milk
$^1/_2$ cup Parmesan cheese, grated	4 egg yolks, beaten
4 egg whites, whipped	$^1/_2$ cup cooked lean ham, diced

This fancy sounding "gourmet" dish is simply "dandelion greens and ham soufflé," but it's a real treat and easy to prepare. Wash and cook tender dandelion greens until tender. Melt 1 tablespoon butter in a pan and add the dandelion greens. Cook over medium-high heat, stirring constantly until the water is gone, being careful to avoid scorching. Add the flour, salt and pepper, nutmeg and hot milk, mixing thoroughly. Bring to a boil, cover, and cook 10 minutes. Remove from heat and add half the Parmesan, the ham, the remaining butter and 4 beaten egg yolks. Beat this mixture thoroughly and fold in the 4 whipped egg whites. Turn into a buttered soufflé pan and round surface into a dome. Sprinkle with the remaining grated cheese and bake at 350 degrees for 30 minutes or until well puffed and lightly browned.

By the way, men, unlike a cake, a soufflé is supposed to "fall" when you take it from the oven. You can use wild boar or any other cooked meat in place of the ham if you are making a main meal soufflé, or you can substitute sweet fruit like strawberries or really ripe wild plums if you want a dessert soufflé.

"Gourmet" Coffee

clean dandelion roots
water

dash of cream

Save the dandelion roots from your salads and soufflés. Clean them well and place them on a cookie sheet in 100-125 degree oven with the door propped open. Heat until dark brown and crispy. Grind in your coffee grinder or between two (clean) rocks (that aren't sandstone) and brew as you would your regular coffee. You will have a naturally sweet "gourmet" coffee that is caffeine-free, but you may want to add a dash of cream if you like it light — or a dash of Jack Daniels if it is after-dinner coffee.

You can also roast your roots on a hot rock near a campfire or in front of the fireplace and store them until needed. You can even dry your dandelion roots on a piece of screen above a lamp. And you can use the roots of chicory just as well, although you won't need as much unless you like it strong.

Armenian Royal Soup

$^1/_2$ pound ground venison
$^1/_2$ small onion, chopped
2 quarts chicken broth
juice of 2 lemons

$^1/_2$ cup uncooked wild rice
$^1/_4$ cup parsley, chopped
3 eggs, well beaten
salt and pepper to taste

Combine venison, rice, onion and parsley. Add salt and pepper to taste. Form mixture into half-inch balls and drop into simmering chicken broth. Cook about 1 hour. In a soup tureen, combine beaten eggs, lemon juice and ½ cup of the hot soup broth. Remove soup from heat and drain off liquid. Pour this broth into the lemon-egg mixture, beating constantly. Add poached venison balls and serve immediately.

Of course, I'd like to think that the real beauty of these recipes is that you can substitute whatever wild meat or vegetables you have on hand or available and improvise, using the recipes as guidelines or inspirations. You can use a turtle shell instead of a soup tureen if you are out there somewhere where you don't have one. Wild duck or goose eggs make this a very rich recipe!

Fillet of Bass Royale

6 medium bass, filleted
2 tsps. paprika
8 green olives, chopped

salt and pepper to taste
1 stick butter

Rub butter over one side of each fillet and sprinkle with salt, pepper and paprika. Broil 3 minutes in preheated broiler with buttered side 2 inches from heat. Turn, butter the other side and broil 4 minutes longer or until fish flakes easily. While the fish are cooking, melt remaining butter in a sauce pan and add chopped green olives. Heat thoroughly and pour sauce over fish when they are done.

Food for the Gods

from the SNAIL CLUB OF AMERICA

Ralph Tucker, President
4849 North Seventh Street, #R • Fresno, CA 93726 • U.S.A.

All over the world, snails are known to be a gourmet food, and very expensive in American restaurants. In the Caribbean they are known as "caracoles," and are called "escargot" in France. My friend Ralph Tucker says, "It is time to call them what they are — snails!" Ralph says that these easy-to-raise creatures are the answer to a need for an economical source of protein in third-world counties and an excellent capital venture in this county. After retiring from his first career, Ralph, who is known as the "Snail King," started the Snail Club of America. Since then he has launched hundreds of others in a new, alternative farming endeavor that is increasing in popularity every year. I am proud to be a "charter member" of the club! In mid-1994, I heard from Ralph that he had signed up his 1,000th snail-raising member.

I have eaten snails all over the world in restaurants and native villages, and wild in North Carolina, California and Florida. Here is a "gourmet" recipe from the Snail King.

Ralph Tucker's Venison Terrine with Snails

1 pound venison	1 cup red wine
1 tsp. thyme	2 bay leaves
4 shallots, peeled	2 garlic cloves, peeled
$^1/_4$ tsp. allspice	24 cooked snails, drained
1 pound ground pork	$^1/_4$ cup Brandy
1 tbsp. peppercorns	2 tablespoons parsley, chopped
1 tbsp. salt	2 eggs, beaten
12 slices bacon	$^1/_2$ cup flour
$^1/_2$ cup water	

Cut venison into 1-inch cubes. Combine wine, herbs except parsley, and snails in a bowl. Add venison. Marinate in refrigerator for 3 days (I have to start with about 72 snails, and by the third day I might have 24 left if I'm lucky), stirring occasionally. Preheat oven to 350 degrees. Strain marinade, remove snails and set aside. Grind meat, shallots and garlic fine, and add snails, ground pork, brandy, chopped parsley, cracked peppercorns, salt, eggs and $^1/_2$ cup of strained marinade. Blend well. Line a terrine with bacon, letting ends hang over the edge. Add the mixture, fold over bacon to cover. Add flour to water to make a thick paste and spread over the terrine to seal. Set in a bath of boiling water and bake for 2 hours at 350 degrees. Allow to cool. Refrigerate overnight. Bring to room temperature before serving.

My grandfather never taught me to eat snails, but we ate about everything else wild there was. My first recollection of eating snails personally came around the same time Chubby Checker was shaking America to "The Twist." My father came home from World War II with some wounds and memories, but my Uncle Linden Squier brought home an Italian bride. I thought Aunt Rae was one of the most beautiful women I had ever seen. I could hardly understand her sometimes, but she looked and sounded like Sophia Loren. And she kept snails in her refrigerator! In the lettuce crisper, mind you!

I like my snails a little more on the simple side than the "gourmet" side. The basic preparation method is to keep snails in a box with flour on the bottom for a couple of days, changing it as it gets damp or dirty. Don't give them any lettuce at this point, as you are trying to "clean them out." Soak an hour in salted water with a little vinegar to remove the mucus. Blanch clean snails 5-8 minutes in boiling water, drain, and cool. With a toothpick, remove from shell and cut off the green tip. Simmer snail meats in your favorite sauce until tender. You can use a cream sauce, or a combination of wine, butter and garlic, or a tomato sauce for an Italian taste. You can serve them on a cracker with cream cheese or you can slip them on a pizza!

Cheese, That's Wild!

"Versatile" is an accurate description of the word "cheese" as it is used in our everyday language. There are dozens of cheese varieties used in literally hundreds of recipes, so "cheese," referring to a popular food product in our kitchens, is one of the most common words in many cookbooks. It is also a common word in our spoken and written language.

Cheese is found not only in the kitchen these days, but also in the woods. When the Army still had C-Rations, nearly every meal had a little can of cheese in it. A lot of them ended up in the fire where they exploded, sending super-hot cheese flying. Some of the worst burns I have ever seen were caused by this boiling cheese sticking to soldiers' faces or whatever parts it happened to hit and adhere to. Nowadays, you can get cheese packed in plastic with plenty of chemicals, so it doesn't need refrigeration, often in combination with beef sticks, similarly treated. They are popular with just about everyone who goes into the out-of-doors because we are conditioned to eating cheese and they are handy. And you can hear the word in many of our conversations, if you listen closely.

The expression "cheesy" refers to sub-standard quality in products or behavior in people. My son says at his school, a "cheesy" guy is the boy who tries to look up the girls' dresses. However, bosses or persons in charge or in the limelight are often referred to as "the big cheese!" When I was growing up in the fifties and sixties a very popular expression was to call someone a rat-fink because they would "eat cheese" on somebody, telling what they knew. Tattle-tales in the Army were also known as "cheese eaters," among other things. Being a "rat" or a "snitch" was synonymous with "cheesing," a generally frowned upon activity. It has led to a lot of "pink bellies" over the years. I suspect, though, that with the expected reduction-in-force of hundreds of thousands of troops and promotions at a premium, "eating cheese" will assume epidemic proportions.

Some people who try to be clever and think they are avoiding being blasphemous by saying "Cheese!" instead of J-e-s-u-s might be in for a surprise someday because the intent is there and from what I've read, a sin in your heart is just as bad as the deed. Some even say "cheese and crackers," but in such a way that their meaning is perfectly obvious. Clever, eh, but what do George and Tammy say in their song? "God's gonna get you for that!"

Even Murphy Brown has cheese in her refrigerator. Because it comes in so many varieties and flavors, cheese is one of the most adaptable and versatile foods there is. I believe that the American Dairy Council has been lying for years with the aid of their pawn the government about how good cheese (and other dairy products) is for you. Too many people are lactose intolerant, and that fact is fairly well-known these days. You can get vitamin D from the sun and calcium in a more digestible form from green leafy vegetables, especially dandelions! The creator designed cow's milk for baby cows, goat's milk for real kids, and human milk for human babies. The spigots are okay for Dad to enjoy, however. I read that somewhere. However, if you like cheese, you love it! Cheese comes in such an endless variety that it can be used in almost any recipe or with any type of meat or vegetable, or by itself. Wild-foods recipes are no different. They just naturally (no pun intended) go well with cheese.

The following recipe can be used with any of your favorite wild foods instead of venison by substituting flakes of fish, crawfish tails, dove or quail meat, or chunks of "Carthage Hedge eels" (known as Jake No-Shoulders in the Army and as a damned snake to my mother and countless others). Or you can turn it into a lacto-vegetarian dish using no red meat and substituting chopped lamb's quarters, dandelion greens or wild onions or a combination. Use whatever you can find or catch!

Venison and Cheese Loaf

6 eggs
1¼ cups flour
½ tsp. salt
3 cups ground venison
1½ cups grated Monterey Jack
   (hot optional) or Swiss cheese

¾ cup milk
2½ tsps. baking powder
½ cup bacon bits
1½ cups Cheddar cheese, grated
1 pinch red pepper

Whip eggs in a large bowl until foamy and stir in milk and dry ingredients, blending well. Shred cheeses and meat, fold into egg mixture, mixing well. Pour into a greased and floured loaf pan and bake at 350 degrees for about 1 hour or until a broom straw (or toothpick for you cleanliness freaks) comes out clean.

Let me point this out now. Most of the recipes in this book mention pepper. Americans are used to sprinkling ground black pepper on their food — if they can. Many persons are sensitive to this seed from an African vine and their kidneys won't allow them to eat it. Use red pepper instead, like they do in Louisiana. Not only is it better tasting, but the active ingredient, capsaicin, is found in medicines for everything from relieving pain to improving digestion and sexual vigor in men. One popular medicine for rheumatoid arthritis pain and shingles called Zostrix runs about $40 for a 6-ounce tube. The active ingredient is capsaicin — ground red pepper — at a strength of ¼ of 1 percent — .025! The rest is emollients. That is not enough to burn your tongue. Bend over when you buy this drug! Or you can use the seeds of pepper grass or poor man's pepper, *Lepidium virginicum* and *L. campestre*. This weed is found nearly everywhere. The seeds look like the seeds that come out of a bell pepper.

Wild Mushroom and Cheese Delights

2 pounds wild mushroom caps
1 egg yolk, beaten
1 pinch salt
1 tsp. wild onion or garlic, chopped

4 ounces cream cheese, softened
1 cup Cheddar cheese, shredded
1 pinch paprika
1 pound ground venison or pork

Combine all the other ingredients, mixing well, and stuff the mushroom caps. If you're not a mushroom hunter, use shiitakes or cremini from the store. Place on an oiled cookie sheet and bake at 350 degrees for approximately 15 minutes depending on size until stuffing is done and mushrooms are tender. As an option, you can make a batter, dip each stuffed cap and deep fry until done.

Fisherman's Sunrise Muffins

6 slices cheese (or equivalent)
1 cup leftover cooked fish
½ tsp. curry powder

3 English muffins (leftover biscuits in the South)
½ cup green onions, chopped

Halve the muffins (biscuits) and place on a cookie sheet. Place a slice of cheese or a half-handful of shredded cheese on each. Spread with fish, evenly dividing the flakes among the muffins. Sprinkle with chopped green onions and curry powder. Place under broiler and heat until the cheese is softened and biscuits are warm.

Wild Hors d'Oeuvres

4 packages cream cheese, softened
$^1/_2$ cup violet flowers
$^1/_2$ cup crawfish tails, cooked
1 package pimento cheese spread
$^1/_2$ cup smoked fish, shredded
$^1/_2$ cup peanut butter

$^1/_2$ cup green onions, chopped
2 cups open daylily flowers
$^1/_2$ cup wild fruit preserves or Polenta All Fruit,
    if tapped out
6-12 thistle leaf stems (tender)
unsalted wheat crackers

Wild foods are in vogue now at parties and you can make hors d'oeuvres easily and tastily in many varieties. Do the hard one first. Carefully slice off the stickers on the outside of the thistle leaf stalks, then cut them in half lengthwise and use them like pieces of celery. Spread with peanut butter, cream cheese or pimento cheese spread or a combination. (It's amazing how many people have eaten "Nabs" — cheese crackers and peanut butter — all their life, but balk at combining the two in other situations.) Rinse daylily flowers if you feel you have to, and stuff with cream cheese mixed with one of the other ingredients. Be creative and add chopped nuts, game meat, whatever. Mix the ground wild onions or the smoked fish or both in a package of cream cheese and use as a dip or spread on crackers. Spread cream cheese on crackers and top with crawfish tails, violets, wild preserves or your own favorite.

Cheese, ain't that wild! When 8-track tapes were the cutting edge of technology, fondue pots where the hottest thing going (again, no pun intended) and they were filled with melted chocolate for fruit or melted cheese or hot tomato sauce for dipping meat, bread and veggies. This next recipe isn't a real fondue, but the flavor is the same:

Game Fondue Bread

2 loaves French bread, halved
    lengthwise
1 cup melted butter
2 cups cooked game meat, shredded

1 pound Swiss or Cheddar cheese, shredded
hot peppers or sliced olives
$^1/_4$ cup fresh parsley, chopped

Shred cheese and chop parsley very fine. Mix cheese, parsley, butter and shredded game meat. You can use any kind you like — bear, venison, rabbit, even fish if you prefer. I guess you could use chicken or beef, but who would want to if wild meat was available? Spread on bread-loaf halves evenly and if you want to, add the hot peppers or sliced olives at this time. Bake at 350 degrees until bubbly — about 20 or 25 minutes and serve hot!

Game Loaf With A Secret

2-3 pounds ground game meat
1 egg, beaten
6-8 slices smoked bacon
1 cup tomato sauce

1 medium onion, diced
$^1/_2$ cup raw rolled oats
salt and pepper to taste
$1^1/_2$ cups cheese, shredded

You can also use any type of game meat for this recipe and you can use any type of cheese you prefer. Cheddar or Swiss are relatively mild and the Monterey Jack with jalapeños gives a special spicy taste. I like to use bleu cheese once in a while because it is one of my favorites. When I'm feeling really adventurous, I use feta. Combine beaten egg, tomato sauce, diced onion, oatmeal, and half the bell pepper, also diced with the ground venison or whatever you are using. Season to taste and mix well, forming into a wide loaf. Make a depression in the center and fill with shredded cheese. Fold meat over to seal the top and shape the loaf well. Slice the other half of the bell pepper into rings and add to the top with bacon slices. Bake 2 hours at 350 degrees.

Prickly Pear Cactus Earning a Tasty Reputation

One problem with eating plants, or for that matter, studying them, is that everywhere you go they are called something different.

Take for example the prickly pear cactus. It is known as the *Opuntia* genus to botanists because there are several related species or varieties. Out West you might hear the big leaves or pads referred to as *nopales,* and the young tender leaves referred to as *nopalitos* and the fruit called *tunas,* their Spanish name. The prickly pear also goes by such names as Indian fig, desert rose, and Cherokee rose. Out West, there are some that grow tall and tree like, but in the South and East they tend to ramble along the ground.

Depending on who (whom, — so what?) you are talking to, this plant may be an ornamental in the yard or landscape, planted for its beautiful rose-like yellow or orange flowers, a fodder plant grown for cattle feed, a medicinal herb or a staple food. You might even find it in the gift shop in the form of jelly, candy or syrup. I found it in the gift shops at Mesa Verde National Park, former home of the Anasazi Indians who long ago vanished mysteriously. Wonder if it was the new neighbors?

While out West, I found cactus candy, jelly and even soda being sold at the tourist traps, the leaves and fruit being sold in grocery-chain stores and the live plants for sale at nurseries. The Utes and other Native Americans eat the seeds because of their high protein content, but also make them into a tea which fights diarrhea by drying up the mucous membranes of the intestines. The large green pads can be split in half and used much like the aloe vera plant as a poultice on burns, skin ulcers and sores. Of course, we've all heard that cactus is a good source of water, and the prickly pear is no exception.

In Texas, the pads are gathered into great heaps and the needles are singed off to provide nourishing feed for cattle that also adds moisture to their diet in an arid region.

The prickly pear grows in one form or another from California to North Carolina, down to Florida and the Gulf Coast and as far north as Vermont and Minnesota. Every paratrooper who has ever "hit the silk" over the Army's Friar Drop Zone at Fort Benning has cursed the acres of beautifully blooming cactus plants there while picking the hundreds of stickers from his or her butt — I mean, fourth point of contact!

Peeling a Prickly Pear

Courtesy of Jim & Sue Willoughby and
Golden West Publishers

Lately, these plants have become chic, in vogue, *nouvelle cuisine* or some other French phrase for the "in" thing to eat. In the big chain grocery stores you can buy cactus leaves for around $5 a pound. Even in little Carthage, North Carolina, of all places, you can buy jars of nopalitos on the shelves of Don's Food Pride because of the many Mexican farm workers in the area. In the Southwest they are sold in every grocery store. We don't have to buy them, though. We can pick them! The prickly pear grows in unwelcome abundance in much of the Sandhills where I live, and probably where you live, too. If not, I'll be glad to send you a cutting! If you try to chop it out with a Rototiller or similar device, it is likely that every little piece if you leave it behind will take root. New plants come back from the roots after some of the terrible forest fires we have around here in the summer.

One local chain grocery store sells the pads for $4.95 a pound, a bargain to some, because "in" foods aren't usually that cheap. The sign above the cactus pads advises the buyer to "Remove thorns with a potato peeler or knife. Slice or dice and serve raw or boil 10 minutes until almost tender. Use in salads or any Mexican dish. The flavor is similar to green beans." The Apaches use bundles of grass to sweep the spines off the plants before they pick them. Use tongs if you have them to avoid the tiny spines known as glochids. If you get them stuck in your finger, coat the area with Elmer's Glue and let it dry. Usually, when you peel it off the glochids come out with the glue.

Stewed Cactus Leaves with Country Ham

2 pounds fresh cactus leaves	¼ pound country ham
salt	1 onion, diced

Remove the spines carefully and slice the cactus leaves thinly. Boil in salted water 5 minutes or until they start to become tender and change color. Rinse well and drain. Fry the ham in a little water and oil until crisp, and break into small pieces. Fry the onion in the ham grease until golden brown. Add cactus pieces and cook until tender. Drain and top with ham pieces.

I have found the leaves, when eaten raw, have a texture and taste like a raw cucumber, but often with a lemony tang. When the big pads are sliced and boiled they are very slimy like boiled okra because of mucopolysaccharide, but in a change of water the sliminess is lost and they do taste more like French cut green beans. The purple or red fruits can also be eaten after removing the spines — and the seeds! They can be eaten raw or added to salads, made into a jelly or wine. They have a great vitamin C content and you can make a nice marmalade or relish with them.

The seeds are very hard and have to be ground to be used in flour. Once at a "Wild Foods Day" at the North Carolina Aquarium, my friend Susie Clontz had volunteered to make the dessert. I gave her a recipe for Prickly Pear Fruit Pie which basically substitutes the cactus fruit for the fruit in any fruit pie recipe. Anyhow, the pie turned out delicious and people loved it. I just forgot to remind her to remove the seeds, which are as big as peas in many cases. Pttding! Pttding! You could hear them hitting the plates like buckshot as people spat them out. I was the dinner speaker, so I further embarrassed her by pointing out who made the pies and that people could just swallow the seeds and "like it says in the Bible, this too shall pass."

The prickly pear that grows tall can be cultivated into a very effective hedge. The fruits can be peeled, split and seeded and dried in the sun like big purple raisins for later use. After they are freed of their spines, the leaves can be used in all sorts of recipes as a cooked vegetable. They can be used in stir-fry recipes, in salads and in omelets and tacos.

Jim and Sue Willoughby's Pepper Steak Nopale Style

$^1/_2$ pound flank steak
$^1/_4$ cup beef broth or bouillon
$^1/_2$ clove garlic, minced
$1^1/_2$ tsps. corn starch
4 cherry tomatoes, quartered

$^1/_2$ cup onions, chopped
1 tbsp. soy sauce
$^1/_2$ cup nopale strips
5 tbsps. cold water

Brown meat. Add onions and cook until soft. Add broth, soy sauce, nopales and garlic. Cover and simmer 10 minutes. Blend together corn starch and water, and add to meat mixture. Cook until thickened. Add tomatoes and cook until heated through.

That recipe comes from Jim and Sue Willoughby's book *Cactus Country*. The drawing of how to clean a cactus fruit is from the same source.

Now, let me share a few more of my favorite prickly pear recipes:

Mexican Style Cactus Leaves

2 pounds cactus leaves
1 tbsp. chili pepper, minced
salt to taste

1 cup tomato, diced small
$^1/_2$ tsp. cilantro, minced

Dice the leaves after removing spines and boil in salted water about 10 minutes until tender and the color changes. Drain and rinse. Add tomato, cilantro and salt. Warm about 10 minutes over medium heat and serve alone or over rice, or add it to an omelet.

As with all recipes, spice quantities are just suggestions. Some people like more garlic, pepper or cilantro and some like less. Suit yourself!

French Fried Cactus Leaves

2 pounds cactus leaves
olive or peanut oil

2 cups pancake batter
salt to taste

Chop cactus leaves into strips after removing spines. Boil 10 minutes in salted water, rinse and drain well. Dip pieces into pancake batter and deep fry in oil or fat until golden brown. Place on paper bag to drain, and salt to taste like French fries. If you're out of pancake batter, use a batter made from two old favorites:

Bisquick Beer Batter

2 cups Bisquick

$^1/_2$ cup beer

Blend well and dip whatever you are deep frying in this mixture. It is good for cactus strips, oysters, fish, quail breasts — just about anything.

Cactus Salad

2 pounds cactus leaves
$^1/_4$ cup wild onions, chopped or
   1 large onion, diced
2 garlic cloves, minced

1 jar pimentos
1 cup Italian dressing
$^1/_2$ cup tomato, diced
sliced hard-boiled egg (optional)

Remove spines from leaves, wash and cut into cubes. Boil with onion and garlic until tender. Drain and rinse, then drain again. Arrange cactus pieces on plate, garnish with tomato and pimento and pour Italian dressing over all. Garnish with hard-boiled egg if you like. Best served chilled. You can sprinkle chopped pine nuts, mint leaves or cilantro over this salad for a different taste.

You can use the fruits in place of cranberries in breads and relishes, and they make a nice sauce for venison or ice cream. With a good jelly bag to filter the spines from the juice, you don't have to be so picky about the spines. The juice can be used to make jelly, candy, punch or wine. You can use the jelly recipe without the pectin to make some excellent pancake syrup.

Prickly Pear Jelly

7 cups cactus fruit juice
2 packages fruit pectin

1 cup lemon juice
9 cups sugar

You will need a very large pot for this — at least 8 quarts — or you can halve the ingredients for a smaller batch. Mix the cactus juice and pectin and bring to a boil, stirring constantly. Add the sugar and lemon juice, stirring all the while, and return to boil. Keep at a rolling boil 5 minutes, until jelly sheets from a spoon. Remove from heat, stir, and skim the foam off. Pour into sterilized jars and seal.

You can always boil a dozen or so crushed crab apples and use the juice instead of commercial pectin if you don't have any, or prefer not to use it.

I have some good friends, Jack and Marian Van Atta. He's retired now and "tinkers" and grows tropical fruits. She edits and publishes *Living Off The Land: A Subtropical Newsletter*, containing recipes and growing tips for various exotic fruits and vegetables. Jack has learned how to use store-bought bread in place of yeast when making wine, in case yeast isn't available.

Jack Van Atta's Cactus Pear Wine

4 cups prickly pear juice
wine yeast

5 cups sugar

Put juice, sugar and yeast in a one-gallon glass jug. Add enough boiled (and cooled) water to almost fill. Put on an air-lock and ferment, which should take about two weeks in 70 degree weather, and longer in colder weather.

Then you just siphon it off, decant it and wait a few weeks to drink it, if you can wait.

Beavertail is another name this plant goes by. Out West, you might find recipes for beavertail stew using real beaver tails or prickly pear pads. You could use both! Read the ingredient list to see which recipe you have. The cactus version is considerably less trouble to put together.

Beavertail Stew

1 pound prickly pear
2-3 onions, cut up
1 pound potatoes or Jerusalem
    artichokes, cut up
salt and pepper to taste

1 pound carrots, sliced
1 tbsp. flour
2 cloves garlic, minced
2 pounds beef, pork or venison
1 quart water

Cut meat into cubes, dust with flour and salt and pepper and brown in a Dutch oven or large pot in a little oil or bacon drippings. Remove the spines from the cactus and cut into cubes or strips. Add to the pot along with all the other ingredients. Bring to a boil, reduce heat, cover and simmer until done — about an hour to an hour and a half. Add more water if needed.

Beaver Tail Stew

1 gallon water
2 garlic cloves, crushed
2 bay leaves
3 large carrots, sliced
6 potatoes, diced
2 turnips, diced
$\frac{1}{2}$ tsp. each sage, rosemary and parsley
salt and pepper to taste

1 beaver tail
2 large onions, chopped
1 tbsp. salt
1 cup celery, diced
1 cup stewed tomatoes
1 cup whole corn
1-2 chili peppers (optional)

To skin the beaver tail, roast it in a very hot oven or a bed of coals until the skin blisters. Remove the skin and cut the meat into cubes. Simmer beaver tail meat in water with onions, garlic, salt and seasoning for $1\frac{1}{2}$ hours or until bones can be removed. Discard bones and any hair you find and return the meat to the pot. Add other ingredients and simmer another hour, adding water if necessary.

Some people like to add a little flour for thickener and $^1/_2$ cup wine or so for taste. Others like to make it a vegetarian beaver tail stew the second time they fix it, leaving out the meat.

I tell you, it ain't all that great, more of a novelty.

Cactus Pickle

2 quarts prickly pear fruits
2 cups sugar
4-5 cinnamon sticks

$^3/_4$ cup apple cider vinegar
3 tbsps. whole cloves

Skin the fruits, halve lengthwise, and remove the seeds. Cook in syrup of vinegar and sugar until they are sort of transparent looking. Place fruit and syrup in standard canning jars and add cloves and cinnamon sticks. Seal and process 15 minutes in a boiling water bath.

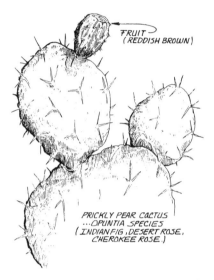

Sharon Gave Me Warts!!

When my wife, Frances, saw the title of this chapter on my computer screen, you can believe she was doing some real serious looking over my shoulder. Not only is Frances pretty good lookin' herself, but occasionally she can be real tolerant and understanding — like the time Reba gave me a big hug when we went backstage to see her. Still, I had better explain before I get into more trouble than I can get out of.

When I went to the annual conference of the Outdoor Writers Association of America (OWAA) in Salt Lake City, there were all sorts of classes (actually they were called seminars) about improving outdoor writing skills. I still had a chance to cross the street to the Salt Palace and give one of my books to Bocephus — Hank Williams, Jr. And, in addition to the educational displays, there was a hall full of manufacturers' booths where the representatives of various hunting, fishing and other outdoor gear companies had sent their public relations people to pitch the newest stuff.

Some of the greatest hunters and fishermen were there to tell why they had been so successful using a certain rifle, bow, fishing pole, or lure, bait or bullet. All sorts of "secret" techniques were shared with us writers. Some of those bearded old guys looked like they could catch a fish in the parking lot where a radiator had overflowed. It was a memorable conference. Fellow Tar Heel Charles Kuralt was there as the keynote speaker, and he was bragging on our young people and their concern for the environment. But OWAA members wanted to know what innovations the lure companies had come up with.

At least one company took the approach that "you can catch more flies with honey than with vinegar!" because the Storm Lure Company from Norman, Oklahoma had a great idea. The lure companies had grizzled old men giving away samples of their fish catchers. Storm Lures hired Sharon Andrews as "Director of Press and Consumer Relations," which is a fancy way to say "attractive and knowledgeable young woman to give away fishing lures and advice." Sharon knows her business. Over the years since then, Sharon has proven that if I tell her the color of the water, the flow and general location, she can match a perfect lure to my fishing conditions. Sharon knows her business! There is nothing wrong with having a good-looking woman promoting your product — if she knows what she is talking about. Sharon and my wife have become friends since then, and I have come to depend on her for advice on what new lure will work best where I live, or when I am fishing away from home.

Storm has lures with names like "Thunderstick," "Tubby Eel," and "Little Mac." Sharon knows a lot more about lures than I do. Myself, I have always been more of a traditional cricket, worm and bread-dough fisherman. I do have some Rebel lures by PRADCO from their "Critter" collection which look exactly like crickets, hellgrammites and tadpoles, but you can use them over and over unlike the real critters. They have one drawback, though. I have caught fish every time I used the "Crickhopper," but unlike the real crickets, you can't dip any leftover baits in chocolate and serve them as snacks!

Well, "I digress....," as they say. I told Sharon I would be fishing in black water ponds and creeks in the North Carolina Sandhills, often full of weeds and waterlilies. She thought a minute and said, "Let me give you some warts!"

"Warts," she explained are a line of lures — colorful little bubbles with big eyes that look like fat goldfish, shiners and baby bream. They were plumb cute! They apparently look pretty good to the fish, too, because the bass love them and I haven't lost any in the weeds (yet!). They have a line of "Wiggle Warts," "Steelie Warts, " "Magnum Warts," and Sharon gave me a couple of each. That is why this chapter is called, "Sharon Gave Me Warts!!" You see, I needed a catchy title and the Storm Lure had already taken "Fishing Up A Storm!" Okay? Got my wife's attention and yours, too, didn't it!

Sharon Andrews shows some top lures to research assistant and editor Frances Squier.

Now, when temperatures start cooling down for the day — about the time the races are over on a Saturday or Sunday afternoon and you are needing a little break from the hard work of cheering on Dale Earnhardt, Kyle Petty and Jeff Gordon, "The Kid!" — reel in a few fish and try these recipes.

Kyle Petty

Grilled Bass with Ginger Marinade

4 medium bass or fillets	$^1/_4$ cup lemon juice
salt and pepper to taste	$^1/_4$ cup soy sauce
wet hickory chips	$^1/_4$ cup sesame oil
lemon wedges	1-3 tbsps ginger, grated

In a baking dish, sprinkle fish with lemon juice, soy sauce, sesame oil and ginger. Salt and pepper to taste. Refrigerate covered overnight. Cook over a gas grill or charcoal, adding the wet hickory chips. The hotter the fire, the stronger the smoke and flavor. Grill, covered, 6-9 minutes per side until done. Serve on heated platter and garnish with lemon wedges. You can sprinkle with hickory smoke salt or Liquid Smoke and broil it in the oven and still get good results if you can't use hickory chips. For a stronger ginger flavor, mix the marinade ingredients a couple of days before you need them and pour over the fish when ready.

You can use wood for smoke and taste on a gas grill if you have those lava rocks in it.

When this was written, some of the readers were "out of town" and might have been eating sea bass from the Persian Gulf. The next recipe works well with any large fish and is known in the Arab world as *Samak Harrah*. The large fish is divided into serving sized portions and eaten with the fingers, a common eating utensil, but NEVER, NOT EVER eaten with the LEFT hand in the Arab world. Suffice it to say that this is the "unclean" hand and replaces "Charmin!" Southpaws have to be extra-careful there to act like they are right-handed.

Baked Fish with Walnut Stuffing

1 large bass, gutted but whole	4 tbsps. olive oil
1 large onion, chopped	1 cup green pepper, diced
1 cup walnuts, chopped	1/4 cup parsley, chopped
3 tbsps. pomegranate seeds	lemon slices
salt and pepper to taste	

Marinade Ingredients

1/2 cup olive oil	salt and pepper
1/2 cup lemon juice	1 or more cloves garlic, crushed
1 sprig rosemary	

Combine marinade ingredients and pour over fish. Turn several times while soaking — at least 4 hours in the refrigerator. Preheat oven to 400 degrees and oil a baking dish large enough to hold the fish. Heat olive oil in a pan and sauté onions until brown. Add pepper and walnuts and cook 5 minutes. Add pomegranate seeds and half the parsley and salt and pepper. Fill fish with this stuffing and skewer shut with toothpicks. Place in dish and bake 30-45 minutes or until done — flesh will come away in flakes with a fork easily. Baste as needed and turn once while cooking. Serve with lemon slices and the rest of the parsley and extra pomegranate seeds as a garnish.

Save the rind of the pomegranate, by drying it well. It serves as an effective, traditional worm remedy. Today we use "California" walnuts produced by the Diamond Walnut Growers of California, but when I was a child they were called English walnuts if they came from there or Carpathian walnuts if they came from Russia. They all come from trees that originated around the Mediterranean world and were originally known as Persian walnuts and are mentioned frequently in the Bible. They are easy to crack and get out of the shell, but I prefer the flavor of our native black walnuts, which are a real bear to shell, even after running over them in the driveway. You can make a black tea from the outer hulls which is great for curing jock itch, ringworm and athlete's foot. Just one note — it is a strong dye and whatever it touches will be dark brown to black for several days! Herbalists know that it is a powerful anti-fungal.

Poached Whole Bass

1 6-8 pound whole bass	2 lemons, sliced
1 large onion, sliced	1 dozen whole peppercorns
2 cups dry white wine	1 handful fresh rosemary

Line a turkey roasting pan with cheese cloth, a cotton kitchen towel, or a *new* cloth diaper. Be sure enough material hangs over the pan's rim to be used for handles later on. Place whole fish in pan and put half the rosemary inside. Sprinkle the remaining rosemary on the fish, pour wine over it and cover with onion slices. Dot with peppercorns and poach in oven at 350 degrees for up to an hour or until fish flakes easily with a fork. Use cloth to lift from poaching liquid. Skin if you like and serve hot or cold.

You might like a nice horseradish sauce or hot pepper jelly with this dish. You can get a completely different flavor by substituting fresh dill weed for the rosemary.

People who have been to the Caribbean or to Central America might miss the dish called *seviche* when they get home. Generally, it is made from white sea bass or "Corvina."

But boneless fillets of our own "hawg" bass will work well, too. The meat is cooked chemically by the acid in lime juice. Here is a typical recipe from Chuck Laudenslager, which looks suspiciously familiar. I wonder who stole it from who — or is it whom? Anyway, when we were in Panama we put away a lot of seviche using variations of this recipe. I like to use more hot peppers in mine than Chuck does and I also like to throw in some cilantro sometimes. I think the flavor of cilantro can be addictive to some people. I wonder if you can smoke it.

Chuck's Fish Seviche

1 pound boneless bass fillet
3 onions, minced
$^1/_4$ tsp. salt
juice of 5-8 limes

2 drops Tabasco
1 bell pepper, minced
1 garlic clove, minced (or to taste)
1 chili pepper, minced

Remove any skin from fish and chop into small, coarse cubes. Combine with all the other ingredients, mix well, and refrigerate covered for 10-15 hours or overnight. Drain and serve with crackers. Decorate with parsley.

This recipe is called "fish" seviche because you can also make it with octopus, shrimp or even conch meat. Conch meat is tough and takes more soaking and chopping.

A couple of years ago, I had the privilege of contributing several recipes to *America's Favorite Fish Recipes,* published by Cy DeCosse Incorporated as part of the Hunting and Fishing Library. Here are a couple of my recipes from that book, which I highly recommend:

Butterflied Barbecued Northern

1 whole drawn northern pike
    or lake trout, $3^1/_2$-$4^1/_2$ pounds
1 tbsp. fresh lime juice
1 tbsp. molasses
$^1/_2$ tsp. salt

$^1/_4$ cup tomato paste
2 tbsps. water
1 tbsp. Worcestershire sauce
$1^1/_2$ tsp. olive oil
$^1/_8$ tsp. garlic powder

Butterfly the fish by cutting along both sides of the backbone and removing it, being careful not to cut through the skin. Combine the rest of the ingredients in a small mixing bowl and set aside. Spray the grill with nonstick vegetable oil. Place fish skin-side-down on the grill and cook for 5 minutes, covered. Spread sauce evenly over fish. Grill, covered, for 6-10 minutes, or until fish is firm and opaque and just begins to flake. Garnish with snipped fresh chives and lime slices, if desired.

Baked Bass Italienne

2^1/$_2$ pounds bass fillets
2 cups onions, finely chopped
1 tsp. Italian seasoning
^{1}/$_2$ tsp. salt

1 tablespoon olive oil
3 large tomatoes, peeled, seeded and chopped
^{1}/$_4$ cup pimento-stuffed olives, sliced
^{1}/$_4$ tsp. pepper

Heat oven to 375 degrees. Remove any skin from fish. In a 12-inch skillet, heat oil over medium-low heat. Cook fish and onions for 4-5 minutes, or until onions are tender crisp, stirring frequently. Stir in tomatoes and seasonings. Increase heat to medium. Simmer mixture for 8 to 10 minutes, or until liquid evaporates, stirring frequently. Remove from heat. Set aside. Spray 13x9 inch baking dish with non-stick vegetable cooking spray. Spread tomato mixture evenly in dish. Arrange fillets on top of mixture, spooning some of mixture on top of fillets. Sprinkle with olive slices. Bake for 20-25 minutes, or until fish is firm and opaque and just begins to flake.

Wild Plums Are Peachy In The Kitchen

"Peachy" is a word that we can use seriously to mean something is just right, very good or really keen, if you are old enough to remember that phrase. In fact, we used to say that things were "peachy keen!" Use that expression now at a party and see how people look at you. I think Robert D. Raiford on the *John Boy and Billy Big Show* might still say that once in a while, but you don't hear it often.

On the other hand, we can use the word facetiously or sarcastically in an expression like, "Well, ain't that just peachy!" In this case, we obviously mean that whatever we are discussing is not peachy at all, but cheesy! "Plum," on the other hand, usually means "very," such as when we say that something is plum beautiful or a situation is plum peachy, if you know what I mean. As a child I heard the same tired old expression for living a good ways out of town over and over again. When asked where they lived, old men who thought they were clever, would respond with "Why I live in plumnearly. Plum out of town and nearly out of the county!" *Spit!* "Har har har!" *Spit!* "Har har har!"

Why all this sudden interest in plums? Because they are such a peachy fruit! (Don't hit me.) And in the summer, you can get them for free over much of the country. Wild plums have been around here a lot longer than golfers and *they* seem to have been here forever. And they are just about as common. If golfers had as many uses as our wild plums, they would be pretty valuable! I think I could make my fortune if I could buy golfers for what they are really worth and sell them for what they think they are worth (like lawyers!). Just kidding. Where I live, golfers keep food on a lot of tables. There are over 50 golf courses within a radius of that number of miles.

There are so many varieties of wild plums that many people just lump them together as the *Prunus* species. To make it more confusing, wild cherries may also be lumped together with the *Prunus* species, too. Obviously the two are related. Another "stone fruit" we are all familiar with used to be considered another member of the *Prunus* species, until recently. The peach is now known as *Amygdalus persica* instead of *Prunus persica* because botanists have been successful in finding enough differences to make it a separate genus. Where I live and forage, there are two types of wild plums — the ones that are red when ripe and those which are yellow when ready to eat.

Some plums have descriptive or romantic names that clue us into their natural history or historical uses. Beach plums grow near the ocean on short bushes. Our native plums are named Chickasaw plums after a once-powerful tribe. The Native Americans would boil bark of various plum trees for medicine. Ojibwas made a tea from the roots which was effective as a vermifuge or worm medicine, and which was pretty gentle on the patient, unlike some other worm medicines which are poisons. The Meskwakis scraped the inner bark from the trees and boiled it for curing mouth sores.

Television commercials tell us how healthful and full of fiber a snack of prunes is for us. We can make our own prunes by drying wild plums in the sun. Store-bought prunes usually are made from Damson plums, but the wild ones work just fine. Sometimes you can find them hanging on the tree already dried out, but still attached. At that point they are referred to as "fruit mummies." They also make a good wine, sauce for ice cream or game, and preserves. A favorite Japanese snack is made from plums which have been salted to dry them. I think I prefer my plums either eaten out of hand, or the old fashioned way — stewed.

Stewed Plums

3 quarts wild plums	1 quart water
3 cups sugar	1 stick cinnamon

Gather plums carefully. Give the tree a little shake so the ripest ones will fall. Watch out for the yellow jackets and gather the soft plums because they don't really get sweet until they are plum (very) ripe. Check them over carefully and discard those which have lots of little pinholes in them because these are infested with bugs. You might want to bite into one just to make sure you aren't wasting good fruit. Combine plums, sugar, cinnamon and water. Bring to a boil and simmer covered for about 15 minutes, or until the plums soften and skins split. Serve hot or cold in the syrup from cooking them. Remember that wild plums are about half seed, so don't bite down on them too hard just because they taste so good.

Wild Plum Sauce for Game or Ice Cream

$^1/_2$ cup butter	2 cups plum pulp
$^1/_2$ cup white wine	$^1/_2$ cup honey
$^3/_4$ tsp. seasoned salt	$^1/_8$ tsp. dry mustard
1 tbsp. cornstarch	

Combine butter, plum pulp, wine, honey, mustard and salt. Heat until butter melts and simmer on reduced heat 15 minutes. Use as is for an ice cream topping, or, if using as a sauce for game, combine the corn starch with a little cold water and add to plum sauce to thicken it before pouring over the meat. It will take about 2 quarts of plums or a little more in a blender to get two cups of pulp.

If you have some stewed plums on hand as you are cooking game, a variation of plum sauce is to combine $^1/_2$ cup each of meat drippings and plum pulp with $^1/_2$ tbsp. of dry mustard, 2 tbsps. sugar or honey, salt to taste, and a pinch of rosemary. Combine all the other ingredients and simmer, mixing well, blending in the rosemary just before serving.

This one gets its name because like a new bride, it is quite hot yet still sweet:

New Bride Meat Sauce

$^1/_2$ cup sugar	2 cups wild plum pulp
1 cup horseradish, freshly grated	$^1/_4$ cup apple cider

It will please and tantalize the palate, help cure colds and open the sinuses. And — it tastes great when spread on a ham while baking or when freshly roasted venison or other game is dipped into it. Combine all ingredients and use like we just talked about.

Plum Cake à la Frances

3 cups sugar	2 cups plum pulp
3 eggs, beaten	2 cups self-rising flour
1 tsp. cinnamon	1 tsp. cloves, grated
1 cup Wesson oil	1 cup nuts, chopped

Simmer plum pulp and 1 cup sugar for 10 minutes and set aside. When cool, combine with all other ingredients and beat 2 minutes in a mixer or 300 strokes by hand. Pour into a greased bundt pan and bake 1 hour at 350 degrees.

Wild plums can be halved, the seed removed, and then boiled in an equal quantity of sugar and enough water to prevent burning, until transparent for use in making cakes for Christmas. Slowly cook the fruit until the water is gone. The not fully ripe ones are best for this. They are also good if picked ripe, but still firm, quartered and de-seeded and added to a bottle of vodka, tequila or rum, along with a little rock candy, and put up until the holiday season arrives. Remove a couple of ounces or more of the liquor and do something useful with it. Add a couple of tbsps. of rock candy and half a dozen quartered plums and put it in the closet out of sight and out of mind until the carolers come around again.

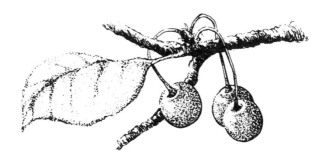

Wild Plum Jam

1 gallon ripe wild plums	**8 cups sugar**
1 lemon	**1 package pectin**

Halve and pit the plums. Where I live, you can get orange, yellow or red plums. I like to combine the colors because the flavors vary. You can leave the skins on the plums or remove them. It's up to you. Add ½ cup sugar to each cup of pitted plum halves. Let stand overnight. Pour into a saucepan and add the pectin and cook until the fruit reaches the jelling point. Pour into hot sterilized jars and process 20-30 minutes in a hot water bath.

A nice conserve can be made by adding 1 or 2 cups well-chopped pecans or walnuts, 4 cups raisins, and 2 finely chopped oranges to the recipe above and substituting either brown sugar or molasses for white sugar. This recipe needs to simmer for 2 hours. Add some ground venison and you have a great mincemeat recipe!

Frances Squier's Plum Cake

2 cups plum pulp, sweetened	**2 cups self-rising flour**
with ½ cup sugar or honey	**3 eggs, beaten**
1 cup corn oil	**1 tsp. ground cloves**
1 tsp. cinnamon	**1 cup (black) walnuts, chopped**

Mix all ingredients 2 minutes in an electric mixer or until smooth by hand, adding walnuts last. Pour into a greased and floured bundt cake pan. Bake at 350 degrees for 1 hour. Cool 10 minutes, remove from pan and drizzle with icing.

Icing

½ cup sugar	**1 tsp. butter**
½ cup milk	**½ cup brown sugar**
½ tsp. vanilla	

Combine, bring gently to a boil, stirring constantly, and pour over cooled cake.

"Mudbugs" Welcome in the Kitchen

The truth of the matter is that you can find more bugs than you want in many of our kitchens, like it or not — especially after the lights are turned out. No matter how clean you keep your kitchen, insects just aren't easy to get rid of. All the ripening fruit just seems to create hundreds of fruit flies. It is no wonder that for years, people believed that flies came from rotting meat and fruit. Here is a quotation designed to get you thinking — "Time flies like the wind; fruit flies like bananas." Use it as a diversion, don't try to figure it out. You'll come to the conclusion it is like comparing apples to Volkswagens or oranges and bustieres, and not worth much serious effort.

The humble crawfish.

If you want to see your own bugs scurry, turn on the kitchen light about 2 a.m. and watch them scramble. Sneak out to the fridge for a midnight snack and you won't be alone. We use all sorts of sprays (organic, safe pyrethrins, I hope) to get rid of pesky insects. We can see people riding around with big plastic bugs on their roofs, and it makes us wonder if we have bugs at home. Some people have used a poisonous mushroom named the fly agaric, floating in a saucer of milk, to get rid of flies, and pioneers used the fruits of the China berry tree to kill flies while they dried fruits or vegetables. Various mints, including pennyroyal, spread around the kitchen will repel bugs naturally. In some parts of the country, geckoes or other lizards are used to get rid of unwanted insects.

One kind of bug that is not unwelcome, but rather brought into the kitchen at great expense sometimes, is the "mudbug," which isn't a bug at all. As scientists say, it is an arthropod crustacean, which means in plain language simply a crusty-skinned animal with jointed legs. There are over 200 species of "fresh water shrimp" alone, so field guides often lump them together as *Cambarus* species.

They are native to the Eastern United States and old maps don't even show them in Louisiana where they have been elevated from the status of pest in the levees of rice farmers to a multi-billion-dollar industry. This is one real-life case where the farmers learned that the old saying "If you can't lick 'em, join 'em" has paid off. Some of our local grocery stores now sell "mudbugs" for just under $5 a pound — a buck less on sale. These freshwater relatives of lobsters are quite tasty and a necessary part of the now-so-popular Cajun cuisine. If you want to get into a heated argument (fistfight) just try to tell your friends whether the correct name is crawdad, crawfish or crayfish!!

We have our own "wild" crawfish just about everywhere there is water. The Reader's Digest book *North American Wildlife* says they live "in streams, ponds, lakes; under rocks or in mud." There are some varieties that live in wet fields and build large chimney-like structures to keep moisture in their holes. Their size varies from an inch long to over 8 inches, if you are lucky enough to find such a monster crawfish, er, uh, I mean crayfish, I mean mudbug! Whoever invented that little promotional name surely must have prevented a bunch of black eyes! In Louisiana, there are festivals in honor of this little fresh-water lobster, and people pay a lot of money to eat them in New Orleans restaurants. Some local folks eat them, too, whether or not they admit it.

Carolina Crawfish

One of South Carolina's newest industries produces a delicious product — Carolina Crawfish. Well known in Cajun and Creole cookery, Crawfish are freshwater crustaceans which can be grown commercially in specially constructed ponds and harvested with nets or traps. The two species grown commercially in South Carolina are the Louisiana White River Crawfish, *Procambarus acutus* and the Red Swamp Crawfish *Procambarus clarkii*. They are trucked in from Louisiana, placed in ponds, and allowed to grow. After a full cycle of reproduction and growth, the Crawfish can then be harvested, allowing South Carolina Crawfish producers to offer their delectable crop to local consumers.

A Food Favorite

Crawfish are a versatile food product. They may be cooked and eaten from the shell or parboiled, peeled, and used in Crawfish dishes such as Etouffee (pronounced A-2-Fay), Stuffed Bell Peppers, and Jambalaya. Although the largest portion of the Crawfish is the inedible head, it yields a tasty treat — a pocket of rich yellow "fat" which is actually an organ known as the hepatopancreas. The fat is an essential ingredient in Cajun dishes, and adds a delicious distinctive flavor to any Crawfish recipe.

Crawfish are consumed in Louisiana much as shrimp or crabs are in South Carolina. Folks gather round for a "Crawfish Boil" and great mounds of crustaceans, along with potatoes, onions, and corn boiled in the same pot, are poured out onto a table for all to enjoy. Boiled Crawfish are usually highly seasoned, so plenty of beverage is required.

In addition to being exceptionally tasty, Crawfish are high in nutritive value and low in calories. Crawfish meat is an easily digested form of high quality protein and an excellent source of phosphorous, iron, calcium, and the B-vitamins. And the fat content of Crawfish is low — only about 2 percent of the meat.

Basic Preparation

Crawfish are purchased live and should be cooked or parboiled on the date of purchase. You will need 5-6 pounds of live Crawfish to yield a pound of peeled tails. To serve them boiled and whole, purchase two pounds per person if there are

several other dishes on the menu, or four pounds per person if not. Some heartier appetites may require larger servings. If you have leftovers, they can be peeled, and the meat saved for another meal.

Before cooking or parboiling Crawfish, place them in a large washtub or other container and rinse well with fresh water. Discard those that show no sign of life. Never place live Crawfish in small airtight containers, containers full of water, or in direct sunlight. In addition, never place heavy objects on the sack of Crawfish or handle the sack roughly, as this could crush or injure many of them.

Crawfish should be parboiled for use in recipes. Boil enough water to cover Crawfish. Either pour the boiling water over the animals or place them in the water. Let stand for 10 minutes. Drain. When cool enough to handle, peel and store in the refrigerator for up to one week. Crawfish meat may be frozen, but must be separated from the fat, as its enzymes break down the flesh. The meat should be covered with water, and kept for no more than a month.

Crawfish are cooked alive. Upon cooking, they become bright red. This cooked Crawfish is ready for picking.

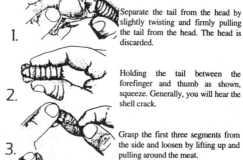

1. Separate the tail from the head by slightly twisting and firmly pulling the tail from the head. The head is discarded.

2. Holding the tail between the forefinger and thumb as shown, squeeze. Generally, you will hear the shell crack.

3. Grasp the first three segments from the side and loosen by lifting up and pulling around the meat.

4. This piece can easily be pulled off now and discarded.

5. Firmly grasp the last segment and tail fin between the thumb and forefinger of one hand and the meat with the other hand and gently pull.

6. The meat should slide out of the shell and the vein should pull free from the meat.

This meat is now ready for eating, freezing, or addition to your favorite Crawfish dish.

(Courtesy South Carolina Department of Agriculture.)

No matter what you call them, mudbugs are fairly simple to clean and prepare. If you go out and catch a good mess, you can keep them alive a couple of days in a wading pool or large bucket with about an inch of water in it and lots of pond weeds or a bubbler meant for keeping minnows alive. When you are ready, fill a large pail with fresh water and dissolve $\frac{1}{4}$ to $\frac{1}{2}$ cup of salt in it. Dump in the crawfish. Paul Prudhomme says that it may be alright to call them crayfish in other places but not to try that in Louisiana. Leave the "mudbugs" in the salt water about 15 minutes. Bring a large of pot of salted water to boil and drop the crawfish into the boiling water. Cook about 3 minutes after they turn red, remove and cool. Shuck off the tails and look for a tiny little wing-like structure in the bottom center of the tail. Pulling it off will remove the small black line that is the intestine. If the claws or pinchers are big enough to fool with, they contain some excellent meat, too.

Crawfish Cocktail

cooked crawfish tails
$\frac{1}{2}$ cup tomato catsup
juice of 1 lemon
horseradish to taste

1 cup mayonnaise or tartar sauce
1 tsp. salt
salt and pepper to taste
lemon wedges

Combine all ingredients except crawfish tails and lemon wedges. Mix thoroughly and pour into cocktail or margarita glasses. Line rim of glass with shelled crawfish tails and serve on plate lined with lettuce leaves. Add lemon wedges.

Fried Mudbugs

1-2 pounds mudbug tails, cleaned
$\frac{1}{2}$ tsp. salt or garlic salt
4 tsps. half-and-half

$\frac{1}{2}$ cup flour
1 egg

Whip the egg and half-and-half together well. Combine flour and salt in a brown paper bag. Dip mudbug tails in the egg mixture and then shake them around in the flour and salt bag. Repeat if you like. Drop into 350 degree hot oil and cook until golden brown. Drain on the brown paper bag and serve with lemon juice or your favorite seafood sauce.

Those are a couple of pretty simple recipes, but actually mudbugs make good ingredients for several types of dishes: in a stuffing with cornbread for gamebirds or turkey or stuffed seafood dishes; in gumbos (of course) with our two wild spices — filé powder made from ground sassafras leaves and wild bay leaves *(Persea borbonica)* from the Carolina Bay in our swamps; and in quiches and other exotic dishes. Man, what a long sentence! "You get a line. I'll get a pole. We'll go down to the crawdad hole!"

Crawfish Étouffée

2 cups crawfish meat
$\frac{1}{2}$ tsp. black pepper
1 stick butter
1 cup tomato, diced
$\frac{1}{2}$ tsp. cayenne pepper
3 tbsps. tomato paste
1 tsp. salt

$\frac{1}{2}$ cup onion greens, chopped
2 or more garlic cloves, minced
$\frac{1}{4}$ cup parsley, chopped
$1\frac{1}{2}$ cups onion, chopped
3 tbsps. flour
$\frac{1}{2}$ cup celery, chopped
2 cups fish or chicken stock

Melt butter in a large saucepan and remove from heat. Stir in flour until smooth to make a roux. Return to medium-low heat and stir for 20 minutes or until dark brown. Stir in onions and celery and cook about 10 minutes. Add tomato paste to stock and stir into roux. Add tomatoes, crawfish, parsley and seasonings. Cover and simmer 20-30 minutes and serve over rice.

Bon Temps
Y'all

Our daughter Jessica will be the first to tell you not to miss the annual South Carolina Crawfish Festival. Write P.O. Box 598, Pawley's Island, SC 29585 for more information. Don't get between "Jack" as we call her and her crawfish!! — or frog legs, either!!

There is one dish they always serve at the Crawfish Festival that I really like. Here is my version of the recipe.

Crawfish Patties

1 cup wild rice	1 cup long grain brown rice
1 tbsp. butter	salt to taste
1½ cups cooked crawfish meat, chopped fine	6 cups water
	hot oil

Add wild rice, butter and salt to taste to the water, bring to a boil and cover. Reduce heat and simmer, covered, 25 minutes. Add the brown rice, more water if needed, and simmer another 25 minutes, being careful not to scorch the rice. What we want here is overcooked rice so that it is real gelatinous and sticks together well as it cools. Remove from heat and stir in the crawfish, mixing well. Rub a little butter on your hands and form the rice and crawfish mixture into patties. Lay aside and allow to cool thoroughly. Heat a little oil in the bottom of a skillet and brown the patties lightly on both sides, heating thoroughly. Be sure to use a vegetable oil.

I usually say cholesterol, schmolesterol!... If you eat enough garlic and stay active, you don't have to worry about eliminating bacon grease from your diet. How can you season greens without it? I have a friend, Dick Tippett, who once addressed the members of the North Carolina Herb Association saying "we are trying to encourage the use of herbs in cooking and to have herbs replace 'grease' as the official North Carolina seasoning!" I use lots of herbs, in cooking and medicine, but there's always a coffee can full of bacon drippin's in my kitchen. In this case, though, you don't want the delicious flavor that grease from smoked bacon imparts overpowering the delicate crawfish taste and the nutty flavor of the wild rice!

Think you're good in the cooking department? There are people who can mold the patties, get them firm enough, and cook them on the grill over charcoal. That's "to die for" mudbugs! You can use them in any recipe that calls for shrimp, including spaghetti sauce and shish kebabs.

"Hasen Pfeffer" Is a Fancy Name for "Rabbit Stew!"

While talking to my friend, Helen Upchurch of High Falls, North Carolina, she revealed to me that she "just adores rabbit!" It is important to note that she said "rabbit" and not "rabbits"! I believe she *adores* rabbit in the same way as Elmer Fudd does — in a stew pot!

Helen went on to tell me about her grandchildren refusing to eat rabbit and wondering if there was any way to get them to try it. She knew that once they had eaten rabbit they'd adore it, too. I told her to do what I do, when necessary: Cut up a couple of rabbits and make them into chicken and pastry or chicken and dumplings — same dish, different names. You can even throw in a small pack of chicken wings to make it look realistic. There's a squirrel and dumplings recipe later in the book. Check it out and substitute rabbit. It's no big deal — in Panama, they substitute iguana for chicken in lots of recipes — chicken and dumplings, pot pie and chicken à la king. An observant person can spot the difference because the iguana bones are flat and chicken bones are round. Iguanas are a lot cleaner in their eating habits than chickens, and so are rabbits!

Hasen Pfeffer is a well-known gourmet dish that originated in Germany, but now comes in many variations. Roughly translated, it means "marinated (or pickled) rabbit stew." Even Bugs Bunny makes reference to Hasen Pfeffer from time to time, though I doubt if he has any first-hand experience! Here is a typical recipe.

Hasen Pfeffer

1-2 rabbits, cut up	3 cups cider vinegar
3 cups water	$^1/_2$ cup sugar or honey
1 medium onion, diced	2 tsps. salt
1 pinch black pepper	1 cup olive oil
1 cup flour	1 tbsp. pickling spices
$^1/_2$ tsp. liquid smoke	

Cut up rabbits and place in a crockery pot, a glass bowl, or even a Tupperware container, but never in anything metal — especially aluminum! Cover with vinegar and water in equal parts and sugar or honey, onion, salt and pepper, and pickling spices. Marinate for two days in the refrigerator or on a cold back porch in winter. Remove rabbit pieces, drain and dry, and dredge with flour. Brown in hot oil in large skillet or pot and gradually add 1 cup of the marinade. Cover and simmer 1 hour or until tender. Use a little of the flour to thicken remaining liquid for gravy and add Liquid Smoke if desired. Serve hot with homemade biscuits or pumpernickel bread.

Rabbit recipes can be very simple or truly gourmet, depending on what you add to them. Rabbit, like chicken, lends itself well to a variety of regional dishes. It is as much at home in a spaghetti sauce as it is in an oriental stir-fry, just as good in some old-world German recipe as it is in a much newer fried rabbit dish from the American South or added to Mexican fajitas. All you need to become an excellent rabbit cook is a good imagination.

Some good Grandfatherly advice:
"Boy, when you find yourself gettin' in a rut, it's time to quit digging!"

San Francisco Rabbit Hash

You can find plenty of rabbits (and ground squirrels) in the shadow of the Golden Gate Bridge. Believe me; I've been there picking mushrooms and there were rabbits everywhere. But this dish gets its name from the inclusion of "the San Francisco treat!"

2 cups rabbit meat, cooked	**1 package Rice-A-Roni, any flavor**
4 tbsps. butter	**¹/₄ cup onion, minced**
¹/₄ cup fresh mushroom, chopped	**1 clove garlic, minced (opt.)**

In a large skillet, melt butter and sauté the onion, mushroom and garlic, if you use it. When tender, add the rice and vermicelli mix and continue stirring and sautéing until vermicelli is golden brown, like it tells you on the box. Add 2³/₄ cups hot water and the seasoning mix. Bring to a boil, cover and reduce heat. Simmer for 15-20 minutes until all water is absorbed. This calls for a little more butter and water than the box says, because the rabbit, onions and mushrooms call for a little extra moisture.

The above can be served at any meal of the day, even breakfast. It is also good if you melt a little cheese over the top before serving. Tame rabbits have tender white meat, while their wild cousins have dark meat, also tender in most cases except for jack rabbits and real old cottontails — which there are very few of.

Fortunately, being almost strictly vegetarian (rabbits may resort to cannibalism in captivity, but then so do chickens), rabbits don't get "gamey" as they get older, a condition uncommon to bunnies. They can get tough, especially old tame rabbits or jacks, and may eventually only be suitable for stews or baking.

(Old, Tough) Rabbit Baked In Milk

1 old rabbit, cut up	**1¹/₂ cup flour**
2 pinches salt	**1 pinch pepper**
2 tbsps. butter	**3 sprigs fresh rosemary**
milk to cover	

Roll rabbit pieces in flour seasoned with salt and pepper and brown in skillet in butter. Transfer to baking dish and add hot milk to cover. Add the butter from the skillet and bake 45-50 minutes at 350 degrees or until tender. The milk makes good gravy.

Rabbit is now considered to be a very healthy meat because it is low in cholesterol, almost totally fat-free and high in protein. Talking about rabbits gets Albert Snipes licking his chops and talking about how good rabbit is — wild ones. He won't eat the tame ones — says they don't have any taste. I've seen him turn down cage rabbits already cleaned. That is what I call sticking to your guns.

Albert Snipes' Special Fried Rabbit

Editor's Note: This recipe is missing because Albert says it is a secret like his secret hush puppy recipe and he isn't ready to reveal the ingredients.

Snowshoe hares can be used in any rabbit recipe. They tend to be tougher than Southern cottontails. Rabbits are born naked with their eyes closed, while hares are born fully covered with fur, eyes open and ready to hop. You can actually skin a wild rabbit with your fingers, but the tougher hides of tame rabbits need a knife or a broken piece of glass or something sharp. They have been bred for tough hides as well as for their meat.

Herbs and Rabbit Sauté

2 rabbits, cut up
8 fresh sage leaves
12 juniper berries
$^1/_2$ cup olive oil
5 tbsps. wine vinegar

3 sprigs fresh rosemary
4 or more garlic cloves
4 bay leaves
salt and pepper to taste
1 large onion, minced

Combine all the herbs in a small bowl, crumbling and mashing them together. If you can't find juniper berries in the store, use cedar berries for the same flavor or $^1/_4$ cup gin. Rub thoroughly into rabbit pieces and season with salt and pepper. In a large bowl, combine herbs and rabbit with oil, vinegar and onion. Marinate in the refrigerator for at least 2 hours, turning several times. Pour rabbit and marinade into large kettle and bring to a boil. Simmer 1 hour, covered, stirring occasionally. Remove cover and increase heat. Cook until most of the liquid is gone and rabbit is tender. Serve hot, maybe over rice or pasta, with juices spooned over top.

Barbecued Rabbit

2 rabbits, cut up
$^1/_2$ tsp. salt
$^1/_2$ cup brown sugar
$^1/_2$ cup vinegar
1 tbsp. paprika
$^1/_2$ cup peanut oil

1 tbsp. Worcestershire sauce
1 medium onion, chopped
$^2/_3$ cup catsup
1 tbsp. pepper
1 garlic clove, minced
1 cup water

Brown rabbit pieces in hot oil and place in a heavy skillet or Dutch oven. Combine other ingredients, mixing well. Pour sauce over rabbit and bake uncovered at 325 degrees for 70-90 minutes, or until done. Baste and turn every 30 minutes or so.

Here are a couple of recipes brother Chuck Laudenslager came up with when he experimented with raising rabbits, soon finding out that one plus one equals a whole bunch and discovering how much room rabbits can take up in the freezer. Of course, it also works well with other small game animals like squirrels and muskrats, game birds like dove and quail and even armadillos.

Chuck's Simmered Rabbit

2 cut-up rabbits, minus backs
1 tbsp. salt or to taste
$^1/_2$ cup flour
(big pinch) nutmeg
2 tbsps. butter
2 medium sized onions, diced

$^1/_2$ pound bacon
big pinch black pepper
big pinch garlic powder
2 cups rabbit stock
$^1/_2$ pound fresh mushrooms

Fry bacon in pan and remove, leaving 2 tbsps. bacon drippings in pan. Combine flour and spices in bag, add cut-up rabbit pieces and shake to coat well. Add butter to grease and brown rabbit well over medium-low heat. Add rabbit stock and onions and bring to boil. Reduce the heat, add mushrooms and crumbled bacon, cover and simmer 45-60 minutes. It makes its own gravy, so serve with potatoes. (Rice for me, thank you.)

Rabbit Stock

rabbit backs
1 large onion, diced
1 cup carrots, diced

water to cover
salt and pepper to taste
1 cup celery, chopped

Salt and pepper rabbit backs and cover with water. Add onion, carrots, and celery and cover, simmering for 2 hours. Add water as needed and remove all bones before use.

You've Got a Dandy Lawn
If You've Got Dandelions!

I used that title for a newspaper column in which I wrote about Peter Gail's new book, *The Dandelion Celebration*, and I like it better than the old title for this chapter — "Dandelions Good Source of Nutrition." A very true statement, but it lacks oomph as a title. The dandelion is perhaps most evident in the early spring when there hasn't been any color for a while, except perhaps the white of snow. Then each time we have our "last" cold snap and spring arrives again, the hordes of dandelions with their bright yellow faces just seem to take over the yard. Of course, after a long dry summer spell they seem to be everywhere when we finally get a good rain. I guess that besides Peter Gail, I may be one of the few people who welcomes them back.

Much more than a troublesome yard weed!

As with all greens intended for the pot, the leaves are more tender and tastier before the plants bloom. However, each time there is another cold snap or long drought spell, the dandelions lose some of their bitterness.

They are so good, though, that if you don't like the bitter taste you can boil it away in a change of water or two to reduce the latex which is the cause of the bitterness. You could serve them in combination with other less bitter greens in salads or as cooked greens. You can add a little extra sugar and more bacon drippin's when boiling them to compensate for the bitterness as we do with late-season collards.

Dandelions are considered by many to be the worst pest afflicting the lawns or golf courses, although some golf courses consider me to be a bigger pest as I try to determine which chemicals they are dumping on the greens and how they affect our drinking-water supplies. Dandelions give their presence away by their golden flowers, and also because where they grow the grass around them thrives. This is due to their long tap roots which bring up trace minerals from far below the surface and share it with their grassy neighbors.

Dandelions have been here a lot longer than golf courses and hopefully will always be here for us to enjoy.

Dandelion Corn Dodgers

1 cup House Autry cornmeal	2 tbsps. honey
1 pinch salt	2 eggs, beaten
1 cup boiling water	½ cup butter (2 sticks)
¾ cup milk	1 cup dandelion blooms without
1½ tsps. baking powder	green parts
1 cup all-purpose flour	

Combine the cornmeal with the honey and salt and stir in the boiling water. Add butter and stir to melt. Add milk, eggs and dandelion petals. Sift in flour and baking powder, then blend until smooth. Drop by spoonfuls onto greased, hot griddle and cook, turning to brown both sides. Serve hot with syrup or drain on paper bag and wrap them up as a trail food when hiking, hunting or fishing.

Biblical scholars consider dandelions to be one of the "bitter herbs" of the Old Testament. They have been grown for centuries as a nutritious green in the gardens of Europe. The dandelion's name is a corruption of one of its names abroad: *diente de leon*, as it's called in France. It means "the lion's tooth" and refers to its sharply indented (toothed) leaves. They also call it *pis-en-lit*, you remember, which means "pee the bed." It has the distinction of bearing two scientific names. Some sources refer to it as *Leontodon taraxacum*, while others use the name more commonly accepted today — *Taraxacum officinale*. That one translates as "official cure for disorders" and refers to all the medical values that have been attributed to it. In Spanish, the name *amargon* means "bitter," referring to the already mentioned latex and its flavor. In Italian cooking, where it may be a staple in some regions, it is called *ciccoria*.

We find recipes for dandelions in a variety of cookbooks from gourmet volumes from *Great Good Food* by Julee Rosso to one called *White Trash Cooking* and everything in between. Julee Rosso says, "Dark greens have the most beta-carotene, a potent cancer-fighter (the orange color is masked by chlorophyll). Popeye was right about his spinach — not to mention... dandelions. Just one cup provides 100 percent of the USRDA for vitamin A. And only 10 calories." What more could you ask? A weight-loss food that fights cancer and lets you see better in the dark!

Posters in the weed control section of most garden stores are almost like "wanted posters" for dandelions, a primary target. This noted "pest" even has its picture on the label of some weed killers — herbicides. It is ironic that in the same garden centers these days we can find dandelion seeds so we can enjoy their flavor and health benefits.

Boiled Dandelion Greens

2 quarts dandelion leaves	1 quart salted water
salt and pepper to taste	2 tbsps. bacon drippin's
1 lemon cut into wedges	

Rinse the chopped greens well in the sink in three changes of water. Boil for 20 minutes in the salted water or until tender. Add drippin's while cooking or olive oil if you prefer. Drain and serve drizzled with a little olive oil and lemon juice. You can also use apple cider vinegar, if you prefer, or hot pepper vinegar.

Dandelions have long been listed in herbal medicine manuals and even official government directories called pharmacopeias as therapeutic. Any plant with the word "officinale" in its name has been accepted as beneficial at some time in its history. Dandelions were listed by Arab physicians in the tenth century and have been used since then for treating various liver disorders, as a diuretic, blood thinner and tonic, and in diabetic diets because of their high nutritional content. The leaves are used as a mild laxative and are valuable in supplying calcium to nursing mothers. A green tea is used to treat colitis.

The U.S. Department of Agriculture handbook number 8, *Composition of Foods*, lists the dandelion as the fourth most-nutritious green, wild or cultivated, if you wade through their charts comparing values. A 3½-ounce serving contains 11,700 international units of vitamin A when cooked and 14,000 raw. Both figures exceed carrots, which we think of as our traditional source of vitamin A for good vision. Dandelion is also high in calcium, phosphorus, and potassium and the B vitamins, as well as vitamin C.

Dandelions and Grits Baked Casserole

4 cups water	2 cups dandelion greens, cooked
⅓ tsp. salt	1 cup uncooked grits
8 ounces shredded cheese,	2 eggs, beaten
Swiss, Cheddar or a blend	1 tbsp. prepared mustard
2 cups ham, finely diced	½ cup grated Parmesan cheese

Add grits to boiling, salted water in a large saucepan and stir to prevent burning or sticking. Cover, reduce heat, and simmer five minutes. Add well-drained, chopped dandelion greens, Swiss or Cheddar cheese and ham. Stir until cheese melts. Fold in eggs and mustard and pour into greased baking dish. Sprinkle the grated Parmesan cheese on top and bake at 325 degrees for 25 minutes, or until a broom straw inserted in the center comes out clean.

Of course, we also make wine from dandelion flowers, and dandelion beer. The dried and roasted roots make an excellent coffee substitute. The greatest consumption, though, of dandelions remains as cooked greens or as a salad ingredient. Theresa Karas Yianilos tells this story in *The Complete Greek Cookbook:* "During a Sunday drive in the country, you may have noticed a neat well-dressed old lady, perhaps in black, digging in fields by the roadside. She works alone while the occupants of a nearby car wait for her. Chances are you have witnessed the spring rite of a Greek woman. She has discovered a patch of dandelions (*radikia*) native to her countryside at their most delicious moment, before they flower and become too bitter to cook. The tender plants are dug up, sometimes roots and all, and taken home to be boiled that very night." Brother Chuck Laudenslager told me that they are also excellent as a substitute for bok choy in stir-fried pork.

Layered Dandelion Green Salad

1 quart dandelions, chopped	¼ cup wild onions with tops, or scallions,
½ cup green pepper, diced	chopped
½ cup celery, chopped	2 cups tender pea pods or redbud
½ cup plain yogurt	tree pods
2-3 tbsps. honey	½ cup mayonnaise
1 cup bacon bits	1 cup Cheddar cheese, shredded
2 cups sprouts, alfalfa or	Chopped hard-boiled egg
bean	

Drain the well-washed dandelion leaves and tear into pieces. Put a layer in the salad bowl. Add a layer of celery, onion, pepper and sprouts. Sprinkle with cheese and bacon. Drizzle with yogurt combined with honey and mayonnaise. Repeat these three layers until you run out of ingredients. Top with hard-boiled eggs and refrigerate overnight to allow cooling and the flavors to mix. Greens must be well-drained to prevent soggy cheese.

When you dig the entire dandelion out of the ground, you will have no waste and won't need chemical pesticides. The roots are eaten as a vegetable if tender and flexible, or roasted for a coffee substitute; the greens are used as salad or cooked; and the flowers are used in fritters and wine. The leaves, when bought in the stores, are going to remain expensive until they catch on more. The real gourmet part is the crown, however. It is the tender, pink part where the leaves and roots come together at ground level. It can be pickled, marinated or added to salads. It is delicious battered and fried. No waste, no mess. If your dandelion has already made its seed ball, you can make a wish as you blow them away!

You can order canned dandelions and dandelion root coffee from Goosefoot Acres, Inc. at P.O. Box 18016, Cleveland, OH 44118.

Dandelion Wine

1 gallon dandelion flowers	5 pounds sugar
4 oranges and 2 lemons	1 gallon water
vintner's yeast	

Remove any insects and the green parts of the flowers. Cover with boiling water and soak for 2 days. Add chopped oranges and lemons and return to a boil. Simmer for at least 15 minutes. Strain through a jelly bag or cheesecloth and add sugar, stirring to dissolve completely. When cooled to room temperature, add the yeast. Pour into a fermenting jug with an air-lock or an open crock which you cover with cloth. Rack (siphon into a clean bottle) when the wine clears and store up to 6 months before sampling. If you can't wait, it is okay to go ahead and drink it.

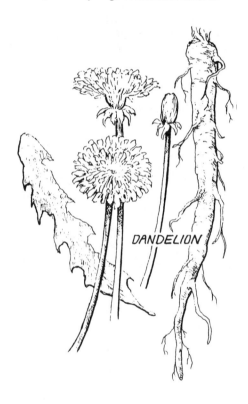

DANDELION

Tricks of the Blueberry Trade

There are "ropes" to learn, short-cuts and tricks of the trade, in virtually anything we could write or talk about or take up as a vocation or avocation. Harvesting wild blueberries is no different. One friend suggests it would be much easier to find a suitable substitute for cooking pies, muffins and maybe even jams, especially in those years when there is a late season frost to make the harvest even scarcer than normal or a long hot, dry spell when the berries need rain, making real blueberries hard to find. "Real" blueberries are hard to find anyhow in some parts of the country, where they could be going by names carried over from the "Old Country." Some of the field guides call them whortleberries or bilberries as they do in Scotland. A bigger argument ensues when we try to determine whether we are dealing with blueberries or huckleberries.

You may have heard this before, but the old wild foods master, Euell Gibbons, says this: "Long before the last blackberries are gone, the blueberries and huckleberries are begging to be picked... In this section (Pennsylvania) all such fruits are called 'huckleberries'— as many as five species are often mixed in the same pail. Since they are all equally delicious, no one cares. Those who like to be more precise reserve the name 'blueberry' for blue or bluish-black members of the genus *Vaccinium*, and use the term 'huckleberry' for berries of the genus *Gaylussica*. If you really want to know which genus the berry you have belongs to, open it and look at the seeds. Blueberries or *Vaccinium* species have many soft seeds, while huckleberries or *Gaylussica* species, have exactly ten hard, seedlike nutlets inside."

I say, "Who cares!" They all pretty much taste the same and are used the same and look alike, except maybe for size. Recently, I found some on plants barely six inches tall — small, dark blue berries — and within stone-throwing distance, larger berries on bushes well over eight feet tall. They all seem to like acid soil, and prefer to keep their feet wet. This propensity for moist locations, at least here in the South, is why so many blueberry pickers run into snakes. I did find lots of blueberries in the dry mountain meadows of the beautiful Green Mountains in Vermont, though, come to think of it. And, when I went through the Master Gardener Course, I discussed at some length with Extension Agent Al Cooke how tame and wild blueberries seem to require and/or tolerate different conditions.

Edelene Wood is President of the National Wild Foods Association, started and inspired by Euell Gibbons. This next recipe is from her book, *A Taste Of The Wild*.

Edelene Wood's Blueberry-Molasses Muffins

2 cups self-rising flour   1 cup molasses
2 tsps. margarine   ½ cup water
1 cup blueberries

To make these, combine flour, molasses, margarine and water and mix well. Add blueberries and bake at 350 degrees for 20 minutes. "This deprivation of sugar will make you understand how the 'South' suffered and how important knowledge of 'make do' wild food can be."

Keep reading, and you'll find out how to use blueberries to make pemmican — the Native American trail snack and survival food. Blueberries can also be made into some fast but elegant desserts at home.

Blue Heaven

1 angel food cake
$\frac{1}{2}$ cup regular sugar
$\frac{1}{4}$ cup confectioner's sugar

4 cups blueberries, divided
1 pint heavy cream
$\frac{1}{2}$ cup blueberry liqueur

In a blender, combine 3 cups blueberries with the blueberry liqueur and the regular sugar. Blend well and set aside. Cut the angel food cake in half so that you are making it in two layers — top and bottom. Whip the cream and confectioner's sugar until it peaks. Wash your hands well, if you haven't already, and, using your index finger, punch a series of holes every so often in each layer of cake down to the first finger joint. Put the bottom layer on a plate and spread half the blueberry mixture on top, filling the holes well, and then spread a thin layer of the whipped cream. Add the top layer and repeat the process, using all the berry mixture up. Use whatever whipped cream is left to cover the top of the cake and the sides. Use the remaining cup of berries to decorate the top of the cake, in a chain around the outside top and wherever else you have enough to put them. Refrigerate the cake at least 2 hours before serving.

Once, I had the good fortune of having my friend Joe McDonald explain to me the rules of berry picking. Joe owns and operates Wildlife Habitat Realty in Hoffman, North Carolina, and I have seen him both in lecture halls where I was speaking and out in the "boonies" up to his butt in snakes and weeds, showing a client a piece of land. Joe specializes in what he calls restricted properties. Not restricted in the old sense when skin color or income was important; no, Joe restricts his land sales to people who want to buy up some acreage and keep it as wild as possible — a man after my own heart! His motto is "Dedicated to Saving Rural Land," and he wants people to leave the berry bushes and the rest of the natural beauty intact. Anyhow, Joe said that when picking berries with womenfolk, you have to work out a system, like being able to eat one for every ten you put in the bucket so you can enjoy some for yourself. Also, he advises, negotiate a little so that you can eat the ones that feel "a little too soft to eat." Thanks. Good point, Joe!

Here are a couple of my own secrets. People always want to know why my blueberry muffins and pancakes aren't blue. Well, don't tell anybody else, but when you are making blueberry pancakes, don't add the berries until just before you pour the batter onto the grill. You can even pour the batter, then sprinkle the berries in. Works great! As for the muffins, it's a little tougher to keep them from looking like they came from a Smurf's kitchen, but not impossible if you drain the berries well (save it to drink), rinse them and add them just before you pour the mixture into the muffin cups. I won a blue ribbon at the county and state fairs with my blueberry jam, so that's not so tough. Just remember to "stem" them real well and add a little extra pectin because they are normally low in it.

Blueberry Jam

3 pints blueberries	2 tbsps. lemon juice
7 cups sugar	2 packages fruit pectin
$1/2$ tbsp. butter	

Boil jars and lids while preparing the jam. Remove the stems from the berries and crush with the bottom of a glass. Measure sugar exactly and set aside. Mix berries and sugar in a large pan and add the butter, which reduces foaming. Bring to a full rolling boil over high heat, stirring to prevent burning. Add fruit pectin and stir well, returning to full boil. Continue boiling one minute, remove from heat, and skim off any foam. Pour into jars, filling to $1/8$th inch from top and seal quickly, using lids and bands. Invert for 5 minutes. Turn rightside-up and, after an hour, tighten rings again.

Hillbilly Blueberry Parfait

leftover grits	blueberries
sugar	cornstarch
parfait glasses	fresh mint leaves for garnish

Cook blueberries in just enough water to prevent burning over medium heat, stirring in sugar to taste for sweetness and just a little cornstarch to thicken. Alternate layers of blueberries and sweetened grits in parfait glasses, ending with blueberries. You can garnish with a mint leaf or two if you want to be elegant.

In the Navy, they referred to grits as "Rebel ice cream." You probably already know what they called creamed beef on toast and I can't tell you the nickname they had for hot dogs. You can make these Hillbilly Parfaits with leftover white rice as well as grits and use about any kind of fruit you have on hand.

Old Fashioned Blueberry Muffins

1 cup blueberries	2 cups flour, divided
3 tbsps. sugar	$1/2$ tsp. salt
1 tsp. baking powder	1 beaten egg
2 tbsps. butter, melted	$3/4$ cup buttermilk

Toss berries in $1/4$ cup flour and set aside. Combine remaining flour with sugar, salt and baking powder in a large bowl and add the liquid ingredients — milk, egg and butter, stirring thoroughly. Just before pouring into greased muffin tins or cupcake papers, fold in blueberries. Fill cups half-full and bake at 400 degrees for about 18 minutes.

Quick and Easy Blueberry Muffins

1 egg	2 cups Bisquick
$1/3$ cup sugar	$2/3$ cup milk
2 tbsps. vegetable oil	1 cup blueberries

Heat oven to 400 degrees. Grease the bottoms only of a 12-muffin or 2 6-muffin pans or line with paper baking cups. Beat egg slightly in medium bowl; stir in remaining ingredients, except blueberries, until moistened. Fold blueberries into batter and divide batter evenly into cups. Bake 15 to 18 minutes or until golden brown.

No matter how you fix them, blueberries are delicious. They are a high source of fiber and contain fair amounts of vitamins C and E, yet only provide about 80 calories per cup. You can store them by drying or freezing, in which case they will last up to 2 years. Boil blueberries in a little water with an equal amount of sugar for a delicious syrup for pancakes or ice cream. Throw a handful into fruit salads or compotes. Add dried ones to chopped jerky and bear fat to make pemmican. Cut into chunks, it makes a delicious (not!) and sustaining trail food.

BLUEBERRY

Pemmican

venison or other jerky
chopped nuts

dried blueberries
bear, buffalo or pork fat

You'll get the best flavor here with melted pork fat, better known as "lard." Buffalo fat is hard to come by and bear grease is better suited to waterproofing moccasins and slicking down your hair. Grind together the nuts, jerky and berries and stir into the melted fat, just enough to hold the mixture together. You can use any type jerky, nuts, and berries without changing the flavor much. Pemmican was a Native American trail food and kept many hunters and warriors alive, but it doesn't taste all that good.

Here are a couple of blueberry recipes that offer more flavor and are more popular, but when you need what pemmican provides, you can't beat it. The nuts provide oil and protein, the fat contains warmth-providing calories and the berries have vitamins and a little sugar, with additional protein coming from the jerky.

Blueberry Pie

4 cups blueberries
3 tbsps. cornstarch
1 cup water
1 double pie crust

1 cup sugar
big pinch salt
2 tbsps. butter

Bake the bottom pie crust in the pie pan and set aside. Combine remaining ingredients in saucepan and simmer over medium-low heat 10-12 minutes. Pour into pie crust, add top crust and seal edges firmly. Cut several slits to allow steam to release and bake at 350 degrees 45-50 minutes or until crust is browned.

Purple Cow for Kids

1 quart milk
$^1/_2$ cup plain/blueberry yogurt

$^1/_4$ cup sugar or honey
3 cups blueberries

Blend at high speed all ingredients until smooth and serve chilled.

Purple Cow for Grown-ups

$1^1/_2$ pints milk
$^1/_2$ cup plain/blueberry yogurt
1 cup blueberry liqueur

$^1/_4$ cup sugar or honey
3 cups blueberries
fresh mint sprigs

Blend at high speed milk, berries, honey, yogurt and blueberry liqueur. Pour over ice cubes and garnish with mint sprigs. Because blueberry liqueur tends to be overly sweet, some of the guys prefer to use half liqueur and half vodka or bourbon.

Keep Local, Natural Fishing FREE!

"A resident may fish with natural bait in his county of residence without a basic fishing license. 'Natural bait' is any bait which may be beneficially digested by fish." That quote comes from the current North Carolina *Inland Fishing and Hunting Regulations Digest*. Every state is different, of course, but here according to law a person may fish in the county in which they live with crickets, worms, minnows, crawfish or even little rolled-up balls of bread dough or kernels of corn, unless they are specifically banned. There are some trout waters where you can't use corn. A lot of people fish using the natural baits and simple equipment such as a cane pole or even a hand line.

Certain others can also fish without a license, too. These include youths under 16 in the company of their parents with proper license(s) in their possession, landowners on their

Jessica and Cousin Charlie Crisp with the catch of the day.

own land, and the legally blind. I hope this is not about to change, but with the economy like it is all the government agencies are seeking new sources of revenue.

Usually people don't send out surveys unless someone wants some ammunition to make a change. I received a survey from the North Carolina Wildlife Federation once in reference to the license-free fishing issue. Although a private conservation organization, they have a lot of influence on the Wildlife Commission and commissioners. The survey went to members, people who can afford to pay dues and buy whatever fishing equipment they desire and don't *have* to fish with worms and crickets if they want to eat fish.

The first question on the survey asked if we should retain the exemptions above or require everybody to have a fishing license. Well, the persons who benefit most from that law didn't get surveys because they can't afford the dues of the Federation, so they aren't really represented.

The people who fish with natural bait and only in their own county are mostly poor or elderly (or both) and probably on fixed or limited incomes. They often walk to where they fish. Many of these people literally "live off the land," eating dandelion greens and poke sallet when the time is right, squirrels and rabbits in season, and fish all year 'round.

Yeah, this is a little political, but requiring some people to have a license would literally take food out of their mouths, or cause them to break the law in order to keep food on the table. So, if the issue comes up again, be sure and let the officials know that the law is good in its present condition and not to tamper with it.

Here are a few easy recipes for panfish. It seems people tend to fish more when hunting season is over and might be looking for a quick new way to use their harvest.

Herbed Broiled Catfish

1-2 fish per person	butter
lemon juice	salt and pepper to taste
parsley flakes	chopped rosemary

Clean and wash catfish. Cut nearly in half along the backbone and butterfly, removing the bone and placing on an aluminum foil "boat." Pour on melted butter and sprinkle with lemon juice, salt and pepper, and herbs. Place 6 to 8 inches away from broiler and cook about 8-10 minutes per side, or until done. Occasionally baste with drippings while cooking, turning once or twice as needed. This recipe goes well with cole slaw and ice tea. I like grits with my fish.

Fish and Rice Made Easy

3 pounds bass/catfish fillets	4 large onions, quartered
1 tsp. salt	1$\frac{1}{2}$ cups uncooked rice
$\frac{1}{2}$ tsp. pepper	1 cup sunflower or peanut oil
big pinch saffron	

First, let me say that saffron is expensive and hard to find sometimes. It adds a nice flavor and color to the rice, though. If you can't find it, use either yellow chrysanthemum petals or calendula petals (pot marigold). Cut fillets into chunks and fry in hot oil until golden brown. In separate pan, sauté onions until they are tender. Place onions in large sauce pan and add saffron or flower petals, salt and pepper and $\frac{1}{2}$ cup of water. Add fish and additional water to cover. Bring to a boil and add rice and additional 2 cups water. Reduce heat to medium-low, cover and simmer until rice is done and water is absorbed. During cooking, add water if needed. Serve immediately.

The author with his upcoming dinner.

This is a staple dish in many parts of the world and can be personalized by adding wild onions, chopped dandelion greens, mushrooms or your own favorite herbs. It adapts easily to cooking in a Dutch oven in the campfire. In some places, the fish heads are used to cook with rice, avoiding waste and using the rest of the fish in other recipes.

Fish Chowder

2 pounds fish fillets
2 cups potatoes, diced
3 slices hickory smoked bacon
1 cup onions and tops, chopped
$\frac{1}{2}$ tsp. salt or to taste
$\frac{1}{4}$ tsp. thyme or rosemary
4 cups milk
1 cup water
big pinch paprika
$\frac{1}{4}$ tsp. black or red pepper
1 cup whole kernel corn

Fry bacon until crisp, remove and sauté onions over moderate heat until brown. Add potatoes and cover with water. Cook until tender, but not mushy. Cut fish into chunks and add to potatoes. Add corn and simmer until fish flakes easily. Stir in milk and spices, then add salt and pepper to taste. Stir to mix thoroughly and heat until simmering, but not boiling. Serve steaming hot.

Of course, you don't have to do anything fancy to enjoy our local fish. Just clean them and rinse lightly. Pat dry. Roll in a little milk (and egg if you like) in a bowl, shake them in a bag with flour, salt and pepper, and fry them in hot oil or butter — about ten minutes per side. Don't forget the cole slaw, grits, iced sassafras tea and hushpuppies.

What's that? Oh, sure, Jimmy, you can have a beer instead of the sassafras tea.

Wild Cherries Provide Some Interesting Desserts

Elderberries, blackberries, mulberries, strawberries and blueberries have all been written about frequently in the paper because Wednesday is "food day," and when they are in season, people want to know how to use them. About the only berry not discussed is dingleberries, unless you count that expression for a stupid or confused person: "He/she don't know sheep sh@#! from huckleberries!"

Since we have run out of berries, let's look at an often-neglected fruit--wild cherries. I always encouraged my survival students to try to learn as much as possible about the botanical names of the plants we discussed, but in the case of the wild cherries, the common names might work just as well. The wild black cherry is *Prunus serotina*. You can get away with calling blackberries *"Rubus"* species because all the *"Rubus"* fruits are either blackberries or raspberries or one of their cousins — with similar shape, flavor and taste. Not so with cherries, though, because even though the *Prunus* genus means cherries, it also means other fruits as well. *"Prunus"* is Latin for "wild plum," and one of our wild plums is *Prunus americana* in some books, *Prunus persica* used to be the peach (*Amygdala persica*, now), *Prunus armeniaca* is the apricot and all the other cherries are *Prunus* something.

Besides the black cherry, there are a couple of other wild cherries to be found here in the southeast and several others across the country. The Carolina laurel cherry is *Prunus caroliniana, P. virginiana* is the choke cherry and *P. pennsylvanica* is the fire cherry or pin cherry. They all share a tart flavor. The pea-sized black cherries are tart-sweet and make excellent jelly and wine and have been used in herbal medicine as cough syrup, expectorant and sedative. The fresh bark is used in flavoring for many commercial cough syrups and cough drops.

The trees bearing the *Prunus* name are easily recognized by a characteristic strong burnt-almond smell in the wood, and this is highly pronounced in the black cherry. That smell indicates the presence of dangerous chemicals. The flesh of the fruit is safe, but the seeds, leaves and woody parts contain toxic glycosides including amygdalin, prunasin and prulaurasin, components of the hydrocyanic or prussic acid found in this plant. This extremely dangerous poison is destroyed by heat and drying, but wilted leaves of freshly-cut trees can convert it into the hydrogen cyanide used in gas chamber executions of Death Row inmates, which there needs to be more of it, it seems. Except for the flesh of the fruit, all parts of the plant should be avoided for cooking, either as firewood or as hot-dog skewers. Cyanide poisoning is rapid and often irreversible, even if identified quickly. Fatalities have occurred among children, and wild cherry leaves cause more livestock poisoning than any other wild plant.

The little fruits are excellent in making jelly, wine and sauces for game, if the seeds are removed, and are delicious, if tart, when eaten out of hand once they ripen. One of the greatest uses for these fruits is as a wildlife plant — the birds love them, and so do many other small animals. They are attractive landscape plants and when they are loaded with cascades of white blossoms, they act as magnets to butterflies seeking their sweet nectar and perfume.

Black Cherry Cordial

ripe black cherries
2-3 ounces rock candy

1 fifth (750 ml) vodka

Pit the cherries. Remove about $^1/_4$ of the vodka from the bottle and do something with it. Drop in the rock candy and as many black cherries as you can fit in the bottle. Shake well and then place in a closet for about 6-8 weeks. Strain if you like and serve in apéritif glasses.

The black cherry is also known as the whiskey cherry or rum cherry in some places because the fruits were added to liquor to extract their *medicinal* properties. Alcohol is an excellent solvent for many plant chemicals, and the resulting black cherry drink could be taken for respiratory ailments, allergy symptoms and as a sedative.

Hungarian Sour Cherry Soup

2 pounds seeded cherries	**1 cup sugar or honey**
10 cloves	**1 6 or 8-inch cinnamon stick**
1 tsp. allspice	**peel from $^1/_4$ lemon**
1 tbsp. arrowroot or kudzu powder	**$^3/_4$ cup dry red wine**
pinch salt	**1 cup heavy cream**

This is a classic recipe that adapts well to our wild black cherries (and other fruits). Pit cherries, saving juice and pulp. Add enough water to make three cups. Combine cherries and juice with sugar and spices in large saucepan. Wrap cloves in cloth bundle for easy removal later if you like. Bring to a boil, stirring constantly. Reduce heat and simmer 10-15 minutes or until cherries are tender. Remove cinnamon stick, cloves and lemon peel. Dissolve arrowroot or kudzu powder in 2 tbsps. cream and stir into remaining cream. Add mixture and wine to cherries and simmer 1 minute. Cool to room temperature and then refrigerate until cold. Serve in chilled bowls with garnish of whipped or sour cream.

Wild Cherry Preserves

2 cups black cherries, pitted	**1 cup sugar**
1 tbsp. lemon juice	**1 tsp. cornstarch**
$^1/_4$ tsp. cream of tartar	

Strain juice from cherries into saucepan and add remaining ingredients, stirring to dissolve sugar. Bring to a boil and add the cherries. Boil about 10 minutes until juice thickens, stirring to avoid scorching. Cover the last 3 minutes. Remove from heat and set pan in a larger pan of cold water to halt further cooking of syrup. Pour into half-pint jars, seal and process 15 minutes in hot water bath.

Wild Cherry Icing for Cupcakes

2 cups black cherries, seeded	**1 cup confectioner's sugar**
1 package cream cheese, softened	

Blend all ingredients well by hand or in a blender. Use this icing for about 18 large cupcakes or for a regular-sized cake.

It is amazing how many people are misinformed about wild cherries. I frequently speak at a local nature preserve called Weymouth Woods. The Ranger/Naturalist there is a friend of ours named Kim Hyre. She has a degree in forestry from West Virginia University, and she nearly freaked out when I ate black cherries during a presentation there. "I thought you were crazy. My dendrology professor at school told us that black cherries are poison!" Remember, it is the seeds and wood that contain the poison, not the fleshy part of the fruit. Enjoy!

Snakes in the Kitchen Can Be Special

"Snake Eaters" is a nickname that soldiers used to associate with Green Berets, but I suspect that no matter how proudly they retain this moniker, many of my cohorts at the Special Forces Association have never eaten any serpents! I guess that a few of the old timers like George Heib, Bob Folwell, Bruce Binas and Jimmy Dean helped to eliminate and consume their share of pythons off the Vietnamese landscape, but these old warriors aren't the only "snake eaters" around. My wife likes rattlesnake and it is not a wise man who gets between our daughter Jessica and a plate of snake meat when she's hungry!

I have been on the *John Boy and Billy Radio Network* to cook rattlesnake on the air. That was a trip! They set up a microphone near the little deep-fat fryer that I had brought with me so people could hear the meat sizzling on the radio. Then it came time to try it. I ate a couple of pieces and John Boy ate some loudly over the air. Naturally, he said it "tastes like chicken." Billy did eat a little nibble so he could say that he did, but Jackie Curry refused. They finally shamed Randy Brazell, Director of Network Operations, into tasting it. I don't think he really tasted it, though. I know for sure he didn't eat it. He moved like a streak across the studio to spit it in the trash can, looking much more like "The Flash" than Chatsworth Osborne III (the *Dobie Gillis* show), whom he more closely resembles most of the time. The photograph John Boy autographed for me says "Tom — Thanks, I'm Still Hungry!"

John Boy, the author, and Billy on the air in Charlotte.

I also fixed it for the Fayetteville Chamber of Commerce once when they came to visit the survival school. I fixed it for about 600 people during a live production of *The Chevy Chase Show* with the help of my host. Chevy was cool! He helped me skin a rattlesnake I had brought with me on the airplane and we chatted like old friends while I cooked it. Later he gave me a photograph which he signed, "Tom, Thanks! You Were Great!" He laughed, "You don't think people will take that the wrong way, do you?"

The author, Chevy Chase, and Frances enjoy a fun-filled day of taping.

One day I received a phone call from Debbe Lowell who had been following my column in the newspaper. She said that a friend of hers had given her a "cleaned" rattlesnake and was looking for a good recipe so they could feed it to a bunch of Girl Scouts at camp!

Chicken Fried Snake

cleaned snake, cut up in pieces	salt and pepper to taste
flour	paprika and rosemary
hot oil	

Rinse and pat dry the meat. Mix salt and pepper to taste with the spices and flour. Roll the snake pieces in the mixture. Fry in hot oil until golden brown. It fries rather quickly, like fish. Don't overcook. Eat like fried chicken!

Eat snake pieces carefully, especially with smaller snakes. They all have over 200 pairs of ribs for navigating and the meat lies along the inside and outside of the backbone. Big snakes like pythons can be cut into pieces about like pork chops once they reach mature size. Some folks prefer to boil the snake, strip the meat off the bones and then use it in any recipe they like.

When you go camping on purpose, always take along some aluminum foil. Even while you are driving, you can wrap meat in it and cook it on the engine's hot block.

Baked Snake-1

1 or more snakes	butter
onion	aluminum foil
wild or store-bought spices	wine, if you have it

Clean the snake, cut (if you desire) into pieces and season with whatever spices you have brought or found and add onion and butter if you have it. Ditto the wine. Wrap the snake securely in two layers of aluminum foil and place the package in the coals or ash bed of a campfire or grill. Cooking time will vary depending on the size of the snake and the coals, but should take 20-40 minutes. Open carefully, avoiding the steam and enjoy!

The kind permission of Mr. Donald Wheeler to reproduce this cartoon in the interest of reptile conservation is gratefully acknowledged.

I see nothing wrong with eating a snake, but I don't believe in killing snakes just because you get the chance. Snakes perform a very important task in controlling disease-bearing rodents and pests. Give a snake a break!

Baked Snake-2

1 or more snakes	**butter**
onion	**river bank clay**
wild or store-bought spices	**wine, if you have it**

This is a recipe similar to the one above, with one exception. You will want to cut off the head and the tail from about an inch away from the vent (on the side closest to the head) to the tip. Slit all the way down the belly skin. Remove the entrails. Keep the snake whole — don't cut it up. Peel the skin almost completely off, leaving just a little attached at one end or the other. Rub with butter, season with wine and spices (if you have them) and then put the skin back in place. Fold meat against meat or close the belly and curl it up. Wrap the whole snake in clay, making a ball with about an inch of clay all the way around. You can use mud in some cases. Put the clay ball in the campfire coals and bake it this way for a couple of hours. Again, time varies according to size and the actual coals. When you open it, the skin should stick to the clay and you can pull the meat free. At any rate, the skin will keep the clay off the meat.

Some people will want to eat a little white clay anyhow on camping excursions — when they get "traveler's diarrhea." Have you seen those ads for that book called *The Doctor's Book of Home Remedies*? They were on television and in the Sunday papers and loads of magazines. When I was still at the Army's John F. Kennedy Special Warfare Center and School, they called me up to ask about natural cures. Here's what the book says:

"A Survivor's Survival Guide"

"Okay, you're out in the boonies. Your Pepto-Bismol, Metamucil, antibiotics, yogurt tablets and loperamide washed away in the rapids, which are running almost as fast as your bowels. Now what?

"We asked, SFC Thomas Squier, an instructor in survival training for the U.S. Special Forces at Fort Bragg, North Carolina, what he tells his survival training students. He says he's tried the following and they work — but you may only want to use them as his men do — as a last resort.

"**Clay.** 'We teach them to eat clay,' Sgt. Squier says. 'Many commercial anti-diarrheal medications, like Kaopectate, contain kaolin, which is a type of clay often found on riverbanks.'"

They also quoted me talking about ash from bones and campfires and tannic acid. Anyway, I took a lot of ribbing from my peers — "You can't say Squier don't know sh@# anymore. He's a sh@# expert!" Well, that's enough of that sh@#! Back to the snakes. Oh, I did catch one little mistake on the part of the publishers *of The Doctor's Book of Home Remedies.* They list Metamucil among the anti-diarrheal medications. Actually, it is a laxative. The generic name is Psyllium hydrophilic mucaloid with dextrose — it is weed seed (a plantain species) husks and sugar! You can make your own much cheaper than you can buy it.

Snakes are considered a delicacy in many parts of the world. The meat of large snakes can be chopped up and served as a "seafood" salad, fooling people as to its true origin. Bill Faust and I pulled that trick on about 200 people, including wild foods experts, at a Wild Foods Weekend in Reidsville, North Carolina.

Chinese Style Snake Soup

cleaned snake pieces	$^1/_4$ cup garlic, minced
2 cups chicken stock	1 tbsp. cilantro, chopped
$^1/_4$ cup ginger, sliced	1 or 2 tbsps. sherry
2-3 drops sesame oil	2 tbsps. rice vinegar
corn starch	olive oil

Brown garlic and ginger in hot oil, remove and set aside. Lightly dust snake meat with corn starch and brown in the same hot oil. Return ginger and garlic to pan and add chicken stock and remaining ingredients. Bring to a boil, cover and reduce heat, simmering 5-10 minutes.

You can find snake meat in fancy French restaurants under fancy names and with fancy prices. The following snake recipe translates as "Fried Hedge Eels:"

Anguille de Haies Frite

chopped parsley	6-inch pieces "hedge eel"
flour	lemon wedges
milk	salt and pepper to taste

Score the back of the snake pieces and form into rings. Secure with toothpicks. Soak in milk 15-20 minutes. Dredge in flour seasoned with salt and pepper. Deep fry in hot oil and garnish with lemon and parsley. You can also dip these rings in a batter before frying.

Snakes are widely known as food because of the popularity of snake round-ups in Oklahoma, Georgia and Texas. Some people insist it tastes like fried chicken, but I think it has a distinct flavor of its own. Because of their fish-eating habits, many water snakes taste like they were fried in cod liver oil instead of vegetable oil, but generally snake is pure white like chicken breast meat, maybe a little pinkish.

Rattlesnake: The other white meat!

When cleaning snakes, the most important consideration is to avoid being bitten, obviously. This is best accomplished by shooting or chopping the head off and burying it immediately. A chopped-off snake head can bite for hours. Venom is the obvious problem with poisonous snakes, but the bite of any snake poses the danger of infection. After disposing of the head, cut off the lower portion of the tail, just ahead of the anal vent. With many snakes of uniform diameter, you can just peel off the skin like a stocking. With bulky snakes, you may have to slit the belly skin. When we were teaching a survival course in Panama, and on world-wide television, my friend and fellow instructor Richmond Nail was quoted as saying this "was like peeling the panty hose off a fat lady."

After removing the skin, grasp the entrails at the head end and pull them out all at once. What you have left is a "U"-shaped piece of meat that you can cut into manageable-sized pieces for cooking.

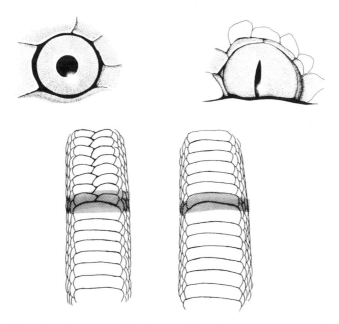

I guess that I should tell you quickly how to identify a poisonous snake in this country. There are four main ones to worry about in the wild: the coral snake and three pit-vipers: rattlesnakes; water moccasins; and copperheads. Many snakes have red, yellow and black color combinations, but only in the coral snake, a relative of the cobra, do the red and yellow bands lie next to each other. Remember this: "Red touch yellow, kill a fellow. Red touch black, won't hurt jack." They are secretive and have small mouths and you just about have to be handling them to get bitten. The pit-vipers all share some similarities. They have a heat-sensitive pit between their eyes and nostrils. Their pupils are elliptical, like "cat eyes," and from their vent to the tip of their tail they have a single row of scales. Native North American non-poisonous snakes have more than one row of scales there and they have round pupils and lack the heat-sensitive loreal pit. You have to be close to observe these details, so just leave snakes alone unless you intend to eat them.

Jeff Eberbaugh's Copperhead Sandwich Spread

Take a bunch of copperheads mashed real flat
Wash em off with water and put em in a vat
Add a little mustard and some real mayonnaise
Let em set in the sun for three or four days
Add sweet pickle that is diced real fine
Mash it all together till it turns to a slime
Chop up a chicken egg and stir it right in
Stir it just a little — don't make it too thin
Spread it on a cracker or some toasted bread
There's nothing like some roadkill copperhead spread

Frances Squier & pet "King Solomon," a great mouser!

Jelly Making Made Easy

It is a well-known fact that men are good at some things, women are good at some things, and everybody is good at *some*thing, regardless of gender. I'm not a sexist or a chauvinist. I believe in people doing what they do best. Those dinosaurs who say women don't have a place in the military haven't met some of the outstanding women soldiers I've known, or served with some of the wimpy guys I have! On the other hand, I don't particularly like to see women in men's suits and ties, either. There must be a happy medium somewhere.

It used to be true that all the great (well-known) chefs were men. This has been proven to be true only because men were in charge of all the cooking contests. Nowadays there are women chefs of equal repute to the greatest male chefs. Still, two of my favorites are Paul Prudhomme and Justin Wilson of Louisiana. They use a lot of ingredients I like, such as turtles, crawfish and wild herbal spices... ground sassafras leaves or filé (fee-lay) powder, bay leaves I can find in my woods, and garlic I can find in my yard. Justin cooks with a lot of wine, and he says, "If it ain't fit to drink, it ain't fit to cook with!" Also, he repeatedly adjusts recipe ingredients "to taste" and tells us "Whose taste? *My* taste!"

Traditionally, though, jelly making has fallen within the realm of women's cooking. Even in such modern places as Moore County, I had to enter my own jellies and jams in the "women's canned and baked goods" category at the County Fair. With an above-average success rate, I won four blue ribbons for five entries one year and twelve out of twelve the next. So it seems that I must be doing something right. Let me share some of my favorite recipes with you.

The author and his many jelly-making prize ribbons.

All you really need to make jelly, jam or preserves is fruit, sugar and pectin. Pectin may be present in the fruit of your choice or it may have to be added. How do you know if there is sufficient pectin or not? There are a couple of simple tests to tell you whether to add pectin or not.

Some fruits are naturally high in pectin. Others are notoriously lacking in this essential ingredient, while still others are high in pectin when unripe, but need added pectin when ripe. These fruits often call for a certain amount of unripe fruit to be included when making jelly.

In the first test for pectin, cook a cupful of the fruit juice you are going to use. Take a tbsp. of the juice and place it on a saucer. Add a tbsp. of alcohol and mix slowly. Any alcohol will work, but use grain (drinking) alcohol if you intend to taste the juice. Jelly will form in proportion to the amount of pectin in the juice — from none to lots.

The second method calls for using a tsp. of Epsom salts instead of the alcohol and if there is any pectin a jell will form in about 20 minutes. If not, add pectin in the form of Sure Jell, Certo or some other commercial jelling agent. Or you could add some fruit high in pectin, such as crabapples, hawthornes or quinces.

The key to success is to follow the recipe instructions. Big problems come when trying to make large batches at one time. Temperature is a major factor in jelly making. You should cook your jelly eight degrees higher than the boiling point of water where you live. At sea level or close to it, this is 212 degrees Fahrenheit. At higher altitudes, this temperature will be just a little higher for every 1,000 feet of change in elevation.

Jelly will be about right for putting in the jars when it "sheets" off the spoon. That means the whole spoonful slides off at once, rather than dribbling off like cough syrup when the spoon is tilted to one side. Avoiding problems is easy if you follow the sequence correctly. Pre-measure the sugar and boil the juice. Add the sugar all at once, along with any additional ingredients such as butter and lemon juice. Return to a full boil and add any pectin if needed. If the pot isn't much bigger than the amount of jelly you are cooking, you are likely to be cleaning up a lot of boiled-over foam. Use a big pot, men!

Goldenrod Jelly

newly opened goldenrod blossoms	3 ounces liquid pectin
1 cup sugar per each cup tea	water

Make a strong goldenrod tea by boiling the flowers with the green leaves removed. Depending on growing conditions, the amount of flowers required varies. The leaves will give it a more bitter, medicinal taste, but the flowers will make a taste more like anise and the jelly will be fruity tasting. Make a tea to your liking and measure the juice. You will need one cup of sugar for each cup of tea. Bring the strained tea to a boil and add the sugar. Return to a boil, stirring constantly, and add the pectin. You will need 3 ounces of pectin per gallon of liquid. Return to a rolling boil and cook two or three minutes, or until jelly sheets. Pour into jars and seal.

This delicate jelly is great for experimenting with. You can add sprigs of mint or rosemary, sticks of cinnamon or herb leaves to create unique flavors. Here is some good jelly-making advice, folks. Once you get the process down pat, look for the fresh fruits of the season and collect them while they are plentiful. You might have to blanch them, but freeze them and make jelly when you have the time. Another good place for finding excellent jelly fruit is on the "Reduced For Quick Sale" rack at the grocery store where the over-ripe fruit is found.

Persimmon Jam

3 pounds persimmons	1 cup sugar per cup of pulp
1/4 cup cold water	2 packages pectin

Clean fully ripened persimmons and cut in half, removing seeds. Crush fruit and add water in a saucepan. Add sugar at the specified rate and bring to a full boil, stirring constantly. Add pectin and boil for a full minute. Skim, pour into jars, and seal.

Blackberry Jam

2 quarts blackberries
4 cups honey (or sugar)

1 package pectin
2 tbsps. lemon juice

Wash fruit, removing green end caps and Japanese beetles from blackberries and combine with honey and lemon juice. Bring to a full rolling boil for 1 minute. Skim foam, cool 3 minutes and pour into sterilized jars and seal.

In the Army, it doesn't really matter whether an objective is actually a real target or not. If it is an easily accomplished task, it is known as a "confidence target." What this really means is that the results are so predictable and the results so certain that this "confidence target" gets a beginner off on the right foot. The "confidence target" is easy to accomplish and offers little risk, but because of the high ratio of success, it builds self-confidence and thus competence so that more difficult tasks can be tackled in the future.

If jelly making were a military operation, then apple jelly would be a "confidence target." Besides almost always providing very tasty results, there is no problem getting the juice to jell. There is nothing more disheartening to a cook than a cake that won't rise, hard biscuits, or jelly that won't jell and ends up as pancake syrup. You don't have to worry about this with apple jelly.

Making jelly from apples or crabapples is fun, because you never know what flavor you will end up with until you are finished. Each tree produces apples of different flavors from year to year due to climactic changes, pollination variances as the bees visit various orchards or trees and just "because."

You can make good apple jelly from apple juice and apple cider that you buy in the stores, but the best and most satisfying jelly is produced when you start with fresh apples, cook them and strain the juice yourself. Today most recipes call for the addition of either powdered or liquid fruit pectin. This is often obtained from apples — green ones and the bouncing jelly attests to the advantage of using one part green apples to 4 parts ripe ones. Good jelly should turn out in one piece, conforming to the shape of the jar or glass it is poured into for storage. Remember that old girl-watcher's comment: "Must be jelly, 'cause jam don't shake like that!" It should jiggle like Jell-O.

Apples should be chopped or crushed with the peels left on, by the way, and the seeds removed. The pectin in the peels is what causes the jelling to take place. It is also harvested as an ingredient in many commercial anti-diarrheal medicines. Ever hear of Kaopectate?

Alright, for the novices, I will give you the basic apple jelly recipe and for the first time or two you try it, follow it closely where the measurements are concerned. Then, once you get the hang of it, you can experiment with some more fancy or exotic recipes.

Basic Apple Jelly

7 cups fresh apple juice or 3 cups
   bottled apple juice
2 ounces pectin

9 cups sugar for fresh juice or
5^1/$_2$ cups for bottled juice
^{1}/$_2$ tsp. butter (optional)

To make fresh apple juice, crush unpeeled fruit and add 1 cup water to 1 pound of apples. Boil, simmering 15 minutes, and strain through a jelly bag, clean T-shirt, or new cloth diaper. You will need 7 cups of juice and it may be necessary to add just a little water. It takes about 3 hours to drip through a jelly bag. Squeeze gently before discarding the pulp. Pre-measure the sugar and the juice. Bring the juice to a rolling boil, add the butter which cuts down on the foam, and the pectin. Stirring constantly, return the juice to a rolling boil and quickly pour all the sugar in at once, stirring constantly. Continue stirring and allow to boil at a full boil for at least 1 minute. The pot will have to have a capacity double the quantity of juice because it will boil up and over. After 1 minute, remove from heat, skim the foam and pour into jars that have been boiled at least 10 minutes to sterilize them. The lids also should have been boiled, even if brand new. Fill jars to within ^{1}/$_8$ inch of the top and seal with lids and rings. Some pectin companies recommend that you now invert the jars for three minutes and then turn upright, checking and retightening ring seals 1 hour later. USDA guidelines also require submersion of filled, sealed jars in a boiling-water bath for 20-25 minutes.

Note: If you enter the North Carolina State Fair and many other similar events, it *must* be processed using either the boiling water bath or a pressure cooker.

This basic recipe for apple jelly works equally well for either apples, producing a golden amber jelly, or crabapples which often yield a delicate pink jelly. This basic recipe also provides excellent results with our wild muscadine grapes, using 5 cups crushed grapes and 7 cups sugar. My daughter, Manda, and I made her first batch of grape jelly one rainy weekend and it was superb. Guess what everybody is getting for Christmas?

Fancy Apple Jelly

1 batch basic apple jelly ingredients
mint leaves
^{1}/$_2$ cup juniper berries

herbs such as rosemary or cinnamon sticks
1 cup chopped sassafras roots
1 tsp. butter (optional)

Follow the basic apple jelly recipe mixture, except add one of the extra ingredients while the apples are cooking — mint leaves, herbs, or sassafras roots. The cinnamon sticks are added to the jelly just before sealing. You can add a fresh mint leaf or two at this time, too. Cinnamon jelly is great with poached eggs and toast, and mint or rosemary jelly makes a perfect addition to game or lamb. Juniper jelly is good for game, goat, pork or lamb. I call it "gin jelly" because the unique, almost medicinal flavor of gin comes from these berries and the flavor is very similar. Just about any fruit can be made into a jelly or jam.

Jelly is made from the juice and jam is made from the whole fruit, with seeds removed. Jam is also thicker and less wasteful!

Enjoying the Wild Foods of Summer

You don't have to be reminded when summer is here in full force, because there aren't many summer days when the temperature doesn't top the 90-degree mark. Even after a thunderstorm, it is like a sweat-box.

We had a rainy July and early August this year, but it has been in pockets and there are still some places where more rainfall can make a critical difference for those crops that weren't already burned up. Some places only had $1/2$-inch of June rain where there are usually 10. As a result, a lot of farm ponds are close to drying up, and you see wading herons foundering themselves on fish in shallow water, and snapping turtles crossing roads and fields in search of water. At least one farmer plowed under his fields of barren corn and misshapen watermelons as green fertilizer to make something else grow.

When the rains finally came, there was a flurry of mushroom growth and my wife, Frances, managed to locate a few nice puffballs. So we had mushrooms for a couple of days in a row — fried slices one day seasoned with Tony Chachere's Creole Spices, and then in salad and cooked in wild rice which was used to stuff Cornish hens. When the thunderstorms cooled things down, I managed to catch a few nice bream and other panfish. Some people are now warning that you should have your farm pond fish and water tested for chemical pollution from runoff. If you are concerned, broiling the fish instead of frying them seems to get rid of chemicals rather than concentrating them further.

Dilled Bream or Bass

2 pounds bass fillets or whole cleaned bream	2 tbsps. butter
	1 pinch paprika
1 tbsp. lime juice	4 tbsps. fresh dill, chopped
salt and pepper to taste	lemon wedges
1 tbsp. green onion, minced	dill weed for garnish

If using whole bream, insert a little dill inside. Melt the butter and stir in the chopped dill, the lime juice and the minced green onion. Salt and pepper the fish to taste. Sprinkle with a little paprika and pour half the butter over the fish. Broil about 5 minutes, being careful not to burn. Turn the fish, pour on the remaining butter, and broil about 5 more minutes or until done. Serve with a garnish of dill sprigs and lemon wedges.

If you feel like you have to fry those fish anyhow, and that's my favorite way of fixing them, just be careful where you catch them. They have closed some lakes around town, on local golf courses and on Fort Bragg, because the fish were contaminated and considered unsafe to eat.

Roll the cleaned fish or fillets in corn meal or flour, or a mixture seasoned with salt and pepper, garlic salt and Cajun spices if you like them, after drenching through a milk and egg mixture. Fry in medium hot peanut, sunflower or other low-cholesterol vegetable oil about 5 or 6 minutes per side, depending on size.

One of the most abundant weeds (depending on your point of view) is the lamb's quarters or wild spinach, *Chenopodium album*. Because it contains more vitamins and lacks the oxalic acid of "real" spinach, it's actually better for you. It is a way we got the kids to eat some wild greens, and they were so good that the youngsters actually ask for them from time to time.

Lamb's Quarters Pinwheels Italiano

1 package lasagna noodles
2 cups chopped lamb's quarters
1 tsp. garlic salt

2 cups Italian tomato sauce
1 15-ounce carton Ricotta cheese

Cook the lasagna noodles according to package directions, adding salt and butter or oil as required. Boil about 8 minutes until tender but not mushy. While noodles cook, steam the lamb's quarters until tender. It will smell a little like spinach, change color and cook down to 1 cup. Drain this well and fold into Ricotta cheese, mixing well. Lay out the noodles flat and spread with the cheese mixture. Roll up like a jelly-roll and place on end in a glass baking dish, not touching each other. Sprinkle with garlic salt and pour tomato sauce over top. Bake at 325 degrees for about 30 minutes. Sprinkle with Parmesan cheese if you like. To keep the heat out of the kitchen, microwave on high for about 7 minutes, rotate $^1/_4$ turn and cook 5 more minutes on low power. You can use low-cholesterol cheese and make this real heart-smart!

Here is a little dish that will help get rid of another weed, sheep sorrel or *Rumex acetosella*. It is nutritious and delicious and can be served hot or cold.

Cream of Sorrel Soup

$1^1/_2$ cups sheep sorrel, chopped
2 tbsps. flour
$^1/_2$ cup whipping cream
sour cream

2 cups chicken stock or broth
1 cup milk
pinch of nutmeg
sorrel leaves for garnish

The arrowhead-shaped leaves make it easy to identify. Boil the chopped leaves in the broth for 10 minutes. Remove from heat and stir the flour into the milk and then add the milk and whipping cream to the broth and sorrel. Heat just enough to thicken, stirring well. Serve hot with a dollop of sour cream and dusted with nutmeg. Garnish with the extra leaves. You can serve this later, chilled.

This delicious soup tastes much like the currently-popular lemon soup. You can also use wood sorrel *(Oxalis)* or French sorrel if you grow it in your garden.

When the rain freshens the mint in the yard, or you locate some down by the creek, you can make a cooling and relaxing summer refresher. If you aren't driving and are over 21, try this version of the classic Mint Julep: Fill your blender with ice cubes and crush well, making what we used to call cracked ice. We made our cracked ice with a hammer after wrapping the ice in a clean towel. Add 1 cup water, $^1/_2$ cup sugar, $^1/_2$ cup bourbon (more or less to taste, but this is just about right) and $^1/_2$ cup chopped mint leaves. Blend again and serve with a mint leaf garnish or perhaps a cherry.

This next recipe isn't really wild food, except for the fact that tomatoes are one of the gifts the Native Americans made to the "Old World" after Columbus landed in this hemisphere (he never did make it to what is now the United States). It is one of my favorite summer foods, and of course goes well with any fish or seafood meal, along with corn on the cob, another Native American dish. Many people don't realize this, but tomatoes were taken back to the British Empire as an ornamental plant. Because they are bright red, they were considered poisonous and grown strictly as a decorative plant.

Of course, their green parts are poisonous, as are the green parts of their cousin the potato. You guessed it! The potato also came from the Native Americans. Both tomatoes and potatoes are related to the deadly nightshades and the potentially deadly Jimson weed. Potatoes came from the natives of South America and were originally small and blue. We often call them "Irish Potatoes" because they have been extensively cultivated in Ireland. However, in Ireland they are called "Virginia Potatoes." Their relatives, the tomatoes, were known as *pommes d' amour* or "love apples."

Fried Green Tomatoes

4 big green tomatoes
1 pinch ground black pepper
2 cups yellow or blue corn meal

7 tsps. salt, divided
1 tsp. garlic salt/powder
grease or vegetable oil

Slice tomatoes into $^1/_4$ to $^1/_2$ inch slices and sprinkle with salt. Let stand 15 minutes and blot away excess moisture. Roll in cornmeal seasoned with garlic salt or powder, depending on how strong you like the garlic flavor, 1 tsp. of salt and the pepper. Cook in the hot grease or oil until browned, turn and repeat on the other side. Serve right away, sprinkled with salt to taste. When they cool, they often tend to get mushy.

I also like green tomatoes, which botanists say are actually a fruit, made into pickles, hot or not, adding peppers if you like.

Wild in the Aisles

Well, once hunting season is over and the spring fishing gets going full-swing, people start thinking about how to fix the game, birds and fish they have in their freezers. Some people, that is, hunters, their relatives and friends, are concerned about wasting this healthy food or letting it freezer burn.

By the time March roars in like a lion, and February, the shortest month, slides off the calendar for another year, the season closes for rabbits, raccoons, 'possums and for quail, too, except on private preserves. A glance in the papers shows all sorts of sales running for fishing equipment. Some people like the idea of eating wild or exotic foods, but don't care much about hunting or fishing themselves. Others don't enjoy the messy job of cleaning stickers from cactus or scales from fish or sliding around the mud at the crawfish hole. You can call 1-800-BUY-WILD and mail order any type of wild meat you want and in just about any quantity. You might also find the answer on the shelves of local grocery stores where you can go "wild in the aisles." You can find some foods that you may consider to be "living off the land" survival-type foods, but they can be pretty good. You can expect to pay "a pretty penny," as they say, though.

Intrigued by the idea of eating crawfish? You could go out with Frances and me and turn over rocks in a cold stream in search of wild ones. Or you could check out the grocery chains which are importing them from Louisiana these days as well as buying them from local crawfish growers. You can find them fresh or frozen, cooked or even live in some cases.

Looking like tiny lobsters, the fresh-water crawfish has a much more delicate flavor when eaten simply steamed, shelled and dipped in butter or when cooked in a gourmet dish. Frances says she likes the texture of the meat much better, more like shrimp and less like the lobster which she says tastes like rubber. No matter how you end up fixing them, they have to be first steamed or boiled until the shells turn from gray to red. Then the tail meat and often the claw meat is removed and eaten.

Crawfish and Zucchini

6 cups zucchini, sliced	1 pound crawfish tails, cooked, peeled and
2 tbsps. peanut oil	deveined
ground cayenne to taste	$^1/_2$ cup fresh parsley, chopped
1 cup dry white wine	salt and pepper to taste
1 cup water	1 tbsp. garlic, minced
2 tbsps. lemon juice	1 cup onion, diced

Heat the peanut oil in a large saucepan over medium-high heat and sauté the onions and parsley until onions are transparent. Add the wine, water and garlic and continue cooking for 10 minutes. Stir in the zucchini and add salt, pepper and lemon juice. Cover and bring to a boil. Add the crawfish, bring back to a boil and reduce heat. Simmer 30 minutes, covered, stirring occasionally.

That recipe works well in a Dutch oven in a campfire. Just remember to take the zucchini. You can catch the crawfish.

Crawfish Salad

1 pound cooked, peeled and
   chopped crawfish tails
2 hard-boiled eggs, grated
juice of 1 lemon
$^1/_2$ cup pecans, chopped

1 cup green onions & tops, chopped
$^1/_2$ cup mayonnaise
     Tabasco sauce to taste
1 head lettuce, shredded
1 cup peas

In a small mixing bowl, combine the eggs, crawfish, peas, onion, mayonnaise, Tabasco sauce and lemon juice with pecans. Put lettuce on plates and top with crawfish salad mixture. Serve chilled.

A little note when cooking crawfish is to rinse them real well before cooking and save a little of the water they were boiled in for cooking rice, pasta or even corn on the cob.

An easy wild food to gather where I live is the prickly pear cactus. What would you expect from an area called the "Sandhills"? However, it is far from one of the more popular wild foods to gather. I can't tell you how many hours I have observed Frances trying to remove the little pickers out of her fingers. When I point out that they aren't "pickers" or "stickers," but are "glochids," it doesn't seem to help her frustration and irritation one tiny bit. I guess some people are just naturally short-tempered!

In our stores now, you can buy raw tender, almost sticker-free cactus in the fresh produce sections, or you can buy cleaned and already sliced-and-spiced cactus in the Mexican canned goods aisle. Look for "nopales" and "nopalitos" in cans and jars. When first boiled, the water is very slimy, like boiled okra, but in a change of water it more closely resembles cooked snap beans.

Cactus Quiche

1 cup cactus, cooked
4 eggs
2 cups cheese, grated
1 undiluted can cream of
   mushroom soup
1 onion, diced

2 tbsps. butter
1 9-inch unbaked pie shell
2 tbsps. flour
2 tsps. Dijon mustard
$^1/_2$ cup half-and-half

Sauté onion in butter and spread in bottom of pie shell. Sprinkle with cheese, using Cheddar, Swiss, Monterey Jack (with or without jalapeños) or a combination. Blend together beaten eggs, flour, mustard, soup and half-and-half and pour into pie shell. Drain cleaned and cooked cactus strips, and stir into quiche mixture. Bake 15 minutes at 425 degrees and then 45 minutes at 325 degrees or until a knife blade stuck in the center comes out clean.

The prickly pear pad or leaf has to be cleaned with either a potato peeler or knife to remove the glochids, and boiled in your chosen number of water changes. Cooked until tender, the cactus strips make an excellent vegetable, especially when a little cilantro and hot peppers are added for flavor. They are also very good when "pickled" in some herb-flavored vinegar after initial cooking and served chilled.

One of the most delicious and dependable wild mushrooms is the oyster mushroom, so named because it looks like an oyster growing out of the side of a dead tree or log and because it has an oyster flavor to some people. Wild mushroom picking requires absolutely positive identification, but oysters and other mushrooms are often available in the store.

Grilled Mushrooms

fresh fleshy mushrooms
lemon juice

olive oil
Italian herb blend/bouquet garni

Combine equal amounts of oil and lemon juice and lightly coat both sides of the mushrooms or mushroom slices. Sprinkle with herbs and grill over charcoals for about 2 minutes per side, serving hot. You can also broil these in the oven under the broiler element.

I have also noticed in the fresh produce sections of some stores little bags of sassafras bark or tea bags for making tea. Latest research is that it's not the dangerous cancer-causing chemical that it was rumored to be a few years ago. It is a delicious tea, hot or cold, that tastes like root beer and flushes the kidneys. Native Americans used it to defeat kidney stones. The government's danger stories are more "read my lips" misinformation. Enjoy it! Drinking beer is far more likely to cause cancer.

PUFFBALL
...CALVATIA SPECIES

A Social History of the American Alligator

One of the first comic strips I remember reading was *Mark Trail*, the nature story. It occasionally talked about alligators, which I found fascinating. The other was *Pogo* and the hero *was* an alligator. Later, "Wally Gator" became a cartoon saurian hero and today is known to millions. After I graduated from high school, I joined the Navy and went to Vietnam. Later I got smart and spent 18 years in the Green Berets.

This design is available on a T-shirt in 4 colors for $20 postpaid from Broken Bear, 4925 Ashemont Road, Aberdeen, NC 28315. Be sure to specify M, L, or XL. Add $2 for XXL.

I joined the Navy on the Delayed Entry Program so I could have the summer free and I went to Ocala, Florida, where, because I was so young, nobody would rent me a room. I moved into a huge live oak tree in the Ocala National Forest and worked at Six Gun Territory doing Indian dances and playing "Billy Clanton" in the gunfighter shows there. I had a ball. I also worked for Ross Allen catching snakes and other reptiles. I ate a lot of armadillos and palm cabbage, fish and whatever else I could catch or find.

'Gators were protected then, but when one was killed because he forgot to look both ways before crossing the road, I found a bunch of ways to cook the firm, white flesh. I also had a friend in a country-club community who occasionally had to shoot one when it took to liking the taste of French poodle, and he would give me the meat. I was surrounded by alligators. On Saturday nights I would head up to Micanopy (home of outdoor writer Tim Tucker, AKA "the Micanopy Flash!") to a little juke joint and listen to 'Gator Lyle and the

Crocodiles. Some of the Seminoles living at the Reptile Institute's village taught me the nuances of alligator wrestling. When I succumbed to the CB craze, my "handle" was "The Blue Gator."

One of my all-time favorite jokes (or is it a parable?) is about the discussion between the fat alligator and the skinny alligator. The big alligator asks his puny friend why he is so skinny and what he eats. The emaciated one replies that he eats mostly second lieutenants, and lots of them. The other alligator notes that as dumb and easy to catch as they are, he should be a fat alligator, too. "How do you fix 'em?" he asks. The skinny one replies that he lies in ambush by the trail to the beach and when they come along he slaps the sh@# out of them with his powerful tail and eats them. "There's your problem!" he says. "When you slap the sh@# out of a second lieutenant, there ain't much left!"

Watch out for second lieutenants... some, but not all, are dips!

In all fairness, I should say that there are some good lieutenants somewhere out there. Lieutenant Emmiko McGraw, for example, helped restore my hearing somewhat when I went to Aural Rehabilitation at Walter Reed Medical Center. Of course, she got promoted to captain and will undoubtedly go higher. Then there were those great colonels I knew and respected — Ted Mataxis, Pete Stankovich, Al Bucknell, and two really great friends and role models, Nick Rowe and Bob Howard, who earned the Medal of Honor. They all used to be lieutenants, believe it or not, and Nick Rowe was even a West-Pointer — but he was not a "ring knocker!" And Major Doug Vermillion will also probably go on to make colonel.

There are a few other good ones, too, but too many would starve a poor 'gator using the wrong capture technique!

Alligators have always fascinated me, as you can see, and I don't think I am alone in that sentiment. A book by Vaughan L. Glasgow, *A Social History of the American Alligator* (St. Martin's Press), is a riveting look at the parallel histories of America and the alligator. Glasgow, curator of the Louisiana State Museum shows us that since the white man set foot here the alligator has been a constant nemesis, companion and source of wonder, as it was to the Native Americans who lived

Alligator mississippiensis, at your service.

here for eons before America was "discovered*." Alligator mississippiensis* has intrigued biologists, poachers, tellers of tales and merchants, and may outlive all us human beings if we don't change our ways.

Glasgow says that alligators have been here virtually unchanged for about 70 million years, along with those other biological successes, the shark and the cockroach. Its closest relative, he informs us, is the Chinese, not the American crocodile. Even Mark Twain, one of our most celebrated writers, found them fascinating. In one story, he wrote that "they were so thick as to form alligator shoals in the Mississippi River which had to be cleared out with dredges."

Although alligators have always fascinated us, they were almost driven out of existence by man's greed. Poachers sold 'gator hides to be made into fashionable and durable leather products. They were almost exterminated and became protected as an "endangered species." Now there are legal alligator seasons in several Southern states where their harvest is strictly regulated. A new market has been developed for their meat which is now outselling the hide. Alligator farms have sprung up from Florida to Texas and they are raised like chickens. Well, not exactly — actually they are fed chickens in some cases. A flooded chicken farm or a tornado can mean some fat, happy 'gators!

On a recent trip to the "Sunshine State," I learned that it is now an offense punishable by a fine up to $500 to feed Florida alligators. They are everywhere, and people are once again fearing for their dogs.

No matter how you feel about alligators and whether your interests are strictly inquisitive, herpetological or culinary, you will be fascinated by Glasgow's book. The alligator was held in high esteem by the native Americans, and his research reveals that even the Senecas in far-away New York revered it. The book opens with a chapter that discusses alligator myths. "Lost in the Mists of Time" explains which alligator legends are true, which are based in fact and which are pure fantasy. Or how was that put the other day? "Interpretations of the truth!" Does alligator fat really cure arthritis? They can outrun a horse for short distances, you know, so maybe it does! Can alligator fat fight fever? Or treat rheumatism? Sprains?

One thing the alligator can cure is hunger pangs! Glasgow remarks, "Among the most interesting phenomena in the past few years has been the introduction of the alligator to the table." The delicious white flesh is high in protein and low in fat, and Americans are seemingly more willing to try something new.

Why, you can even find 'Gator Jerky for sale in some places, and the fresh meat lends itself well to stir-frys, stews and fondues. It is still expensive, though, and a dream come true for the yuppie party giver! It is expensive enough to be fashionable, yet environmentally conscious with the proliferation of farm-raised alligators, and delicious enough that everybody will love it.

"A Map of the British Empire in America," published in 1737, is decorated with a rather large alligator and a couple of Rubenesque Indian princesses. Chapter 4 of Glasgow's book, "The Gray-Green Badge of Courage," explores the position of the alligator in Native American culture, semi-historical writings, and truly accurate diaries of our history. Alligators may not have all the mystical powers attributed to them, but they still serve as mascots for the Louisiana State Museum and University and for Florida State University, one of my *alma maters*. I didn't graduate from FSU, but attended a lot of classes at their satellite campus in the Panama Canal Zone.

Glasgow says alligator hides have been used as musical instruments by Indians, their teeth have been used as "pacifiers" for infants and they have graced the tables of the very richest and the very poorest alike. It is my hope that all our endangered species could recover with the strength of the alligator.

I know I'll never be this young again, but I can't promise that I won't ever do anything this dumb some time in the future!

Alligator Tail Steak

2 pounds 'gator tail steak
$^{1}/_{2}$ tsp. garlic powder
1 tsp. paprika
salt and pepper to taste

1 cup flour
juice of 1 lemon
2 eggs, beaten
$^{1}/_{2}$ cup or more bacon drippin's

Cut the meat into strips and sprinkle with lemon juice. Combine flour, garlic, paprika and salt and pepper. Wipe 'gator meat dry and dip into flour, then into beaten egg and back into the flour mixture. Fry quickly in hot bacon drippin's.

Smothered Alligator

2 pounds 'gator meat, cubed
2 cups celery, diced
2 bay leaves
$^{1}/_{4}$ cup peanut oil
2 tbsps. Tabasco sauce

2 onions, finely chopped
8-10 shallots, minced
$^{1}/_{4}$ cup fresh basil, diced
1 bell pepper, chopped
4-6 sprigs parsley

Sauté onions until tender in oil and add pepper and parsley and continue cooking until tender. Add 'gator and seasonings and simmer covered for 45 minutes or until tender. Add parsley and shallots and simmer 10 minutes more.

Alligator Sauce Piquant

1 large onion, diced
$^{1}/_{2}$ cup celery, diced
1 garlic toe, minced
1 cup dry red wine
3 tbsps. flour
$^{1}/_{2}$ pound butter
1 tbsp. sugar

3 pounds 'gator meat cubes
$^{1}/_{4}$ cup bell pepper, diced
2 cups stewed tomatoes
1 6-ounce can tomato paste
2 tbsps. Worcestershire sauce
3 tbsps. Tabasco sauce
4 cups water, at least

Drench meat with Tabasco and brown in melted butter. Add vegetables and cook 5-6 minutes. Add tomatoes and tomato sauce and sugar. Mix flour with cold water to make a paste and add to mixture. Add remaining ingredients. Simmer with 4 cups water for 4 hours or until tender, adding additional spices to taste.

Jeff Eberbaugh's Alligator Tail

Take a roadkill gator tail from down in mississip
And start some red-hot coals in your Bar-B-Q Pit
Skin out your tail — There's no hair or feathers
Then wrap it in some foil with some halapena peppers
Not too many peppers, cause they do give quite a zip
The first piece I ever had was so hot I almost flipped
Cook your tail for quite a while but check it now and then
To let a roadkill 'gator burn would be an awful sin
Take it out and slice it up and cook some beans and kale
And fetch ya somethin good to drink and enjoy a piece of tail
When you eat your tail, take your time and never eat too fast
Cause a piece of tail is hard to find and it just might
Be your last
So go out early on the beach, before the boats set sail
Who knows, you might get lucky and pick up a piece of tail!

The 'gator-lover's delight!

Alligator Kebabs

alligator meat
hot oil in deep fryer
flour

salt and pepper to taste
garlic salt to taste

Cut alligator meat into bite-sized cubes. Using a wooden kitchen mallet, tenderize it if necessary. Wild 'gator is tougher than farm-raised 'gator, and old 'gator is tougher than young 'gator. Season flour with salt, pepper and garlic salt to taste. Roll 'gator meat chunks in flour and skewer on bamboo or metal skewers. Leave about 1-inch space between meat chunks to allow complete cooking quickly. The longer it cooks, the tougher it tends to turn out. Drop skewers in hot oil and cook until browned on all sides, turning as needed. Serve immediately. Remember the skewers are hot this way.

'Gator Kebabs 2

alligator meat cubes
onion chunks
large pineapple chunks (opt.)

Newman's Own dressing
bell pepper chunks

Marinate alligator meat overnight in Newman's Own dressing. Skewer with chunks of pepper, onion and pineapple if you use it. Cook under the broiler or over charcoal, turning as needed to ensure complete cooking.

'Gator Chili

2 pounds ground 'gator meat
bacon grease
1 tbsp. chili powder
2 garlic cloves, minced

1 pound pinto beans
1 jar Bombolino spaghetti sauce
1 onion, minced
salt and pepper to taste

Cook pinto beans until tender, allowing liquid to slowly cook away without burning. Brown alligator meat in bacon grease with onion and garlic. Combine beans, 'gator, spaghetti sauce, and chili powder in large pan and season to taste. Heat thoroughly and serve hot with crackers and extra hot peppers for those who like them.

I like to top my chili with shredded cheese and minced raw onion. This recipe works for any type of game meat.

Secrets of Snapping Turtle Soup

There aren't many things around here as ugly as the snapping turtle, and some people think there is nothing around here to match the taste of a snapper either. Paul Prudhomme says, "Turtle meat is just exquisite and has its own particular taste. You'd never mistake it for beef. It has a wonderful sweetness to it." A lot of people must agree, because it is one of the most popular dishes in New Orleans with the tourists and the local people alike.

The author, mother-in-law Delphia Whisnant and nephew Charlie Crisp
proudly display a snapping turtle.

It is so popular that some people are concerned about the possibility of over-harvesting snapping turtles. Dr. Peter S. Pritchard, author of *The Encyclopedia of Turtles*, says that this huge and spectacular turtle is one of the most popular exhibits in zoos like the National Zoo in Washington, D.C. where thousands of children see it daily. He also says that it is in danger of disappearing from many places because its meat is so valuable. Pritchard says that what really tells you it is in danger is the fact that some turtle trappers are calling for some kind of control of its capture. A trapper from Georgia agrees with him. He says that it is possible to catch every turtle out of a pond and that is why people have to go to waters in Georgia, Florida and other states to catch turtles for the Louisiana markets, where, according to Pritchard, hundreds of thousands of turtles are sold annually. An indication of their scarcity is the selling value. Turtles once selling for five or six dollars are now selling for over a hundred!

It takes the turtle 7 to 10 years to get to breeding age and about 40 years to reach marketable size. The US Department of Agriculture says in *Composition of Foods* that turtle meat is high in protein and iron and low in fat, but interpretation of the charts indicates that a live turtle is 70% waste. Government specialists are probably a lot more picky about what they eat, so you may get more usable meat than they claim. Plus you can always find uses for other parts — jewelry from the claws, survival weapons from them as well, and all sorts of uses for the shell. You can cook in the shell as long as it doesn't dry out and split into pieces. My friend Frank Sherwood made a very unique musical instrument out of a dried snapping turtle. The long snake-like neck which helps contribute to the scientific name — *Chelydra serpentina* — was stretched out about a foot and dried as good as the neck on any Gibson guitar, but with more "personality."

Though people in most places aren't as enthusiastic about eating snapping turtles as the folks in New Orleans seem to be, it still brings a good price and is served as a delicacy. You can find it on restaurant menus or in cans in the store.

There are really two kinds of snapping turtles, but the one most commonly seen and with the widest range is the common snapping turtle, *Chelydra serpentina*. They are common in North Carolina and I find them often while fishing, but they have a very wide range. I have seen them as far north as Maine, where I caught one crossing a bridge in the first week of June, no doubt looking for a place to lay eggs. A farmer in New York near Niagara Falls told me he located them during nesting season by plowing a bare strip around his ponds and following the tracks to the nesting turtles.

We often see them on the roads in spring, looking for nesting sites and later, as summer's heat dries up ponds, looking for water. A large snapping turtle where I live might

The author and daughter Amanda admire Chelydra serpentina.

weigh 50 pounds, but they can get up to 150 pounds with a 20-inch shell. The larger alligator snapping turtles, *Macroclemllys temmincki*, can grow well in excess of 200 pounds! These turtles are considered non-game animals in North Carolina, and their harvest is unregulated. Check the regs in your state, because some states have seasons and limits, and alligator snapping turtles are protected in some states.

They can do considerable damage in ponds when they are crowding. Snappers grab ducks and geese by the feet while swimming and drag them to the bottom to drown them They use their powerful beaks and claws to tear the birds apart chunk by chunk. They can be expensive pests in ponds where food or aquarium fish are being raised. That is why they are very unpopular with people who raise catfish for meat like other farmers raise cows or chickens. The turtles are very aggressive and fast when out of the water. They can deliver a bone-crushing bite at amazing speed, as children, dogs and fools have found out.

It is possible to buy snapping turtle meat in the stores, especially seafood shops, but most people will be getting their own. These turtles are easily caught by placing a very large hook, like they make for sturgeon or sharks, on a strong metal leader and then tying it with strong twine or heavy-duty fishing cord. Bait it with a turkey gizzard, fish head or parts of a roadkill cat or possum and leave it in the quiet water near a dam, under a bridge or in the bend of a stream overnight. Check regularly. Another way to catch these delicious reptiles and wear them out at the same time is to attach your hook and line as described above to the tip of a long bamboo pole and stick the butt of it deep in the mud with the baited hook suspended in the water. When a turtle is caught, the springiness of the pole offers resistance and wears the turtle out without allowing it to get a grip in the mud to break your line with its strength. A 30-pound turtle can walk around with a 200-pound man standing on his back with no trouble!

There is no easy or neat way to clean the turtles. They have to be killed some way, and usually they are shot in the head or it is chopped off. Cut-off snapping turtle heads remain dangerous for hours, so beware! Then the cleaning progresses. Smaller turtles can be dropped whole into pots of already strongly boiling water where they die quickly. Boil for about 20 minutes and then the skin and toenails can be removed. Turn the turtle on its back and cut around the bottom shell plate. Most of the meat lies in the legs, tail and neck, but there is a strip of "filet mignon" along the inside of the top shell under a series of arching bones that many people overlook. Larger turtles will need to be cut up first and then boiled. After the initial cooking to remove the skin, the meat is used in other dishes by boiling, frying or barbecuing it.

You frequently find leeches attached to snappers. If it bothers you to pull them off, sprinkle with salt to cover and they will die and fall off. You'd be a lot better off to take them off with tweezers or needlenose pliers and put them in a jar of water to use as bait the same day or next, or in vinegar for future use.

Turtle Pie

2 cups turtle or chicken broth	1 cup carrots, sliced
$1/4$ cup sherry	2 small onions, chopped
2 tbsps. corn starch	1 pound boneless turtle meat
$1/2$ cup celery, chopped	1 cup lamb's quarters or other leafy,
salt and pepper to taste	green vegetable
1 cup potato, diced	$1/4$ cup whole kernel corn

Combine (previously boiled) meat, vegetables and broth. Simmer until vegetables are tender and add the sherry and cornstarch mixed in $1/2$ cup cold water. Cook until it thickens, stirring to prevent scorching. Pour into oiled baking dish and cover with a pie crust recipe or with Bisquick mixed 2 cups Bisquick to 1 cup water or milk. Bake at 400 degrees until the crust is brown and pie is bubbling through.

As with all pot pies, you can add or delete whatever ingredients you like. The above recipe is also good cooked in a pot with dumplings added the last 15 minutes instead of baking with a crust.

Turtle Soup

2 quarts water
4 cups stewed tomatoes
2 tsps. salt or to taste
5-6 bay leaves
2 onions, minced
1 cup half-and-half

2 pounds turtle meat, cubed
2 cups beef broth or turtle stock
mixed herbs to taste
$\frac{1}{2}$ tsp. garlic salt or powder
2 cups each potatoes, zucchini and carrots
$\frac{1}{2}$ cup Muscadine wine or sherry

Combine all ingredients except wine, half-and-half and turtle meat. Simmer turtle meat gently for about half an hour in water to cover and add spices and vegetables. Simmer another 40-50 minutes or until vegetables are tender. Just before serving, add sherry and half-and-half. Serve steaming hot with croutons.

Smothered Turtle

1 onion, chopped
$\frac{1}{2}$ tsp. paprika
$\frac{1}{2}$ cup olive oil
$\frac{1}{2}$ tsp. cayenne pepper
flour
$\frac{1}{2}$ cup sherry

3 pounds turtle meat, cubed
6 garlic cloves, minced (to taste)
salt and pepper to taste
$\frac{1}{4}$ tsp. filé powder or 1 tbsp. ground
    dried sassafras leaves

Fry meat in hot oil in a Dutch oven. Dredge browned meat in flour and return to pot. Add sherry, onion, garlic, salt and pepper and small amounts of cold water as needed. Watching pot closely (it'll never boil), simmer about 2 hours until meat is tender. Add filé powder in last 15 minutes and serve hot over rice or pasta.

The powerful jaws of the snapping turtle can deliver a bone-crushing bite capable of removing toes or fingers. (Drawing by Tom Squier, Jr.)

Snapper Kebabs

2 pounds snapping turtle cubes
green pepper chunks
mushrooms

cherry tomatoes
onion chunks
soy sauce or barbecue sauce

Parboil turtle meat and then marinate in either barbecue or soy sauce or do some of each for about 4 hours in refrigerator. Alternate cubes of turtle meat on skewers with vegetables and cook until done over charcoal embers or under broiler.

Muscadine... Fruit of the Vine

We are pretty proud of our agricultural heritage here in North Carolina, and our Commissioner of Agriculture, Mr. Jim Graham, has developed a logo that bears a map of the state for the use of those growers and farmers who produce and market fruit and nuts, meat, flowers and dairy and poultry products. The motto is "Goodness Grows In North Carolina," and it does! We have plenty of good wild foods here, besides all the things our farmers provide.

We have several wild grapes growing here including fox grapes, 'possum grape, and scuppernongs, but the best-known is probably the muscadine. It is certainly my favorite grape, wild or tame! One of the first words my son, Tom, Jr., spoke was "monkeydimes" when he learned to pick them as a toddler. I have to say, I had some fun as he learned to talk. He learned early about cleaning fish and game, too, and I guess now is the time to tell you about another of his mispronounced words. When cleaning rabbits, my mother would wash my mouth with soap, no matter how old I was, if she heard me refer to the little rabbit pellets as sh@#. So I told Tommy to be sure and remove all the fecal matter. His little lips wouldn't form the words, and for years we had a lot of fun talking about being sure to remove all the "frenklelmockers!"

The older you get, the less it bothers people when you drift off the subject, but let me get back to muscadines anyway. I won blue ribbons at the Moore County Fair, the Cape Fear Regional Fair and the North Carolina State Fair with my muscadine jelly. Those wild grapes just have so much more flavor. Down in Texas where Frances and I picked them, the wild grapes were known as mustang grapes. My daughter Amanda's eyes were filled with pride as she made her first ever batch of jelly with muscadines. The hug she gave me and the proud look in her eyes were something that all the money in the world could never buy!

Mandy's Grape Jelly

3 pounds grapes	7 cups sugar
1 package pectin	clean, sterilized jars

Chop grapes well or run them through a food processor. Put grapes and juice in a saucepan and bring to a boil. Reduce and simmer for 10-15 minutes. Strain juice through a jelly bag or strainer. Measure out 4 cups grape juice, adding water if needed, and at the same time measure out 7 cups sugar and set aside. Put juice in a large saucepan and bring to a rolling boil. Dump in sugar all at once and bring back to a boil. Add pectin and return to boil while stirring constantly. Boil for 1 full minute, still stirring constantly. Remove from heat and skim off any foam. Pour into hot, sterilized jars, filling to within $1/8$ inch of the top. Cover with lids quickly and screw on bands tightly. Invert jars 5 minutes and turn upright. You may want to process jelly for 20 minutes in a hot water bath as per USDA recommendations.

Possum and fox grapes grow in clusters like yankee grapes, but muscadines and mustang grapes grow in twosies and threesies or individually. Around home, I usually have to get mine from the ground or high up in a tree because, like other grapes, the fruit comes on the new growth. However, when I was in Mississippi, I found a vineyard that grows muscadines on trellises like other wine-producing species. More than twenty years ago, a veterinarian named Scott Galbreath opened his "Old South Winery," making 12 varieties of wine from muscadines exclusively.

Before I go any further, let me say that Frances and I sampled all 12 varieties and found them all to be truly excellent. I like the dry, red ones but Frances prefers hers a little sweeter than I do. Dr. Galbreath has 12 varieties that run the gamut of flavors and uses. Last time I checked, you could order a case conveniently shipped by bus for $56 by writing the Old South Winery, 507 Concord Street, Natchez, MS 39120. You could pick it up yourself and save ten bucks from your wine's bus ride. But if you ever get the chance, visit the winery yourself. They can process 2,000 pounds of grapes into juice in an hour!

(Being a veterinarian in Mississippi has its funny moments. Dr. Galbreath told me how some years ago he was called to shoot down a bear from a big tree right in downtown Natchez. Naturally, it drew quite a crowd. They thought it was an escaped pet bear, but when the eight men it took to move the downed bear opened its mouth, the tattoo of ownership was not there! What to do with a drugged, wild bear, about to wake up anytime with a nasty headache?

(The veterinarian was friends with a game warden who had been run down by a poacher, not long before, having his life saved by the big farm gate that landed on top of him as the old farm truck passed over his body. Unable to legally arrest the man he knew in his heart had nearly killed him, the game warden waited for the opportunity to get his revenge. You know what they say about "paybacks!" What better place to release a hungover bear than behind a poacher's house? It is told that his screams could be heard for miles around!)

Dr. Galbreath showed me all around his winery and vineyard and shared some of his wine-cooking techniques and recipes with me. "Use a semi-dry, red wine like NOBLE for game and beef or a white wine like CARLOS for poultry and pork." These are two of the wines sold at Old South Winery, and they would meet the strict standards of Justin Wilson: "If it ain't fit to drink, it ain't fit to cook with!" You can make some bounteous feasts with these wines. They're good!

Muscadine Meat Marinade

1 cup muscadine wine	1 bottle Italian dressing
1 tbsp. Worcestershire sauce	

Combine ingredients and pour over the meat. Let stand at least 3 hours in refrigerator prior to cooking. Turn to baste all sides, pouring marinade on meat as it grills, too.

Muscadine Wine Cake

$2/3$ cup dry white muscadine wine	1 butter recipe cake mix
1 stick butter	1 cup toasted pecans and/ or hickory nuts

Prepare the cake mix according to package directions, substituting the wine for water. Stir in pecans. Pour into a greased and floured tube pan. Bake at 375 degrees for 45-60 minutes. Cool before removing from pan. Drizzle with a glaze made by combining 1 cup confectioner's sugar, $1/4$ tsp. vanilla and 1 tbsp. milk.

Muscadine Wine Jelly

3 cups muscadine wine	4 cups sugar
1 box pectin	$3/4$ cups water

Mix pectin and water in large saucepan and bring to a boil over high heat. Boil 1 minute, stirring constantly. Reduce heat to medium and add sugar and wine. Cook 4-6 minutes or until all the sugar is dissolved. Remove from heat, skim off any foam and pour into hot sterilized jars.

During the late fall or early winter, if you go out into the woods you can find some muscadine raisins on the vines, maybe. If you want to get the grapes, you had better beat the deer, turkeys and other animals to them! These grapes are excellent for jelly and wine-making, but they can be used fresh to make other dishes taste better. Here is a good example.

Debbe Lowell's Dove with Grapes and Mushrooms

8 dressed doves
$1/2$ tsp. salt
12 fresh wild mushrooms
$1^1/2$ cups white wine
$1/2$ cup butter

$1/3$ cup flour
$1/2$ tsp. ground pepper
1 cup seeded muscadine grapes, white if you can find them

Naturally, use muscadine wine if you have it. Dredge doves in flour seasoned with salt and pepper. Melt butter in a large skillet and brown birds on all sides for about 10 minutes. Add wine and mushrooms to pan, cover and simmer over low heat for another 35 minutes or until tender. Add grapes and cook another 3 minutes. Stir occasionally. Serve over wild rice. A Waldorf salad is a nice accompaniment to this meal.

Deb's recipe also works well with quail. Other parts of the grape vine are valuable, too. Cut grape vines into 6-8 foot lengths, bend into a hoop and tie with wire for making wreaths for any occasion. Shred or cut grape vines into small pieces and use after soaking to add a smoke flavor to the charcoal grill. This next recipe is a traditional Greek recipe that works well with other meats like goat or pork.

Dolmathes

muscadine or other grape leaves
$1/2$ cup olive oil
ground venison or lamb

cooked rice
$1/4$ cup lemon juice
garlic cloves to taste, minced

Soak the grape leaves in a brine solution if necessary for storage. Combine olive oil, minced garlic to taste and lemon juice and set aside. Blend cooked rice with ground meat and spoon on to grape leaves. Or be traditional and use your fingers. Wrap leaves from ends first and then roll up, placing seam side down in baking pan or dish. Drizzle with olive oil, lemon juice and garlic and bake at 350 degrees for 30-40 minutes.

(From left) Danita Laudenslager, Jessica, Tom's daughter, and Paige Laudenslager and their hand-picked muscadines.

Jeff Eberbaugh's Muskydine Wine

Muskydine wine makes you feel so fine
Sends chills up and down your spine
First you get hot then you start to quiver
If ya drink too much it'll quiver your liver
Go up to the holler to your muskydine patch
Pick a bunch of grapes and fill your vats
You can squish em with your hands or mash em with your feet
Or do the boogie woogie on em out in the street
Then ya pick up your vats and strain it through a sieve
The more wine ya drink the longer you'll live
Put the juices in a barrel and add a little yeast
Let it work in the cellar for two or three weeks
A pro wine taster will say it's the best
Muskydine wine will put hair on your chest.

Battling the Blues With Blackberries

People are funny. The same ones who complain in early spring that they want a hot day spend the summer inside sniveling about the air conditioning not working well enough. Hot weather does make people cranky. Sociologists tell us that some people get very moody in hot weather and others just feel sort of depressed because they don't feel like doing very much when they are pouring sweat with every effort.

I have an idea that will get you out of those doldrums, get you out of a blue mood and turn your skies blue again. No, I am not leading up to blueberries, although they may be ripening at the same time in some places. I want to suggest that you get out and pick yourself some blackberries. Actually, the ones that ripen first where I live are referred to as dewberries. They grow on sprawling vines, close to the ground, with lots of stickers, but have very large and sweet berries.

Botanists fall into two large general categories — lumpers and splitters, depending on how picky they want to be in determining how many varieties of a certain type of plant there may be. The lumpers list blackberries and their cousins simply as *Rubus* species in many field guides, while the splitters claim to be able to identify more than 200 distinct plant species and subspecies in the *Rubus* genus. We know them by such common names as blackberry, black raspberry, salmon berry, red raspberry, wineberry, thimbleberry, blackcaps and, of course, dewberries. The Brits and some mountain people in this country refer to them as "brambles."

Some tame varieties are thornless (and expensive), but many folks find the wild ones to have the best flavor. Even before Br'er Rabbit made his now-famous escape with the words, "...throw me in the briar patch!!," people have thought the delicious berries worth the sweat, heat, briars, mosquitoes and stiff backs that occasionally accompany a trip to the berry patch.

The USDA tells us that fresh blackberries are about 85% water, but they are extremely high in vitamin A and contain a lot of calcium with a fair amount of vitamin C, fiber and potassium with some iron and the B vitamins, too. All are good food that is low in carbohydrates but provides us a lot of nutrition in a flavorful package.

There are plenty of standard pie recipes around, so I'll give you a few others to think about.

Blackberry Ice

2 cups blackberries, crushed
1 cup water
2 tbsps. honey

$^1/_2$ cup sugar
3 tbsps. lemon juice

Combine sugar and honey with the water and bring to a boil. Hold at a full boil for 5 minutes. Remove from heat and mix in the crushed berries and lemon juice, stirring well. Pour into ice cube trays and when frozen place in the freezer. Use in punch, or to chill drinks. Or place in a tray or shallow dish and put in the freezer. When the mixture becomes slushy, stir again to reduce the size of the ice crystals. Do this every 30 minutes or so until the mixture is all coarse ice crystals. Remove to the refrigerator for 15 minutes and serve as a dessert or snack.

Blackberry Mousse

¹/2 cup fresh berries
1 cup plain yogurt
1 ripe banana
3 ice cubes

2¹/2 cups berries, mashed
1 tsp. vanilla extract
¹/2 cup honey or sugar
mint leaves

In a blender, combine banana, blackberries, vanilla, honey and ice cubes. Blend on low to mix, then on medium until smooth. Pour into 4 dessert bowls and refrigerate until firm or until ready to serve. Before serving, garnish each bowl with 2 or 3 mint leaves and fresh berries.

Amanda and her blackberries.

Blackberry Cheese Pie

3 pints blackberries
14 ounces condensed milk
2 cups sugar
1 tsp. vanilla extract

1 large graham cracker pie crust
juice from 2 lemons
8 ounces cream cheese, softened
1 tbsp. butter

Mash the berries and add sugar and butter. Bring to a boil and simmer until thickened. Set aside. Whip cream cheese until fluffy and fold in the condensed milk, lemon juice and vanilla extract. Mix thoroughly and pour into the crust. Refrigerate 3 hours or until it sets firmly. Top with blackberry filling and serve immediately or after chilling.

Quick and Easy Blackberry Cobbler

2 quarts blackberries
¹/2 cup lemon juice
1 tbsp. butter

4 cups sugar
2 packages canned biscuits

Mash the berries and add lemon juice, sugar and butter. Bring to a boil and reduce heat. Simmer for 10 minutes or until berries change color and mixture thickens. Pour into buttered baking dish or a thin pie crust. Top hot berries with store-bought biscuits, just touching, and bake, following package directions for the biscuits. This is usually about 8-12 minutes at 400-425 degrees. Serve hot with whipped cream or vanilla ice cream.

You can use any of these recipes for your favorite (or available) berries, or a combination of berries at season's beginning or end. Use less lemon juice for blueberries. Sugar and freeze some berries to stir into muffins and pancake mix or to add to summer or winter fruit cocktails and salads later. Drop a few berries into a pint of vinegar for a nice flavor change in salads.

Blackberry Cooler

1 quart ripe berries
$^1/_2$ lemon, sliced

2 cups sugar
3 quarts water

Mash the ripest berries you can find and strain the juice if the seeds bother you. Add water and sugar and pour over glasses of ice with a twisted slice of lemon. Repeat as needed. Grownups like to add a dash of vodka to this cooler.

Blackberry Leather

6 quarts blackberries
unflavored gelatin

sugar
lemon juice

Mash blackberries. Force through a sieve. For each cup juice, add 1 cup sugar, $^1/_2$ tsp. lemon juice and $^1/_2$ tsp. gelatin. Bring to a boil, taking care not to scorch. Simmer over reduced heat until thick enough to spread on foil without running. Heat to dry in a low oven until leathery and no longer sticky. Roll in foil or plastic wrap. Enjoy!

Blackberry Dessert In A Hurry

blackberries
those cute little tart shells

strawberry glaze from the store
whipped cream

Combine equal amounts of blackberries and strawberry glaze — about a cup of each. Mix well and fold into the cute little tart cups. Refrigerate to chill and top with whipped cream just before serving. This is a tasty, quick and impressive dessert.

Any recipe for blackberries can be used with raspberries, dewberries and other berries as well. So you have a lot more recipes than you thought. Here's one more to delight you.

Raspberry Lemon Pie

1 Keebler Ready Crust Graham
   Cracker pie crust (6 oz.)
dash salt
1$^1/_4$ cups water
1$^1/_2$ tbsps. butter
$^1/_2$ pint red raspberries

1 cup sugar
2 tbsps. corn starch
2 tbsps. flour
3 egg yolks, slightly beaten
$^1/_4$ cup lemon juice and rind from a whole lemon

Brush crust with one egg yolk and place crust on a cookie sheet. Bake for 5 minutes at 375 degrees. Remove from oven and allow to cool. Mix sugar, cornstarch, salt and flour and slowly add the water, stirring constantly. Cook until boiling, then reduce heat and cook for 2 more minutes. Remove from heat and stir a small amount of the custard into the remaining egg yolks. Blend the egg yolk mixture with custard and return to low heat for about a minute. Remove from heat and stir in butter, lemon juice and rind. Pour into shell and cool. Top pie with raspberries immediately before serving. Use mint leaves for additional color. Preparation time: 15 minutes.

Raspberry Lemon Pie

Catfish Making a Big Splash in the Kitchen

I have been hearing a lot lately about catfish. We have been eating catfish in my family as long as I can remember. My grandfather and I spent many happy summer nights fishing along a riverbank in the dark, listening to frogs and night birds, watching the lightning bugs play their dating games, and enjoying the stars and the fragrance of the magnolias. In the big grocery stores lately, catfish and catfish fillets have become very popular and much more expensive than many of the more traditional fish that have long been popular. They used to be considered almost a "trash fish" because of their ugly appearance, reputation as a scavenger and because they were so easy to catch. Their difficulty in cleaning made them unpopular with many people. The River Lady, my friend and correspondent, tells me that you could pour scalding water over a wooden tub of catfish, let it cover them just a couple of minutes and follow it with an ice water bath to make the skin come right off like a bubble. You can do this with peaches, too. You just rub a little and it comes right off.

Now, largely due to the success of farm- and pond-raised catfish, they have become *haute cuisine*. In many places they are almost considered "the" game fish, and tournaments are held in their honor. There is even a trade publication called *Catfish News* that links growers, buyers and hobbyists. According to the package, feeding catfish in a pond with high-protein food pellets will show a weight increase of about 1 pound per fish per season. The U.S. Army has been stocking channel catfish in ponds on Fort Bragg and many other reservations for years. Purina and other companies make a floating fish chow, and the fish can be trained to eat at a certain time and location. It is an impressive sight to see the water boiling with gaping mouths and whiskers as the smiling cats gobble up the "fish chow!"

There is an old joke that says the way to cook an old river cat is to clean them, place them on a board and bake them until the meat comes off the bone. Then you throw away the fish and eat the board. That's a little harsh, although many river cats do taste muddy, especially the bigger, older ones. Actually, boards can help flavor the fish and allow for the mud and juices to drain off.

Baked Catfish

1 large catfish	untreated cedar plank
$^1/_4$ cup vinegar	$^1/_4$ cup coarse or rock salt
1 large can tomato juice	1 large onion, sliced

Clean the catfish. Soak overnight in refrigerator in 1 gallon of water with vinegar and rock salt added. Remove and marinate for 2-3 hours in enough tomato juice to cover in refrigerator. Remove and place catfish on cedar plank in a large baking dish or pan. Cover with onion rings and bake at 325-350 degrees until meat flakes easily. Pour the pan drippings over cat food.

Catfish are cleaned by skinning them as mentioned earlier. They aren't scaled. Some people drive a spike through a plank and stick the catfish's head on the spike to hold it. Cut a line through the skin from the top fin to under the chin, just behind the head, grasp skin with pliers and pull the skin all the way off.

The Southern Sportsman, Franc White, said on his show that South Carolina biologists had brought some yellow cats into the Pee Dee region, stocking lakes and the river, and they were being caught in the 65-70 pound range in just a few years. Don't expect those results with farm-raised catfish, but several hundred pounds per acre is easily achieved. The USDA says that in the single month of December 1989, catfish farmers processed over 25.8 *million* pounds of fish. The industry has grown by leaps and bounds since then.

Catfish Creole

2¹/₂ pounds catfish fillets
salt and pepper to taste
¹/₂ bell pepper, chopped
2 tbsps. dill weed, chopped
1 tsp. cayenne pepper (opt.)

4 tbsps. butter
1 tomato, peeled & sliced
1 medium onion, chopped
1 tsp. paprika

Rub baking dish with butter and lay fillets in 1 layer. Season with salt and pepper. Add tomato, onion and bell pepper. Bake 25 minutes at 350 degrees, sprinkle with dill weed, paprika and cayenne pepper. Bake 5-10 more minutes until fish flakes easily and serve.

With your favorite adaptations, catfish, especially fillets, can be a real hit at dinner time.

Deep-Fried Catfish

2-3 pounds catfish fillets
salt and red pepper to taste
white or yellow corn meal
peanut oil

1 cup milk
¹/₂ cup dry red wine (optional)
cracker crumbs rolled out fine

Heat oil to 350 degrees. Combine milk and wine with salt and pepper to taste. Add more milk if needed while dipping fish. Combine finely ground cracker crumbs with corn meal and salt and pepper to taste. Drench fish in the milk and roll in the flour/cracker mixture. Deep fry until they float and are golden brown. Drain on paper bag and serve hot. The cold leftovers make a great snack later.

Bullheads (Catfish) In Fennel Sauce

4 pounds catfish
2 carrots, sliced
3 sprigs each parsley & thyme
2 tbsps. butter
2 tbsps. flour

2 large onions, chopped
salt and pepper to taste
3 tbsps. fennel leaf, chopped
1 cup fish stock or water
2-3 bay leaves

Melt butter in saucepan and sauté 1 chopped onion until transparent. Add flour dissolved in 2 tbsps. cold water, fish stock and salt to taste. Heat to simmer and add fennel leaves. Cover and simmer while cooking the fish. In a large kettle combine catfish with the other onion, bay leaves, carrots and herbs. Add water to cover and season to taste with salt and pepper. Simmer gently until the fish flakes — about 15 or 20 minutes. Remove the fish to hot platter and serve topped with the fennel sauce. It's good over rice, toast squares or pasta.

In some places, catfish is in high regard, even as a "fast food." I first discovered "Mr. Catfish"-type places competing with the fried chicken joints on a trip to Memphis about 1980. More recent trips to Mississippi, Alabama and Louisiana revealed that "Cajun Catfish" and others are among the more popular eating places. Radio come-on ads for the Mississippi State Fair touted the many catfish booths along the midway!

Catfish is good for you, too, according to the USDA. They like fillets because there is 0 percent refuse. One pound contains 467 calories, 79.8 grams of protein, iron, potassium, several B vitamins, and no carbohydrates. A similar portion of standard grade beef contains only 67 grams of protein and is 18 percent refuse.

Smothered Catfish

2 pounds catfish fillets
juice of ¹/₂ lemon
3 tbsps. butter
¹/₄ cup soy sauce

2 sliced onions
2 ounces red wine vinegar
2 tbsps. Worcestershire
salt and pepper to taste

Sauté onion in butter over low heat. Add vinegar, Worcestershire and soy sauce. Place fillets in baking dish. Drizzle with lemon juice and salt and pepper to taste. Put half the butter and onions on the fish and save the rest for sauce. Bake fish at 350 degrees for 8-10 minutes or until it flakes easily. Remove fish and mix drippings from fish into remaining butter and onions. Serve fish on heated plate with sauce served over top.

As you can plainly see, our daughter Amanda knows something about catching a fine mess of fish, too! These aren't catfish, but bream, and actually this was her "beginner's luck" stringer. But, it was fun eating all these fish. I'll take luck like this anytime!

I have learned to take the advice of experts no matter how strange it might sound at the time. In his book, *Masters' Secrets of Catfishing*, fellow writer John E. Phillips comments on the right bait. "Often, the season of the year determines what baits catfish will bite. Their preferences may include hot dogs, frogs, salamanders, freshwater clams, catalpa worms, fish entrails, various kinds of soap — Ivory, Palmolive, Camay and Octagon — as well as cheese balls, soybean meal cakes and flavored sponge baits."

Amanda and her catch!

John Phillips' Smoked Catfish

¹/2 cup salt
1 gallon water
1 pound green hickory

¹/4 cup dark brown sugar
10 pounds charcoal

Prepare brine by mixing salt, brown sugar and water together. Soak whole, dressed catfish, preferably ¹/2- to ³/4-pound fish, skin on, in brine for 12 hours in the refrigerator. Remove, rinse and air-dry fish on rack for one hour.

Prepare smoker. Use ¹/2 of the charcoal first. Put hickory chunks on hot charcoal when the fish are placed on the smoker. The catfish should be one foot from the heat. Smoke four hours. Check fire. Add additional charcoal and hickory if needed. Smoke another two to four hours. If you lift the lid, add ¹/2 hour more cooking each time. (Don't peek!)

When finished, fish will be a dark-saffron color. Let fish cool before handling.

Thanks, John! I use a charcoal smoker at times, but I also like the electric smoker from Luhr-Jensen. It makes things very simple.

Smoked Catfish

For people interested in raising the status of catfish, the American Catfish Association, Rt. 2, Box 285, Lincoln, MO 65338 says, "Catfish Ain't Ugly!"

South Carolina's ELGIN CATFISH STOMP

FIRST WEEKEND IN DECEMBER

Elgin Catfish Stomp

Buffalo — At Home on the Range Again

When I was trying to think of a title for this chapter, I kept remembering the song that says, "Give me a home where the buffalo roam... home, home on the range..." Then I got to thinking that for part of my life a "stove" meant the wood stove we had cooked on for years and a "range" was an electric stove that rich people in town had. So, all sorts of thoughts of buffalo and electric stoves were bouncing around in my head, competing with the more recent images of "buffalo wings." When I went to Oklahoma, my companions and I went to the Phillips Ranch, home of the former owners of the Phillips Petroleum Company. Go there if you ever get anywhere close. The other soldiers who were with me were so fascinated by the buffalo barbecue that I thought they would founder themselves on it. It was delicious, I must admit, and buffalo meat is not so rare these days as you might think.

If you want to see a buffalo up close, you can now find them on farms across the country. They were once wild here in the Carolinas, but were wiped out of our forests by hunters without controls and even more so by habitat destruction. They almost became extinct all across the country, but thanks to government intervention (the rare good example) and protection, there are once again huge herds in many parts of the West and the Great Plains. There are so many in some  of our national parks that once in a while the government gives them away or sells them at auction! You have to be in the right place at the right time to get them and you need a good strong fence and lots of space for them. Buffalo are smart, too. One man near me who maintains a herd had to round them up after they escaped by swimming over the top of a fence in a field that flooded. The fence stretches across a pond and the pond flooded over the top. Herd owner Milton Bass says, "They love to swim." Unfortunately, one of the herd bulls got hit by a truck and had to be shot. "I think the problem was having two bulls," Bass said when the deserter was found five miles from home. "One has to be master and one has to leave."

Buffalo, American bison, were once considered so connected to the Native Americans of the plains that it would be impossible to think about one without thinking of the other. Many Native American reservations now maintain herds of these magnificent animals. There are also many private ranchers who raise buffalo for meat, most notable of which are probably Ted Turner and Jane Fonda, who maintain quite a sizeable herd. One company that sells game meat including venison, pheasants and buffalo is located outside New York City, amazingly. D'Artagnan is a company founded in 1983 by George Faison and a French woman named Ariane Daugin who was here as a student. The company started out producing a pâté that was so authentic-tasting that some thought it had been "smuggled from France." Not so! It is produced in the wilds of New Jersey, but with a flavor reminiscent of Ariane's native Gascony, France. The company now sells a large variety of game and fowl

— some wild, some not. Grouse and woodcocks come from Scotland, rabbits and range chickens come from Arkansas, and venison, wild boar and buffalo come from Texas and other places.

Two foot-long buffalo steaks

Both prices and recipes can be had by calling 1-800-DARTAGN (327-8246). You can order from the same number, using your credit cards (Don't stay at home without them!). While working on this chapter, my son said I should leave it out because all the yuppies will be wanting to try it and there aren't enough buffalo now!

Buffalo (and other game) is a healthy alternative to store-bought beef because it is nearly twice as high in protein, but lower in calories, cholesterol and sodium.

Buffalo Kebabs

$1\frac{1}{2}$ pounds cubed buffalo meat
3 onions, quartered
$\frac{1}{2}$ cup olive oil
salt and pepper to taste
2 bay leaves
1 tsp. cayenne pepper

12 large white mushrooms, halved
2 tomatoes, cut in chunks
2 seeded bell peppers, cut up
minced garlic cloves to taste
2 zucchini, sliced
1 cup red wine

Make marinade of olive oil, wine and herbs. Cover meat with liquid and marinate overnight. Alternate meat and vegetables on skewer. Cook over hot grill or in broiler 2-6 minutes per side. Serve with brown rice and a Burgundy wine.

Barbecued Buffalo Steak

1-2 pounds buffalo steak
1 tsp. dry mustard
1 tbsp. sugar
1 big pinch paprika
2 tbsps. catsup
1 tbsp. honey

2 tbsps. butter
2 tsps. salt
1 pinch ground pepper
1 tsp. Worcestershire sauce
2 tbsps. peanut or olive oil

Blend butter with mustard, 1 tsp. salt, pepper, sugar and paprika. Rub thoroughly into steak. Combine Worcestershire sauce, oil, remaining salt, honey and catsup to make sauce. Brush steak with sauce. Broil 15 minutes or to preferred doneness, turn and brush with more sauce. Brush with sauce while cooking as needed and turn again to heat sauce thoroughly.

Spiced Buffalo Roast

5 pound buffalo roast
$\frac{1}{2}$ tsp. pepper
2 tsps. cayenne pepper
$\frac{1}{2}$ pound bacon slices
3 large carrots, sliced
2 sticks butter
$\frac{3}{4}$ cup water

1 tsp. salt
1 tsp. allspice
1 dozen whole cloves
4 celery stalks, diced
3 large onions, diced
1 cup dry red wine
1 tsp. rosemary (opt.)

Rub salt and pepper into roast. Sprinkle with allspice and cayenne and stick cloves in meat. Criss-cross with bacon and place in baking dish or pan. Add remaining ingredients. Roast 20 minutes at 400 degrees and then $2\frac{1}{2}$ hours at 275 degrees. Spoon pan liquid over meat when serving.

All these buffalo recipes can be used with venison and your favorite venison (or beef) recipes can be used with buffalo. You can also use them for other large animals such as moose and elk and even for bear steaks or kebabs made from bear stew meat. All of these meats make great chili. Just grind cooked leftover roasts and steaks and add beans and you have chili!

Buffalo Rib Roast

5-6 pound buffalo rib roast
1 tsp. ground pepper
$^1/_2$ cup red wine
1 cup apple sauce

1$^1/_2$ tbsps. salt
1 tbsp. garlic salt
$^1/_4$ cup Worcestershire sauce

Put roast in a Dutch oven or roasting pan. Combine all other ingredients and pour over meat. Cover and bake about 30 minutes per pound or until tender. Uncover during last 30 minutes of cooking.

P.O. Box 1051
Reno, NV 89504

If you want some good buffalo meat as well as other things that come from the animal, ensuring that it doesn't get wasted, contact Thundering Herd Buffalo Products. They sell robes, moccasins and buffalo jewelry. Even mounted heads and skulls. Nothing gets wasted! I recommend their Buffalo Meat Sampler.

Buffalo Barbecue For Buns

1 pound cooked buffalo meat
1 minced onion
1 tbsp. Tabasco sauce

1 garlic clove, minced
1 tbsp. liquid smoke
$^1/_2$-1 cup barbecue sauce of choice

Grind or finely shred meat. Combine all ingredients and heat just enough to warm completely. Stir well and cool. Store overnight in refrigerator for a better flavor. Heat thoroughly and serve on onion rolls or buns with slaw.

Richard Petty and Frances Squier

If you don't know where to get good barbecue sauce and you don't make your own, let me offer two suggestions. One is to visit or write the Richard Petty Museum at 311 Bransom Mill Road, Randelman, NC 27317 or call 910-495-1143 and ask for Doris Gammons, manager. Tell her you want to get some of Richard's Honey Barbecue Sauce 43. It is made in the Southern tradition with vinegar, water, tomatoes, sugar, honey, corn syrup, salt, onions, garlic and a blend of spices which is Richard's secret, like the proportions of each ingredient. Richard has a great recipe for stuffed peppers in which he uses ground beef. Here is that recipe with ground buffalo substituted. You could also use venison or other game meat just as well.

Richard Petty's Stuffed Bell Peppers

1¹/₂ pounds ground buffalo
1 cup catsup
1 medium onion, chopped fine
1 cup corn flakes

1 tbsp. chili powder
salt and pepper to taste
2 eggs
6 bell peppers, halved & cleaned

Sauce for Peppers

2¹/₂ cups catsup and tomato paste,
    more catsup than tomato paste
1 tbsp. vinegar

2 tbsps. brown sugar
2 tbsps. ground mustard

Boil peppers for 5 minutes. Mix other filling ingredients together. Stuff peppers with mixture and arrange in bottom of large Pyrex dish. Mix sauce ingredients together and pour over peppers. Bake at 375 degrees for 30 to 40 minutes.

It is a good possibility that Richard Petty will be the next governor of North Carolina. His supporters are urging him to run for it. "King" Richard, NASCAR racing's greatest hero, says he might. If he does, it will be the biggest landslide in voting history. Richard Petty has signed so many millions of autographs that no one knows for sure just how many he has done. For information about the Richard Petty Fan Club, write National Directors Jerry & Linda Ritchie, at 1028 East 22nd Street, Kannapolis, NC.

The other place that I turn to when I need *real good* barbecue sauce *real fast* is the kitchen of Mrs. Jean Cole and her husband James. They make several barbecue sauces, using all-natural ingredients including fresh herbs. The most popular one is probably her "Fast Track" B-B-Q Sauce which I used to serve roadkilled deer to the fine members of the North Carolina Herb Association at one of their annual Wild Herb Weekends. It was so good that one lady was rubbing a roll around the crockpots I served it in to get the last smear of color and flavor. He makes my favorite sauce, "James' Tear Jerkin' Sauce," and it will bring tears to your eyes if you eat it by the spoonful, but it is delicious. I like to use it for marinating meat, especially venison, that I am going to make into jerky. It would make a great buffalo barbecue. Or, although not related, the best buffalo wings!

Write Mrs. Cole's Cottage Industries, Inc. at P.O. Box 7071, Jacksonville, NC 28540 for more details.

Elks and Nettles in the Kettles

You know, one of the constant efforts required of a writer, particularly a columnist, is coming up with new ideas. Well, knock on wood, I have never really had a hard time finding something to write about. I do a fair amount of traveling (153,000 miles in a Dodge Dakota in 3 years. I'll never buy another Dodge. Even staying on the maintenance schedule, it took over $4,000 in repairs for 1 blown transmission, 2 blown engines and replacing the radiator and the entire braking system, cylinders and all, and still the payoff was five times the trade-in value when I got rid of it! The Dodge dealership's mechanics told me to get rid of it, but nobody wanted it. Sorry, I got off the subject there.), I know lots of interesting people — Ralph Tucker the Snail King, Richard Petty the Racing King, John Boy the self-interview king, radio show host and legendary car driver, Jim Graham the Commissioner of Agriculture, and Renelvis the Filipino Elvis impersonator — you get the picture, and I love to eat so I am always trying new foods. Lots of people, including my wife, Frances, are always suggesting story ideas to me. I keep a list, too, of ideas that pop into my own head from time to time. Actually, there is more to write about than most columnists can cover. Like my former editor, John Myers, said, "All the news that fits, we print!"

I try to write like I am talking to people, my friends, and that has always been successful for me. I have made a lot of friends through my column, and through my books. Readers are always calling, writing or visiting. The night I was working on this chapter, we stopped to go and visit some friends in town and when I came back there was a freshly killed rattlesnake on the step in a box and a message on the answering machine. The Parks brothers, Raymond and Julian, had picked her up after the car in front of them ran over it and knew I'd hate to see it wasted. Cleaned, it is now about eight pounds of meat in the freezer!

I know that other columnists read my stuff, too, because I see it excerpted in their columns and articles. Most of them are nice enough to say "Tom Squier said...," but one old codger frequently writes "I read somewhere that..."and adds his own comments. When a man has been using the same photograph with his column for over a quarter of a century, you have to understand if he forgets to mention where he got his material. Besides, you know what they say about "imitation being the sincerest form of flattery." I get ideas from other columnists from time to time, too.

For instance, Brenda Lawlor, one of my fellow writers at the *Spring Lake News,* has a regular column called "Potluck." One issue it was entitled "Don't Look a Gift Elk in the Face." Personally, I like elk meat because it is richer than venison and because even the largest elk are much more tender than their smaller cousins, deer and antelope. Possibly it is because these regal forest monarchs move more slowly and gracefully everywhere rather than dashing about like bumblebees in the manner of our white-tailed deer! Now that they are being raised in fenced enclosures, they are fork-tender, no matter what their age. Well, here is what Brenda Lawlor had to say about "wapiti" in her column:

"My brother called from the airport to say hello and goodbye. He'd been in the States but preferred to spend his time elk hunting on the Pacific coast.

"I'm sending you some meat, but don't worry, it doesn't have much cholesterol."

I wasn't worried about having a heart attack from eating elk meat. I once cooked some venison and then didn't have the courage to eat it. I understand that the herds have to be thinned out and after reading *The Old Man and the Boy,* I understand the ecological importance of hunting.

"It's just that elk meat is not on my list of comfort foods. He went on to explain what I would get and how to cook it. I'll get a few steaks, then some ground elk that will make excellent meat loaf. The sausage will be a bit dry and I should make canapés from the summer sausage. I can use the steaks for country-style steaks or stir fry with onions and peppers.

"I was beginning to understand why he had explained that it had low cholesterol. It sounded as though I'll be cooking elk meat for the next three years. Since the kids went to college I don't cook much anymore. In fact, I usually clean my oven with a Dust Buster.

"I've given our conversation great thought and I'm ready to take up hunting too. I'm hunting for someone who'd like to trade a bunch of fast-food coupons for a bunch of elk meat."

Kathleen Marquardt and Jessica.

Upon reading that article, I became a Brenda Lawlor fan because, as you can see, she is a terrific writer. With a phone call, I also received the promise of some good elk meat when it arrives. I clip the coupons from the Sunday paper inserts, but the fast-food ones have no interest to me, so I was trading something I would throw away for something I wanted.

Funny, the very next day I received a letter with a recipe for elk jerky from Kathleen Marquardt, Chairman and founder of the group called Putting People First. Basically, Putting People First is what some people would call an anti-PETA group, but Kathleen said that she started it because she was tired of people trying to make her feel guilty about eating meat! She was tired of kids being brainwashed in the Washington schools and she was going to fight back. If you eat meat or cheese, drink milk, wear leather, wool or fur, hunt or fish, even if you just have a pet or ride a horse, you should find out what the organization can do for you. Write to them at Putting People First, P.O. Box 1707, Helena, MT 59624-1707.

Kathleen Marquardt says, "Every day, we are struggling to retain the basic freedoms won by our forefathers that we rightfully thought we'd never have to defend against an enemy from within. This is a very serious business, and we have to take it seriously."

Kathleen Marquardt's Elk (or Moose) Jerky

20 pounds elk meat	**3 gallons water**
3 cups salt	**1 cup sugar**

Cut elk meat into strips 6 inches long and $1/4$ inch thick. Soak overnight in 2 gallons of water in which 1 cup salt has been dissolved. Drain and soak in a brine solution made from 2 cups salt and 1 cup sugar dissolved in 1 gallon boiling water and marinate for 72 hours. Drain and hang to dry in a cool place. After 2 or 3 days, smoke in a smoker 5-6 hours. When dried thoroughly, it can be wrapped and frozen.

Kathleen also sent me a recipe for nettle soup, which was strange because I had been lecturing in Boston about eating the weeds in your yard and herbal medicine when a lady named Simone Adams told me how much she loved nettle pie. Originally from Albania, nettles were an important part of her childhood diet. I was thinking what a small world this is when I read Kathleen's letter.

Kathleen Marquardt's Nettle Soup

2 quarts fresh nettles
salt to taste
1½ tbsps. flour
pepper to taste

2 cups water
1 tbsp. butter
3 pints pork stock

Wash nettles well and drain. Cook in lightly salted water until tender — about 10 minutes. Strain, conserving water. Chop nettles finely or pass through a sieve. Melt butter, add flour, the stir well until blended. Add stock, still stirring, and simmer 10 minutes. Add nettle pureé and season to taste. Serve with poached or hard-boiled eggs.

Nettles are among the most nutritious of wild greens. The bad news is that they contain numerous stinging cells and must either be harvested with gloves or chopped with a stick (finally, a good use for a golf club, other than filing it down as a snake hook) and picked up with tongs.

Blackened Elk

elk steaks or backstrap
ripe papaya
olive oil

garlic powder
ground pepper, red or black
butter

Cut into ³/₄-inch thick steaks. Rub meat with papaya to tenderize it about 30 minutes before cooking. This will work with any tough meat — venison, buffalo, or even tough beef. Don't leave it on too long, though, or it will end up like Gerber's strained elk. Mix equal amounts of butter and olive oil in cast-iron skillet and heat to the smoking point. Do this either outside or with the exhaust fan on. Mix garlic powder and pepper and rub into steaks thoroughly. Don't rub your nose or eyes while doing this! Add steaks to skillet and blacken on both sides. You can do fish the same way, using fillets, but I like to add a little finely ground lemon peel (zest) to fish.

Kathleen Marquardt and friend

Brought back from the edge of extinction, elk are so plentiful that they can be hunted again thanks to the joint efforts of hunters, conservationists and people who support the endeavors of the Rocky Mountain Elk Foundation, 2291 W. Broadway, Missoula, MT 59802. Their objective is the conservation of habitat for the North American elk, and its continued success in returning to its former glory. But they also feature elk recipes in their magazine, *Bugle,* from time to time. Reality works!

Nettle Pudding

2 quarts tender nettles	**2 large onions, diced**
1/2 cup uncooked rice	**4 cups cabbage, shredded**

Mix washed nettles with cabbage and onion and combine with rice in a jelly bag or muslin big. Tie the top and boil in a closed container for about half an hour with water to cover or until vegetables are tender and rice is done.

Tom's Nettle Soup

2 cups nettle tops	**1 Irish potato, diced**
1 onion, chopped	**1 tbsp. butter**
2 cups chicken stock	**1 cup milk or cream**
salt and pepper to taste	

Sauté the potato and onion in the butter and add the milk, nettles and chicken stock. Season to taste and simmer about 20 minutes over medium low heat. Serve immediately. Some people like to add 1 or 2 tbsps. dry wine to this recipe. Suit yourself.

Rocky
Mountain
ELK FOUNDATION

Where There's Smoke, There's Fire — I Mean *Flavor!!*

The flavor of smoked game, poultry, or fish is pretty hard to beat. But it is really a lot easier to produce than many people think. There are all sorts of things that can be smoked on the grill or in a smoker, be it homemade or store-bought.

For traditional smoked hams and sausages, there are several recipes that call for soaking the meat in a solution of equal parts of sugar (usually brown) or molasses and salt for a few days in a glass or crockery container to help in the preservation process. Then you rinse the meat and smoke it for flavor and to continue the preservation process.

As I taught in survival classes, there are two ways to use smoke in the meat-handling process. One is to smoke and cook your meat at the same time. This method puts the meat down close enough to the flame, smoke and coals that it gets flavored and cooked at the same time. The other method uses what we call "cold smoke" to preserve the meat and it takes a much longer time. It is usually agreed that the smoke temperature (and smoker temperature) should remain below 40 degrees if possible, certainly no warmer than the outside temperature. The meat is far enough away from the smoke that it doesn't really cook. The antibacterial qualities of the smoke (and the brine bath) help preserve it, while the moving air currents carry off the excess moisture, drying it out. This also aids in preservation and helps prevent growth of fungus or mold. Some may be inevitable. In England, a green mold is often allowed to grow on the meat to seal it and is then removed before use.

In order to achieve cold smoke, we have to hang the meat, fish or poultry some distance from the fire. There are various techniques for accomplishing this. You can dig a pit for the fire and make a tunnel which will carry the smoke to the meat while it (the smoke) cools down enroute to where the meat is hanging. Generally, we figure that meat which has been thoroughly and steadily smoked for 24 hours or more will remain preserved for up to 30 days. Refrigeration extends preservation time.

You can make a large smoke-house with a deep pit to contain the fire, and when it burns down to coals and ashes put on wet wood or green leaves of the proper type to produce smoke. Occasionally more charcoal or burnable hardwood may need to be added to keep the fire alive. It is important to realize that once the fire dries the wet wood or leaves, it too will become fuel and need to be replaced.

Hang the meat at least 3 feet above a "cold" fire and keep it small and enclosed to contain the smoke. Make an "Indian fire." You know what they say: "The Indian makes a small fire and sits close, while the white man makes a bonfire and stays back." No matter how good it smells, don't open your smoker to peek. Leave it closed except to add fuel or smoke-producing material.

It proved to be a waste of time trying to tell some soldiers this, but don't use any resinous wood such as pine for the fire except in the very earliest stages when you are getting the fire lit. ("Lieutenant, why are you smoking your fish with pine knots?" "Because, Sergeant, it burns good and lights easily!") The pine should be long gone before any meat is close to fire or smoke or the results will be a coating of black soot and a flavor like the wild hogs that had to be killed to save the pine trees in the Smokies. In other words, it will taste like Pine-Sol!

You will want to use certain woods known for their ability to add flavor as spits or rods on which to hang your meat, birds or fish. Two that come to mind quickly are sourwood, known for the honey that the blooms flavor, and the sassafras, known for its tea and medicinal properties. The leaves of both, especially sassafras, added to the fire, produce a very special flavor in smoked meats. Some other woods that are common and especially flavorful are pecan and hickory (spicy), oaks and sourwood (tangy) and maple and sycamore (sweet). Sassafras produces a unique flavor with a hint of licorice or root beer and a lot of people like the flavor produced by grape vines. Another old favorite trick that produces clouds of billowing white smoke is to use corn cobs that have been soaked overnight in water. You can add bourbon or rum to the water and the flavor will be imparted to the meat. Or you could rub it directly on the meat.

No matter what type of smoker you use, the addition of a pan of water where possible between the fire and the meat will catch the drippings (although they produce flavor in the fire) but keep the air moister in the smoker, extending the time required. Some people like to put wine in the pan, and as it evaporates it flavors the meat, so use a good port, elderberry or muscadine wine. Remember that meat which is being cold-smoked for storage will need to be as dry as possible. However, a fat Tom turkey which has been hot-smoked overnight or for 10-12 hours will benefit greatly from the additional moisture as it cooks.

An old "2-holer" makes a great smoker.

I have a great electric smoker that I got from the Luhr-Jensen people that produces smoked turkey and salmon of fight-starting quality! But you can build your own, if you prefer, from materials at hand. You can still find an old two-seater in my backyard that I converted to a smoke house after moving it away from its previous site. The smoke helps cut down on mosquitoes and spiders and it's funny to have people stop and say, "Hey, your toilet is on fire!"

You will need a fire pit with a lid that can be closed with a non-flammable top when you are ready to produce the smoke. Half a 55-gallon drum works great after it has been cleaned and burned out a couple of times. You can just dig a hole and line it with rocks or bricks, especially if you live in a place with sandy soil, to prevent cave-ins. From the fire pit, you need to construct a little "tunnel" or run a pipe to carry the smoke — about 10 or 12 feet.

Permanent smokers can be built solid like my old outhouse or something similar. A less permanent structure, but just as effective for a smoke-house, can be made from a tripod covered with old wet blankets or sheets in layers, a tarp, or even a large cardboard box like a refrigerator comes in. No matter how you do it, smoking your meat greatly adds to the flavor. And to your reputation as a cook!

Smoked Trout or Salmon

trout or salmon	coarse salt
brown sugar	charcoal-aged bourbon

Before you can smoke a fish for the purpose of preserving it, it must be soaked first for a few days in a brine-sugar solution. I sometimes add a bourbon like Jack Daniels for the flavor. During the smoking process, the alcohol goes away but flavor remains. You can decide on this option yourself. Clean the fish by slitting it from under the chin to the tail and removing the entrails. You need to leave the head on to have a way to hang it up. Other scaly fish such as bass will have to be scaled in the normal manner first.

After cleaning, dry-salt the fish by packing it inside and out in a half-and-half mixture of salt and brown sugar. Use sea salt if you can get it. Cover and refrigerate for 3 or 4 days. Clean off the salt mixture and store back in the fridge for a couple more days, not touching it until a glaze forms. This protein substance is known as the "pellicle" and ensures even smoking. Set up your smoker and hang the fish safely out of the heat. Smoke cold for 4-5 days. When done, you will be able to pry open the belly and squeeze and it will be completely dry and firm. You can speed up the process by propping the belly open with a stick during smoking. Wrap loosely and store in a cold place.

The same technique can be used with game or game products such as sausage and pepperoni. Apple and alder wood provide a mild flavor, while the other hardwoods provide a much stronger flavor. Paul and Millie Laudenslager say it's worth the effort to go get some sassafras when smoking. "Daddy wouldn't use anything else!"

Making the Most of Quail

As each year's quail season opens, many of us hope that we can finally expect the weather to remain cold. For some it marks the beginning of the winter hunting season. Once quail season opens, the first snow of winter can't be far behind. Of course, I am talking about here in North Carolina, because they hunt quail, funny looking ones, in California in the heat of the year. I guess in many places, it doesn't get cold or snow. But wherever you live, and whatever the weather, the guys who sell shotgun shells are always glad to see the opening of quail season because sales skyrocket about as much as the birds do. Quail are one of the most difficult targets for the shotgunner to hit. They explode out of the covey and then just won't fly fair!

On the radio, John Boy gets tickled at his own self when he does his imitation of a quail hunt. He makes this noise with his mouth that sounds a lot like a horse blowing his breath out with his lips flapping and then adds a couple of sounds that remind us of a shotgun going off. Raw talent if I ever heard it!

Others won't be so happy to see the season open because, in the South, quail are a favorite with birders — those hobbyists who used to be called bird-watchers. People get hooked on that "Bob White... Bob White..." call of theirs. Hunters or no hunters, nature makes a lot more quail than can survive and most won't live through their first summer. Estimates are that only somewhere between 10 and 25 percent will see their first winter. The rest simply don't make it, even where they aren't hunted much. That's just the way it is.

There are many types of quail in this country, some native and some introduced. They are called quail, bob whites and partridges, often pronounced as "potridge." One of the California quail, the Gambel's quail, actually has the little top knot of the cartoon quails! Our Southern quail is the one which identifies himself by calling his own name.

Much to the delight of shotgun-shell vendors, and according to statistics, the average number of shells expended per quail is around eight. Some hunters will laugh at this figure, getting almost a bird per shell, while others will wish with their last breath that they could get a quail for every eight shots! Why do you think some hunters buy their shells by the case?

Even though the opening of quail season was mentioned as a sign of winter's approach, it still may be close to a hundred degrees outside in some parts of the country. Make certain you take along plenty of water or iced tea to the field so you don't end up a heat casualty. Save the beer for Saturday night! Don't neglect your dog's needs for water either, if you take one with you. Beware of snakes as you reach into the briers (a popular place for them to fall) for downed birds. Be sure to either take along some insect repellent or start eating plenty of garlic about 2 weeks before going hunting. Either way, be sure to check yourself carefully for ticks. Rocky Mountain spotted fever and Lyme disease are both serious threats all across the country these days. And please, don't just pull out the bird's breast and waste the rest. Quail are too easy to pluck and the meat is too good to waste any.

When a recipe calls for quail meat, just boil the birds a little until the meat is tender enough to pull off the bones, as if you are making chicken salad. It takes about two or three quail to make a cup of meat, depending on size and variety.

Frances' Quail Casserole

2 cups cooked quail meat	$^1/_4$ to $^1/_2$ cup dry onion soup mix
1 cup uncooked rice	1 cup undiluted mushroom soup
1$^1/_2$ cups water	1 cup broccoli, chopped(opt.)

Wipe a 2-quart casserole with olive oil or butter and add a layer each of quail meat, onion soup mix and rice until you run out of meat or rice — probably about 2 layers. Add a layer of broccoli if you opt to do this. Mix mushroom soup and water and add to casserole. Cover and bake at 325 degrees for 1 hour.

Minted Quail

2 cups mint leaves	10 quail, halved
$^1/_4$ pound streak-of-lean	1 stick butter plus 2 tbsps.
1 garlic clove, minced	1 tsp. fresh, chopped
2 tbsps. cognac (opt.)	1 tsp. each thyme, rosemary
2 shallots, minced	1 cup dry wine
1 bay leaf	salt and pepper to taste

Soften the butter stick and whip with basil and garlic. Season with salt and pepper to taste and chill. When firm, form into balls with a melon baller. Freeze on waxed paper. Sauté shallots in 2 tbsps. butter with cognac added. Brown quail halves in butter and place half of them in a layer in baking dish, on top of the streak-of-lean shredded or sliced thin. Sprinkle with one cup mint leaves, half the shallots and herbs and half the chilled butter balls.

Make a second layer just like the first, pour the wine over and cover. Bake at 350 degrees for 45 minutes, covered, or until done.

Remember as you are "recipe surfing" that quail, dove and pigeon recipes are interchangeable. Or you can make "four and twenty" into a pot pie and it will be a "dainty dish" fit for a king!

Cross Creek Deep Fried Quail

6-8 quail (2 per person)	$^1/_2$ cup milk or as needed
1 cup seasoned flour	hot oil to cover birds

Clean quail and dip in milk, then roll in flour seasoned with salt and pepper, or Cajun spices, or your favorite herb or blend. Mine is made with equal parts garlic powder, chervil and/or chopped fresh cilantro. Heat oil until a bread cube will brown in 1 minute. Drop in whole quail and cook until they are the color of a chestnut. If you use plenty of milk, you can add a little flour, a little hot oil and simmer it into a nice gravy for rice when you finish drenching the birds.

Don't turn your nose up at the idea of deep frying a whole quail. Remember, our friend Justin Wilson deep fries whole turkeys at holiday time. I tried it and it works well. Use a good oil like canola, sunflower or peanut for good results.

Stuffed Quail

8 quail	1 cup chicken broth
2 cups Italian bread crumbs	$^1/_2$ cup real bacon bits
$^1/_4$ cup chopped celery	$^1/_2$ cup white wine
8 slices smoked bacon	butter

Preheat oven to 350 degrees. Combine bread crumbs, bacon bits, celery and broth. Stuff quail with this mixture and wrap each with a slice of bacon. Place quail in a baking dish, add wine and cover. Bake at 350 degrees for 35-45 minutes, remove cover and bake at 425 degrees for 10 minutes or until browned to your satisfaction. Serve hot.

Quail are rather fat-free and small. Use them in other recipes such as pot pie or quail and dumplings. Marinate them overnight in half soy sauce and half Tabasco sauce for some excellent "buffalo birds." Quarter them before frying or baking.

Because quail are so lean, they tend to freezer burn quickly, so use them up as soon as you can. Besides, they are just too good to keep for long without using them. They are also excellent smoked or marinated and used in quail kebabs, quartered and spitted with vegetables, or cooked in a special herbed cream sauce.

BOBWHITE

As great as quail are in the pan, they are relatively useless as medicine. I am, of course, saying this as a joke. Historically, birds have been used in medicine, or so I've been told. Kenny Ruggles of West Virginia said that the exposed flesh of a still-living chicken would pull the poison out of a snake bite. I've had more than my share of snake bites, almost always my fault, but the furthest thing from my mind was slicing open a chicken to get the venom out!

When I was in the hospital at Fort Sam Houston, Texas, a hospital ward administrator named Marie Pawelek told me that when she was a child, her mother would cook road runners whenever her father could get one. They may have been roadkills because they are too fast to shoot! Road runners are muscular and don't have much spare meat. They would be very tough. I never ate one myself. I did eat a seagull once and it was the Godawfulest thing I ever dined on. People always say a certain wild animal "tastes like chicken!" This seagull did — like a chicken fried in cod liver oil! I ate it two times in one day — the first and the last! Anyhow, Marie couldn't remember how the road runners tasted, but said that it was an old Texas remedy to use the juice from road runner soup on skin lesions and other cutaneous problems. So there is at least one medicinal use for birds — two, if you believe Ruggles!

My friend Dr. Dwight Bundy (real name Earl Dwight Bundy — not a lot to choose from, so we usually called him "Doc" and left Dwight for his wife Carla and his Mom!), told me that when he first moved from Louisiana to West Virginia he was having a little problem with the Ridgerunner dialect. One of his first patients had body lice — "the crabs" — and he asked the other doctor what he would use in this case. His response was to rub him with *quail!* Not sure if it was the accent barrier or if he was the butt of a joke, Doc asked again. The answer was the same, "Tell him to rub it with *quail*." Doc Bundy kept repeating "Quail, quail are you sure?" "Yes," the other doctor was getting frustrated now. "*Quail,* put some lindane cream on it, *quail,* K-w-e-l-l! *Quail!*" Get it? I hope you don't ever need any *quail* cream for anything!

Cookin' 'Coon in a Crockpot

These days, cooking is a lot different than when I was growing up. We had a wood stove and cooked nearly everything in either a Dutch oven or cast iron skillets. Beans and other vegetables were cooked in big enamel pots like you occasionally see nowadays in somebody's yard with flowers growing profusely from them. The rusted-out holes in the bottom provide good drainage and ensure they won't be stolen for cooking pots. Today we use microwaves, crockpots and indoor grills that make food taste like it was cooked over charcoal.

I have to confess that I like old-fashioned, slow-cooked jelly and jam and big pots of beans and stews that simmer for hours, maybe even a couple of days. Those old enameled pots bring back lots of fond memories — I always liked to eat! And questions, too! I still haven't figured out to this day how my grandmother, grandfather and my mother kept the pots separated, because we had three or four alike. One was for beans and stew, one for canning, one for making soap and washing clothes and small children, and the fourth — ah, yes, the fourth! It went under the bed on those snowy, wintry nights when it was too cold to run across the back yard to the toilet! It was also my job, being the oldest, to dump it in the morning, along with cleaning it and putting a little fresh water in it before toting it back upstairs. Maybe the "good old days" weren't all that great in some respects.

My wife, Frances, will kill me for telling you this, because she is trying to help me improve my image, not an easy task considering the way I was raised (no complaints) and having spent 20 years in the Green Berets! Anyway, this is a story I should have submitted to *Reader's Digest* for their most embarrassing moments. My ex-wife and her family were the kind of Southerners we read about — deeply religious, devoted and tee-totalers. If you took a drink of liquor, even one beer, you were a drunkard. Well, I was in the Army and that was a part of life. They punish you for drinking now, but it used to be a social requirement — unit parties, happy hour and "right-arm night" where you drank with your supervisors. To make a long story short, one day my ex and my son were returning from church with a bunch of other ladies who had given them a ride. Naturally, they had to chit-chat in the yard, and my son quickly went in and got out of his church duds, returning to the porch in his BVD's. That's how I used to play in the rain, but because of the company I said, "Son, you can't be out in the yard in your underwear." With his six-year-old logic, he returned, "Why not, Dad? You pee out here when you get drunk!" That's one of the top ten reasons for moving to the country. Well, back to the story of 'coons.

People always seemed to have more spare time in the "old days," yet still managed to get a lot more done than we do now. I never seem to have enough hours in the day to finish my work, and my son appeared to have even less time than I did to sit and just listen to the birds — even when he had no job. Now that he's in the Air Force, I rarely see him, but when he does come home he manages to spend a little time down in the woods by the creek. Poor Frances! She works all day at her job and then spends all the remaining daylight hours making the yard look like a cross between a botanical garden and the grounds at Silver Springs or Cypress Gardens. Everybody tells me how great it looks, but she's the one with dirt under her fingernails and cactus stickers from here to yonder. (Thanks, honey!) Sometimes she doesn't even get to see *The Guiding Light* and I have to tell her what happened!

Frances Squier at work.

I never have enough hours, and still make jelly slowly, but my microwave, crockpot, and electric Luhr-Jensen smoker have greatly changed the way I prepare some other dishes.

Stews are one of the easiest things to make in a crockpot, because you don't have to keep stirring and adding water. One day, company was coming to dinner and I wasn't sure what I was going to fix. They wanted something "wild" and as luck would have it, the Great Spirit was watching over me again. As I headed out to work, I left the driveway and there

was a young, tender raccoon that had forgotten to look both ways before crossing the road. It was fresh and undamaged, and in no time at all it was soaking in salted water and vinegar while I went to work on the rest of the things I needed to fix Crockpot 'Coon Stew. Sometimes this helps the flavor of a 'coon's meat.

I wasn't quite as fast as I thought, it turned out. Next day, my neighbor Geneva Hodges knocked on the door and asked, "Tom, wasn't there a 'coon in front of your house yesterday?" "Yeah," I told her. "We ate it for supper last night." Dancing down the steps, she left. "I knew it. I won that bet!"

There are dozens of ways to fix a raccoon, and some wild-food cookbooks say that it was almost a Southern staple food. They are so well known that raccoon meat is included in the USDA's *Composition of Foods,* which lists it as a good source of protein. The standard 3^1/2-ounce or 100-gram serving contains 29.2 grams of protein — double that of pork! It is also high in vitamins A and B.

Of course, like any other meat, the young ones are most tender. Older raccoons, especially, tend to have a lot of fat on them when it gets close to cold weather. Though not as greasy as a 'possum, this fat should be removed before cooking, with a knife or by parboiling if necessary. The little glands or "kernels" along under the back and under the forearms need to be removed, as well. Tom, Jr. prefers his raccoon baked or roasted in sour cream and herbs, but I decided to stew this one for guests Debbe and Gordon Lowell. They said they loved it, and ate several bowls full.

Crockpot 'Coon Stew

1 small raccoon	2 stalks celery, diced
3 medium carrots, diced	4 small potatoes, cubed
4 carrots, sliced	1 pint tomato sauce
1 cup okra, sliced	1 cup cabbage, shredded
2 small turnips, cubed	1 cup mushrooms, halved
4 cloves garlic	4 Jerusalem artichokes, quartered
1 tsp. Italian spices	1 cup zucchini and yellow summer squash, sliced
salt and pepper to taste	hot peppers to taste (opt.)
4 bay leaves	1 onion, diced

Quarter the raccoon after cleaning and either bring it to a boil, simmering for 45 minutes, or cook it in the crockpot on high with 1 onion and 2 cloves of garlic until the meat can be taken off the bone. De-bone and return the meat to the crockpot with just enough liquid to cover. Add spices, minced garlic and other ingredients. Cook on high until it comes to a boil and turn down to low. Cook all day or until vegetables are tender. Some people like to serve it over boiled rice, brown rice being better for you than white rice, of course.

Raccoons can be baked, fried like rabbits or chicken, ground into burgers or made into pot pies. Tommy, as I said, prefers his baked and so does my mom, Helen Squier Blakely.

Mom's Baked 'Coon and Sweet 'Taters

1 cleaned 'coon	1 cup Madeira sherry
4 apples, cored	8 small sweet potatoes
1 cup water	1 large onion, sliced
salt and pepper	hickory smoked bacon

Season raccoon with salt and pepper and place in a roasting pan with apples and onions inside and sweet potatoes around it. Lay strips of bacon across the raccoon and add water and wine to pan. Bake at 350 degrees for 60-90 minutes or about 20 minutes per pound, basting with pan drippings, until done.

Of course, you can leave out the apples and onion and fill the raccoon with your favorite stuffing recipe. Corn bread and either chestnuts or (ocean) oysters works well!

Braised Raccoon

1 small raccoon, cleaned
1 tsp. celery seed
1 cup flour
1 tsp. mustard seed
$1/2$ cup dry red wine

6 bay leaves
3 tbsps. lemon juice
4 tbsps. bacon drippings
12 whole cloves
1 tsp. rosemary, chopped

Cut raccoon into serving-sized pieces and dredge in flour. Salt and pepper to taste and brown in bacon drippings in a Dutch oven or large skillet. Add other ingredients and simmer covered for 2 hours or until done (tender). Add 1 cup water initially and more as needed. Remove meat when done and use pan liquids to make gravy.

Fried Raccoon, Panamanian Style

1 dressed raccoon
4 tbsps. milk
8 tbsps. flour
1 tsp. salt

3 eggs, beaten
2 tbsps. peanut butter
1 tsp. paprika
$1/2$ cup bacon drippings

Cut raccoon into serving-sized portions. Combine eggs, milk, peanut butter, flour, salt and paprika into a batter. Coat raccoon pieces with batter and brown in hot bacon drippings in skillet or Dutch oven. Add $1/2$ cup water and cover tightly. Simmer over medium-low heat until tender — about 1 hour or more, depending on size.

The Joys and Sorrows of Small-Game Hunting

When rabbit season opens each year, some people I know take a whole week off so they can follow their beagles through the fields in pursuit of those cotton-tailed little speed-demons. As a youngun', some of my earliest memories are hunting rabbits by myself with a little .22-caliber rifle that my grandfather had owned for many years.

It was easy tracking the rabbits through mud, sand or winter snows because their distinctive tracks are like little arrows pointing the way. Of course the point is in the wrong direction, but as long as you keep this in mind, you'll be okay. Their larger back feet are placed side-by-side and their smaller feet make their round marks one behind the other and to the rear of the front feet's tracks. Think of a pattern that looks about like two Almond Joys or Mounds bars side by side the long way and about three or four inches apart. Put a miniature peanut-butter cup roughly center-ed and about four inches behind these and a second miniature peanut-butter cup two inches behind that one and slightly to the right. Got the picture?

Next time you see this track in the sand or snow, you will know what animal was passing through the area.

When I have the occasion to ask my mother if she needs anything or what does she want for, oh say, Mother's Day, she has been known to ask if I have a rabbit or two in the freezer I could spare! I remember that when I could just see over the top of the wood stove and into those old cast-iron skillets, we ate a lot of fried rabbit. Mom was never what you would call a gourmet cook, but she could fry rabbit to a "T" and there were never any leftovers.

My father used to call me "The Buzzard" because I would hang around the kitchen and eat all the food that was left when everyone else was finished eating. Later he took to calling me "Ears," like some of my schoolmates did — for obvious reasons. Then, as I got older, he called me "Buck," a common appellation and also the daily name for one of my uncles who you all'll be hearing more about soon. Mom, bless her heart, called me "Poinsettia," because I was her little Christmas-season baby, and embarrassed me calling me that in front of my service buddies after I went to "Vietnam on my senior trip." It unofficially became the Native American name that many people knew me by. Every cloud has a silver lining and one pain-ridden night after my parachute accident, the name "Broken Bear" came to me in a vision. Thank you! Thank you!

When my grandfather was still alive — which means still hunting and fishing, because he hunted and fished until the day he died — Mom always cooked the heads for him. Not much was wasted in our house. There were always heads in Mom's squirrel, rabbit or muskrat gravy. Now they are Mom's treat! A lot of people look back fondly on childhood memories when times were harder but life was simpler. Kids have always had it easier than adults. Journalist and editor Pat Allen Wilson told me that she could remember eating squirrels, rabbits, and venison in her Arkansas childhood days. She says, "We didn't think of them as 'game.' They were just 'food!' for us."

Even in his old age, my grandfather, Joseph Thomas Jones, was a skilled stalker and could often sneak up on an animal such as a groundhog or rabbit while it was eating or playing. When he was hungry, he obtained food in this manner, but when he wasn't he would use this "game" of stalking to keep his skills honed or just for the fun of it. I can remember his laughter filling the woods as a deer blasted its way between the trees after he had tip-toed up on it and slapped it on the rump! He would laugh even harder than when he tip-toed up on Mom-Mom (my grandmother) in the kitchen and slapped her on the rump playfully and she pretended to be mad about it. When I do that to Frances, I always say "Excuse me!" She always says, "I'm going to excuse you alright — upside the head!" But I see her smiling!

One of the worst fights between two old men occurred once when Pop-Pop, as my grandfather was known to me, and my Great-uncle Buck were out hunting rabbits together. Buck's real name was Rothburn, but only Aunt Elsie and his parents were permitted to call him by his Christian name. To everyone else, he was always "Buck!" Many of my uncles had funny names — there were Uncle Corb and Uncle Harm, Uncle Sonny was really James Medford Jones, and I don't know what Uncle Pee Wee's real name was. I don't think I ever heard it. He was deaf, but he could wiggle his ears at will like a rabbit and we all loved him.

Uncle Buck had killed a rabbit — must have been with a stick or a rock, because no shot had been heard. Pop-Pop was somewhere in the area stalking and Buck carefully propped up the cotton-tail to look like it was testing the air for some scent of danger. Pop-Pop was pretty old by then, a fact which probably accounted for Buck living a few more years. Pop-Pop was still sharp-eyed, and from a long way off he spotted the rabbit and began his sneak. Carefully angling around so that he was inching his way up from behind, the minutes ticked by until he finally grabbed the rabbit by the ears in victory, a trick he had often performed in the past. Buck wet his pants, doubling over in laughter, as Pop-Pop clutched the lifeless bunny, prepared to break its neck swiftly. It is only because Pop-Pop was too mad to run fast and Buck was a little younger that his life was spared that day!

A THOUSAND AND ONE REASONS TO TAKE THE WIFE HUNTING!

There have been times when I have been accused of treating my family "like a dog," and taken out of context that sounds pretty bad. Let me defend myself. It is popular to hunt squirrels with little dogs called "feists" because their barking keeps a squirrel occupied so a hunter can get a good shot. I never had a squirrel dog of my own, so I conned my sons into walking around the other side of the tree like a terrier would, and of course the squirrel would slip back around to my side of the trunk and would soon be in my pot or pan. When I tried to get my wife, Frances, to do this she said, "Ha! Ha! Buddy, you know what you can do with that little idea!"

STALKING THE "WILD RABBIT"

I did, however, get my ex-wife to do this once when we were out in the country and saw a nice fox squirrel run up a tree. There are only about eighteen counties in North Carolina where you can legally harvest these giant squirrels. I asked her to run around to the other side of the tree so the squirrel would move. He refused to budge! Unbelievably, after convincing her that there was no one else around and that I would never tell, I talked her into jumping up and down and *barking* at the squirrel! It was a comical sight, but it worked. I was laughing so hard I didn't know if I could keep still long enough for a good shot. I had to bite my tongue and squint to stop the tears from rolling down my cheek, but we ate that squirrel a couple of days later. That was a few years ago, and wouldn't work now. She was slim at the time and light on her feet, but last time I saw her she had obviously been eating ordinary food on a regular basis. She had plumped up considerably and if she could still jump, would look more like a pit bull than the little feist dogs the rich squirrel hunters prefer!

Once, as a child, I shot a squirrel in a dead tree and rather than just fall, it managed to drag itself up into a hole with nothing but its tail hanging out. I barked, hollered and cussed that day, all to no avail. Nowadays, we try to leave these dead trees, called "snags" when weather is good and "widow makers" when there are storms in the area, as homes for wildlife, but I had to go and find an axe to cut down the tree. There were no branches to climb, it was too big around to shinny up, and the old dead tree had my hands bleeding before I got it down and retrieved the squirrel.

There are some bad hunting memories, of course, and that is one for me, but on the whole it is great to get out into the woods and just get a little closer to the Earth even when I don't harvest any game or gather any weeds. The ethical hunter is an important game-management tool. It is now against the law in North Carolina to interfere with anyone who is legally pursuing game or fishing. It should be so everywhere! As the bumper stickers say, "Take your boy (girl) hunting, instead of hunting your boy (girl)."

There are so many reasons for me to remember my grandfather and the things that he taught me. Even though he was uneducated, he knew more than many professors I have known and college-boy lieutenants ("The first thing I'm going to do is straighten these Master Sergeants out!" NOT!) I have had to wet nurse, with their inflated sense of self-value. What is that old saying? "If I could buy him for what he's worth and sell him for what he thinks he's worth, I'd be rich!" Many of them wouldn't even deign to speak to an old Indian root-doctor who couldn't even write his name, but they would do well to listen to his teachings. I'll never forget the day Uncle Buck tricked Pop-Pop into sneaking up on that dead rabbit!

Pop-Pop never met my mother-in-law, but he would love her as much as I do. She has helped me chase squirrels (No barking! "There he goes, honey. Shoot him! Shoot him!"), cut poke and look for snakes for a class I was giving. She raised my orphaned raccoons after I got them on the (milk) bottle and turned them into the spoiled brats they are today.

Delphia Whisnant's Bubbly Bunny

1-2 rabbits	1 cup catsup
2 cups Sun Drop	flour
salt and pepper	oil

Roll the cleaned and cut-up rabbit in flour that has been seasoned with salt and pepper to taste. Brown in hot oil on all sides. While the rabbit is browning, combine the catsup and Sun Drop in a large bottle and shake thoroughly with lid on. In the Southern mountains we drink Sun Drop, but you can use Mellow Yellow (Go Kyle Petty, driving the number 42 Mellow Yellow race car to victory!), Seven Up or whatever similar yellow soda is available. In the Southwest, they have a soda made with cactus juice that would be perfect and where there are lots of Hispanics, the coconut flavored Coco Rico would be a great taste. Shake well and pour over the browned rabbit in a baking pan or dish and bake at 350 degrees for one hour. The taste will amaze you!

Kyle and #42 at Rockingham's NC Motor Speedway.

Well, you will find Kyle Petty fans at every race still wearing shirts with his old Mellow Yellow car on them. Now that he has changed sponsors from Mellow Yellow soda to Coor's Lite beer, we might want to change how we use Kyle's sponsor's products. Mellow Yellow is great for Bubbly Bunny, but Coor's Lite is more suited to boiling shrimp and crawfish, making a tempura or pancake batter, or for a leavening agent.

Mom's Simmered Muskrat

2-3 muskrats	1 onion, chopped
1 carrot, chopped	1 stalk of celery, chopped
2 bay leaves	1 cup sherry wine
flour	salt and pepper
garlic to taste	1 stick butter

Clean and cut up muskrats, saving heads if Mom is eating with us. Roll in flour that has been seasoned with salt and pepper. Brown in butter. Add vegetables and seasonings, wine and water to cover. Simmer for 30 minutes or until tender.

Tom's Mom, Helen Blakely.

*Frances' Mom, Delphia Whisnant
and her grandson, Billy.*

Pop-Pop and Uncle Buck and all the other uncles trapped muskrats and beavers because they were hungry or didn't want to get that way. Today these animals are pests in many places and people will be delighted to find out how tasty they are.

Braised Beaver

1 cleaned beaver, cut up	1 cup flour
1/2 cup oil or drippings	salt and pepper to taste
water as needed	3 cups carrot slices
3 cups diced onions	3 cups snap (green) beans

Brown the floured and seasoned (young) beaver meat in hot oil. Add the veggies and water to cover in a large kettle or Dutch oven. Cover and simmer 1 hour or until tender. Some people like to add a cup of dry red wine and some minced garlic for flavor.

At my house we eat a lot of green beans. Heck, we eat a lot of beans, period! But when we have an abundance of fresh string beans, we snap them and hang them on strings to dry in the traditional Cherokee method of making "leather breeches." They will keep well for a long time and you "bring them back to life" by soaking in water for an hour or two. Of course, now we usually string them and our mushrooms and peppers for drying on dental floss. It lasts longer than cotton thread and is much easier than weaving fibers from plants.

Small Game Makes for Big Meals!

Small game means different things to different people. To some, only rabbits are included and even squirrels are not eaten. Some will try both. Still other more adventuresome cooks will find a way to make a meal of just about any small animal that they are able to harvest or get as a FORD (Found On the Road Dead). If worse comes to worst, there is almost no animal you can't grind up and either add to pizza or seal in a wrapper as egg roll, empanada or ravioli!

I had to add that part about FORD animals because as a teenger living in Florida (after graduation, before the Navy and Vietnam), I ate a lot of FORDs, especially armadillos! There were always plenty to harvest from the highways because they had the stupid habit of jumping straight up in the air whenever they were scared and rolling into a ball. They could really hop and would rise up to the height of a car's bumper. After a while, I could tell you which side of the a road one of these "possums on the half shell" would land on just by whether he sort of kissed the bumper or backed into it. Mountain people will understand what I mean when I say that I nearly "foundered" myself on these little armored pig-eyed critters. My father really got mad when I fixed one for him on the barbecue grill and told him it was a suckling pig. Despite their armored-car appearance, armadillos are easy to clean. You just cut off the head and tail, cut down either side of the belly and pass your hand down inside the shell to remove the meat. Then you will probably want to remove the skin from the belly.

In Latin America, they make pocketbooks from the dried and varnished shells of armadillos, tanning the skin and installing a zipper in the belly. I don't know of any use for the discarded tails, but I have seen the cured heads made into walking canes and gear-shift knobs! You see a lot of FORD armadillos on the side of the road in the Gulf states and now Georgia. Most people just drive right by them. Me, I get a "better idea!" as the light bulb comes on!

Stuffed Armadillo

1 medium armadillo	your favorite stuffing recipe
salt and pepper to taste	1 cup red wine (optional)
1 pint cider vinegar	1 tbsp. peppercorns, crushed
2 or more garlic cloves, minced	1 tsp. each chervil, rosemary, sage, thyme
1 tbsp. dry mustard	and celery seed
1 lemon, chopped	$^1/_4$ cup salt

Clean the armadillo and wash inside and out with hot water. Marinate overnight in a large pot with vinegar, wine, mustard and the herbs (tied in a little bag if you prefer) with the lemon and enough water to cover, stirring in $^1/_4$ cup salt. Remove from marinade next morning, rinse and drop in a pot of boiling water to cover. Reduce heat and simmer 30 minutes. Remove and when dry, stuff with your favorite stuffing or one made from cornbread and wild rice. Apples or apricots are good additions to stuffing for armadillos. Lace loosely and dust with salt and pepper to taste and a light coating of flour. Roast at 350 degrees 1 hour or until tender and done to preference, basting as needed to keep moist.

One of my favorite pastimes in Florida was to sit very still at dusk as the armadillos were feeding in the woods and throw pebbles in their direction, slowly bringing them closer and closer to me. Their eyesight is so terrible they would often get right up to my toes before they put it in high gear to haul buggy! The recipe above can be used with any small game, but works especially well with raccoons, ground hogs, porcupines and, of course, possums! It will even take the toughness out of an old wild goose. Old tame geese are very greasy. I bake them for about 20 minutes on 450 degrees until the skin swells and the fat melts and they look like they are in a water balloon. Then I drain the fat off and lower the heat to finish baking them.

Tom and armadillo.

Maybe you are more interested in recipes for more conventional small game, so here are some for squirrels and rabbits before I get back to the unusual but delicious and often overlooked little critters.

Rabbit Belle Chase

3 small rabbits	**lemon**
flour	**salt and pepper to taste**
peanut oil	**sour cream**

Cut rabbits into 6 or 8 pieces, wash well and rub with lemon. Salt and pepper to taste. Roll in flour and fry in hot oil until browned on both sides. Place in a baking dish and cover with sour cream, baking at 350 degrees for 35-45 minutes, until tender. Serve on a bed of rice or pasta.

Easy Squirrel Pie

4 squirrels	**1 double pie crust**
¹/₂ cup minced parsley	**2 onions, chopped**
¹/₄ pound salt pork, diced	**2 tbsps. butter**
1 can mixed vegetables	**4 cups boiled small diced potatoes**
salt and pepper to taste	

Cut up squirrels and boil gently in lightly salted water, simmering gently for about an hour or until meat can be pulled from the bones. Remove meat and set aside. Save stock for cooking rice or pasta. Sauté onion and salt pork in butter and stir in a mixture of the flour and enough cold water to dissolve well. Combine with squirrel meat, parsley, vegetables and salt and pepper. Pour into pie shell and top with second crust, making a few slits in top. Bake at 400 degrees for 50 minutes or until crust is lightly browned. Some times I add some diced celery or carrots to this recipe or Jerusalem artichokes or mushrooms if I can find them.

Barbecued Rabbit

rabbits, $1/2$ to 1 per person	barbecue sauce
1 tbsp. Italian herbs	1 tbsp. soy sauce
honey	garlic salt to taste

Cut rabbits into manageable-sized pieces. Small ones can be barbecued whole. In a pressure cooker or covered pot simmer rabbit in enough water to cover with herbs and soy sauce, for 15 minutes. Remove and pat dry. Sprinkle with garlic salt and coat with your favorite barbecue sauce. Drizzle with honey and then cook it on the grill until done or broil or bake it in the oven for 30 minutes at 350 degrees or until done. If you bake it, broil it on the higher setting 5 minutes before serving, turning while cooking. You might leave the door open to prevent burning.

Pearl Pulley's Barbecue Sauce

$1/2$ cup onion, chopped	2 tbsps. brown sugar
1 tbsp. paprika	1 tsp. salt
1 tsp. dry mustard	big pinch cayenne pepper
$1/4$ tsp. chili powder	2 tbsps. Worcestershire sauce
$1/4$ cup vinegar	1 cup tomato sauce or juice
$1/4$ cup ketchup	$1/2$ cup water

Mix above and simmer for 15 minutes. Pour over meat and bake or grill.

Frances Squier's Quick B-B-Que Sauce

8 ounces Carolina Treat or	$1/2$ cup brown sugar
Kraft BBQ sauce from store	$1/4$ cup Worcestershire
2 tbsps. garlic powder	1 tsp. dry mustard

Blend all ingredients, simmer to heat thoroughly and pour on meat or use as marinade and basting sauce.

Frances Squier's Wild Lasagna
(Meat Sauce Mixture)

2 cups mushrooms	$1/2$ cup (wild) onion, chopped
1 tbsp. garlic, minced	$1/2$ cup bell pepper, chopped
2 tbsps. corn oil	$1 1/2$ pounds ground rabbit, squirrel,
15 ounces tomato sauce	pheasant or venison
$1/4$ cup wine	$1/2$ cup water
1 tsp. sugar	1 tsp. Italian herb blend
4 cups tomato wedges	1 tsp. oregano
1 or 2 drops Tabasco (optional)	

Sauté mushrooms, onion and pepper. Remove. Sauté game to brown and drain. Combine all ingredients and simmer 1 hour.

Noodle Mixture

1 package lasagna noodles	2 packages mozzarella cheese
cottage cheese	Parmesan cheese

Cook noodles and drain. Or use slices of puffball mushroom. Line buttered or oiled baking dish with noodles or mushroom slices and then alternate layers of meat and tomato sauce, cottage cheese, mozzarella cheese and repeat, ending up with mozzarella cheese. Top with Parmesan cheese and bake at 350-375 degrees until bubbly and slightly browned on top.

Small game (all game, in fact) is more healthy for you than most store-bought meat because it usually is low in cholesterol and has very little fat on it, except for some fur-bearers like raccoons and possums and baby pigeons which are known as squabs, which may be French for "expensive" in restaurants. Venison, squirrel and rabbit generally are

Tom with Danita Laudenslager and possum
in a persimmon tree.

higher in protein and fiber than grocery market meats, and lack the added growth hormones, steroids and antibiotics. At one time possums were great eating, as Dan'l Boone's progeny can tell you, but they have changed from forest feeders to garbage gourmets and can't be eaten these days, freshly shot or captured. Forget FORD possums! You have to put them up for a few days in a pen and "sweeten them up" with fresh fruit, corn bread and perhaps buttermilk! Occasionally, you can find a possum who has spent a week in a persimmon tree and is already "sweetened up." This will be a rare occasion these days.

The rabbit hunter would do well to wear a pair of latex gloves to clean his bunnies, or any other game these days, any time of year, because the little cottontails can harbor the ticks that carry Rocky Mountain spotted fever, Lyme disease and even tularemia — rabbit fever. Remember Elmer Fudd with "spots before his eyes?" This can be spread to the hunter or collector of FORD rabbits through blood, and as you snap the brittle leg bones it is easy to get a cut or injury from the sharp ends. In the meat, tularemia is destroyed by cooking, so it is only a danger while cleaning or if you eat rabbit sushi! It is said that rabbits

The author inspects his dinner.

are the most popularly hunted small-game animal in the country. Wild rabbits are the easiest to prepare in the field or kitchen! You can snap the leg bones to remove the "lucky" rabbit feet and pull off the fur from a wild cottontail rabbit without a knife.

When cleaning any small game, avoid getting hair on the meat as much as possible, avoid breaking the stomach and bladder, and remove any fat you find. Check under the "arm-pits" and in the small of the back for any glands or "kernels." Some people call them "lights," while to others "lights" means the lungs. You usually eat the lungs of KFC's chickens — the dark spongy (tasty) mass on the back of the breast portion — and you can eat many animals' lungs by cubing, parboiling and then frying. Parboiling makes many types of game, small or large, more tender and may help to remove unpleasant odors and flavors from what they have been eating — pine roots, other animals or your garbage.

Braised Porcupine

1 porcupine, cut up
$^1/_4$ cup bacon grease
$^1/_2$ cup or more water

1 cup flour
salt and pepper to taste
1 cup red wine (optional)

Soak porky overnight in salted water. Rinse and pat dry. Dredge through flour seasoned with salt and pepper. Brown in large skillet in bacon grease. Add water and wine. Cover and reduce heat. Simmer until tender and fully cooked. Make gravy from pan drippings and flour. Serve over rice.

Porcupines tend to be tender because they move so slowly. Unless they have been feeding heavily on pines, they usually are pretty tasty, too. You can catch them where there is a lot of salt deposited — on toilet seats in campgrounds, for example, where they can be very destructive. When they are dead, turn over and carefully remove the skin. Native Americans and craft makers value the quills for vests and chokers. Boil them until softened, dye them and flatten with a flat iron or hot rock.

"How do porcupines make love?"... *"Very* carefully!"

Red-Eye Gravy

$^1/_4$ cup pan juices from game
Tabasco sauce to taste
1 cup water

salt and pepper to taste
instant coffee to preference
$^1/_4$ cup flour

Mix flour and cold water to form a thin liquid and combine with other ingredients, using instant coffee for color and not for flavor. Bring to a boil, reduce heat, cover and simmer until it is done the way you like it.

Baked Possum

1 whole dressed possum, skinned
$^1/_2$ pound smoked bacon
1 can cream of mushroom soup

stuffing
1 cup red wine

Parboil the possum for 20-30 minutes. Fill with your favorite stuffing, sew or skewer to close, and lay in a roasting pan or Dutch oven. Pour mushroom soup over possum and criss-cross with bacon strips. Add water and wine and bake covered at 350 degrees for about $2^1/_2$ hours or until done, depending on size.

Tom, Jr. and Richard Whisnant with a pair of possums
to go in the pen for a few days.

The second newspaper editor I worked for was named John Myers and he related to me a story about how his father long ago, with much difficulty, had buried a mule when it died, just barely getting it covered. A few days later John, his father and their black farm worker were in the field where the mule was buried. They noticed some movement and went to investigate. The wide-hipped mule's head was covered, but now his butt was exposed and fur could be seen. The worker reached in and pulled out a possum, handing it to John, who was by now gagging! Reach in and pull. Reach in and pull. Reach in and pull. They ended up with six possums and a happy helper because neither John nor his dad wanted to share in the bounty! Since that time, John says he has not been able to eat possum!

That is a true story and not racist. Just like this next story which I think is worth sharing. Joe Carpenter was working as a hunting guide for a big plantation owner when he was a youngster down in Georgia, I believe he said. The plantation owner also had several black men working for him. A friend gave the owner of the place a bottle of untaxed liquor, and being unsure of its origin and safety he gave it to the hard-working foreman. Next morning the plantation owner asked the black man how the liquor had been. "Jest right!" was the reply. Confused, he asked for an explanation. "Well," he was told, "If it was any wuss, I couldn't have drunk it. And if it was any better, you wouldn't have gib it to me!"

Armadillo Sausage

2 pounds ground armadillo meat	$^1/_4$ cup apple cider vinegar
minced garlic to taste	$^1/_4$ cup brown sugar
juice from 1 squeezed onion	$^1/_4$ tsp. ground red pepper
1 tbsp. ground sage	salt and pepper to taste

Make sure meat is well ground. Add garlic and vinegar to $^1/_4$ cup boiling water and dissolve the other spices in this water. When cool, pour over meat and mix in thoroughly. Regrind the meat and refrigerate for 5-7 days. Pack in parchment paper or pork or sheep casings and refrigerate for use or freeze for later.

Remember about interchanging the various game meats in these recipes and you will always have something interesting to serve your guests.

Beaver Meat Loaf

4-5 cups ground beaver	2 eggs, beaten
1 onion, minced	$^1/_2$ cup corn flakes or oat meal
$^1/_2$ cup tomato paste	2 tsps. Worcestershire or soy sauce
$^1/_2$ cup mushrooms, chopped (opt)	minced garlic to taste
salt and pepper to taste	

Combine all ingredients, mixing well. Form a loaf and place in a well greased loaf pan. Bake at 350 degrees for 2 hours or until done.

The third annual Beaver Dam Wild Game Cookoff was held at the Roseboro National Guard Armory in late January 1995, with nearly 300 people attending. The Wild Game Cookoff is a fundraiser for the Beaver Dam Community Center. This year's judges included Cumberland County Sheriff Moose Butler, Senator Tony Rand, Spring Lake realtor Charlie Wellons, NC Superintendent of Schools Bob Etheridge, chef Bill Faust, and yours truly.

There were three categories of entries — small game, large game, and a composite category called fowl, fish and reptile. An overall trophy called the "Cooper Cup" is named in honor of Reverend Donald Cooper. "This whole thing was Preacher Cooper's idea," said Paul Maguire, one of the big winners. Reverend Cooper started the wild game cookoff three years ago as a fund raiser for the Beaver Dam Community Center, where the first two cookoffs were held. Reverend Cooper is the pastor at Beaver Dam Baptist Church, and he believed the many hunters in his congregation would enjoy the fellowship of the cooking contests and contribute funds for the community center. The contest got so big that it moved into the Roseboro National Guard Armory and is hopefully going to be held in the Charlie Rose Agri-Expo Center next year. "It's bigger than Christmas for us," said winner Leonard Smith. "It causes a closeness. It's something we can talk about all during the year."

A first and second place winner in each category was chosen by the 8 judges. All of the winners with the exception of one were prepared by two friendly rivals — Leonard Smith and Paul Maguire. Iris Lucas earned first place in the large game category with fried deer steak medallions. Large game second place was Leonard Smith with bear stew. The competitors share recipes and hunting stories. Leonard Smith was justifiably proud of his bear stew, cooked just that morning. "A lot of bear hunters from down around Garland said it was the tenderest they had ever eaten." He added, "It's almost like the Andy Griffith show here, where Aunt Bea keeps entering her pickles in the fair."

The two winners in fish, reptile and foul were Leonard Smith in first place with pheasant in sauce and Paul Maguire with broiled pheasant breasts with melted cheese, mushrooms and bacon. I was delighted to get Leonard's recipe because I was the only one of the judges who guessed the secret ingredient. I kept saying it had a hint of chipped beef gravy flavor — what we used to call "S.O.S." in the mess hall — and the recipe confirms it.

Pheasant Supreme

1 pheasant, skinned and cut up	1 jar Armour dried beef
2 cans mushroom soup	1 pint sour cream

Arrange dried beef in bottom of cassorole dish. Place pheasant on top of beef. Mix cream of mushrom soup and sour cream together and pour over pheasant — covering all pieces. Cover with foil and bake for 3 hours at 275 degrees.

First place in small game was Paul Maguire's Beaver Dam spiced beaver. His marinated beaver strips took second place. It was strange that with all the delicious rabbit and squirrel dishes, beaver would win the two prizes. Perhaps more people will make use of this tasty meat. They can now be hunted with a gun anytime there is an open season on any game animal here, and many farmers will be glad to get rid of them. What was Paul's "secret" marinade? "I soaked it overnight in some sauce I got at Sam's Club called Yoshida's Original Gourmet Sauce. Then I grilled it until I thought it was done." His only regret, like the other contestants, was "I didn't get a chance to taste it. By the time I got to it, it was all gone." The winning Beaver Dam spiced beaver went quickly, as well. Sheriff Butler said he had never tasted beaver before and "hadn't had anything that good very often!" It is good enough that you can serve it under the name Beaver Dam special pot roast if you want to. The meat for this recipe came from the two back legs with all the fat removed.

Beaver Dam Spiced Beaver

6 pounds beaver meat	6 or 8 carrots
6 or 8 potatoes	6 or 8 small onions
$^1/_2$ cup fresh mushrooms	2 pkgs. beef stew seasoning mix
water to cover meat	

Mix seasoning and water in bowl. Put meat in bowl; make sure it is covered with sauce. Add more water if necessary. Refrigerate overnight. Put meat in roaster. Surround with peeled and halved vegetables. Place sliced mushrooms on top of meat. Pour sauce from bowl over meat and vegetables. Bake covered at 350 degrees for $1^1/_2$-2 hours.

The Cooper's Cup was shared for the first time, as the judges were split in favor of Leonard Smith's pheasant in sauce and Paul Maguire's Beaver Dam spiced beaver. Other groups thinking about sponsoring such a popular fundraiser will want to take into account that an odd number of judges will eliminate ties. Both winners graciously shared the

Cooper's Cup. Leonard Smith said, "Paul knows I would have been tickled for him to win and he said he would have been happy for me to win." Then Smith told me that Paul actually had another pheasant dish that he thought could have won easily. "He had to take it out of his van to make room for his son's carrier seat and forgot it on the step." Cookoff jitters, Paul?

Leonard Smith (left) and Paul Maguire (right), winners of the
3rd Annual Beaver Dam Wild Game Cookoff, flank
Billy Ray Underwood, Chairman of the event.

Admission to the cookoff included a performance by country entertainer Pegi Allen which ended in an autograph session, a display of trophy bucks, and a barbecue plate. Donald Ray Underwood, President of the Beaver Dam Community Center, had cooked seven pigs and shredded them into barbecue. This would be an excellent fund raiser for other church and community groups and hunting clubs as success has shown here.

Persimmons Prime For Picking (Up)!

Usually, by late October we have had a couple of frosts already, and since they say that you can't eat persimmons until they have been frosted, many folks are waiting for the right time. I don't know how much truth there is to that because persimmons grow in some places where there is no frost. I have had mine ripened by *drought* some years or by placing them in a bag with apples or in the freezer when they are real close to ripe. I do know that you can't eat American persimmons until they are ripe or they will really pucker your mouth up. This was one of our commonest childhood pranks — getting kids to eat them green, thus making them unable to whistle or speak. It ranked right up there with snipe hunts, getting innocents to pee on electric fences and tricking people into eating "Indian chewing gum"— the red berries of Jack-in-the-pulpit.

If you can find a place where they are on the ground, then you are in luck because the soft persimmon fruits are always sweet and tasty. They are also mushy and will squish in your hands as you pick them up. That is why we don't find American persimmons in our stores. They don't ship or keep well after they are ripe. The bigger, tennis-ball-sized persimmons in the markets are the oriental varieties. They lack the seeds and the taste of our native persimmons. It isn't always easy to find ripe persimmons on the ground, because the animals love them — deer, turkey and all the little animals of the forest.

Don't ever eat a green or hard, light-orange persimmon. To be tasty they need to be soft and either bright orange or dark colored like "Reduced For Quick Sale" produce. A neighbor and friend, Victoria Weaver, called to talk about persimmons once when she had plenty to share. "They are at their best when they look their worst," she said. "They should be on the ground, wrinkled, and almost black!" Mrs. Weaver said she uses persimmons to make an excellent preserve using a standard orange marmalade recipe and substituting persimmon pulp for orange and cutting the sugar in half.

Although the fruits are the best part of the persimmon tree when they are ripe, other parts of the tree are useful as well. The seeds from ripe fruits can be cooked either by boiling or roasting, and the kernels eaten. They are tasty and protein-rich. The leaves can be picked and dried to make a robust tea that is high in vitamin C. The bark has been used medicinally for years by Native Americans. The Cherokees chewed it for heartburn and bilious stomach conditions, and chewed the bark mixed with the bark of wild cherry and walnut for toothache. The Rappahannocks used the bark tea for sore throats and thrush.

Probably everyone's favorite recipes for dealing with the orange-colored fruits are for what is known as persimmon pudding, but which is more like a cake and very close to a tradition at our house and many others. It doesn't have to be fancy to be good. In fact, experimenting doesn't always turn out good. The "River Lady" said her Mama was always a good cook — *until* she tried to get fancy! "She made the most God-awful persimmon pudding I have ever et," and she adds, "Many years later, I found some good recipes, one-by-one."

River Lady Persimmon Pudding #1

3 cups persimmon pulp	2 cups buttermilk
3 cups sugar	¹/₂ cup melted butter
3 eggs	¹/₂ cup sweet milk
1 tsp. baking soda	1 tsp. vanilla
1 tsp. cinnamon	3 cups flour

Mix eggs and sugar and combine with pulp and milk. Mix well. Add soda and cinnamon to flour and fold into pulp mixture. Add vanilla and beat well. Bake at 350 degrees until brown and a broom straw comes out dry. This should be about 35-40 minutes.

River Lady's Persimmon Pie

1 cup persimmon pulp	1¹/₂ cups sugar
2 eggs, beaten	1 13-ounce can evaporated milk
1 tbsp. flour	1 tbsp. melted butter
¹/₄ tsp. nutmeg	¹/₄ tsp. vanilla
1 uncooked pie shell	whipped cream

Mix sugar and pulp and add beaten eggs and milk. Stir in spices and mix well. Pour into pie crust and bake 1 hour at 350 degrees covered with oiled foil. When done, remove foil and serve with whipped cream.

River Lady's Persimmon Pudding #2

2 cups pulp	2 cups sugar
2 cups sweet milk	2 eggs, beaten
1 tsp. vanilla extract	2 cups self-rising flour
1 cup grated coconut (optional)	

Combine all ingredients and bake at 350 degrees about 40 minutes or until light brown. The optional coconut makes a nice addition.

I have found that persimmons can also be made into a cold dessert.

Persimmon Ice Cream

1 pint persimmon pulp	1 pint vanilla pudding, prepared
1¹/₂ quarts milk	1 can sweetened condensed milk
1 tsp. vanilla extract	

Thoroughly mix all ingredients. Put in the ice cream maker, either electric or hand-cranked, adding ice and salt as required, and mix until thickened. This recipe also works well with prickly pear cactus fruit pulp or whatever else you have handy.

River Lady's Persimmon Fruit Cake

3 eggs, beaten	3 cups all purpose flour
1 tsp. cinnamon	1 tsp. baking soda
2 cups persimmon pulp	2 cups sugar
1 cup oil	1 cup nuts, chopped
1 cup candied fruit, diced	1 cup raisins or currants

Whip oil and sugar together and add eggs and persimmon. Fold in flour and soda, cinnamon, raisins and fruit and nuts. Pour mixture into three oiled and floured 10-inch tub pans. Bake at 350 degrees for 1 hour or until done. Cool and remove from pans. Sprinkle with powdered sugar.

(Tom's Note: Originally, River Lady used nuts *or* candied fruit in her recipe. I like both! and I use either 1 cup of pecans or hickory nuts or both or ¹/₂ cup black walnut pieces, which can be overpowering if you use a whole cup. I also like this recipe with an optional cup of dark rum or bourbon for flavor because the alcohol bakes out. Then I set it aside for a few weeks to let the flavors really reveal themselves.)

I had the distinct pleasure of having lunch with Julee Rosso, of *Silver Palate Cookbook* fame, to help promote her *Great Good Food Cookbook,* and I shared my ideas and recipes with her. She was very gracious, and agreed with me that there are times when you should use the less healthy, more tasty necessities such as butter instead of margarine for flavor and bacon drippings on greens, despite their cholesterol warnings. I treasure the cookbooks she autographed for me. In one she wrote, "Tom, I'll come for dinner anytime!" You couldn't buy that book from me for any amount of money! Julee puts her own touch on our humble persimmons with this recipe from the *Great Good Food Cookbook.*

Julee Rosso's Persimmon Pudding

1 cup ripe persimmon purée	$1/2$ cup skim milk
1 tbsp. unsalted butter	1 egg
$3/4$ cup packed light brown sugar	1 cup all-purpose flour
1 tsp. baking soda	$1/2$ tsp. salt
1 tsp. ground cinnamon	$1/2$ tsp. ginger, ground
$1/4$ tsp. nutmeg, grated	sour lemon sauce

Preheat oven to 350 degrees. Lightly spray or wipe a 9-inch pie pan with canola oil. In a small bowl, whisk the persimmon purée, milk, melted butter and egg. Set aside. In a large mixing bowl, combine the sugar, flour, soda, salt and spices. Stir the persimmon mixture into the flour mixture. Pour the mixture into the pie pan. Place the pan in a large shallow pan, and pour boiling water into the larger pan to a depth of $1/2$ inch. Bake for 1 to $1 1/4$ hours, adding water if necessary. The pudding is done when a knife inserted in the center comes out moist but clean. Cool the pudding slightly, cut it into wedges, and serve warm or at room temperature with sour lemon sauce.

Julee Rosso's Sour Lemon Sauce

1 tbsp. cornstarch	$1/4$ cup sugar
1 cup fresh orange juice	$1 1/2$ tbsps. lemon juice
1 tsp. grated lemon zest	pinch salt

In a heavy saucepan, combine the cornstarch and sugar. Slowly whisk in the orange juice. Cook, stirring, over low heat until the mixture is thickened and begins to boil. Stir in the lemon juice, zest and salt. Serve warm or at room temperature.

My wife makes a delicious persimmon pudding herself. Once after I got crippled — not physically challenged — Frances, the girls and I were at Fort Bragg harvesting persimmons. It was a bad day. I got my cane stuck in the tree and had to back the truck up so Jessica could stand on the roof and retrieve it. Then about a mile down the road after we left, I noticed one of my hearing aids was missing. We went back where I had been painfully jumping up and down and fortunately Amanda heard it making katydid noises before I stepped on it. We did get a fine bait of 'simmons, though.

Frances Squier's Persimmon Pudding

Measure **1 quart whole persimmons.** Wash, cap and put in food mill to separate pulp from seeds. Optional: add **nuts, coconut or raisins.**

2 eggs	$3/4$ cup milk
2 cups self-rising flour	$1/2$ tsp. salt
2 cups sugar	$1/2$ stick butter, melted
$1/2$ cup grated raw sweet potato	

Combine all ingredients, including persimmon pulp. Bake $1 1/2$ hours at 350 degrees.

Persimmons may be a little scarce some years, or too much trouble for some people to fool with, especially after working all day. Dymple Green produces an excellent canned persimmon pulp (the only source I know of) which I first tried at the Persimmon Festival in Indiana, but have used several times since then when I needed persimmon pulp in a hurry or out of season. You'll have to write for a current price list to Dymple's Delight, Rt 4 Box 53, Mitchell, IN 47446.

●●●●●

I am really proud of how my first born son turned out. I hope that some of the credit is mine! I believe Tom, Jr. has the right idea.

Earth Song

Dream of the flower,
Budding anew.
Dream of the oak
Standing so true.
Linger on wings
Atop the wind.
Linger on scents
The wind will send.
Sing of the mountain
Its deep rolling bass.
Sing of the cliff wall
Its hard stony face.
Touch the sea
Rolling along.
Touch the soil softly
And know you belong.
Listen to the earth
Singing its song.
Listen to its voice
And try to sing along.
	— Thomas K. Squier, Jr.

"Keep following the trail you're on, Son!"

The Many Faces of the Elder

Well, I may get into trouble with some of the guys I used to work with if I'm not careful, so I have to be certain to word this just right. There are still a lot of male chauvinists in the Army who think women are good for two things. One is typing and the other definitely isn't cooking! But it seems to me that women may be smarter than men, or at the very least they seem to think more logically. Women just seem to be able to solve problems more easily and see things in a clearer light at times — sometimes too clear!

I keep a list of things to write about when inspirations don't present themselves, but just to be on the safe side, I often ask my wife, Frances, if she has a suggestion to write about. Wednesday can be the hardest or the easiest because it is considered "food day" in most papers and I want to go with the flow. ("Since when?" I hear people asking.) One week I asked Frances for a suggestion and she said "Write about elderberries. They are in season now." I replied that I already had written about them, but her logical and brutally honest thinking prompted her to ask, "Did you say everything there was to say about them?"

Obviously not, or this whole book would be about elderberries! Actually, the elder is a very interesting plant, found around the world, and steeped in mystery and legend. Elderberries make good pies, jam and great wine, and are also used for treating some of life's aggravating ailments.

There is a terrific herbal medicine book by Bianchini, Corbetta and Pistoia named *Le Pianta Della Salute*, which translates as *The Plants of Health*. Those authors, if you will permit me, have this to say about elder: "Not only was it unthinkable for a witch of any standing not to have an elder in the garden; quite often they actually lived in it, and country folk rarely chopped down this tree for fear that the branches would drip blood, the witch having been chopped in error, with disastrous consequences for the woodsman. From this belief stem others: that the elder should never be planted too near the house, nor used as firewood, nor to make a cradle." I don't know about the witch and elder connection, but when my ex-wife moved out, taking everything but the waterbed which she couldn't figure out how to drain, the elder bushes along the fence died! Probably no connection at all. I do know that the dangerous practice of making pea-shooters from elder branches should be discouraged. The green parts of the plant are mildly poisonous, but a straight piece of branch makes an excellent pea-shooter when dry. The pith in the center pushes out easily, making a perfect tube. I guess you could use a well-dried one for a straw!

Elderberries are readily available and, as Frances points out, are easily recognized. They are blue to black and found in great clusters so you can't mix them up with the poisonous gallberries which form singly or in small bunches along the stalks. And, if you cut the stem of elders, the white central pith will be readily visible. Raw, elderberries can be pretty bland, although they are very nutritious. Dried or cooked, they assume a much sweeter flavor. Because they are found in such large clusters, they are easy to gather — except for their habit of growing in swamps and wet places where muskeeters (mosquitos) and snakes abound!

Years ago it was found that winos drinking cheap port weren't bothered by a back problem that others who weren't drinking the same wine were suffering from. This cheap wine was adulterated with elderberries where it was made in the Mediterranean area, and a chemical they contain relieved the pain of sciatica sufferers. Here are some more traditional uses for the berries:

Elderberry Cheese Pie

4 cups elderberries	9-inch graham cracker pie crust
8 ounces cream cheese, softened	14 ounces condensed milk
$^1/_2$ cup lemon juice	1 tsp. vanilla extract
2 cups sugar	

Stem elderberries and remove critters. Simmer berries and sugar with water to just cover until thickened and set aside. In a mixer bowl, whip cream cheese until fluffy. Beat in condensed milk until smooth. Fold in lemon juice and vanilla, mixing thoroughly. Fold into pie crust and mold to shape. Top with elderberries and chill until firm.

Elderberry Pie

4 cups elderberries	2 cups sugar
1 pint water	3 tbsps. flour
3 tbsps. lemon juice	$^1/_4$ tsp. cinnamon
1 pinch salt	pastry for 2 crusts

Combine berries, water, and lemon juice and add the dry ingredients and mix well. Pour into unbaked pie crust and top with second crust. Pinch edges and trim excess. Slit top in 4 places. Bake at 425 degrees for 25-35 minutes or until done.

While working on this chapter, I was interrupted by a phone call from David Smith of Roseland Road. He had recently taken the Hunter Education course with me and, of course, I talked about saving our dwindling snake population. He called to say he had two freshly killed rattlesnakes and I was welcome to them if I wanted to come and get them. I say, if you have to kill them, put them in the freezer, don't waste them. I get a lot of headless snakes from farmers "bush-hogging" their fields. For some reason, a rattlesnake will lie flat along the ground, perhaps coiled, with its head lifted straight up about half a foot, as the vibrations of the bush-hog mower approach. Dumb idea! Now with the meat in the freezer, Frances tucked in, and the clock ticking, I can get on with this chapter.

Because of their medicinal value, elderberries are added to tinctures or elixirs to draw out their healing properties. What is the difference? Tinctures are meant to be taken by drops, often under the tongue. Elixirs are swigged down by the spoonful or capful. Elderberry wine is drunk shamelessly from large glasses or out of the bottle. Elderberry wine is of course the famous drink in the play and movie, *Arsenic and Old Lace*.

Elderberry Jam

4 cups elderberries
3 cups sugar

6 crabapples, cored
2 tsps. lemon juice

Crush the elderberries and chop crabapples (or substitute 1 package fruit pectin) and combine with sugar. Add lemon juice and simmer over medium heat until thickened. Jam is finished when it sheets off a wooden spoon. Pour into sterilized jars and seal.

Elderberry sauce can be used on ice cream, pancakes or game. To eliminate stems and bitterness, simply take a pocket comb and comb the berries off the stems to harvest from the bushes.

Elderberry Sauce

2 cups elderberries
$^1/_4$ cup water
$^1/_2$ cup honey or sugar

1 tsp. cornstarch
4 tbsps. lemon juice

Combine berries, water, cornstarch and lemon juice and simmer gently about 15 minutes. Add sugar and continue to stir until sufficiently thick. Refrigerate unused portion.

Obviously, there is a lot you can do with elderberries. The Italians have figured out one more thing to do with the berries and leaves. They make a liqueur called Sambuca Romana that tastes like anise and clouds up water so it looks like milk. Enjoy! Keep in mind, however, that many authorities consider the fresh green parts to be poisonous, so let the wood dry out thoroughly before making your pea-shooter or whistle! Herbalists make a cream from the flowers for removing freckles, but they are more commonly used to make a tasty snack.

Elder Flower Fritters

elder flower clusters
1 egg
big pinch salt
hot oil

$^1/_2$ cup flour
milk
confectioner's sugar

Sift together flour and salt and beat with the egg. Stir in enough milk to make a creamy batter. Wash and dry the elder flowers (some folks call them elder "blows") and remove any insects. Dip flowers in batter and fry in the hot oil until crisp and brown. Serve hot, sprinkled with the powdered sugar.

Both elderberries and elder flowers will add a nice flavor to vinegar.

Doves... A Delightful Dish

To the delight of some and the chagrin of others, around Labor Day weekend each year, opening day of dove season marks the beginning of a new hunting season.

Many people object to the hunting of doves, and in some northern states they are considered by law to be song birds and therefore protected. About 75 percent of the doves hatched each year die of natural causes anyway, and it seems that hunting them has little effect on their numbers. We must not forget what happened to the passenger pigeons, but sensible hunting and wise use won't hurt the dove population. I think it is nearly criminal, certainly it is shameful, when hunters throw away half the dove, saving only the breast.

The whole bird is good, easy to clean, and the wings and legs are perfect for dove-and-dumplings, pot pies and other stew-type recipes. And talk about bite-sized buffalo wings! What a way to use what too many people discard.

Dove season can signal the beginning of each year's hunting accidents, too. Even though the shot is small, many injuries have occurred as hunters shoot out of their zone-of-fire, or get careless because of the light loads and small pellets. Also, dove season often opens during "dog days" when the weather is still very hot, and after a long period of inactivity, some hunters suffer heat-related injuries, heart attacks, dehydration and even snake bites from reaching into the briar patch to recover a downed bird.

Take along a cooler when you hunt doves, and not for beer, either! In the heat of the early season, many doves are lost to spoilage. Here is a suggestion. As you recover the birds, pluck off the breast feathers, slit or tear the bird from anus to breastbone, and remove the entrails. Be sure to save the heart, liver and gizzards for yourself and put the rest of the guts in another bag for catfish bait. Place doves inside a plastic bag and ice them down. You'll find it much easier to get womenfolk to eat doves which have been properly handled and taste as delicate and delicious as they should.

Paprika Doves

6 doves, halved
2 tbsps. butter
$^1/_2$ cup chicken stock
4 tbsps. flour
salt and pepper
2 tbsps. olive oil
1 tbsp. rosemary

2 tbsps. paprika
1 garlic clove, minced (to taste)
1 tbsp. parsley, chopped
$^1/_2$ cup dandelion or other white wine
1 medium onion, diced
$^1/_2$ cup orange juice
2 tbsps. sour cream

Put flour, salt and pepper, and paprika in a bag and shake to mix well. Shake dove halves in the flour mixture. Brown doves in butter and olive oil in heavy skillet, about 3 or 4 minutes per side. Add garlic, onion, parsley, rosemary and chicken stock. Cover and cook on medium heat for a ½ hour. Add wine and orange juice and cook until fork-tender — about 15 minutes more. Stir in the sour cream just before serving and serve hot. Over rice is good.

Microwave Glazed Doves

10-12 doves
1 cup honey
$^1/_2$ stick butter

salt and pepper
$^1/_2$ cup orange juice concentrate

In a covered casserole, microwave doves whole or halved about 10-15 minutes on high until tender. Do not overcook. Salt and pepper to taste while cooking after rubbing with butter. Drain and roll in a mixture of the honey and orange juice concentrate. Broil in oven until honey and doves are browned. If you don't have a microwave, boil the doves in a little water until tender and proceed as above.

There are two main types of doves that are hunted in this country — the familiar mourning dove whose plaintive cooing we associate with sadness or longing for a lost mate, and the ring-necked or turtle doves. Other species are sometimes seen. In the Southwest, tiny Inca doves are so small that two can fit in your hand easily.

Grilled doves.

Country Fried Doves

doves
flour
butter and/or oil

salt and pepper
hickory-smoke salt

Rinse and dry the doves. Halve or quarter. Roll in flour and salt and pepper to taste. Sprinkle with hickory-smoke salt if desired. Fry in small amount of hot oil or oil and butter, about 4-5 minutes per side. Serve with gravy made from pan drippings over wild rice for a taste treat.

Here are two cooking tips: First, a combination of butter and oil produces a more flavorful and crispy skin or crust than just oil. Second, anytime you have a taste for wild rice but a search of the cupboard turns up empty, use long-grain rice and add finely chopped pecan or hickory nuts. It ain't the same, but will do in a pinch.

Doves with Rice In Wine

6 doves
4 tbsps. butter
1 cup chicken broth
1 cup uncooked rice
1 tsp. rosemary

8 small white (pearl) onions
salt and pepper to taste
1 cup Madeira sherry
1 tbsp. lemon juice
$^{1}/_{2}$ pound mushrooms

Sauté the rice in the butter, browning but not burning. Put the rice in the bottom of a casserole. Rub the doves inside and out with lemon juice followed by rosemary, and then salt to taste. Arrange doves on rice and surround with mushroom pieces and onions. Pour broth and wine over all and cover. Bake at 350 degrees for 40-60 minutes, until rice is fully cooked. Remove top, raise temperature to 400 and bake 3-5 minutes to brown if desired.

Doves In Cream Sauce

10 doves	12 ounces bacon
3 egg yolks	salt and pepper
1 tsp. paprika	2 cups whipping cream

In a large skillet, fry bacon until crisp and drain on brown paper bag. Sauté doves over medium heat in the bacon grease, turning until browned on all sides. Sprinkle with salt and pepper while cooking. Remove doves and keep warm. Pour off all grease except 4 tablespoons. Beat egg yolks with cream and pour into hot fat. Thicken over low heat, stirring constantly. Stir in paprika and pour over doves on a bed of rice. Garnish with bacon crisps.

Dove Breasts With Bacon

12 dove breasts	12 slices bacon
1 tsp. salt	$^1/_2$ cup bell pepper, chopped
3 tbsps. onion, minced	$^1/_2$ tsp. pepper

Soak dove breasts in salted water for about 4 hours. This is optional. Pat dry and sprinkle with pepper and salt. Put a little mixed onion and bell pepper in breast cavities (I know it's not easy. Just do it.). Wrap with bacon and secure with a toothpick. Bake at 300 degrees for 45 minutes or until done.

Doves Hannibalese

6-8 doves or more	1 4-inch cinnamon stick
1 cup dried apricots, chopped	$^1/_2$ cup pitted prunes, chopped
$^1/_2$ cup fresh or maraschino cherries, pitted and halved	$^1/_2$ cup pine nuts
1 cup mushrooms, chopped	1 tbsp. cloves
2 tbsps. white wine	$^1/_2$ tsp. saffron or $^1/_2$ cup chrysanthemums
$^1/_4$ cup apple cider vinegar	$^1/_2$ cup brown sugar

Place doves in a clay cooker, if you are lucky enough to have one, which has been prepared by soaking. If not, use a glass baking dish. Combine other ingredients, mixing well and pour over doves. Cover and bake at 325 degrees for 45 minutes to 1 hour until done.

When Davey killed his first squirrel, a fine specimen of a fox squirrel, he learned a lot about self-confidence and life. First he confidently shot his first squirrel and he learned to be patient until it decided to fall. He found out how strong the will to live can be. He then learned to confidently clean a squirrel and, finally, learned to cook it himself.

A Bird in the Pan is Worth Two in the Bush!

Only a birder would disagree with that statement, and they're entitled to their opinion, too. Besides, it leaves more for me to eat!

When I was a youngster and the weather was either unseasonably cold or abnormally hot, it was expected that the grownups, who at that time, were all veterans of World War I or II, would blame the problem on the "danged Roosians!" They were always accused of messing with the weather again. These days, it is more fashionable (and surely more accurate) to blame the vagaries of weather on global warming caused by damage to the ozone layer.

Here in North Carolina, at least, the calendar and the regulations digest say that it is prime time to hunt small game sometime around the middle of November. Just about everything is in season at that time. However, some old timers say they want to wait for cold weather to get here before they hunt birds and small game — it kills the "warbles" in the rabbits. I have usually had to burn several fires to keep Frances as warm as she likes by then. I got a special grill from Lowes which allows me to cook birds and other meat in the fireplace (yeah, I'm going to say it!), allowing me "to kill two birds with one stone!" Here are some more traditional ways to prove that a bird in the pan is worth two in the bush. Some are from my friend Ken Laws, an overachiever in the life-insurance business. This one is simple enough for a lieutenant to follow.

Ken Laws' Pheasant In A Slow Cooker

1 pheasant, cut up
1 can cream of mushroom soup
$^1/_3$ cup onion, chopped
2 chicken bouillon cubes
1 stick margarine

1 cup apple cider
$^3/_4$ tsp. salt
$^1/_2$ tsp. black pepper
$^1/_3$ cup celery, chopped
$^1/_2$ cup carrots, chopped

Put in a slow cooker for $8^1/_2$ hours.

Thanks, Ken! I like a recipe with simple instructions. Pheasants originally came to us from China but have done very well in the Midwest and around the Eastern Seaboard and Chesapeake Bay areas. One nearly flew into me at Tom Brown's Survival School in western New Jersey. Around North Carolina you have to hunt them on preserves, although we have grouse in our mountains which can be substituted in pheasant recipes.

Ken Laws' Pheasant Bake

Cut **pheasant** into serving sized pieces. Dip pieces in **milk**, then **flour** to coat. Bring to a sizzle in a pan $^1/_2$ **cup margarine** and brown pheasant on all sides. Arrange the brown pieces evenly in the bottom of a pan and add:

2 carrots, sliced
$^1/_2$ tsp. Italian herb blend
$^1/_2$ tsp. salt

2 stalks celery, sliced
2 large onions, cut in large pieces
$^1/_2$ tsp. pepper

Cover and put into a 375 degree oven for 1 hour, then turn down to 325 degrees and bake for 1 hour. Make sure you have **2 cups of broth** from the pan and combine until perfectly smooth with:

2 tbsps. flour   **¹/₄ cup sherry**
¹/₂ cup cream or evaporated milk

Add this liquid into a saucepan and bring to a slow boil. Simmer for 5 minutes to make a gravy. Serve pheasant and gravy over rice or noodles.

If there aren't any wild pheasants where you live or hunt, you can look up a shooting preserve in the Yellow Pages of the phone book or find a copy of the latest edition of Black's *Wing & Clay*, which lists about 1,200 shooting preserves in the United States. The editors tell us that "Hunting preserves are state-licensed hunting areas that offer extended season or year-round hunting for ring-necked pheasants, bobwhite quail, chukar, Hungarian partridge, mallard ducks, wild turkey and other birds, depending on locale. They are open to the public on a daily-fee basis or an annual membership basis or both." If you can't find *Wing & Clay* in your library or bookstore, write to P.O. Box 2029, Red Bank, NJ 07701 for more information or call (908) 224-8700.

399 ST. PAUL AVENUE,
JERSEY CITY, N.J. 07306

If you are in a hurry or just don't want to go out and shoot your birds, then you might want to call a company called D'ARTAGNAN at 1-800-D'ARTGN (327-8246). Or you can write them at 399-419 St. Paul Avenue, Jersey City, NJ 07306. A recent price list offers 2 pound pheasants at $15 — more than chicken, but well worth it. Besides, that is about 5% of the cost of an average trip to go out and shoot your own, if you count driving, lodging and meal costs. They also offer grouse, woodpigeon, red leg partridge and quail as well as guinea hens and squab. More about squab in a minute. One of the specialties at D'ARTAGNAN is smoked duck breast or "magret."

Magret À La D'Artagnan

2 sides of magret (duck breast)   **1 shallot, minced**
*2 glasses Madiran wine   **2 tbsps. duck demi-glace**
fresh-ground black pepper   **salt to taste**

Score the skin of the magrets crosswise and sprinkle both with salt and pepper. Heat a skillet over low heat. Cook the magrets skin-side down for 15 minutes. Pour off the fat. Turn the magrets and cook for 5 minutes. Remove from the pan and keep warm. Add the shallot to the pan and cook until soft. Add one glass of Madiran and reduce by half. Add the duck demi-glace and reduce by half. Slice the magrets and arrange on warmed plates. Pour the sauce over and serve.

*"A good cook must always taste the quality of the ingredients, hence the second glass of wine."
I'll bet you can get Justin Wilson to "second that."

Squabs are, of course, baby pigeons and are considered standard food by some folks who raise them and gourmet fare by rich people who eat them in restaurants with French names.

Soused Squabs

6-8 young pigeons	**2 large onions, quartered**
3-4 sprigs fresh rosemary	**$1/2$ cup melted butter or more**
1 cup dry white wine	**$1/4$ cup good Scotch whiskey (opt.)**

Preheat oven to 350 degrees. Wipe squabs inside and out with a damp cloth (or a halved lemon) and sprinkle with salt and pepper. Place onion and rosemary inside each bird. Place birds breast-side up in a baking dish, drizzle with melted butter, wine and Scotch if you choose. Bake 35-40 minutes or until fork-tender. Baste as needed and brown last 5 minutes at 375 degrees.

D'ARTAGNAN describes squabs as "large, yet young pigeons that have never flown, yielding a tender full-flavored red meat." I would say that is kind of like nature's own version of veal, but in the form of a bird! My grandfather had a half-dozen holes cut in the back of the barn which led to boxes where pigeons made their nests, coming and going as they wanted, basically wild. We ate squabs every second clutch or so. When I lived in Fayetteville, I sometimes got mine under the highway overpasses and railroad bridges where they nest. The good news is that there are plenty of squabs out there. The bad news is that you have to go after them about 4 o'clock in the morning so that some speeding drunk doesn't knock you off the ladder while you are "squabbing!" Don't bring any nest material home because of insect parasites, and wash your hands well when you get home. Expect some strange looks and questions while you are on the ladder.

"What the hell are you doing up there, buddy?" "Good evening, Officer!" "Oh! It's you, Tom!"

The folks at D'ARTAGNAN have done some research and found that pheasants, squabs and quail are much better for you than chickens! Check out these (per serving) statistics. Calories: chicken-239; pheasant-151; quail-168; and squab-294. Grams of fat: chicken-17.9; pheasant-5.3; quail-6.8; and squab-23.8. Milligrams of cholesterol: chicken-83; pheasant-49; quail-56; and squab-n/a. Protein in grams: chicken-18.2; pheasant-24.3; quail-25.0; and squab-18.47. Well, it looks as if I might want to stay out of the hen house! Squab is tender and tasty, and the meat is rich because the parents feed the young birds with a "milk" produced in part from seeds and grain they eat and regurgitate for the squabs. Statistics are different for mature pigeons, but the more they fly, the tougher they get!

Quail are one of the most popular upland game birds, but seem to be getting scarce in places where golf courses are changing the face of the landscape without creating "wildlife areas." George Thompson leaves wild areas at The Country Club of North Carolina and the call of quail can be heard all over the property. Quail are one of the more popular birds hunted on hunting preserves like Joe Carpenter's Hunt Club. The season can be greatly extended, making quail available longer and success more certain.

Ken Law's Fried Quail

5 quail	**1 tsp. salt**
$1/4$ tsp. black pepper	**$1/2$ cup self-rising flour**
$1/2$ cup margarine	**$3/4$ cup white wine**

Cut quail into pieces, leaving the legs and thighs together. Salt and pepper each piece. Place flour and quails in plastic bag and shake. Fry slowly in margarine until brown. Remove quail and place on platter. Pour wine into pan drippings and bring to a boil. Pour over quail pieces.

Perhaps it's just brand loyalty to a Southern company, but I prefer to use Martha White flour for two reasons. I always get great results, no matter what the recipe, and one of the first cooking tips I learned as a child was hearing Tennessee Ernie Ford on the radio telling me to use Martha White flour with "hot rise!"

Lots of people don't like the taste of duck and goose because they can be greasy. My friends, here is a tip from me. I bake my fatty duck or goose in a very hot oven — 425 degrees or more — for 20-30 minutes and remove the cooked-off fat before continuing the recipe. D'ARTAGNAN *sells* duck fat. "Duck fat is, like olive oil, low in saturated fat while high in mono- and poly-saturated ones. That is probably why people from Gascony, in the southwest of France, have less coronary disease than anywhere else in the world. They use duck fat in all recipes in place of oil or butter, or spread it on country bread when possible with a few slices of truffle. And, of course, they always enjoy it with a few glasses of red wine."

Roast Goose or Duck

1 goose or 2 ducks	**¹/₂ cup melted butter**
salt and pepper	**fresh sage (opt.)**

Clean ducks or goose and rub inside and out with butter. Salt and pepper well. Rub with fresh sage if you like. Stuff with cornbread dressing. Wrap in foil and bake at 350 degrees for 20 minutes per pound. To make slicing easier, allow to cool one hour before you carve the bird. Save the bones to make soup!

Canadian geese

Cornbread Stuffing

4 cups cornbread	**1 large onion, chopped**
2 tsps. sage	**1 cup apple, chopped**
1 tsp. salt	**pinch black pepper**
2 eggs	**1 cup celery, diced**
2 cups turkey broth	**meat from cooked giblets**

This recipe works for 1 duck. Double for a large goose or a turkey. Combine crumbled cornbread with apple, onion, celery, giblets and seasoning. Whip the eggs in the cool turkey broth (from boiling the giblets) and mix well. Stuff bird, baking any left-over stuffing in a baking dish.

"Eat Crow" is an old expression that means "eat your words," and doesn't have a good connotation. Realistically, however, crows are large birds and can be tasty, if fixed properly. In North Carolina, they can be hunted, and are, according to the game laws, on "Thursday, Friday, Saturday of each week from June 1 to June 30 plus Labor Day and Christmas Day.

Bag Limits: No Restriction." So, next time you go crow shooting, remember that old Native American saying: "Waste not; want not!"

Sautéed Crow

2-3 crows, quartered	1 stick butter
1 cup flour	salt and pepper to taste
$^1/_2$ cup water	$^1/_2$ cup sherry
$^1/_4$ tsp. each thyme, basil, rosemary and mint	1 small onion (or garlic), minced

Roll quartered crows, plus giblets, in flour seasoned with salt and pepper. Brown on all sides in butter and reduce heat. Add onion or garlic, herbs, water and wine and simmer, covered, 45 minutes to 1 hour or until tender. Serve over rice.

These crow recipes are in honor of my wife's Aunt Katie who loved crow. It is a shame more people don't try it. It makes excellent pot pies.

Baked Crow

1-2 crows per person	1 cup bread crumbs
$^1/_2$ cup apple, chopped	$^1/_4$ cup onion, diced
$^1/_4$ cup celery, chopped	$^1/_4$ cup raisins
$^1/_4$ cup walnuts, diced	salt and pepper to taste

Adjust ingredients as necessary to accommodate the proper quantity of crows. This amount will work nicely with 3-4 birds. Rub crows inside and out with salt and pepper. Combine remaining ingredients, adding a little water or wine for moistness if necessary. Stuff each bird. Bake at 350 degrees for about 45 minutes.

You can make a really great Curried Crow (or other game bird) dish using the Sautéed Crow recipe and adding 2 or 3 tsps. curry powder and 1 cup of sour cream while it is simmering.

Pluck crows to clean, removing entrails and saving heart and liver. Remove the oil gland at the base of the tail. On a chicken this is called "the parson's nose" and is often left on. It is the last part of the chicken to go over a fence. Young birds, naturally, are the tenderest.

Here is the beginning of one of those recipes for you *not* to take seriously!

Jeff Eberbaugh's Old Crow Pie

Get some crows off the road or anywhere you can
When crows get old you can catch em with your hand
They're old and they're tough and sometimes they stink
Just cook a crow pie and see what you think
Drive to the store to buy shells for your pies
It would only take a minute as an old crow flies
Throw your crows down on an old choppin block
Ya only need three or four — ya don't need a flock
Chop em into pieces about two inches square
Add some Old Crow whiskey — as much as you dare...

Bring the Flavor of the Sea Into Your Kitchen

When summer draws to a close, everybody scrambles to make one more trip to the beach before school starts. That might be the ideal time to enjoy some of the bounty of the sea and the nearby shore. Seafood is generally considered to be very healthy for those persons worrying about high cholesterol and extra calories — depending on how you fix it. I mean, after all, there are a lot less calories in a clambaked lobster cooked over coals in a pit than there are in using the same lobster in a rich cream sauce or if you float the chunks of lobster meat in a bowl of melted butter!

New England fast-food restaurants feature lobster. In Mississippi, it's catfish!

It is easy to see how times change. I used to go to our coast around Holden Beach, Sunset Beach and Wilmington's port, where there are big fishing piers. I would take a cooler with a couple of bags of ice and a couple of inches of milk, and I would come home with a cooler full of delicious meat — shark meat and eel. I'd volunteer to remove eels and sharks from frantic anglers' lines and get rid of these "trash fish" for them. I'd clean the sharks and throw them in the cooler with the cold milk and bring them home. The meat was exquisite — firm, sweet and white in most cases. Many "fish-and-chips" places have been known to sneak shark meat into their dishes under a variety of names which hide their origin. Now shark meat is one of the more expensive seafoods in the stores — right up there with catfish — and the sharks are becoming scarce and threatened in many places.

Shark Steaks in Tarragon Mustard Sauce with Macadamia Nuts

4 large shark steaks
3 tbsps. butter
½ cup toasted whole macadamias
1 egg, beaten
1 cup sunflower oil
2 tbsps. tarragon, chopped
2 tbsps. Dijon mustard

1 cup Italian bread crumbs
salt and pepper to taste
2-3 ounces macadamia nuts, chopped
½ cup water
½ cup dry white wine
¼ cup heavy cream

Beat egg and water together. Mix finely chopped macadamia nuts with bread crumbs, salt and pepper. Dredge shark steaks through crumbs, through egg and water combination, and back through crumbs. Set aside. In a large skillet, heat oil and fry steaks 5 minutes per inch of thickness. Turn and finish frying until done, about the same amount of time for second side. Drain and place on warm platter, drizzle with tarragon mustard sauce and garnish with toasted macadamias. Make tarragon mustard sauce ahead of time by melting butter in medium sauce pan and adding wine, mustard and tarragon. Simmer until liquid is reduced by one half. Stirring constantly, pour in cream and simmer for 1 minute more, adding salt and pepper to taste.

By the way, this recipe works well with pork chops, turkey or chicken breasts, or venison steaks as well, and is great with any fish that can be cut into steaks. Cooking times change according to the meat used. This next recipe works well with a variety of meats and types of fish as well.

Orange Broiled Shark

shark steaks
onion rings
tequila (optional)

undiluted orange juice concentrate
bell pepper cut into rings
toasted, sliced almonds

The ingredients aren't given in specific quantities because you adjust to the amount of shark steak you have. Marinate shark steaks in orange juice concentrate overnight in refrigerator, adding tequila (to taste) if desired. A jigger or two is plenty.   Place marinated shark in baking dish and decorate with rings of onion and bell pepper. Sprinkle with almonds. Broil about 7-9 minutes in preheated oven until meat flakes easily. Watch carefully to avoid burning. Turn and broil about 3 minutes on other side. Serve immediately on bed of rice.

As an alternate recipe, use a can of frozen piña colada drink concentrate and garnish with toasted coconut.

Bluefish are well known along the coast because of the many tournaments held in their honor. Some readers told me they went down to reel in some of the big blues for big bucks, but high seas forced them to play golf instead. Talk about a bummer! Franc White, known as "The Southern Sportsman" because of his television program and books, has an interesting view of fishing tournaments. He thinks that they may be bad for the fish population, and he takes the stand that they are legalized gambling! He's right, if you look at it carefully. People pay a big entry fee to get in the tournament, catch all the big bluefish they can, often without eating them later, and whoever has the biggest or most wins the pot. It is a gamble. Some people do it for the money alone, not for enjoying the sport of fishing.

Grilled Bluefish

2 pounds bluefish fillets
2 lemons, cut in wedges

2 cups Italian dressing
2 tbsps. fresh rosemary

Remove skin from fish and place in a baking dish. Pour dressing and chopped rosemary over fillets and marinate 2 hours, refrigerated. Place fillets on a hot, oiled grill and cook about 10 minutes, basting frequently with marinade. You may need to place foil on your grill and punch a few holes in it. Turn, baste and cook about 8 more minutes until fish flakes with a fork.

It is believed that bluefish are an excellent source of omega-3 fatty acids which are now considered to be effective in lowering blood (serum) cholesterol and reducing the risk of heart disease. This is true of many ocean fish, including flounder, also an excellent source of flavor. I love fried, whole small flounder, another fish which doesn't need scaling. Just dip in flour and spices of your choice and fry until golden brown. Serve with cole slaw, fries (I prefer grits) and cold beverage of your choice.

I mention Italian dressing in many recipes throughout this book. I usually make my own because I like my garlicky version, but when you buy it I have to recommend Paul Newman's brand which of course is called "Newman's Own." Not only is the flavor excellent, Mr. Newman donates *every cent of the profits* to charity. Paul Newman says, "What I like is when life wiggles its hips and throws me a surprise." Newman's products use only natural ingredients and no preservatives. I think the latest addition to the line is a spaghetti sauce called "Bombolino," which I have used with great success as a cooking sauce for game and fish dishes.

Paul Newman's Italian Baked Scrod

2 pounds scrod filets	**2 tbsps. chopped fresh basil**
salt	**2 tbsps. chopped fresh parsley**
pepper	**1 clove garlic, crushed**
sliced onions	**clam juice**
chopped stewed tomatoes	**sliced pitted ripe olives**

Wash and dry filets. Arrange in a single layer in 13″ x 9″ x 2″ baking dish. Season with salt and pepper to taste. Cover filets with onions, tomatoes, olives, basil, parsley and garlic. Moisten with a little clam juice and bake in preheated 375 degree oven for 20 minutes or just until fish separates easily when touched with a fork. Drain off most of the liquid before serving. Serves 4.

I have learned to love a crockpot because you can cook great dishes when you are out fishing, er, I mean researching a story!

Bombolino Seafood Supremo

2 jars Newman's Own Bombolino
  spaghetti sauce
1 large onion, diced
2 small zucchinis, sliced
2 garlic cloves, minced
6-8 artichoke hearts, quartered
1 cup chick peas (opt.)

1 pound shark steak, 1-inch cubes
1 pound small raw shrimp, shelled
1 green bell pepper, diced
1 yellow bell pepper, diced
1 fennel bulb, sliced and diced
2-3 chili peppers (opt.)
¼ cup dry red wine (opt.)

Combine all ingredients in a crockpot, stirring well to mix. Add optional ingredients — if you like them, and if there is room. Put crockpot on high while you are getting ready to go out, change to lower power setting when you leave for the day, and come home hungry!

Elegant Low-Calorie Flounder

4 flounder fillets
4 cups chicken broth
¼ cup shallots, chopped
1 pinch paprika
1 lemon, cut in wedges

2 tomatoes cut into wedges
2 cups dry white wine
1 tsp. garlic powder
1 tsp. lemon-pepper seasoning
1 tsp. minced onion

Cut flounder in small strips and roll around tomato wedges. Skewer with toothpicks. Poach flounder in broth and wine until it flakes. Sprinkle with remaining ingredients and serve with lemon wedges on a bed of lettuce — or better yet — dandelion greens.

Foragers can hardly go to the beach without eating some weeds that just can't be found away from the beaches. Go to the beach at low tide and pick some sea lettuce, *Ulva lactuca*, and make it into soup using any good cream of broccoli soup or sorrel soup recipe.

Sea Lettuce Soup the Easy Way

2 cups chopped, washed sea lettuce
  leaves
1 cup chicken stock

1 can cream of mushroom soup
1 cup milk

Combine all ingredients, mixing well. Bring to a boil, reduce heat and simmer for 15-20 minutes. Some people like the sea lettuce in coarse flakes, while others prefer to purée it in a blender. Either way, it tastes great. You can also use sea lettuce to make an excellent won ton soup if you like oriental food, substituting it for bok choy, and you can use it as a wrapper when making sushi.

Gather some leaves from the yaupon holly, dry or roast them, and make some coffee. This plant is the only plant native to North America known to contain caffeine. A small quantity makes a nice tea pick-me-up. Too much makes a nice black tea throw-me-up! The scientific name, *Ilex vomitoria*, alludes to its use by Native Americans as a purgative. It can be made into a natural replacement for syrup of ipecac and used to empty the stomach in case of poisonings, so might be good to have around if you have little kids.

Another under-foot weed at the ocean's edge, related to our goosefoot or lamb's quarters, is glasswort or saltwort, known to botanists as *Salicornia*. It looks like a swollen, jointed stem with no leaves, and though it is normally green, it may also be red. It is high in sea salt, so can be used in place of store-bought salt in recipes. It can be made into some interesting pickles, too.

Susie Clontz works at the North Carolina Aquarium at Fort Fisher where she is in charge of housekeeping. She is also a turtle watch volunteer, a wildlife rehabilitator, and is learning to be a wild-foods specialist. She gave me this recipe for a way of fixing *Salicornia* that I think you will like.

Susie Clontz's Saltwort Casserole

1 cup saltwort, chopped	1 cup water
1 cup fresh mushrooms, chopped	½ cup onion, chopped
2 cups French style green beans	1 stick butter
1 can cream of mushroom soup	2 cups herbed or bread crumb stuffing mix

Simmer saltwort in water for 15 minutes. Drain. Sauté mushrooms and onion in butter until tender and mix together all ingredients except stuffing, mixing well. Pour into casserole dish. Sprinkle stuffing mix on top and bake at 350 degrees for 30 to 45 minutes until top is golden brown. Do not add salt!

I still like a little saltwort pickle now and then. It even goes well as a condiment with the saltwort casserole above.

Saltwort Spicy Pickle

freshly picked *Salicornia*	1 quart apple cider vinegar
½ cup brown sugar	3 tbsps. pickling spice blend
2 small onions, sliced	hot peppers to taste
garlic cloves	bay leaves

You can increase the recipe for the pickling mixture as necessary by doubling or tripling everything. Put a couple of onion rings in the bottom of sterilized pint jars. Add garlic cloves and hot peppers to taste, and fill half way with *Salicornia* snapped into 1- and 2-inch lengths. Add more onion slices, garlic and hot pepper and fill jar to ½ inch from top with *Salicornia*. Repeat the layer of onion, garlic and hot peppers. Combine remaining ingredients and bring to a boil, simmering about 12 minutes over reduced heat. Pour into *Salicornia* jars to within $^1/_8$ inch of top, making sure to get some of the pickling spices in each jar, and seal. Process in hot water bath for 20 minutes. Re-tighten tops when cool.

If you can't find a commercial pickling-spice blend in the store, you can make your own by combining very coarsely ground dried ginger root, chopped dried cayenne peppers, chopped cinnamon stick, mustard and dill seeds, crumbled bay leaves, coarsely ground allspice and black or white peppercorns. Some blends also contain coarsely ground mace, turmeric and cardamom as well as fennel seeds. You can even add juniper berries, or any other flavor you like.

I hope that next time you make it to the beach you can enjoy some of nature's bounty that you can't find at home. A lot of people like to make a chowder from those tiny little clams you find in the wet sand while looking for shark's teeth or collectible shells. You can also eat those little locust-looking critters called mole crabs, *Emerita talpoida*. Like mole crickets, they are very fast diggers. Some people call them beach fleas, but another, smaller animal also shares this name. The mole crabs are edible. In the *Nature Guide to the North Carolina Coast*, Peter Meyer says: "Mole crabs are edible. Hundreds (one to two pounds) must be gathered to make a meal. The mole crabs are steamed to make broth for an interesting chowder." Another better-tasting-than-sounding snack is made from these little crustaceans:

Mole Crab Munchies

mole crabs	1 cup Bisquick baking mix
1 cup self-rising corn meal	garlic salt to taste
1 egg, beaten well	1 cup butter milk or milk
2 tbsps. oil	hot oil for frying

Be kind. Kill the mole crabs by freezing them to death or by plunging in boiling water just long enough to kill them and then drain well. Allow to come to room temperature from either method while preparing batter. Combine remaining ingredients, except hot oil, to form a heavy batter. Coat mole crabs and drop into hot oil. Fry until batter is golden brown and looks like a hushpuppy. Just serve these crunchy, tasty tidbits with lemon juice to drizzle over them or sauce to dip them in. Adopt Bill Clinton's homosexual policy about what they are: "Don't ask! Don't tell!"

Coquina Chowder

4 cups coquina clams, live	**4 cups stock, chicken or fish**
½ cup green onions, minced	**salt and pepper to taste**
2 cups diced potatoes	**2 tbsps. butter**
2 cups light cream or milk	

Melt butter in large pan or Dutch oven and sauté onion. Add potatoes and half the stock, then simmer until potatoes begin to get tender. Add the rest of the stock and season to taste. Bring to a boil and reduce heat to a simmer. Drop in the washed coquinas and the milk and simmer for 12-15 minutes, covered. Serve with oyster crackers.

In the method above, each diner has to pick out the opened coquina shells from his or her bowl. An alternate method is to boil the clams separately in stock to cover until they open. Pick the meat out and discard the shells. Add clams and the stock they were cooked in to the rest of the ingredients as above.

Everybody has their own favorite recipe for a seafood chowder. It is a great way to combine the various flavors of the ocean while disguising the fact that you were only able to catch a little of this and that, a few shrimp and a couple of fish — maybe even just one! A couple of potatoes, some herbs and you're in business.

Tom's Seafood Chowder

1 pound shrimp, headed and cubed	**1½ pounds fish fillets**
1 dozen mussels, whole	**3 blue crabs, cooked**
4 cups potato, cubed	**1 stalk celery, sliced**
1 cup whole kernel corn	**1 46-ounce can tomato juice**
1 large onion, diced	**2 garlic cloves, minced**
2 tbsps. sugar	**2 tsps. salt**
1 tsp. black pepper	**1 tbsp. Italian herb blend**
¼ cup dry white wine	**4-5 bay leaves**

Sauté onion, celery and potatoes in butter until onions are transparent in a large pot. Add tomato juice and bring to a boil. Add fish chunks. Simmer 5 minutes and add remaining ingredients except for blue crabs. Add water as necessary to cover all ingredients and stir well to mix. Simmer, covered, while preparing crabs. Remove apron and top shell and get rid of dead man's fingers so that you end up with two end portions of crab with meat and legs intact. Break each in half, so you are quartering the crabs. Drop these in the pot, adjust water and seasoning if needed and simmer for 30 minutes.

The author's father,
Richard Keith Squier.

I seriously doubt if my grandfather ever saw the ocean except when he crossed the Atlantic on a troop ship bound for France to fight in World War I. He was very fond of seafood, however, and I believe I inherited that trait from him. I could eat fish every day. Fish, crabs, shrimp, oysters, clams — it doesn't matter. I think Pop-Pop preferred the clams and oysters from the ocean to the fresh-water mussels at home in the mountains. But we ate plenty of those, too! He taught me early that when we saw piles of their shells on the river bank we could feel around in the mud and sand like raccoons and fetch ourselves a nice mess in no time at all. He really loved blue crabs, too, and my uncles and my father knew when they went to the beach on one of those party boats to bring him back a bushel or so. I remember my mother complaining about those party boats and my father's fishing trips to the coast. He always complained himself, jokingly, that "the trouble with those fishing trips is that somebody always wants to fish!" For some reason, those boats were required to haul a lot of beer, and it had to be consumed to allow for the weight of the fish.

Dad had a regular fishing buddy named Lawrence Collins. The thing I remember most about him, even as an older man after my father had died, was how much he loved and adored his family, especially his wife Phoebe. A gray-headed grandfather, he would lie on the sofa with his head in her lap watching television. But I remember once when I was very young, Mr. Lawrence, as I called him, came to pick up Dad and show off his brand new car — a station wagon. I got to ride in the middle and listen to fishing stories being told while they drank more and more beer. Mr. Lawrence ran the passenger side of his new car into a bridge and Dad said something like, "Damn it, Lawrence, you've torn up the whole side of the car." He leaned over me to look out Dad's window and metal crunched as the driver's side of the car was raked along the other side of the bridge. It all happened in a matter of seconds. Later, he told the insurance company that a truck had forced him into the bridge and tore up the car on both sides.

What's the point? Mr. Lawrence owned a beer joint and Dad went there. I went along too, sometimes. They often served crabs, to make people drink more beer, I think. My mother told me that if I drank beer, I would start peeing and never stop until I died! I believed that for a good while. They only fixed crabs one way (the same way my Grandfather fixed them): boil them in water with a lot of vinegar and Tabasco sauce. Here is a recipe I think they would all have enjoyed:

Crawfish boil

**Shannon Allison's
(The Damned Crawfish Didn't Show Up!)
Blue Crab Boil**

live blue crabs	whole small Irish potatoes
corn on the cob	plenty of garlic toes (cloves)
crab boil spices	

Bring 20 gallons of water to a rolling boil in a 20-gallon restaurant pot or other similar container. Dump in 4 or 5 boxes of crab boil spices and as much garlic as you like. Add about 5 pounds of potatoes, cut into halves and quarters if they are really big, and a dozen ears of corn, broken into 3 or 4 pieces each. Return to a boil and after 5 minutes, dump in 2 or 3 dozen blue crabs — all that the pot will hold and cover. Cook until the crabs are all bright red. Scoop out corn, potatoes and crabs with a mesh sieve or colander and dump onto newspapers spread on tables. It's every man (or woman) for himself (or herself) now!

That recipe came about when Shannon got promoted and invited about 50 friends over for an old-fashioned Louisiana (he is a coon ass!) crawfish boil and ordered 200 pounds of mudbugs delivered by air from home for the occasion. Unfortunately, U.S. Air sent them to Fayetteville, Arkansas, instead of Fayetteville, North Carolina. Blue crabs from every store in the area were substituted and turned out good. Later in the evening, the airline called and asked Shannon, "What should we do with the crawfish, which are now in Arkansas?" What do you think he told them?

You can always make delicious patties from crab meat, spices of your choice and finely crumbled corn flakes. Here is another idea:

Curried Crabmeat Spread

1 pound (2 cups) crabmeat	8 ounces cream cheese, softened
¼ cup plain yogurt/sour cream	salt and red pepper to taste
¼ tsp. curry powder	¼ cup chives, chopped
1 tbsp. capers, drained	

Capers aren't always easy to find. You can make your own imitation capers by pickling the new seed pods of your nasturtium plants. It is just as good and a lot cheaper! Combine all ingredients, mixing well. Chill before serving to allow flavors to meld.

In the popular spirit of giving things more attractive names, many persons like to refer to plants that come from the ocean as "sea vegetables." Larch Hanson and I still prefer to call them as they have always been called — sea*weeds*!

Hanson owns the Maine Seaweed Company. You can write him at P.O. Box 57, Steuben, ME 04680, or call (207) 546-2875 and get their current price list of seaweeds that the Hansons harvest off the New England coast. I have tried their dried seaweeds in some of my favorite recipes and they work just as well as the fresh seaweeds Frances and I gather on trips to the beach. If you live in Kansas, or some other place far from the ocean, this is the way to go.

Fried Kelp Chips

½ pound kelp fronds   **peanut or olive oil**
raw sugar

Cut dried kelp (*Laminaria*) into squares or small rectangles and drop into hot oil, frying as is. Remove to absorbent towels or paper bags and drain. Sprinkle with sugar.

Dulse Salad

1 cup dried dulse   **2 apples, diced**
3 carrots, grated   **1 cup sprouts (bean, alfalfa, or wheat)**
½ firm avocado, diced   **¼ cup golden raisins**
juice of 1 lemon   **½ cup shredded cooked ham, turkey or**
1 cup canola oil   **venison**
4 tbsps. soy sauce

Obviously, vegetarians can leave out the meat. "Dulse" sounds a lot like "dulce" which is Spanish for "sweet," and describes the taste of this seaweed — salty and sweet — like the sweat of a beautiful woman! (That's you, Frances!) Combine oil, lemon juice and soy sauce to make a dressing and chill in the refrigerator. Shake well before serving. Chop the dried dulse very fine and mix with the other ingredients, tossing well. Sprinkle with turkey, ham or venison (browned tofu for vegetarians) and pour the dressing over the salad. I sometimes add a half cup of pecans, hickory or walnuts and/or a half-cup or so of shredded Cheddar, Swiss or hot pepper Monterey Jack cheese over the top, too.

Seaweeds are very nutritious and supply many trace elements and minerals lacking in our diet. They dry and store well. Some people prefer them to popcorn as a movie or television snack! They are also excellent additions to the compost pile or garden soil and well worth the effort of bringing back a truckload.

Dock — A Plant for All Seasons

We've already talked about the problem of identifying plants and finding that the same plant has many different common names in different areas. Here is a plant with several different names in the same area — dock! A person might call dock by as many as four different names depending on the season. Although there seem to be several species known as greater dock, curly dock, yellow dock or common dock, the botanists refer to them all as *Rumex crispus*, leading us to believe that they are variations of the same plant. In some books, you may find mentioned *Rumex sanguinea* mentioned as the red-veined dock, but other authors tell us that all the docks are subject to developing the red veins if damaged by insects, disease or big feet. Because the large-leafed variety reminds them of the familiar garden plant, some folks refer to it as wild rhubarb. Gets a little confusing, doesn't it?

Now, people may go out early in the spring and gather this plant for a salad green while the leaves are small and tender. At this time of year it is referred to as dock salad and eaten raw like spinach or lettuce. A month later the forager may call it dock sallet and/or wild spinach and go to the same place to gather leaves to boil as a potherb. The older leaves of dock get a little bitter for some people's taste and may have to be boiled in a couple of changes of water. I have found some to have a lemony taste, but they are bland after changing the water a couple of times. Some authors and cooks suggest combining with other available wild greens such as pepper grass, *Lepidium virginicum*, or wild mustard, *Brassica* species, or even the ever-popular dandelions.

Even though the cooked leaves might be bland tasting, the US Department of Agriculture says this plant is very nutritious. Their book, *Composition of Foods*, says that a 100-gram portion (about $3^{1}/_{2}$ ounces) contains 28 calories, 2 grams of protein, 66 grams of calcium, 41 milligrams of phosphorus, 338 milligrams of potassium, a whopping 12,900 International Units of vitamin A and 119 milligrams of vitamin C. No doubt that's where the lemony taste comes from. When I mentioned these nutrition values to my unofficial editor, Frances, she said, "Too bad it doesn't taste better!" It is all a matter of taste, because a lot of people like dock salad or greens.

I personally like dock a lot, and others agree. In *A Heritage of Herbs*, Bertha Reppert says, "Dock (*Rumex hymenoseplus*) is a large perennial weed; grows everywhere; called wild spinach or wild-pie plant and used in the same ways; Indians, Eskimos, and pioneers sought out these wild greens." There is a different scientific name to confuse us and there are two possible uses — as a "wild-pie plant." It could be like a rhubarb pie from the stems or like a nettle pie from the leaves.

Dock Soup

8 cups tender dock leaves	6 cups water
2 cups potatoes, diced	1 large onion, minced
4 ounces salt pork/smoked bacon	2 beaten egg yolks
salt and pepper to taste	$^{1}/_{2}$ cup milk

Chop and fry the meat in a large pan or Dutch oven. Sauté the onion in the grease and add the potatoes and the dock leaves finely chopped. Cover with water and season to taste. Bring to a boil, reduce heat and simmer 30-50 minutes until tender. Add the milk and the beaten egg yolks and simmer 10 more minutes. Serve hot, adding croutons if desired.

When the dock is young and slimy, early in the season, you can make some unique concoctions from its leaves and stems.

Dock Wine

5-6 gallons dock leaves and tender stems   **8 ounces raisins or currants**
2 tbsps. sourdough starter   **3 pounds sugar**
2-3 gallons unchlorinated water

Chop leaves and stems very fine and put in a crock or glass vat. Bring water to a boil and pour over leaves a little at a time, mashing constantly. Add raisins and sugar and stir to dissolve sugar. When water cools to room temperature, add sourdough starter and cover loosely with cheesecloth. Stir and mash daily for a week and a day. Strain leaves and stems out and let ferment until bubbling stops — about 30 days in a warm corner. Strain into bottles and cork. Allow to age about 6 months if you can wait that long.

Sourdough Starter

2 cups flour   **$^1/_2$ cup sugar**
2 cups water or milk

Stir ingredients together well and store in a warm place in a glass jar, uncovered. In 3-4 days it will be ready for use, perhaps doubling in size. Store after this in refrigerator or cool place.

As the dock plant gets about 3 feet tall and the stems toughen, they develop those mucopolysaccharides (slime) that lets it be used as sham rhubarb in pies. Like real rhubarb, it seems to be better combined with strawberries. The sliminess of the stems gives rise to another common name — wild okra. This recipe only works well when the stems are very tender and contain a lot of sugar and slime.

Wild Okra

6 cups tender dock stems   **$^1/_2$ cup flour**
$^1/_2$ cup corn meal   **1 egg, beaten**
$^1/_2$ cup milk   **salt and pepper to taste**

Chop stems about 1 inch long, peeling if necessary. Roll in egg beaten with milk and then shake in flour and cornmeal mixed together in a bag. Fry in hot oil or bacon grease until golden brown and drain on paper bag. Salt and pepper to taste.

Dock.

You bring home the paper bags from the grocery store, use them to drain the grease from fried fish, okra, and other foods, and then you put them in the fire place. They make excellent fire-starters and serve a lot better purpose than cluttering landfills. You can use the same bag initially to mix your flour and cornmeal to coat whatever you are frying.

In the fall, the large heads of triangular-shaped seeds make this plant easily recognizable. They also give it another name, as if we need another name to add to the confusion. Dock at this time is known as wild buckwheat and it is, in fact, in the buckwheat family — *Polygonaceae*. When the seeds turn brown, they are simply removed from the stalk and ground up as flour. They can be used alone for a strong buckwheat flavor or they can be combined with "refined" flours from the store to lessen their taste and food value.

Dock is a perennial, which means that there is always a large root in the ground storing food for the new season's growth. The old roots are tough and fibrous and can be quite large, but the young tender roots of the season can be used like a root vegetable — a carrot or potato. They can be baked, fried or boiled. They may be stringy and many might consider them to be survival food rather than everyday table fare. Dock roots, when boiled, yield an antifungal that can be used against athlete's foot and similar problems. Once at an herb festival where I was lecturing about alternative medicines, I suggested that it might be used as a cold tea wash against yeast infections. One young lady actually came up to me afterwards and asked me if I could look at her yeast infection to see if I thought dock would work for her? First of all, you need a microscope to see yeast plants; and secondly, my wife overheard the conversation and rescued me: "No, NO, *Absolutely NOT!!*" I didn't want to look, anyway!

Sweet and Sour Dock Greens

1 gallon small dock leaves
3-4 wild onions, chopped
1 hard-boiled egg
pepper or peppergrass seeds

4 ounces bacon, fried crisp
$^1/_4$ cup apple cider vinegar
$^1/_2$ cup honey or maple syrup
salt

Tear or chop leaves into small pieces, boil 10 minutes and drain. Add cooked bacon and drippings. Add salt and pepper or pepper grass seeds to taste. Mix honey and vinegar and pour over hot greens, stirring well to coat. Garnish with slices of egg.

Dock is found widely in North America, but has a relatively short history here, I'm told, although it is found from coast to coast and even as far north as Alaska. There are other uses for dock besides as a food and herbal medicine. The roots of yellow dock were used to produce an orange dye, and crafters still use it. In the winter, people like to add the seed heads to dried flower arrangements. I have even seen them in "boutiques" sprayed silver and gold along with okra pods and other *objets d' art!* Dock is truly a plant for all seasons.

Creamed Dock Greens

3 cups dock greens, chopped
1 tbsp. flour

1 tbsp. butter
1 cup half-and-half

Boil greens until tender and chop finely. Drain and set aside. Melt butter in sauce pan over low heat and blend in flour. Add the greens and the half-and-half. Heat thoroughly, stirring to prevent scorching, and serve over rice or toast squares or as a vegetable. You can even use it as a cream soup, garnishing it with a thin lemon slice or parsley or both.

When Frances went to Tom Brown's Survival School, she cooked her campfire trout wrapped in dock leaves.

Oysters — Ya Either Love 'Em or Ya Hate 'Em!

One of the most controversial dishes that a wildfoods enthusiast can offer his or her guests is the oyster. There are lots of myths about this two-shelled relative of the snail. One persistent rumor that remains to be proven is that oysters are good for your sex life or that they are an aphrodisiac. Down at the coast, you see bumper stickers and T-shirts that read, "Eat fish — live longer; Eat oysters — love longer!"

Mock Rumaki

Rumaki is normally made with chicken livers, but any liver of sufficient size works well. And so do oysters!

shelled raw oysters
green, stuffed olives or
   water chestnut halves

bacon slices, cut in half
soy sauce

It ain't easy, but wrap each oyster around a water chestnut half or an olive and then wrap a piece of bacon around this, securing it with a toothpick. Marinate in or drizzle soy sauce. Place on cookie sheet and cook under broiler until the bacon is done. The oysters will be done and curly on the edges by then.

One of the biggest challenges for many oyster eaters is swallowing the critter raw — especially when you're sober! Many prefer them right out of the shell with either a shot of lemon juice or Tabasco juice or both. Should you be one of these hearty souls who likes them uncooked, the government says in *Composition of Foods* that less than 4 ounces of oysters contain 8.4 grams of protein and only 66 calories. Oysters are also high in vitamins and minerals with more than 3 milligrams of combined B vitamins, 310 International Units of vitamin A and high levels of iron, potassium, phosphorus and calcium. We, of course, would expect a lot of calcium from oysters, because their crushed shells are fed to chickens so that their eggs will have firm shells. And oysters are a good source of zinc — the best natural source, in fact! Three ounces of raw oysters contain 63 milligrams of zinc. Contrast that with a much touted zinc source — beef liver — which contains only 3 milligrams of zinc in the same quantity. Zinc treatments have been proven to cure some forms of impotence, hence the value of oysters as an aphrodisiac. They increase testosterone levels and production.

There seems to be a common belief that oysters can only be eaten in certain months. As far back as 1600, William Vaughan wrote in his book, *Directions for Health*, that "Oysters must not be eaten in those months, which in pronouncing want the letter R." Many still hold that they can only be eaten from September through April. It does seem to be true that they taste better when harvested during these months.

Oysters On The Half Shell

6 oysters or more per person   lemon wedges
cocktail sauce   garlic butter
freshly grated horseradish

This is the most popular way to serve raw oysters. They are usually served on a bed of crushed ice with half the shell removed and the oyster resting in the deeper half. Side dishes of either horseradish or hot garlic butter are also provided along with Saltines or other soda crackers.

Of course we know that pearls come from grains of sand that the oyster encases with the mother-of-pearl material to protect itself from the irritation the grain of sand causes. Cooking destroys the pearl, so they are only taken from raw oysters.

Each year on the Columbus Day weekend's Saturday, there is an Oyster Festival — all you can eat for $15 — at Chincoteague Island, Virginia, about 185 miles southeast of Washington, DC. This is the same island where wild ponies are rounded up the last Thursday of each July and swum across the ocean by the fire department to be auctioned off as a fund raiser. For more information about either event, contact the Chamber of Commerce at P.O. Box 258, Chincoteague, VA 23336. There are many fun things to see and do.

Creamy Oyster Stew

1 pint fresh oysters   salt and pepper to taste
1 cup milk   1 cup heavy cream
$\frac{1}{2}$ stick butter   pinch cayenne pepper
$\frac{1}{4}$ cup white wine (opt.) $\frac{1}{2}$ cup whole kernel corn, cooked

Some people consider the corn and cayenne pepper as optional as the wine. You can add whichever you like before serving. In a large sauce pan, heat the oysters and their juices over low heat until their edges start to curl. This won't take much longer than a three-minute egg takes. Add the cream, milk and butter and season to taste. Heat slowly, but avoid boiling or scorching.

Roasted Oysters

There are two common ways to roast oysters. The easy way is to scrub them, then wrap them in a wet towel which is placed in a turkey roasting pan in a hot oven (450-500 degrees) for 7 to 10 minutes until you can smell the oysters as their shells open. The more traditional and most flavorful way is to get a real good bed of coals in a charcoal grill or a deep hole in the sand with a heavy grill above the embers. Put a good layer of wet seaweed or burlap on the grill, lay the oysters down, and add a second layer of seaweed or burlap — or close the lid on the grill if you can do that. Wait about the same amount of time — 7 to 10 minutes — and they will be ready when their shells are open. You can fix large clams the same way.

You may have known the pleasures of harvesting your own oysters in the past but can't seem to find a place to gather them now, or you may have noticed that they are more expensive in the stores now. In 1975, the annual harvest was around 175 million pounds (in North Carolina) but it is now down to around 50 million. That explains the price jumps.

Deep Fried Oysters

plenty of fresh shucked oysters
seasoned bread crumbs
hot oil

beaten egg
paprika and red pepper
salt and pepper

Roll oysters in egg and then in seasoned bread crumbs — herb or Italian flavor. Cook in hot fat until browned. Drain on a paper bag and serve immediately. Sprinkle with paprika and red pepper or salt and pepper.

Oyster Fritters

shucked fresh oysters
4 eggs, beaten
salt and pepper to taste

1$\frac{1}{2}$ cups flour
4 tsps. baking powder
$\frac{1}{4}$ cup fine yellow corn meal

Beat eggs well. Sift together dry ingredients and blend in the eggs until a smooth batter is formed. Dip oysters one at a time in batter and drop in hot oil. Cook until golden brown. A couple of interesting variations are to add some chopped herbs — cilantro or chives — to the batter or some finely grated Parmesan cheese.

Of course, every oyster eater has friends or relatives who will never share our enjoyment because they would rather die than put an oyster in their mouth. Good! Leaves more for us!

In those last "R" months — March and April, you can find the poke sallet to make Reba's Poke Salad Delight on page 16. It goes good as a green dish at an oyster feast!

The author and Reba McEntire photographed by (the watchful) Frances Squier.

Oysters In Champagne

1 pint oysters & juices, shucked
1 tsp. Bouquet garni herbs

1 cup champagne
1 tbsp. butter

Bring champagne, herbs and butter to a boil. Drop in oysters and simmer 2 minutes or until edges curl and oysters are done. Serve over toast squares.

Oyster Pie

1 quart oysters	1 9-inch square baking dish
3 tbsps. butter, melted	$^1/_2$ cup celery and onion, minced
2 cups Bisquick baking mix	1 cup buttermilk
salt and pepper to taste	1 can cream of mushroom soup

Preheat oven to 425 degrees. Place butter, celery and onion and mushroom soup in baking dish, stirring to mix. Add oysters. Mix buttermilk and Bisquick and pour over top. Bake for 25 minutes or until crust is browned on top.

Gobble Up Those (Wild) Turkeys!

It had been impossible to hunt a wild turkey legally around my home in the Sandhills of North Carolina for many years. Why? Because they had been wiped out, it is said, not by overhunting, but when New Castle disease unfortunately and accidentally escaped years ago due to the actions of men with good intentions. They used manure from poultry houses to fertilize feeder plots for wildlife out in the woods. The tame birds had been inoculated against the disease, but it took a heavy toll on the wild turkeys. The flocks were devastated by it. Now, they are hunted again, not in spite of man, but because of him!

Hats off to the persistent wildlife biologists in our area who kept restocking wild turkeys, the game wardens who have protected them, and the hunters who paid for the restocking efforts with monies from the purchase of hunting licenses and ammunition, as well as direct donations to conservation organizations such as the National Wild Turkey Federation in Edgewood, South Carolina. The NWTF has done wonders in research, education, protection and restocking. They offer a reward of $400 for information about poachers (game thieves) shooting turkeys out of season, or of the wrong sex. Only males, "Toms" or "gobblers," may be shot during the spring season here and they must have a visible "beard" hanging from their chest. Another $100 provided by the North Carolina Bowhunters Association brings the reward to $500 for each conviction. Good work, men (and ladies)!

A brief look at turkey history tells us that Benjamin Franklin wanted the native turkey as our national bird, saying that it had much more character than the eagle. Although we always think of Native Americans introducing the pilgrims to turkey at the first Thanksgiving, actually the Spaniards had already brought the turkey to England years before. It was considered second-rate food for humans.

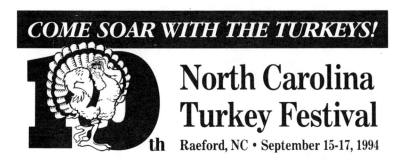

COME SOAR WITH THE TURKEYS!

North Carolina Turkey Festival

10th Raeford, NC • September 15-17, 1994

Not so here! North Carolina is one of the major turkey producing states, if not the premier turkey producer. Nearby Raeford is home of the North Carolina Turkey Festival, and a week or more of celebrations, parades and feasts honor this bird annually. Still, nearly everyone who has tasted wild turkey prefers it over our barnyard variety. Here are some recipes that work well with either type.

When I roast a turkey, I rub a lot of butter into the skin, season it, stuff it, and bake it at 425 degrees for about an hour to seal the skin and contain the juices. Then I lower the temperature to 350 degrees and bake it about 20 minutes per pound, covered, basting it regularly. Stuffed turkeys take about an hour longer on the average than ones that aren't.

I usually whip the butter I rub on my turkeys in a bourbon like Jack Daniels which has a strong charcoal flavor, and the alcohol cooks away.

The author and a savory turkey dinner.

Roast Turkey With Sausage And Oranges

1 turkey
1½ tsps. salt
3 cups mandarin orange segments
1 tsp. cinnamon
½ cup brown sugar
½ cup flour
1 tsp. pepper
2 pounds Jimmy Dean sage sausage
½ cup bacon drippin's
½ cup butter

Cut turkey into manageable-sized pieces. This is a good recipe for old birds. Depending on the turkey's size, you may have to double the quantities of flour, salt and pepper. Combine these in a bag, add turkey pieces and shake until all parts are well coated. Heat ½ cup each of butter and bacon drippin's in pan until it sizzles. Brown turkey pieces on all sides. Grease a large baking dish well and line the bottom with ⅓ of the sausage and 1 cup mandarin orange segments, drained. Insert browned turkey pieces and cover with the rest of the sausage. Add 1 cup of water and roast at 350 degrees for 1 hour. Lower the heat to 300 degrees and roast 1 hour more. Cover the top with brown sugar, the remaining mandarin orange slices and cinnamon. If necessary, add a little water to keep moist. Cover and roast 45 minutes more. Enjoy!

When teaching our daughter to cook at age 12, we looked for things that would be relatively easy as well as offer good results. It's amazing how many grown-ups won't try to fix a quiche, which, incidentally, real men *do* eat!

Jessica's "Child's Play" Turkey Quiche

Jessica Squier and a quiche.

1 dozen eggs
6 cups Cheddar cheese, grated
1 pint half-and-half
1 onion, minced
salt and pepper to taste
1 cup mushrooms, sliced
pie crust mix (opt.)
1½ pounds ground turkey meat
½ cup Monterey Jack cheese with
    jalapeño peppers, grated
minced garlic to taste
butter
½ cup bell pepper, minced
½ cup tomato, minced & drained

Butter the bottom and sides of a 9 x 13 inch baking dish or put a pie crust in it. Whip eggs and half-and-half together and pour into baking dish. Stir in half the cheese, mixing well. Sprinkle in other ingredients, including remaining cheeses, getting a good spread throughout the egg/milk-/cheese mixture. Bake in preheated 425 degree oven for 15 minutes. Lower heat to 325 degrees and cook 45 more minutes or until broom straw inserted in center comes out clean. Rub top with softened butter and allow to set in oven for 5 more minutes. Serve hot immediately or chill and serve cold.

German Turkey And Sauerkraut

1 turkey
1 or 2 onions, chopped
4-6 slices hickory-smoked bacon
6 carrots, quartered

3-5 pounds sauerkraut
2 tsps. salt
3 cups water
1 dozen small potatoes, halved

How much sauerkraut and onions you really need depends on how big the turkey is and how well your guests like the taste of them. Combine sauerkraut, onion and 1 tsp. salt in the bottom of a deep baking pan or turkey roaster. Rub turkey inside with the other tsp. of salt and lay it on the sauerkraut. (Stuff it at this time if you wish.) Lay bacon strips across turkey. Roast covered at 325 degrees for 2 hours (3 if stuffed), basting as needed. Surround the turkey with potatoes and carrots, add a little water if needed. Roast another 2 hours (adjusting for size), covered. Remove cover, baste well and bake uncovered for 30 minutes or until browned the way you like it.

Roast Wild Turkey

1 10-15 pound wild turkey
1 pound Jimmy Dean sage sausage
3 sticks butter
6 cups dry bread crumbs
2 tbsps. rosemary, chopped

salt and pepper to taste
1 onion, chopped
2 apples, cored and chopped
2 tbsps. fresh parsley, minced
2 cups chicken broth

Melt butter in pan and sauté onion and torn-up sausage for 10 minutes. Blend well with apple, herbs, salt and pepper and bread crumbs. Add enough broth to moisten. Fluff with a fork and stuff into the turkey, fore and aft. Place in a roaster and cover with a double thickness of clean or new dish towel soaked in melted butter. Roast at 325 degrees at the rate of 20 minutes per pound, adding a pound for the stuffing. Baste with pan drippings every half hour. Remove towel and bake 15 minutes uncovered to brown.

Those are just a few suggestions for cooking your wild (or not) turkey. Down in Louisiana, let me tell you, man, dem crazy Cajuns, dey even deep fry turkeys in hot peanut oil to cover about 5 minutes per pound of fresh or well-thawed turkey. Get the oil hot, almost boiling, before you put the turkey in.

My own favorite turkey is smoked with corn cobs, grape vines, sassafras or hickory wood.

How many turkeys do you see in this photo? Ben Franklin wanted the wild turkey to be our national bird because he said it was more elegant and genteel than the eagle!

If you want to get kids into a conservationist frame of mind and do something to help the wild turkey as well, you can sign

The author and his prey... in this case, a wild turkey!

youngsters up in the JAKES program of the National Wild Turkey Federation. For kids under 17, it costs $5 a year. JAKES is the name given to young male wild turkeys, but stands for **J**uniors **A**cquiring **K**nowledge, **E**thics and **S**portsmanship. For more information, write NWTF, P.O. Box 530, Edgefield, SC 29824.

Taste-Tempting Gourmet Game Dishes

In North Carolina, by late November we are halfway through the deer season, into the second dove season and well into the rabbit and squirrel seasons. A lot of people have finally gotten their fill of fresh venison and doves and have started to get some accumulating in the freezer at last. Some wives are already tired of the same old venison stew and deer steaks, fried rabbit and squirrel and gravy. Well, you don't have to keep fixing the meat the same way or keep it until it gets freezer burned. I want to suggest a few ways of cooking your game that may be different to you and offer a welcome change.

Barbecued Bear Loin

3-5 pounds bear tenderloin
1 cup tomato sauce or paste
1 onion, diced
salt and pepper to taste
$^1/_2$ tsp. Tabasco
$^1/_4$ cup Madeira sherry (opt.)

1 cup apple cider vinegar
1 cup water
2 cloves garlic, minced
$^1/_4$ cup maple syrup or honey
1 tsp. dry mustard
$^1/_2$ cup raisins

Slice bear meat $^1/_2$-inch thick and lay in a pan. Roast in the oven at 350 degrees for 30 minutes. Combine all other ingredients, bring to a boil and then reduce heat, simmering, covered, while bear meat cooks. After 30 minutes, drain the pan juices off the meat and cover with the sauce. Return to oven and cook 1 hour more.

I discovered that people don't always know how to best prepare the feasts from the field and woods when one of my co-workers asked me how to soak meat to take out the gaminess. Well, you know, venison shouldn't ever have a gamey taste if it is shot well, properly and expeditiously cleaned and refrigerated as early as possible. Some male animals such as goats and hogs may have a musky taste. Sometimes, people may want to soak their venison or other game a little to change the flavor. I have used milk, vinegar, salt water and Newman's Own dressing and other marinades with great success. If you use vinegar, you have to use a lot of water and a little vinegar.

I'll just make up a name and call my friend Jimmy Barker. Jimmy was given some venison — and the advice to use vinegar to soak it in. They forgot to tell him how much. He called me to ask how to get the vinegar taste out of it or if I knew a better soaking method. Seems he had soaked his deer meat overnight in about 2 gallons of pure vinegar and by morning it was just about pickled! Some people use salt and water, but in that case you have to rinse off the salt water and excess salt before cooking. There are lots of popular marinades and their flavors vary greatly. Many folks soak their game in wine or bourbon and water, using a whiskey with a strong charcoal flavor.

Stewed Squirrel and Dumplings

Stew

2-4 squirrels, cut up in pieces
$^3/_4$ cup vegetable oil
1 dozen wild onions or 1 diced
   tame onion & 1 garlic clove
8 carrots, sliced
$^1/_2$ cup mushroom slices

$1^1/_2$ cups flour
2 quarts water
8 Jerusalem artichokes or potatoes
salt and pepper to taste
1-2 stalks celery, sliced

Dumplings The Hard Way

2 cups flour
¹/₂ tsp. salt
1 cup milk

1 tbsp. baking powder
1 tbsp. melted butter

Short Cut Dumplings

2 cups Bisquick

²/₃ cups milk (approximately)

Cut up squirrels into stewing-sized pieces. Sprinkle each with salt and pepper and dredge in flour. In a large kettle, brown squirrel on each side and drain on a brown paper bag. Pour off excess oil from kettle and return squirrel. Add water and simmer covered for about 2 hours. Add vegetables and cook until tender — about 1¹/₂ hours on a low simmer. Mix up dumplings according to one of the recipes, blending ingredients thoroughly. I often add some Italian herb blend into my dumplings. Drop dumplings by spoonfuls into boiling stew, cover and simmer about 15 minutes to cook. You can substitute rabbit, raccoon or doves for the squirrel — even armadillo or porcupine, or....

Duckghetti

3-4 ducks
¹/₂ cup celery, chopped
1 large onion, diced
2 tsps. chili powder
1 can tomato juice (46 oz.)
salt and pepper to taste
1 pound spaghetti

1 cup bell pepper, chopped
1 cup mushrooms, sliced
2-3 garlic cloves, minced
1 can tomato paste
2 tbsps. Worcestershire
2-3 ripe tomatoes, quartered
grated cheese

In a large pot, boil ducks with water to cover until they are tender enough to pull the meat off the bones. Cool and de-bone. Save the broth in another container. Return shredded duck meat to pot and add all the remaining ingredients except for spaghetti noodles and cheese. Bring to a boil, reduce heat and simmer about 3 hours if you can stand waiting that long and smelling it cooking. Boil spaghetti noodles in broth and drain. Pour sauce over spaghetti and top with grated cheese.

It's high time that you should be thinking about substituting your favorite meat or whatever meat is available when you read these recipes. Use your imagination!

Tom & Jessica with doves.

Tandori Grilled Dove Breasts

1 dozen dove breasts
2 tbsps. sunflower oil
1 tbsp. curry powder
2 tsps. ginger, minced
1 tsp. paprika
¹/₂ cup plain yogurt
2 tbsps. lime juice
2 garlic cloves, minced
1 tsp. grated lime peel

Place dove breasts in a plastic bag. Combine remaining ingredients and add to dove breasts. Shake to cover well and marinate overnight in the refrigerator. Coat the grill with vegetable cooking spray. Cook breasts over hot coals 5 minutes per side or until done.

Sweet and Sour Venison Balls

$\frac{1}{2}$ pound seasoned sausage
1 pound ground venison
4 tbsps. cider vinegar
$\frac{1}{4}$ cup brown sugar

$\frac{1}{2}$ cup bread crumbs
$\frac{3}{4}$ cup catsup
4 tbsps. soy sauce

Combine venison, sausage and bread crumbs, mixing well. Form into small balls and brown in a hot skillet in oil or bacon grease. Drain. Combine remaining ingredients and pour over meatballs. Simmer 30 minutes, adding water as needed. Serve over noodles or rice.

Leftover Venison Barbecue

4 cups chopped, cooked venison
$\frac{1}{4}$ cup butter
$\frac{1}{2}$ cup celery, chopped
salt and pepper to taste
$\frac{1}{4}$ cup brown sugar
1$\frac{1}{2}$ tsps. chili powder

1 tbsp. Worcestershire sauce
1 onion, chopped
$\frac{1}{2}$ cup bell pepper, chopped
1 cup catsup
$\frac{1}{2}$ tsp. hickory smoke flavor, liquid or salt

Sauté onion, celery and bell pepper in butter until tender. Add remaining ingredients except venison and simmer 10 minutes, stirring constantly. Add cooked chopped venison and heat thoroughly. This gets better if you can make it up ahead of time and let the flavor develop overnight.

These are just a couple of ideas for making use of late-season game in new ways. They can be real crowd-pleasers.

Fried Frog Legs

2-3 pairs frog legs per person
$\frac{2}{3}$ cup fine corn meal
peanut oil
salt and pepper to taste
2 brown eggs, beaten
$\frac{1}{3}$ cup all purpose flour
$\frac{1}{2}$ cup buttermilk or beer

Combine beaten eggs and beer or buttermilk in a bowl and add cornmeal and flour. Mix well to form a creamy batter, adding liquid a little at a time until it's just right. Sprinkle with salt and pepper. Drop into hot oil in a large skillet and brown on all sides. Serve hot. Drizzle with lemon or lime juice.

Frog legs should be frozen or at least chilled well before cooking. Fresh frog legs will jump out of hot grease or when lemon juice is poured on them before they are cooked.

Jessica with frog.

Antelope or Elk Chili

2 pounds elk or antelope,
   coarsely ground
1 tsp. garlic powder
1 tsp. salt
4 cups cooked tomatoes

$^1/_6$ cup bacon drippin's
4 onions chopped
1-2 tsps. ground cayenne
$^1/_2$ tsp. paprika
12 ounces tomato paste

Brown meat in a large skillet in the bacon drippin's. Add the rest of the ingredients and enough water to cover. Bring to a boil. Reduce heat and simmer, covered, for 1 hour.

Tender Fried Rabbit

2-3 rabbits, cut up
salt and pepper to taste

flour
hot oil

Cover rabbit with water and simmer until tender. Dry rabbit, sprinkle with salt and pepper, dust with flour and fry in hot oil until browned.

Bears have always held a special fascination for Native Americans who called them the "people of the forest."

Person of the forest.

Wild Rice Bruin

2 cups diced, cooked bear meat
1 diced onion
2 cups V-8 juice
$^1/_2$ cup wild rice
salt and pepper to taste

$^1/_2$ stick butter
2 tbsps. bell pepper, diced
1 cup whole kernel corn, cooked
$^1/_2$ cup brown rice
1 tsp. chili powder

Brown bear meat in butter and add onion and bell pepper, sautéing until tender. Add corn, V-8 juice, chili powder and salt and pepper. Add rice and bring to a boil. Reduce heat, cover and simmer 45 minutes or until rice is done, adding water if necessary.

Roast Bear

4-5 pound bear roast
¹/₄ pound bacon
salt and pepper to taste

minced garlic cloves
¹/₄ cup red wine

Rub meat with salt, pepper and garlic. Place in roaster pan and cover with bacon strips. Add minced garlic and wine to the pan and bake at 350 degrees for 2 hours. Add water if necessary, cover and bake about 2 hours more or until tender. This is the time to add any potatoes, carrots, onions, etc.

It is essential to cook bear meat fully to avoid any possibility of trichinosis, a disease once common in pork and now a problem in bear meat in some areas.

Bear paws are like deer neck roasts in many places — something that most people don't want to fool with. They miss a lot of good eating by wasting this meat.

Simmered Bear Paw or Venison Neck Roast

2 bear paws or 1 deer neck
garlic
¹/₂ cup red wine

flour
sage, rosemary & cloves
salt and pepper to taste

Roll meat in flour seasoned with salt and pepper. Brown on all sides in a Dutch oven or roaster in a little bacon grease. Add herbs, wine and minced garlic and enough water to reach halfway up the meat as it cooks. Cover and bake at 350 degrees or simmer on stove top until tender, turning as necessary.

Lots of folks think of a really good pasta as a nice addition to any meal. Others, like my friend Adrian de Pasquale, consider pasta to be the staff of life. So, especially for all of you noodle lovers, here are a couple of pasta dishes for the sportsman's palate.

Venison Fried Won Ton Noodles

1 package won ton noodles
1 tsp. grated ginger
¹/₂ tsp. sesame oil

2 cups ground cooked venison or elk or buffalo or whatever
minced garlic to taste

Combine venison, ginger and garlic and sesame oil. Mix well. Spoon into center of won ton noodles and fold over to form a triangle. Seal the edges and fry in hot oil until brown, turning to cook on both sides. Serve with hot mustard or horseradish sauce.

If you can't find fresh won ton noodles in your store, you can make do with phylo dough or with pie crust cut into 3- or 4-inch squares. In Panama they call these "empañadas" with a "ny" sound and which means "meat pies." In Italy they make them square and call them ravioli. "We are the world....."

Game Bird Lasagna

1 cup cooked game bird meat
1 cup ricotta cheese
1 tsp. each salt & sugar
4 cups spaghetti sauce
¹/₂ cup onion, chopped
1 cup cottage cheese
¹/₂ cup basil, chopped

2 garlic cloves, minced
2 tbsps. olive oil
1 cup mozzarella cheese, shredded
¹/₂ cup Parmesan cheese, grated
¹/₂ cup parsley, chopped
¹/₂ cup mushrooms, chopped
1 package lasagna noodles

Boil 1 duck or 3-4 quails, crows or doves until tender and pick the meat off the bones. Chop fine. Sauté the onion, garlic, mushrooms and herbs until tender in oil. Add spaghetti sauce and meat and simmer for 30 minutes. Boil lasagna noodles for 7 minutes and drain well. In a square baking dish, pour ¹/₂ cup of the meat sauce. Layer with half the noodles and half the ricotta, mozzarella and cottage cheeses and more meat sauce. Add another layer of noodles and repeat the other layers, ending with meat sauce. Sprinkle with the grated Parmesan and bake 20-30 minutes in a 350 degree oven.

Use other wild foods in your favorite "regular" recipes and you will be pleasantly surprised!

Rabbit Croquettes

4 cups cooked rabbit meat	**2 cups bread crumbs**
1 egg, beaten	**$^1/_2$ cup Parmesan cheese, grated**
minced garlic to taste	**salt and pepper to taste**

Whip egg and add rabbit and half the bread crumbs and the Parmesan cheese. Season to taste. Form into croquettes and roll in the remaining bread crumbs. Fry in hot olive oil or bacon drippings until browned.

Marinated Wild Boar Chops

wild boar chops	**juice of 1 lime and 1 lemon**
1 tsp. each marjoram, basil, mint,	**apple cider vinegar**
rosemary	**cloves**

Mix 1 part vinegar with 5 parts water, add herbs and blend well. Marinate chops overnight in refrigerator in mixture. Remove and pat dry. Insert one or two cloves in each if desired. Broil in oven or grill over hot charcoal, turning as necessary until done.

Thanksgiving in the First Tradition

"Over the river and through the wood,
Now grandmother's cap I spy!
Hurrah for the fun!
Is the turkey done?
Hurrah for the pumpkin pie!"
— Lydia M. Child, "Thanksgiving Day"

When that turkey and pumpkin pie time of year comes again nearly 400 years since the first Thanksgiving dinner, we must realize that it wasn't called that then. In fact, many of the foods we associate with this popular holiday weren't even known to the Pilgrims and Native Americans in early Massachusetts, which also wasn't called Massachusetts.

In the fall of 1621, Governor William Bradford, the leader of the Plymouth Colony, invited neighboring Indians to share in a three-day celebration marking their survival and a successful and bountiful harvest. By the end of the 19th century, this habit had spread throughout New England, but it was President Abraham Lincoln who first proclaimed it as a national holiday in 1863. Traditionally celebrated on the last Thursday in November for many years, Congress determined in 1941 that it would be henceforth celebrated on the fourth Thursday of November. Don't ask me why, but the official Canadian Thanksgiving appears on the calendar on the second Monday of October. That day usually turns out to be the "day off" for Columbus Day here, and "D" Day for Native Americans!

The contemporary Thanksgiving feasts contain ham, pumpkin and apple pie, and turkey. There was, in all probability, no apple pie there at the first Thanksgiving. Apples aren't native here, came over later from Europe, and our native hawthorns don't make a particularly good pie. They do, however, make a great cardiac medicine which strengthens and tones the heart muscle and beat. A few sources speculate that there was no turkey, but most think there was,

myself included. There was no ham at the first Thanksgiving, though, for hogs came over later as well. What was found there were the wild birds like ducks and doves, venison and rabbit, and various fish such as cod and bass. There were oysters, grapes, persimmons and wild nuts — hickory, walnuts and hazelnuts. We now call the hazelnuts "filberts" in our Christmas mixtures.

I'm not going to offer any special turkey recipes here, because they are all roasted pretty much the same way — 425 degrees in the oven for about 20-30 minutes, then 400 degrees for about 4 or 5 hours, depending on size, until done. Figure about 20 minutes per pound and add another hour if it is stuffed. Where the real flavor differences come in is what you put on the turkey (or goose) and what you stuff it with. You can make an endless variety of glazes and come up with an incredible number of stuffing recipes. I like to whip butter with a charcoal flavored *bourbon* and rub it inside and out the turkey, then let it chill a couple of days in the refrigerator before proceeding. The alcohol bakes away and the charcoal flavor stays behind. Even though most have a nice charcoal flavor, don't use Scotch whiskeys because your bird will end up tasting like "tincture of turkey!"

REPORT WILDLIFE VIOLATIONS!

1-800-662-7137

Edelene Wood, president of the National Wild Foods Association, says, "I have never reached the place where I prefer one kind of wild meat; however, wild turkey is certainly one of the favorites of many other wild food devotees... A complete wild meal, particularly a fancy dinner, always includes some type of meat, and that, depending on what is available, can be anything, including fish, reptiles, game birds, game animals and shell fish." That statement probably sums up what was served as the first Thanksgiving so long ago.

Oyster Mushrooms.

Wild Mushroom Stuffing

1 cup mushrooms, chopped
$1/2$ cup butter, melted
1 tsp. parsley or sage
$1/2$ cup hot water
4 cups bread crumbs
$1/4$ cup onion, grated
salt and pepper to taste

Melt butter in pan and sauté mushrooms and onion. Mix into bread crumbs and add sage or parsley and salt and pepper. Mix well and add sufficient water to moisten, but don't make it soggy. Stuff into bird or bake in a dish.

For this next recipe, you can use ocean oysters, mountain oysters, or even oyster mushrooms off a tree.

Oyster Stuffing

1 gallon stale bread cubes
1 cup celery, sliced
salt and pepper to taste
3 eggs, well-beaten
1 quart fresh oysters

Pour boiling water over bread cubes to moisten and allow to steam for 15 minutes. Combine with other ingredients, leaving oysters whole or cutting them up. Stuff turkey and roast. Adjust quantities as needed for larger or smaller birds.

Hazelnut Stuffing

$^1/_2$ cup hazelnuts, chopped
1 stick butter, melted
4 cups bread crumbs or cubes
$^1/_2$ tsp. rosemary, sage, thyme,
   or a combination

1 medium onion, diced
$^1/_2$ cup celery with leaves, diced
$^3/_4$ cup giblet stock
salt and pepper to taste

Sauté onion and celery in butter until tender. Combine with bread crumbs and nuts and mix well, adding stock to moisten and herbs to flavor, but not overpower. Stuff into bird and roast. You can use other types of nuts as well — even pine nuts, which aren't really nuts at all.

A nice combination of flavors comes by substituting cranberries for nuts in the recipe above and glazing the outside of the bird with cranberry sauce — the whole berry type, puréed, not the jelled stuff from cans.

Cranberry Relish

1 pound cranberries
1 red apple, cored & diced
1 orange, peeled & chopped
$^1/_2$ cup water

$^1/_2$ cup honey or maple syrup
$^1/_2$ cup walnuts or pecans, chopped
1 tbsp. grated orange peel

Chop the orange well and combine with other ingredients. Bring to a boil in a saucepan and reduce heat, stirring to prevent burning and avoid bubbling over. Simmer until all the berries have popped, cooking to desired thickness. Remember, it will thicken as it cools, and some people like to add more honey or a little sugar.

I like my cranberry sauce tart. I also like to make up a batch and use it as a seasonal pie filling.

Apple Cider Venison Roast

3-5 pound venison roast
$^1/_2$ cup raisins
oil
salt and pepper

flour
1 cup apple cider
pinch nutmeg

Season flour with salt and pepper to taste. Roll venison roast in flour and brown on all sides in hot oil. Rub the inside of a brown paper bag with oil and place the roast, raisins and cider inside, folding the top to close. Place in a roaster pan or baking dish and bake 2-3 hours at 350 degrees, depending on size — about 40 minutes per pound. Serve, sliced, with a gravy made from the raisins, cider and juices from cooking. Combine $^1/_2$ cup flour and $^1/_2$ cup cold water, stirring until smooth. Mix with hot pan juices and heat thoroughly, stirring while it thickens.

Walnut or Hickory Pie

2 cups nuts, chopped
$^1/_2$ cup corn syrup or molasses
1 cup honey or maple syrup
1 tsp. vanilla extract
1 single pie crust recipe

$^1/_2$ cup whipping or heavy cream
3 large eggs, beaten
$^1/_4$ cup melted butter
pinch salt

Preheat oven to 400 degrees. Blend cream, molasses or corn syrup, honey or maple syrup, salt, vanilla extract and butter. Mix well. Fold in nuts and pour into pie crust. Bake 10 minutes and reduce heat to 350 degrees. Continue cooking 25-30 minutes or until a broom straw inserted in center comes out clean. Pie will rise up initially, but will settle as it comes from the oven and cools.

Traditionally a sassafras tea or wild lemonade made from the berries of sumac would be served along with sweet potatoes, baked as they are or in a pie. Though the sweet potato is a Native American traditional food, here is a modern recipe for it:

French Fried Sweet Potatoes

sweet potatoes   **hot oil**
salt and pepper to taste

Simply cut washed sweet potatoes into French fry-sized pieces and fry in hot oil in a deep fryer. You can also fry slices if this is an easier way for you to cut them, and they are just as good. When they float, drain on a paper bag and season to taste. This might be a good way to get kids to eat these healthy veggies. They are said to be a great cancer preventative.

Sassafras is easy to recognize with its green bark and three different shapes of leaves — one "regular," one shaped like a three-toed track, and the other looking like a catcher's mitt or a mitten, giving it the nickname of "mitten tree." The leaves are used as a spice, the wood for smoking meat, and the roots alone are used to make the tea. They can be used over and over if dried between times so they don't mildew, until they no longer produce any flavor. Sassafras made one of the original "root beers."

Sassafras Tea

washed sassafras roots   **water**
sugar (optional)

Boil the roots in water until you get a satisfactory flavor. Serve hot with milk and sugar if you like or cold with sugar or not.

Old Timey Black Walnut Fudge

1 cup black walnuts, chopped   **1 pound sugar**
1 cup evaporated milk   **1 tbsp. corn syrup**
1 tsp. vanilla extract

Combine sugar, corn syrup and milk in a saucepan and bring to a slow boil, stirring constantly. Simmer 20 minutes on reduced heat and add the walnuts and vanilla extract. Stir well. Place saucepan in a larger pan of ice water or on a cold back porch to thicken. Spoon into a large buttered dish and let harden. Cut into squares.

You can use any type of native nuts for this — hickory, walnut or hazelnut. Chestnuts don't work all that well, and forget peanuts altogether. That relative of peas and beans isn't really a nut at all, and is better in peanut brittle, which is made by melting butter and sugar, heating it to caramelize, adding the "goober peas" and cooling. When I was a child, everybody had vanilla extract around, just like in the Pilgrim days. I have known some of my kin to use it like cologne, rubbing it behind their ears. We kids would use it for a beverage base.

Homemade Cream Soda

water   **vanilla extract**
sugar or honey

Add about $1/4$ to $1/2$ tsp. vanilla extract to a large glass of water and sweeten to taste.

The Native Americans and the Pilgrims at the first Thanksgiving ate some type of fish — some in a chowder, some smoked over the fires and some cooked either in the iron stoves of the Pilgrims or in balls of clay *in* the fires. Here's a much easier way.

Baked Fish

6-7 pound salmon or trout   lemon slices
diced wild onions or scallions   butter
salt and pepper to taste   parsley or mint

Rub fish inside and out with lemon and salt and pepper. Stuff with lemon slices and onion. Dot with butter inside and out. Wrap in foil. Bake at 400 degrees for 25 minutes. Uncover and bake an additional 15-20 minutes until done. It will flake with a fork. Drizzle with butter and lemon juice from cooking and serve with a garnish of mint or parsley.

Native Americans usually ate corn as meal or hominy, almost never "on-the-cob" the way we do today. Due to the difficulty in digesting whole-kernel corn, it is not really all that nutritious. If you don't believe me, ask any chicken how much trouble digesting whole corn can be!

Around the time of the first Thanksgiving, way up north at Plymouth, Massachusetts, the meals of the Native Americans were kind of bland for the most part. The food was eaten for nourishment, not to provide gourmet fare, and was often cooked in the same manner day in and day out. Life was more demanding and required much more time to handle the hunter-gatherer chores of the day. In the Native American version of the "crockpot," foods were cooked in large pots or bowls for hours on end while the work was being done (by the fairer sex, by the way!). Surely you have seen some of those plaques that read something like this:

"When the white man arrived in America,
the men hunted and fished all day,
the women did all the work,
and there were no taxes!
The white man
thought he could improve on a system like that!"

The many Native American museums around the country are good places to learn about their culture. Near me is the Indian Museum of the Carolinas, located in Laurinburg, North Carolina. The museum's director, Dr. Margaret Houston, says that "the typical dish of the day was a very boring and predictable stew. Whatever meat, bird or fish there was available, was boiled. As the meat cooked, whatever vegetables that could be found were added to the pot." This would include dried corn and dried green beans, known as "leather breeches," Jerusalem artichokes, wild carrots and onions, mushrooms and possibly even some dried fruit such as plums or cherries. Then, as it was nearing doneness, a couple of handfuls of chopped nutmeats were thrown in to thicken it up and to add flavor and the oil needed to keep the body warm in winter. A pinch of white campfire ashes was used as spice and maybe even some sea salt, if trading with coastal tribes had been good.

The "black tea" made from the Yaupon holly was drunk by men at harvest celebrations when they ate too much, so they could throw up and begin anew, enjoying the fruits of the harvest.

Acorns were an important part of the Native American diet from coast to coast. The nuts from white oaks could be eaten raw after they dried out, but the nuts of the red and black oaks are much higher in tannin or tannic acid and this had to be leached out before they

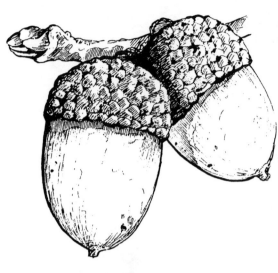

could be eaten. The Native Americans would soak acorns in a basket in a moving stream or repeatedly boil them to get rid of the bitterness. Leaching in the modern kitchen is easy.

To leach the tannin from your acorns, shell them and grind them into a coarse meal, using a coffee grinder, pepper mill, food processor or blender. Cover with boiling water in a pot and simmer half an hour. Dump the water and repeat the process until the water remains clear and the nut meal is no longer bitter. Drain off as much water as possible, using a jelly bag or cloth sack. Roast in a warm, but not hot, oven with the door open to finish the drying process. Store like flour when completely dry. You can continue to roast some until completely roasted dark and crisp. You can then use this as a coffee substitute.

Acorn Venison Stew

3 pounds venison, cubed
2-3 pounds acorn meal
salt and pepper to taste

2 quarts water
2 large onions, diced

Simmer meat and onions in water with salt and pepper to taste for 1-2 hours or until tender. Add water as necessary. Add acorn meal and simmer another 30 minutes to an hour. Try serving with herbed nut butter!

My friend, Karen Sherwood, teaches plant classes at Tom Brown's Survival School and has some excellent wild foods recipes to offer her students.

Karen Sherwood's Acorn Bread

1 cup acorn meal
1 tsp. salt
1 tbsp. baking powder
$^1/_4$ cup maple syrup
1 cup milk

$^1/_2$ cup cornmeal
$^1/_2$ cup whole wheat flour
$^1/_4$ cup nut or salad oil
1 egg, beaten

Combine dry ingredients, and mix in the wet ingredients until all are moistened. Pour into greased 8 x 8 baking pan and bake 20-30 minutes at 350 degrees.

In the interest of providing some recipes which the modern reader might care to fix in the modern kitchen, here are some based on wild or traditional Native American foods, but modified for modern cooking methods. Feel free to further modify them, add your favorite spice combinations or experiment with them, but enjoy!

Hickory Nut Soup

2 cups hickory nut meat
2 tbsps. honey
2 tbsps. parsley

3 pints water
2 wild onions, chopped

Combine all ingredients and simmer for 1 hour before serving. Black walnuts, pecans or acorn meal can be substituted. Hickory nuts are well worth the trouble to get them shelled. Shelling nuts would make a good family project while watching the "boob tube."

Hickory Nut Cheese Sticks

$1/2$ loaf store-bought bread
1 egg, beaten

2 cups cheese, shredded
2 cups hickory nuts, chopped

Preheat oven to 350 degrees. Cut bread into 1-inch slices. Dip into beaten egg, roll in shredded cheese and then in the chopped hickory nuts. Place on ungreased cookie sheets and bake until golden brown.

Venison Roast With Spices

5-6 pound venison roast
1 tsp. allspice
$1/2$ pound bacon
4 medium onions, diced
1 cup red wine
1 cup water

salt and pepper to taste
1 dozen whole cloves
2 cups celery, diced
2 cups carrot, sliced
2 sticks butter
1-2 tsps. cayenne pepper

Rub salt and pepper into roast and sprinkle with spices and herbs. Wrap bacon around roast and secure with toothpicks. Place roast in roasting pan or Dutch oven and surround with remaining ingredients. Cover and bake 1 hour at 400 degrees. Spoon pan liquids over roast and continue baking at 275 degrees until done to your liking.

Roasted Yams with Maple Sauce

1 dozen sweet potatoes
1 cup maple syrup

3 sticks butter
1 cup nuts, chopped

Bake yams at 350 degrees until they can be pierced with a fork. Combine butter, nuts (hickory, pecan or black walnuts) and maple syrup in a sauce pan and warm until butter is melted. Split yams lengthwise and make 2 crosswise slits in each one. Drizzle with butter and syrup mixture and bake 5 more minutes. You can also add marshmallows in each one at this time if you like.

This next recipe comes out similar to the brown bread that the Yankees in New England are so fond of (and so good at making), but uses ingredients more suitable to a Southern palate.

Persimmon Bread

$1/2$ tsp. nutmeg
$1/2$ tsp. salt
4 eggs, beaten

$1/2$ tsp. cinnamon
1 cup oil
3 cups sugar

Mix these ingredients all together, beating well. And then add —

2 cups persimmon pulp
2 tsps. baking soda

$2/3$ cup water
3 cups self-rising flour

Mix it all well, stirring out the lumps. Half fill 3 one-pound coffee cans which have been greased (buttered) and floured. Bake 1 hour in a 350 degree preheated oven. Cool and slip from the cans.

This next recipe can be made hot if you like by adding some cayenne pepper. Corn, squash and beans were staples of Native Americans. They are often referred to in legend as "the three sisters."

Indian Bean Balls

2¹/₂ cups coarsely ground cornmeal
3 tsps. baking powder
3 eggs, beaten
1 cup water
bacon drippings or oil

3 cups cooked, mashed pinto beans
3 tbsps. all-purpose flour
1 onion, minced fine
salt and pepper to taste

In a bowl, combine all ingredients except the bacon drippings or oil. Mix well, using your hands if you have to. In a large skillet, Dutch oven or deep fryer, get the oil hot. Form the bean mixture into balls and when the oil just begins to smoke, drop the bean balls in one at a time, not touching. Fry until golden brown and crisp on all sides. Scoop out with a slotted spoon and drain on paper bags. Serve hot.

Indian Pudding

5 cups milk, scalded
pinch sea salt
pinch nutmeg
1 tsp. ground ginger

¹/₂ cup coarse yellow corn meal
1 cup dark molasses
1 cup freshly grated corn

Preheat oven to 350 degrees. Grate corn off cob and combine with cornmeal. Add to scalded milk, stirring constantly. Add salt, molasses, nutmeg and ginger, and simmer, stirring to prevent burning for about 30 minutes. Pour into a buttered or greased baking dish and bake at 350 degrees for 1 hour and 45 minutes. Check with broom straw. It's done when straw comes out clean.

Here is a more recent recipe, but one that seems to be essential at all pow-wows, tribal meetings and other Native American festivals these days. I usually make a mess in the kitchen fixing it, but the way the kids eat them, it's worth the fussing I get from Frances.

Indian Fry Bread

1 cup flour
2 tsps. baking powder

big pinch salt
³/₄ cup milk

Combine ingredients to form a stiff dough. Drop into hot oil and brown on both sides. Drain well and drizzle with something sticky and sweet like honey or maple syrup!

Sassafras Remains Popular Despite Controversy

Sassafras is one of the most common of our small trees and is the source of a popular natural tea with a history which is entwined with that of our country.

Some legends say the sweet smell of sassafras being swept to sea was the key to convincing Columbus' mutinous seamen that land was near, and they shortly thereafter discovered America. The Native Americans had been using this plant for a variety of ills and it fell into popular usage immediately among the settlers as a medicinal tea and also as a key ingredient in the drink that later became known as root beer. Natural root beer drinks today are flavored by sassafras. The Native Americans here called it "winauk" and it was the first cash crop exported back to Great Britain from the "colonies in the New World." It was so valuable and popular that one of the search parties sent here to locate the now famous "Lost Colony" abandoned their quest and instead harvested sassafras roots which were bringing a high price back home in London. So greed helped to contribute to the development of one of the Cape Fear region's greatest mysteries.

Money was a prime motivator in spreading the popularity of sassafras around the world and money now threatens its usage here. A government study says that sassafras contains a cancer-causing agent called safrole which now must be removed before any sassafras products can be sold. Studies show this chemical causes cancer in mice when they are subjected to very large quantities, but studies in other countries show that humans metabolize sassafras in a different manner. Two employees of the USDA explain the controversy like this: Dr. Bruce Ames did a study which rates the carcinogenicity of various substances. "Carcinogenicity" is a big word that means the "cancer-causing ability" of a material. To make it simple and to have a starting point, Dr. Ames said that common tap water in most cities would have a base rating of "1" because of chemicals it contains if we drink a liter per day. Because of the safrole, 12 ounces of sassafras is rated at "200." Sounds bad, doesn't it? Well, the same studies indicate that one can of beer of virtually any brand is rated at "2,800," or 14 times the danger of sassafras! Why then, we ask, has sassafras been branded so dangerous?

"Money," says Dr. Jim Duke, who is also a government researcher in the Department of Agriculture and has written a dozen or so books and hundreds of articles on herbal medicine and plants. The industry which provides sassafras teabags, roots, and extracts to the markets doesn't have the powerful lobbying ability of the giant brewing industry. So the truth, it seems, is that sassafras may have a chemical in it which could cause cancer, but it is doubtful if you could drink enough of it to develop any cancer. Just to give you the proper perspective on the situation, 2 slices of "fortified" white bread is rated at "400," or twice as dangerous as sassafras, and a 12-ounce soda is rated at "2,700". Think about that the next time you say "Pepsi, please!"

Sassafras tea was brought to the attention of the television watching public by Granny Clampett of the *Beverly Hillbillies* program, but it has always been a favorite drink in the area of America known as Appalachia. It has always been drunk in my family and I remember my mother sending me out for sassafras roots as a boy. My grandmother, Miss

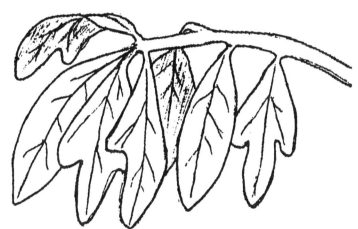

The three different shapes of sassafras leaves make the tree easy to recognize.

Edna, born in 1896, has been drinking it for all her life as a spring tonic and as a refreshing summer iced tea, and she is still going strong. My teenaged son Tommy likes it so well that he encouraged me to do this article and provided the artwork.

Known to botanists as *Sassafaras albidum*, and having many common names, including tea tree, ague tree, cinnamon wood, green stick, and mitten tree, it is easy to recognize. It has green bark, hence the name green stick, and has three distinctly different shaped leaves. One is shaped very much like a catcher's mitt or a snow mitten, and that is why that name came about. Its two scents are its real giveaway, though. The wood and leaves smell like cinnamon or a mouth wash, while the roots smell much like root beer. The scents of the leaves and roots are distinctly different. So are the uses.

The roots are used to make root beer or sassafras tea, but the leaves are sold in the stores as "filé powder," so if you are fond of Cajun cooking you have tasted the leaves. They are ground and sold in the spice section or gourmet food section as filé powder, pronounced fee-lay. The same ground leaves that bear Paul Prudhomme's name and sell for around $4.50 an ounce can be duplicated wherever this tree grows. This spice is used in gumbos and other soups for its particular flavor and as a thickener, as well.

Varro E. Tyler's book, *The Honest Herbal,* is a study of various herbal medicines, and he confirms or denies the effectiveness of various plants as medicines and their safety. Taylor says that studies in Switzerland in 1977 confirm the metabolism of safrole into a carcinogen in rats, but not in humans. Other books describe a wide range of medicinal uses, including stimulant, diaphoretic, diuretic, blood thinner and tonic, aromatic, and alterative. It is said that the oils in sassafras will relieve a toothache if it is chewed, and that a poultice of the roots will heal ulcers and sores on the body. According to Alma Hutchens in her book, *Indian Herbalogy of North America,* "if given in painful menstruation... it soon relieves the sufferer," because it thins the blood. It is used as a corrective in rheumatism and varicose ulcers, and is effective in after pains of childbirth, and in all skin eruptive diseases, according to Hutchens.

The strong tea also makes a delicious jelly when used in any juice-based jelly recipe which requires added pectin. The tea will increase the flow of urine, which leads to its usage as a diet aid and also to dissolve kidney stones and nephroliths. Herbalists use the leaves in a salve or ointment for bruises and wounds. These same leaves can be ground at home to save the cost of filé powder. You can gather your own roots for teas, remembering that the roots are most potent in winter when the sap is down. Just boil them until the water turns red or pinkish-brown and add sugar if desired. They can be saved and reused until they don't work any more. Out in the woods, chewing on the twigs freshens the mouth and breath — much like many commercial mouth washes.

Sassafras is a well-known, long-used and still-popular tree, despite the controversy about possible carcinogenicity.

After this column ran in the paper, I was talking to Suzanne Johnson in the Country Bookshop in Southern Pines and she told me this story:

"This really isn't much of a story. In fact, it's barely even an anecdote, but here it is.

"I wear a cologne called Mitsouko. The main reason I like it is it smells like sassafras when it's fresh. (At least I think it does.) One day in the early seventies, I'd just opened a new bottle, put some on, and gone to work. One of my co-workers became hysterical when she smelled me! She said that she couldn't understand why anyone would want to smell like that. She'd been in one of the death camps during World War II, and that the delousing solution she'd been sprayed with there smelled of sassafras.

"I guess the reason the episode stayed with me was that I love the smell so much. It reminds me of warm, happy things, and it was startling to hear that someone else had such different memories. I read somewhere that scent triggers emotion more strongly than any other sense, and I guess it's true."

Thanks, Suzanne, for your comments. The remark about delousing solution reminds me that a chemical in sassafras is reputed to be an insect repellent and that farmers have been known to use large sassafras branches as roosts in the hen house to keep mites off the chickens.

There's Just No Best Recipe for Tasty Venison!

Well, by the time people are doing a lot of last-minute Christmas shopping around the first of December, many hunters have already gotten at least one deer and maybe more if they were lucky. The next thing you know they are looking for a very special recipe to fix that venison with. Some people have been given deer meat by successful hunters as the holiday spirit takes over, and a few have even gotten some roadkills. After writing in my newspaper column about eating roadkills, it was two women who surprised me by confessing to eating FORD animals. Vicki Layton at my bank said that her family got a roadkilled deer in front of their house. Peggy Colvin at the ABC store told me, "I have eaten roadkill all my life." I stopped in Southern Pines one spring day to check on a dead deer along the road and a little red pickup pulled over. Michelle Bohse stuck her head out of the window and said, "That deer has been there a couple of days." Her husband, David, added: "Yeah, we already checked it out." Well, see, there are lots of ways to get a deer or some meat, but there are lots more ways to fix 'em!

There seem to be many favorite ways for handling deer meat initially, and everyone has their favorite way of cleaning

The author and his venison shish kebab!

them. Some hang them head up and some head down — the way I prefer to do it. Others clean the deer on the ground. The one common denominator that determines how a deer is going to taste later on when cooked is how soon the heat is released from the body after harvest. Making a clean and quick kill also helps the flavor, because animals that have run a long way tend to be tough. Ted Nugent, a very avid hunter, has this advice: "If we apply ourselves, we can all become expert hunters, attaining the ultimate goal of swift, clean, humane kills. To kill is not necessary to have hunted, but to aspire to kill cleanly is the only killing goal. We've got what it takes if we use what God gave us. We are a specialized predator, capable of effective, intelligent, and uniquely compassionate killing... Put forth the effort to do it right."

BOWHUNTING REPRESENTS THE SANCTITY OF PEACE FOR ALL HARDWORKING AMERICANS

TED NUGENT

Ted Nugent's Venison Stroganoff

**2 pounds venison steaks
fresh mushrooms
cooking sherry
curry powder
butter
1 envelope Lipton Onion Soup
1 beef bouillon cube
1 cup sour cream
garlic salt**

Cut meat into strips (eliminating fat). Brown quickly in 3 tbsps. or more butter with mushrooms. Stir in $^2/_3$ cup liquid ($^1/_3$ cup water, $^1/_3$ cup sherry). Add the onion soup mix, a dash of garlic salt, a dash of curry powder, and the bouillon cube, mix well, cover and simmer for $1^1/_2$ hours or until meat is tender. Stir every 15 minutes, adding liquid when necessary. Just before serving add sour cream and increase heat. Serve over rice or noodles for 4, unless Ted's eating over, then it'll serve 2!

Ted is actually quite a conservationist and sportsman as well. In the summer he operates Ted Nugent's Kamp for Kids, where he teaches sportsmanship and fair play, conservation, and a love of nature, and of course — archery.

*Tom Squier,
My Rock N Roll Bloodbrother,
Keep the Spirit of the Wild with you always,*

Blood Trails '92
A Fact of Life

Here is a little tip I like to use in my classes. Lots of hunters say that you have to run up to a deer after you shoot it and cut its throat because the blood will ruin the flavor of the meat if you don't. That is like saying the water in your car's radiator will rust your engine if you don't drain the cooling system after the fan belt breaks. That may be a bit of oversimplification, but both are closed systems designed to get rid of the excess heat by carrying it off. Excess heat will cause the engine to seize up, and excess heat will make the meat spoil much faster by promoting bacterial growth. That is why a deer needs to be either bled or cooled down and cleaned immediately after complying with the legal requirements of tagging it. Ted Nugent says, "Time is of the essence for getting the carcass cooled down to 35-40 degrees Fahrenheit. Rush, I say *speed* to the nearest cool spot."

The way in which a deer is handled at first is going to affect its flavor when it is cooked later on. You have to prove it to old hunters, but it is no longer absolutely necessary to hang a deer a couple of days before freezing it. Our newer lower-temperature freezers will properly age a packaged deer even if it is frozen the same day it is harvested. I like the aging process best. Ted Nugent agrees with me. "On some occasions in the past, I have cut up meat into small enough portions to wrap and put in the refrigerator at home. This will certainly do. I've heard two theories: 1. Cut it up right away and freeze it, or 2. Hang the carcass in a cooler for a week of aging to break down the enzymes that make meat tough. Both ways work, but I prefer the aging process. Bug free at 35 degrees Fahrenheit."

The big problem is that too many hunters don't know to cut up and package a deer properly. At Fort Bragg's Rod and Gun Club, there is a cleaning facility where successful hunters can clean and butcher their own deer after a productive hunt. "Butcher" is a good word! After a couple of visits there watching new hunters clean and cut up a deer for the first time, I decided they could have filmed the movie *The Texas Chainsaw Massacre* right there! Unfortunately, the same thing is true at many hunt clubs that have their own facilities. You can't just grind up the meat for burgers and sausage without

Before.

After.

some preliminary steps such as removing the membranes and the rare fat you find on a deer. You have to add some pork fat for flavor and moisture when cooking deer meat, because venison cooks drier than beef or pork. You can't just whack off chunks of meat and call them steaks. But where do you learn the process without paying a butcher to tell you how? I know of one place.

There is a videotape called *Venison Processing: A Meatcutter's Way* that shows you very professionally, in a step-by-step way, how to turn a deer into some excellent eating. I took it with me one weekend when I went to visit the in-laws and we watched it twice — even the women! It shows you how to handle deer from the time it enters your sights until the final preparations as fine cuts of meat are made and the table is set. Though it was so tastefully done that the ladies enjoyed watching it, I am sure they learned enough to be more critical of the men's efforts in the future.

The author examines a dead deer...
it looks good enough to eat!

The purpose of the videotape is to show you how to keep the meat from becoming "tainted" and to obtain the maximum flavor from your venison. The hunter who takes pride in being an expert will be just as picky about how he handles his meat and in the video Mike McDermott shows how it can be done easily in a garage or your kitchen. A professional meatcutter for 16 years, Mike is also a hunting guide and avid hunter himself. He makes skinning, boneless meatcutting and sausage-making look easy. It is much more fun to put strip steaks, chuck roasts, steaks, and tenderloins in the freezer than simply wrapping hunks of "venison."

Everyone has their favorite cuts of meat and the special recipes they like best when preparing them. There is no "best" recipe — just the ones we like the most! I have had venison fixed in elegant style in wine and sour cream sauces with herbs and mushrooms, and I have had it on a stick cooked over a campfire, and it was all great! I cooked a bit of venison over the fire for an El Salvadoran guest and he loved it, saying he had never been able to enjoy "venado" at home. He had been tempted many times to shoot a deer, but didn't want to risk giving his location away to the terrorists his unit was after. And, in his country, deer hunting is illegal. In this country, we take so many freedoms and privileges for granted — like just being able to own a gun. We may lose that if we don't defend ourselves from our own government!

A briefcase full of recipes? Only
Chuck Laudenslager knows for sure.

Chuck Laudenslager's
Korean Fire Venison

1¹/₂ pounds tender venison cut bacon thin,
but long enough not to fall through the grill
¹/₂ cup soy sauce
1 large bell pepper, minced
3 garlic cloves, minced
3 green onions, minced
3 tbsps. peanut oil *or* **¹/₄ cup sesame oil**
3 tbsps. sugar
2 tbsps. sesame seeds

Toast sesame seeds in a frying pan without oil until golden and fragrant. Combine with all other ingredients in a bowl and mix well. Marinate meat 3-4 hours in this mixture. Place on well-oiled grill over charcoal, turning once, until done (medium rare), about 10 minutes. Serve with rice.

Chuck says these two recipes are the "best" venison recipes! They are so good, in fact, that he carries copies of them in his briefcase and gives them out to anybody who talks about eating venison.

Marinated Venison

6–8 pounds venison
salt & pepper
1 stick butter

2 anchovies
1 pint cream

Marinade

1 cup white wine
2-3 ounces vinegar
1/2 cup water
2 tbsps. oil

1-2 whole cloves
1 bay leaf
1 onion
parsley

Parsley and onion are chopped fine and mixed with all other ingredients for the marinade. Put salt and pepper on the meat and pour marinade over meat and refrigerate 2 days. Drain meat and put in oven with butter all over. Let brown and pour marinade over. Roast 1 hour at 400 degrees and pour cream and anchovies into pan. Reduce heat to 300 degrees and cook 1 hour or until done, basting frequently with pan juices. When done, drain pan juices and thicken for gravy.

As I said earlier, the flavor of the meat depends greatly on how it is handled in the beginning. Really careful hunters don't drive around all day with a deer tied across a hot hood or their fender. It would be half-cooked by the time they got it home, half-spoiled and loaded with flies. Toughness of the meat depends on the age of the animal and its physical condition, the circumstances surrounding its death and whether it is aged — by hanging or freezing. Deer don't normally have much fat on them to marble the meat, so it is often necessary to lard the meat with a larding needle or strips of bacon, especially late in the season. Cooking it in moist heat, or covered, also keeps it from drying out. Does and young deer are naturally more tender. Biological studies and laws determine which may be hunted legally and how many. Traditionally, however, many huntmasters like Joe Carpenter are against the killing of does, even on the days when it is legal.

Many people like deer burger and sausage, and both are easy to make as long as you remember to add one part of beef or pork fat to four parts venison to prevent it from sticking, burning or drying out. Otherwise, you just remove the membranes, grind the meat, add the spices you prefer and mix by hand or with a machine. After a second grinding, it is ready for packaging. You can either pack it in parchment paper like Neese's sausages, in casings made from sheep or hog intestines or in freezer containers. I prefer it in casings, so that some can be smoked. Sausage's flavor

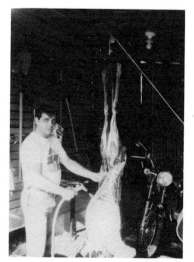

Chuck Laudenslager cleaning venison.

improves with age. Because it has such a fine-grained texture, venison is also excellent for pickling or making corned "beef." It makes excellent jerky, too, sliced thin, marinated and dried in the oven or sun. You can use a food dehydrator, a low oven with the door open or a piece of screen over the top of a lamp shade. The important thing is to remove all the moisture with circulating air.

The author marinating venison in a soy sauce and garlic mixture.

Roast Venison

6-7 pound venison roast
1 tsp. thyme
2$\frac{1}{2}$ cups beef stock
$\frac{1}{4}$ pound softened butter
salt and pepper to taste

2 garlic cloves, thinly sliced
4 tbsps. flour
10 larding strips or $\frac{1}{4}$ pound bacon
1 tsp. rosemary

Using a larding needle, poke the larding strips into the meat in ten different places about 1$\frac{1}{2}$ inches deep and follow with a slice of garlic. If you don't have a larding needle, stick a slice of garlic on a toothpick, followed by a piece of bacon, and stick these on the meat at intervals. Mix salt and pepper with flour and herbs. Rub meat surface with butter and dust with flour mixture. Roast uncovered in roasting pan with half the stock at 325 degrees for about 2 hours. Venison should be served rare and hot, but not bloody. Figure on about 15 minutes per pound. You may turn the oven up to 400 degrees the last 10 to 20 minutes to brown the meat. Remove the meat from the pan, but keep it hot. Mix remaining flour into pan, stirring out lumps, and place the pan over heat to brown the flour and dredge mixture. Stir in the remaining stock and water if needed to make a gravy, stirring as it thickens. Serve hot at once.

If you ever get the chance, get a set of those metal plates that you heat up to keep steaks sizzling. They are heated and then placed in a hard plastic holder so you don't burn yourself on them and are the best way to serve game and lean meats. You can find them at restaurant-supply houses and yard sales — that's where I got mine.

Another version of roast venison, and there are hundreds, calls for boiling 2 cups of cranberries in one cup of water until they are popped, and pouring this sauce over the roast as it is cooking. The British add juniper berries to the original recipe above. This will sometimes help remove a gamey taste and adds a unique flavor of their own.

The "Iron Man," the "Intimidator," or whatever you call Dale Earnhardt, drives every race to win. He has a simple philosophy: "If you aren't going out there to win, you don't need to be in the race!" Probably by the time you are reading this,

Dale Earnhardt

Earnhardt may have tied Richard Petty's record of winning seven NASCAR season championships and going for a record eighth win of his own. He also has a simple but excellent recipe for preparing a venison tenderloin. Dale Earnhardt says this is the "best recipe" for venison, so maybe there is one after all! How can you argue with a man who can start 39th out of 42 drivers in a race and makes it all the way to the front to lead the pack?

Dale Earnhardt's Grilled Tenderloin

1 venison tenderloin
bacon
1 bottle Italian dressing

Slice tenderloin into 1 inch-thick steaks. Fill bowl with bottle of dressing. Place tenderloin steaks into mixture in a glass bowl and marinate overnight. Remove when it's time to cook, wrap bacon around edges of steaks and pin with toothpicks. Don't allow charcoal to burn down in grill because you need a hot fire. Add hickory chips soaked overnight in water. Place steaks on grill and cook quickly so venison won't dry out.

These next two recipes use ground venison and are tasty, meaning you can use all those "parts" that aren't cut right for steaks or chops instead of wasting them or making the same old chili and quiche recipes.

Venison Hash

1$^1\!/_2$ pounds ground venison	**1 large green pepper, diced**
2 cups tomatoes, cooked & peeled	**1$^1\!/_2$ tsps. chili powder**
1 red bell pepper, diced	**3 large onions, diced**
salt and pepper to taste	**$^1\!/_2$ cup nuts, chopped(opt.)**
2 chili peppers, chopped(opt.)	

Preheat oven to 350 degrees. In a large skillet, cook and stir venison, onion and bell peppers until meat is browned and vegetables are tender. Drain off liquid and add tomatoes. Add salt and pepper and options. Mix thoroughly and pour into a covered casserole and bake 1 hour. Stir once or twice while cooking.

Easy Venison Porcupines

1$^1\!/_2$ pounds ground venison	**1$^1\!/_2$ cups uncooked rice**
1 onion, minced	**garlic to taste**
$^1\!/_2$ cup mushrooms, minced	**2 cans tomato soup**

Combine all ingredients except soup, blending thoroughly. Shape into meatballs and place in a crockpot. Add two cans of tomato soup, but only one can water. Add any spices you like — Tabasco, etc. — and cover. Cook on low about 6 to 8 hours or all day while you are at work. A variation is to substitute a can of Cheddar cheese soup for one of the cans of tomato soup. You can serve this as a main dish or over noodles, spaghetti or rice.

This next recipe also uses ground venison, but is a little more fancy. You probably wouldn't serve this to a guy who counts, "One, two, Earnhardt!, four, five!" But he'd enjoy it even if he couldn't say it.

Venison Burgers with Châteaubriand Butter

2 pounds venison burger	**1 cup dry white wine**
1 tsp. tarragon	**$^1\!/_2$ cup parsley, freshly chopped**
2 sticks butter	**1 tsp. chervil**
3 shallots or 6 wild onions	**1 cup beef stock**
with tops, minced finely	**salt and pepper to taste**

In a small sauce pan, combine the wine, shallots or wild onions, and herbs and bring to a boil. Reduce the heat and simmer slowly until half the liquid is gone. Add stock and reduce to $^1\!/_2$ cup liquid.

Cool. Whip the butter, combining with the cooled wine and herb mixture. Use this to season the venison burger and form into a thick log. Freeze overnight in plastic wrap. Next day, slice into large patties and cook on the grill when thawed, topping each with a large pat of butter.

Tom Squier, Jr.'s Venison Jerky

2 pounds venison, chunks and strips	**mashed garlic cloves to taste**
vinegar	**juniper berries**
teriyaki sauce	**soy sauce**

Slice venison into strips about $1/4$-inch thick and $1^1/2$-inches wide. Make a marinade sauce from equal parts vinegar, soy and teriyaki sauces. Add juniper berries and garlic and some chili peppers or Tabasco sauce if you like it hot. Add your favorite spices — even maple sprinkles or syrup, rum or bourbon. Soak the venison overnight in the marinade in the refrigerator. Drain well and place, not touching, on a mesh of hardware cloth. This is the $1/4$-inch square-holed stuff used to make small animal cages. After the meat drains well, it is ready to be dried. This can be done by placing the screen on the middle rack in the oven and drying overnight or longer as required on very low heat — around 100 degrees — with the door cracked open to allow moisture to escape. If you have a fireplace or insert with a blower in it, you can make a rack by placing the hardware cloth on two bricks or rocks in front of where the hot air comes out. The moving hot air quickly dries the jerky. It is ready when totally dried out and crisp. You can add such things as hickory-smoke salt in liquid form or powder and barbecue powder to the meat after it is removed from the marinade or while still in it.

Girls like to hunt, too!

If venison is properly cared for at the time it is harvested, and then butchered and processed the way a meat-cutter would do it, it is better than any steroid and antibiotic beef you can buy anywhere. The rare fat that you find on venison congeals rather quickly when it cools. That is why it is important to serve venison hot. The meat will turn out exquisitely when used in your favorite recipes.

Venison lends itself well to slow cooking in a crockpot. It also turns out well if you cook it covered all day in a slow oven — about 250 degrees — basted with some of those mushroom, Mexican or other cooking sauces on the market now for beef and pork. You have to either cook it very hot and very fast or for a long while in low heat and covered to get the best results. One reader, Melinda Kemp, called to say that she enjoyed my columns and that she was looking for some tasty venison recipes. Seems a friend had hit a deer and the Toyota was totaled, but there was a lot of good venison left over. Maybe one of the recipes on these pages will work for her. Deer hunting has been an American tradition since B.C. times (Before Columbus), but there are other ways to get your venison besides shooting it.

Here is a perfect recipe for converting those people who say "I don't like venison." You aren't even required to tell them what is in this delicious dish. Wait 'til they beg for the recipe.

Deb Lowell and Frances Squier.

Debra Lowell's Venison Stew

3 pounds venison, cubed
$^{1}/_{2}$ cup olive oil
12-15 small onions
2 tbsps. brown sugar
$^{1}/_{2}$ pound mushrooms
2 tbsps. flour
1 faggot

Raw Marinade (recipe below)
1 cup diced fat salt pork
12-15 pared small carrots
1 garlic clove, crushed
snipped parsley
$^{2}/_{3}$ cup dry red wine

To make the "faggot," tie together: **2 stalks celery, 4 sprigs parsley, $^{1}/_{2}$ bay leaf, 1 sprig thyme.**

Raw Marinade

2 bay leaves
1 carrot, thinly sliced
$^{1}/_{4}$ tsp. dried thyme
2 stalks celery
2 whole cloves
$^{1}/_{2}$ cup olive oil

2 medium onions, sliced
2 shallots, minced
1 tsp. salt
12 whole peppercorns
2 cups dry red wine

Mix all marinade ingredients; pour over venison. Refrigerate 24 hours or longer. Remove meat from marinade; strain marinade and reserve. Dry meat with paper towels. In hot oil in skillet, brown salt pork and set aside. To skillet add onions. When onions begin to brown, add carrots; sprinkle with brown sugar and cook until vegetables are brown; set aside. Sauté mushrooms until brown all over and set aside. Brown meat all over; place in large saucepan or kettle. Sprinkle with flour and cook until flour browns. Add garlic, wine, faggot, marinade and water to cover. Simmer 1 hour or until tender. Add salt pork, onions, carrots, celery, mushrooms and cook 40 minutes.

Once I won a $100 grocery-shopping spree with a recipe for sweet-and-sour Spam! It seems to be a popular flavor. I used tomato wedges and pineapple chunks in my S&S Spam, but here is a fast and delicious way to make sweet-and-sour venison. It is from my friends John and Denise Phillips and is from their book, *Deer and Fixings.*

Sweet and Sour Venison à la Phillips

venison steaks or roast
1½ tsps. salt
2 tsps. mustard

6 tbsps. olive oil
1½ cups brown sugar
2 tbsps. vinegar

Brown meat in oil, place in Dutch oven or covered roaster. Combine remaining ingredients to make sauce. Layer steak with sauce, or if roasting, use sauce to cover roast and to baste. Bake at 400 degrees 20 minutes per pound.

Venison yield varies, but here's an estimate of how much freezer space you'll need.

From The Hoof To The Table

Successful whitetail hunters often face the question, "How much did it weigh on the hoof?"

Experts say the field-dressed weight is about 78 or 79 percent of live weight. So, a deer that weighs 120 pounds at the registration station or butcher shop probably weighed about 152 pounds live.

That same deer should yield about 58 percent, or in this case 70 pounds, of its field-dressed weight in boneless meat. Of course, the actual yield in the freezer will vary somewhat depending on shot placement and how much trimming is required in the butchering process.

Once venison reaches the table, hunters should be encouraged to know that it is very nutritional. A steak or chop has approximately 24 percent protein and only about 1.2 percent fat. An 8-ounce serving contains approximately 325 calories.

Courtesy of North American Hunter Magazine
and North American Hunting Club

What to Do With Those Leftovers?

I got a cookbook from my friends, John and Denise Phillips, titled *Deer and Fixings,* and I think it will make anyone a venison chef! The dictionary says that a chef is literally "the head of the kitchen." That could be anyone from the guy with the French name wearing one of those funny-looking hats that looks like the little cap they put on the end of a pheasant's leg in a fancy restaurant to my grandmother when she was alive. I would defy anyone to tell her that she wasn't "head of the kitchen!" To me, a chef is a cook who can produce delicious dishes consistently and from just about anything, including leftovers.

I called Denise Phillips to talk about this cookbook of theirs a little, because I liked some of the recipes a lot. We were lamenting the fact that neither the Squiers nor the Phillipses would be at the 1994 Southeastern Outdoor Press Association (SEOPA) convention. The Phillips family was already over-committed, and the Squiers were having lunch with Richard Petty. Sorry, SEOPA! See ya another year.

Leftovers can be among the hardest things to turn into something "new and exciting," but the first recipe Denise has in *Deer and Fixings* is for leftovers — cleverly disguised in the ingredient list as "accumulated bones and meat trimmings," "assorted cooked vegetables and pasta products," and "venison that has been precooked." I'm not picking *on* Denise — I'm picking *at* her!

It's a great recipe and you can adjust it to fit your own needs.

Denise Phillips' Venison Vegetable Soup

accumulated bones and meat
  trimmings
2 tsps. salt
2 large cans of tomatoes
1 onion, chopped
pound or more of ground
venison that has been pre-cooked
  with 1 chopped onion and 1 bell pepper

2 quarts water
$\frac{1}{2}$ cup vinegar
assorted cooked vegetables and pasta products
1 clove of garlic, minced
seasonings: celery salt, parsley and/or crushed
  1 red peppers, and freshly ground peppercorns

Cover large pot, and simmer the bones, water, salt and vinegar for a couple of hours, or cook 30 minutes in a pressure cooker. If the odor of vinegar can be detected at the end of this period, uncover the pot, and boil vigorously for a few minutes until vinegar has evaporated. Add all types of cooked vegetables and pasta. (I keep a freezer container in my refrigerator for leftover vegetables.) Add tomatoes to the soup mixture, and any other vegetables you may need to fill out the amount of leftovers. Add to simmering mixture the onions, garlic, pepper, 1 pound ground venison (precooked with onion and bell pepper) and seasonings. Simmer for 1 hour, and serve hot.

I think everybody has a recipe similar to that if they have done enough cooking to be called "head of the kitchen." I like to add some wild rice or barley to mine occasionally so I can call it "hearty" venison vegetable soup! Some folks like to throw in a little red wine for flavor as well, or some flour to make it a stew.

One of the biggest problems facing the world and the environment today is what to do with things we have used before. A plan to solve this problem involves the "three **R**s" of the environment, which are **R**educe, **R**e-use and **R**ecycle!

We can **R**educe waste and spending by not buying in quantities too large to use on the one hand or by co-op buying on the other. When several people buy together, the larger quantities are often much cheaper. If 10-pound turkeys are 90 cents a pound and 20-pound turkeys are 45 cents a pound, it is just smart money sense to buy the larger turkey for half the price per pound — if you can accommodate it. A 20-pound turkey sawed in half can either be baked in two neighbors' kitchens, or eaten half now and the other half frozen for later. The bad thing is that it saws the wish-bone in half!

Re-use the food. You don't even have to change the form. If you get a big turkey, for example, have one friend's family over for supper one night, and another family over the next night, and serve the same meal. The "leftovers" will be new to the second guest family, and many dishes taste better the second day anyhow. The meal is already planned and already cooked, so there is more time for visiting and talking the second or third time it is served. I know these are really leftovers, but it is a good plan if you like to entertain.

Recycling technically involves turning one product or residue from a product — the leftovers — into another. With food this means perhaps turning baked sweet potatoes into a pie, mashed potatoes into pancakes, sliced turkey and venison into any of hundreds of new dishes, and experimenting with leftovers. Although I like to snack on them cold, here is an idea for leftover sweet potatoes.

Sweet Potato Soup

1-2 large baked sweet potatoes	1 medium onion, minced
1 Irish potato, peeled & diced	1 large carrot, shredded
3 cups turkey or beef stock	$^1/_2$ tsp. pumpkin pie spice
$^1/_4$ cup celery, minced	1 cup cream or half-and-half
2 bay leaves	2 garlic cloves, crushed

Bring turkey stock to a boil and add carrot, onion, Irish potato, celery, bay leaves and garlic and simmer until vegetables are tender. Remove the bay leaf and discard it. Drain off juice and reserve it. Combine the half-and-half and one cup of stock in a blender or bowl and fold in the cooked vegetables and the sweet potatoes, peeled and mashed. Blend or mix well until smooth and return to pan, stirring in the remaining stock. Slowly heat to simmer and serve hot, sprinkling with the pumpkin pie spice. Garnish with parsley if desired.

Sweet Potato Pie

baked sweet potatoes	1 cup sugar
5 tbsps. butter	1 tsp. pumpkin pie spice or nutmeg
2 large eggs, beaten	1 cup buttermilk
1 unbaked pie crust	

Peel and mash the sweet potatoes to equal 2 cups. Beat until lumps are smoothed out and sift in sugar and nutmeg. Fold in butter, beaten eggs, and milk; beat or mix until well blended. Line pie pan with crust and fold in sweet potato mixture. Bake at 400 degrees for 50-60 minutes or until crust is done and top is slightly browned.

Murphy Brown told Frank Fontana that she was "fixing a traditional Thanksgiving dinner from the *Betty Crocker Cookbook*." There was no mention of "cacciatore" in it anywhere, but turkey lends itself well to cacciatore recipes since "cacciatore" is the Italian word for "hunter style."

Turkey Cacciatore

$^1/_2$ cup tomato sauce	4 cups cooked tomatoes
2 pounds turkey chunks, cooked	2 large onions, diced
3 garlic toes, minced	6 tbsps. butter
1$^1/_2$ cups turkey stock	$^1/_2$ cup dry white wine
salt and pepper	2 tsps. ground oregano
1 bay leaf	1 cup bell pepper, diced
chopped parsley	1 cup mushrooms, chopped
peanut oil	1 tsp. sugar

Sauté onion and garlic in butter for 5 minutes. Add tomatoes, stock, wine, spices, sugar and tomato sauce and bring to a boil. Simmer for 30 minutes. Heat oil and brown turkey chunks, lightly salted and peppered. Place half the sauce in a baking dish and lay the turkey in a layer. Sprinkle with bell pepper and mushrooms and top with the rest of the sauce. Bake at 375 degrees covered for 45 minutes. Garnish with parsley.

Mary Mihelic was kind enough to give me her first-prize-winning recipe for chili which used ground beef for the meat. The traditional Native American November dinner included venison. Leftover venison from Thanksgiving makes an excellent chili.

Mary Mihelic's (It's No Secret) Chili

1 large onion	$\frac{1}{2}$ pound chopped fresh venison
1 or 2 garlic cloves	2-3 tbsps. chili powder
1 tsp. cumin	cayenne pepper to taste
2 tbsps. oil	

Heat oil in a large cast-iron pot and add minced garlic and stir briefly. Add meat, onions, spices and brown. Then add:

2 cans Del Monte Mexican- style stewed tomatoes	2 cans green chilies, chopped
2 tomato cans of water	1 jar hot Old El Paso salsa
	beans of choice (opt.)

Simmer all day. Add a little more water if necessary or cover when chili reaches the desired consistency. Start early in the day or better yet — the day before. The longer it sits, the better the flavors blend. Mary doesn't put beans in her chili, but some people insist.

Mary is married to "Doc" Chuck Mihelic, another Green Beret surgeon I worked with at the 3rd Special Forces Group (Airborne), and a pretty good-natured guy — most of the time. He bought Mary some kind of a big, ugly bulldog which she said reminded her of me because he looked like me in the face. She named him Tom in my honor. That lasted about two days until Chuck got tired of hearing "Come here, Tom. Here, baby. Oh, you're such a good doggie, Tom. Blah blah blah!" You know how women talk to their pets. In a flash, Tom became "Sarge!"

Here are a couple more recipes from Mary with a Southwestern flavor. They're delicious! I've tried them. They go good with Wild Turkey and water. But, then, what doesn't!

Mary Mihelic's Venison Enchiladas

1 batch chili, above recipe	soft flour tortillas
chopped onion	shredded cheese

Lay tortillas on top of chili to soak a little juice up. Spoon chili onto center of tortilla and top with onion and cheese. Fold ends over and then roll the two sides over to close. Lay "flap" side down in a baking dish just touching and cover with extra chili mixture. Bake $\frac{1}{2}$ hour at 350 degrees.

Mary Mihelic's Venison Tamales

1 batch chili, above recipe, without beans	masa harina corn husks

Soak corn husks until pliable. Combine masa harina with water according to package instructions to make a thick paste. Masa harina is a very fine corn flour found in Mexican food sections of most large grocery stores. Spread paste thickly on each corn husk. Add 1 or 2 tbsps. beanless chili and roll up the sides. Then fold over the ends. Place in rows in a steamer basket or rice steamer, alternating the way the rows face in each layer. This lets the steam cook the tamales most thoroughly. Cover and steam 45 minutes to 1 hour or until the dough is cooked firm.

Frances Squier (left) and Mary Mihelic.

Mary's recipe is based on using fresh venison (or elk or moose, etc.), but you can use leftover meat of about any kind. If you are using shredded, cooked leftover venison, remember it doesn't take nearly as long in the simmering stage. But don't forget that chili, like spaghetti, is better the second day, after the flavors meld together.

Using leftovers is fun as well as challenging. If you have a large quantity of any type of leftovers, you can completely change the flavor and the mood by changing the spices you cook it with. Cut it in strips and use bell peppers, mushrooms and onions and you have a stir-fry. Shred it and use some barbecue sauce and you have great barbecue sandwiches. Cook the shredded meat in tomato sauce with oregano, garlic and basil and you have Italian-style spaghetti sauce. Substitute cumin and chili powder for Mexican-style. Use wine, shallots and garlic with parsley and provincial herbs to make it French-style and use rosemary and garlic with coriander seeds to make it Middle Eastern- or Mediterranean-style and just add lime juice and hot pepper sauce for a Caribbean flavor. Use pineapple chunks to make either Aloha Venison, or add some other ingredients like tomato sauce and wedges, vinegar and brown or cane sugar to make sweet-and-sour leftovers. The possibilities are endless.

Use leftover pumpkin or sweet potatoes to make breads, muffins and pies. Add leftover cranberries to muffins or substitute them for bananas in a banana bread recipe. Use leftover stuffing or dressing, depending on what you call it, to make stuffed pork chops or for stuffing smaller birds, squash — winter squash or zucchini. Top it with Parmesan cheese and tomato sauce before baking.

Here is one more way to use leftover venison that makes an excellent pie or sauce for meat or vegetables:

Venison Mincemeat

4 cups cooked venison, shredded	2 cups tart green apples, crabapples or pears
1 cup ground beef fat	2 cups brown raisins
3 cups mixed candied fruit and peels	2 cups golden raisins or currants
1 tbsp. cinnamon	1 tbsp. nutmeg
2 cups brown sugar	1½ tsps. salt
1 tsp. ground cloves	1 tsp. ground allspice
1 cup apple cider	1 cup apple juice

Shred venison very fine. Peel and chop apples, crab apples, crisp pears or a mixture of these fruits. Grind the suet (beef fat) fine and mix with the venison and apple. Chop the candied fruits and peels. Combine all the ingredients in a large kettle and mix thoroughly. Bring to a boil, cover and simmer 30 minutes, stirring occasionally. Bake in pies immediately or pack into sterilized jars and seal. Process in hot water bath for 20-30 minutes.

Having trouble getting the kids to eat leftovers or even new venison or other game meats? Here's a surefire trick. Shred it or cut in small cubes or rings and use it as a pizza topping!

The Wonders of Winter's Wild Foods

Teaching survival made it apparent that even many instructors think that wintertime survival basically equates to "starvation survival." That is not necessarily true. Even with below-freezing temperatures and layers of ice and snow, we can find something in Mother Nature's larder. Here are some recipes that have made me a success in the kitchen in the middle of winter.

No matter how cold it gets, we can see the blue-green hues of wild onions in our fields and yards. Our trees may be bare except for the pines, hollies, bays and magnolias. There are plenty of bare twigs out there, but our wild onions are really growing strong. They do their resting during the hot months of summer when the trees are full of leaves.

Wild Onion Soup

2 cups wild onion bulbs	8 cups chicken stock
1 tsp. sugar	1 cup wild onion tops, chopped
1 tsp. salt	$^1/_4$ tsp. cooking sherry

Brown half the onion bulbs in a little butter or bacon grease. Add the salt and sugar and the chicken stock and bring to a boil. Add the rest of the onion bulbs and the chopped onion tops. Simmer about 30 minutes or until the onions are tender and add the sherry and some croutons if you like.

The tops of the onions can be chopped and added to cream cheese or sour cream for a dip for vegetables or chips. The small size of the wild onion bulbs makes them perfect for cooking game or other meat that goes well with a garlic or onion accent, such as lamb and pork. Just peel the little onion bulbs, make slits in the meat and insert the bulbs.

The common name of "green stick" makes it easy to find sassafras trees in winter, and it makes an excellent and tasty tea. Also, every time there is a warm spell, we find more oyster mushrooms growing from the trunks of dead hardwood trees. In winter, food is where you find it. Of course, there are always road kills to be cherished and used wisely, but you just never know what else you will encounter.

On the morning of January 8, 1995, I received a phone call from a neighbor named Junior Crouch. Junior is the caretaker of a tract of land known locally as the "Blue Farm." It is on the maps on Blue Farm Road, but everyone around here calls it Rattlesnake Road because so many of those snakes have been captured there. This had been a weird January. On the night of the 6th, it got down to 12 degrees in the country and my pond was frozen in the morning. The next night, the 7th, it got up to 66 degrees and there were thunder storms all night long. In the next day's news we found out there were also tornadoes that night, blowing over trees and wreaking havoc. Junior called to say that he had killed a rattlesnake that night and it was still wiggling the next morning — with no head and no rattles! It is now in my freezer, but will soon be eaten.

It is hard to ignore our pine trees in winter as the needles are falling at their greatest rate and being raked (or "roke," depending on who you talk to) enthusiastically. They make good mulch when brown, but the green needles make a surprisingly good tea which can be used medicinally. Chopped and steeped green pine needles release a great amount of vitamin C and a pleasant flavor. Boiling the needles in a covered pan a few minutes will diminish the vitamin C content, but releases an oil that serves as an expectorant to help break up and get rid of chest congestion. The tea makes a good base for jelly, too. It was such a great hit at Christmas time that we decided to call it:

Christmas Tree Jelly

1 gallon green pine needles, chopped	6 quarts water
8 cups sugar	1 tsp. lemon juice
2 packages fruit pectin	

Chop the needles well and remove the brown sheaths that hold the needles together. Cover with water and bring to a boil. Reduce the heat and simmer for half an hour. Let stand overnight and bring to a boil again. Strain and simmer to reduce to 6 cups liquid. Add the sugar all at once and stir well to prevent burning. Bring to a full boil once again and hold for at least 1 minute until jelly reaches 225 degrees or "sheets" easily from spoon. Pour into hot sterilized jars and seal. After sitting all night the tea may have a cloudy appearance, but this will disappear and the jelly will be a nice golden color and will taste fruity, not piney.

When I was a young weed-eater many years ago, the winter was a favorite time of mine because I could make maple-flavored popsicles in the yard. The sap is moving a little in the trees as the temperatures fall to the 20s at night after a warm day. We used to cut off the end of a maple branch and usually there would be a frozen icicle hanging there in the morning.

As New Year's rolls around and ends the deer season, it means there is a month of squirrel season left, and the bushy tails are doing their best not to be seen until February gets here. Some of us already have a mess of squirrels in the freezer and may be tired of fried squirrel.

Frances got herself into *America's Favorite Wild Game Recipes* from the Hunting and Fishing Library with:

Squirrel Pot Pie

Filling

2^1/$_2$ cups cubed cooked squirrel or substitute	2 cups red potatoes, cubed & peeled
1 10¾-ounce can condensed cream of mushroom soup	1^1/$_2$ cups frozen peas and carrots
^{1}/$_2$ cup squirrel or chicken	^{1}/$_2$ cup celery, thinly sliced
^{1}/$_4$ tsp. ground black pepper	^{1}/$_2$ cup onion, chopped
	^{1}/$_2$ tsp. instant chicken broth bouillon granules

Crust

^{3}/$_4$ cup all-purpose flour	1 tsp. baking powder
^{1}/$_4$ tsp. salt	^{3}/$_4$ cup milk
^{1}/$_2$ cup butter, melted	

Heat oven to 375 degrees. Spray 8-inch square baking dish with nonstick vegetable cooking spray. Set aside. In 12-inch nonstick skillet, combine filling ingredients. Bring to a boil over medium-high heat. Remove from heat. Spoon filling evenly into prepared dish. Set aside. In medium mixing bowl, combine flour, baking powder and salt. Add milk and butter. Stir with fork just until dry ingredients are moistened. Spoon batter evenly over filling, spreading to edges. Bake for 30 to 35 minutes, or until crust is golden brown.

In winter, especially around the end of January, you can get a lot of squirrels on the way to the post office or the store. That's when their first mating season of the year begins. When squirrels are chasing each other with sex on the brain they don't stop to look for traffic, and sometimes you will find three or four in a single block that should have looked both ways before crossing the road! When you get tired of fried squirrel, try this next recipe which made me a big hit with my mother-in-law, Delphia Whisnant.

Squirrel and Dumplings

2 squirrels, cut in pieces
salt and pepper
4 tsps. baking powder
2¹/₂ cups flour

1 cup celery, chopped
2 cups each, potatoes, onion and carrots, chopped
³/₄ cup milk

Cut up squirrels in small pieces and roll in flour seasoned with salt and pepper. Brown in bacon grease and drain. Put squirrel in a cooking pot with vegetables and enough water to cover well. Add salt and pepper to taste. Simmer for an hour or until squirrel and vegetables are tender. Add 2 more cups water to the pot. Make the dumplings. Combine 2 cups flour, ½ tsp. salt, baking powder and milk, stirring milk in a little at a time. Roll dough onto a floured board and cut into 1-inch squares. Thicken gravy in pot by mixing remaining flour with cold water until lumps are gone and stirring into pot. Drop dumplings into the simmering stew one at a time and cook uncovered for 10 minutes. Reduce heat to a slow simmer, cover and cook for 10 more minutes.

A lot of people use flour or cornstarch to thicken stews and dumpling dishes, but put it in too soon. The flour should be added near the end because if you put it in too soon, there is a tendency for burning and sticking to the bottom of the pot.

Even when it is very cold where I live there are still lots of wild things to eat. Those pesky prickly pear cactus pads can be de-thorned and made into a throat-soothing boiled vegetable like okra. Good sources of vitamin C are the berries, actually fruits, on staghorn and other non-poisonous sumacs. Don't boil the stems or your "wild lemonade" will taste like corn starch!

Where they grow, which is in much of the country, the Jerusalem artichokes provide tasty tubers through the winter, and the persistent dandelion greens are sweet in the winter when a warm spell makes them bolt.

Jerusalem Artichoke Chips

2 quarts Jerusalem artichoke roots
salt

peanut or sunflower oil

It's not necessary, but you might want to peel the Jerusalem artichoke roots. Slice very thinly and blot dry. Heat the oil until it just begins to smoke, but don't overdo it. Fry the chips in the hot oil until golden brown. That means about 30 seconds per side, if you don't over-crowd them in the pan. Remove from oil with a slotted strainer and drop into a brown paper bag. Sprinkle with salt and shake well.

If you like sunflowers, which is what Jerusalem artichokes are, and enjoy good eating, you need to start you a little patch. It will soon be a big patch, so don't plant them where you need worry about them crowding other things. You can get starter roots from the wild if you know where they grow, from many seed catalogs, and from the grocery store where they are often sold as "Sunchokes." I've often found them reduced-for-quick-sale because they sprouted in the package. These are the best ones for planting.

Scalloped Jerusalem Artichokes

2 quarts Jerusalem artichokes
¹/₂ cup whipping cream
3 tbsps. butter
¹/₂ tsp. nutmeg, grated

1 large baking potato
salt and pepper to taste
³/₄ cup Parmesan or Cheddar cheese, shredded

Slice artichokes and peeled potato and cover with lightly-salted water. Bring to a boil and simmer over reduced heat for 5 or 6 minutes. Drain and place in a baking dish, mixing in the butter, cream and cheese and adding salt and pepper to taste. Sprinkle with nutmeg and bake at 400 degrees for 20 minutes or until the top begins to brown. Serve immediately.

This isn't really a wild-food recipe, but it's one that goes very well in winter and was almost a family heirloom as we had it so often growing up. It will warm you up on the coldest days. For winter activities it can be made ahead of time and carried in a thermos into the woods or out to fishing holes. For overnight trips it can be taken along without taking up much space. Cut up the onions and potatoes and put them in zip-lock bags and take the corned beef out of the can and put it in a zip-lock bag. Some times it is hard to get those cans open with half-frozen fingers! Takes up less space this way, weighs less and there is no can to pack out!

Corned Beef Winter Soup

2 cans corned beef	**6-8 large white potatoes**
2-4 onions	**1-2 turnips (opt.)**

Mash the corned beef into chunks and place in a kettle or pot that will hold about 2 gallons of soup. Add a quart or two of water to cover and bring to a boil. Dice the onions, potatoes and turnips and add the soup. Simmer until the vegetables are tender, adding water as necessary and for the desired thickness of soup. Don't add salt. That comes from the corned beef.

Here is another winter remedy and recipe combination I really like. It comes from Debra Stark, owner and operator of the Natural Gourmet restaurant in Concord, Massachusetts, and first appeared in her cookbook, *Round-The-World Cooking At The Natural Gourmet*. She told me I can use it in an herbal medicine book I am writing, but I wanted to share it here, too. I like it a lot. I use honey as a sweetner and meat glaze a lot, and cayenne pepper and horseradish are two of my favorite spices and herbal medicines as well. I'll give you Debra's Famous Cold Remedy as it appears in her book, but first let me add that I have discovered that adding a little bourbon and going to bed well wrapped-up will knock a cold out of you just about as well as going into a sweat lodge!

Debra's Famous Cold Remedy

This remedy works! My son, Adam, says I used to torture him with it when he was too little to appreciate its effectiveness. My brother, Daniel, took it on a bike trip to Nova Scotia and said it saved his vacation. If your throat hurts too much to swallow, this will act like balm.

1 cup raw honey	**1-2 tbsps. prepared horseradish**
1-2 tbsps. cayenne pepper	

Place honey in a glass jar. Add pepper and horseradish. Stir until liquidy.

Store cold remedy in the refrigerator until you feel something coming on or have a sore throat. When you use this remedy, take $1/16$ teaspoon dose or just a tiny dot. True, you will feel the heat and may think you are dying, but the honey will coat the throat, the red pepper will warm it and stop the hurt. We all know that horseradish opens blocked passages. Cayenne pepper is rich in vitamin C, higher even than orange juice.

Take remedy as needed.

So, stop laughing and mix some up today while you're feeling healthy. When you're sick, you won't feel like doing anything.

Hunters Defeat Communism

That title, "Hunters Defeat Communism," is an example of how selective reporting can make people see the news from the writer's point of view. Actually, two well-known hunters are credited with helping to bring democracy to parts of Eastern Europe. Ronald Reagan and George Bush are two well-known hunters, but this has little to do with their efforts at bringing democracy to the Eastern Bloc nations. Crediting these two hunters for the success of the freedom movement in Eastern Europe would be accurate, but it would be illogical according to the thinking of the National Shooting Sports Foundation (NSSF).

The NSSF is concerned about newspaper accounts that mislead people in another direction. An example they present involves a Connecticut woman who circulated a letter to a number of New England papers stating that she was almost killed by a "hunter" while walking her dog. It was not hunting season and the person who did the shooting was in an area he had no permission to be in. Press releases prepared in response to the letter suggest that the alleged offender might more correctly be referred to as a trespasser or poacher. He was definitely not a hunter!

Jessica and Tom Squier hunting doves.

As misleading as saying that "two hunters brought democracy to Eastern Europe" is the misuse of the term "hunter" by the largely anti-gun media in referring to individuals with no affiliation to any hunting sport. A prime example occurred a few years ago when a criminal killed a bear in its cage in New York. The papers screamed "Hunter Shoots Bear In Zoo!" There are some hunters living in New York City to be sure, but they have to leave the city to enjoy their sport. There are many more people in New York City who (illegally) have guns than there are hunters. So let's get our terms straight. Regardless of how you feel about the sport personally, "hunters" are those men and women who legally purchase their guns or bows, buy licenses and are subject to obey the hunting regulations which legislators and biologists adjust every year to protect the wildlife population as well as to ensure a suitable harvest of those animals. In this way, populations remain stable and healthy. Those criminals who shoot animals out of season, using spotlights, or kill more than they are permitted to are purely and simply game thieves, "poachers," as we refer to them, and frequently are trespassers and guilty of other crimes as well.

Legitimate hunters are just as anxious to see poachers arrested and punished as are anti-hunters. When protesters and demonstrators smash windshields (and heads) with baseball bats, the headlines call them "rioters" and not "baseball players." Imagine the outrage we'd have here in the golf capital of the world where I live if we labeled the rioters as "golfers" because they smashed windows with a 9-iron! Let's give the shooting sports the same consideration and not refer to criminals as "hunters" simply because they have guns.

Webster's Dictionary's official written definition of a hunter is a "person who hunts game." Most hunters have an unwritten definition of their own that includes ethics, responsibility, safety and respect. A hunter pursues game only during the hunting season. Those who do otherwise are poachers. Hunters are authorized to hunt by their licenses. Those shooters without licenses are outlaws — poachers. Hunters only hunt when and where they have permission to do so. Everyone else is a trespasser or a game thief or both.

According to the NSSF, it was the hunter who first demanded laws restricting the taking of game, and it is the hunter who finances the conservation efforts which guarantee wildlife for future generations. The NSSF says that hunters have contributed over $7 BILLION toward wildlife conservation (benefiting all wildlife, not just game species) through excise taxes, license fees and permits, and continue to spend some $250 million annually to develop wildlife habitats on private land. The Wildlife Management Institute credits hunters' efforts with restoring the whitetail deer populations from near-extinction levels of only about 500,000 nationwide to over 12 million today. In fact, they have been restored to some places where they were totally extinct and are even pests in some places where they have thrived beyond expectations, thanks to hunters and other conservationists. No thanks to poachers and trespassers.

To learn more about the hunter as a protector of wildlife, write to the NSSF at Flint Ridge Office Center, 11 Mile High Road, Newtown, CT 06470-2359, and ask for their free booklet, *The Hunter and Conservation.*

The NSSF has launched a national campaign of education that is available to teachers at all grade levels. The three-part program consists of "Wildlife for Tomorrow" for elementary school levels, "The Un-Endangered Species" for grades 4-7 but also suitable for high-school students, and "What They Say About Hunting," which is especially suitable for high-schoolers. The programs are available free to educators who agree to have them filed in their school's audio-visual resource center or library. Contact the NSSF at the above address for more information. NSSF President Bob Delfay says, "Almost without exception, educators are rating the program extremely high and using it extensively." Environmental-science teachers rate it "very effective in increasing knowledge about wildlife."

Poachers are considered criminals in this state, and penalties are heavy. In response to citizens' complaints, a task force of wildlife enforcement officers (game wardens) captured several night hunters and confiscated their guns and vehicles. These items are sold at auction or destroyed, in the case of illegal firearms. The poachers receive fines, jail sentences or both and the loss of their hunting privileges when they go to court.

The North Carolina Wildlife Commission encourages the reporting of wildlife-law violations. Those making the reports are protected by anonymity, and a toll-free line is provided. When you see a poacher, trespasser with a gun or other criminal violating the wildlife laws in North Carolina, call 1-800-662-7137. Nearly every state has a toll-free number for this, and it is usually found in your state's regulation digest.

I don't believe in hunting just to put a trophy on the wall, but many of my friends and acquaintances "live off the land" part of the year and put food on the table by hunting. Let's not associate or confuse these ethical hunters with lawbreakers with guns. Poachers are not hunters!

Giving game can be a gesture of thanks, but be sure to know the regulations regarding such gifts.

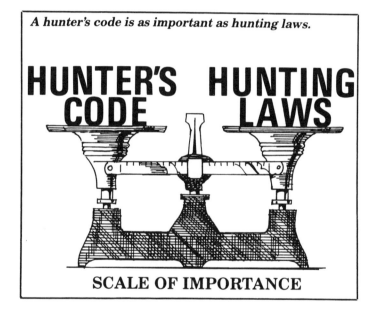

A hunter's code is as important as hunting laws.

HUNTER'S CODE

HUNTING LAWS

SCALE OF IMPORTANCE

You Ain't Really Gonna Eat That, Are You?

One of the questions I get asked most often is: "You ain't really gonna eat that, are you?" When I teach weed walks at herb or wild-foods conventions, I always eat the weeds I talk about to show that they won't hurt you. At the Army's Survival, Evasion, Resistance, Escape School, or SERE, which is often called the P.O.W. School, I ate insects and earthworms to show that they might save the life of some "high risk" Special Operations soldier or "State Department" official or operative under the right circumstances.

What's the big deal? I saved a story from *People* magazine about Lauren Hutton eating grub worms and beetle larvae in Africa. In West Virginia, a wild-foods group inspired by Euell Gibbons adds earthworms to cake mix and sells lots of T-shirts that read, "I Ate The Worm Cake at North Bend," which is the name of the state park where the Euell Gibbons Nature Trail is located. It has a picture of what looks like a birthday cake with little smiley-faced worms coming out of it. I kept the worms I used in class for a few days on wet paper towels "to clean them out," and they were like skinny, wiggling hot dogs, except much better for you!

I also try to practice a "waste-not, want-not" kind of philosophy and lifestyle, so when I am cleaning deer at Joe Carpenter's Hunt Club, I save the parts most hunters discard — the liver and heart, the brains and even the tongue and testicles. Most people know the testicles as "mountain oysters," and depending on where your hotdogs are made, you might be eating them as "beef parts" or "pork parts!" They are considered an aphrodisiac in many cultures. Mountain oysters certainly won't hurt you. Reba McEntire confesses in her autobiography that she "practically grew up on mountain oysters," and you can see how good she turned out!

Basic Mountain Oysters

bull, boar or deer testicles	salt and pepper to taste
paprika	flour
butter	garlic salt optional

Clean the mountain oysters by removing the membrane which covers them. In case you care, this is called the "tunic." Rinse and slice into 1/4 inch rounds — medallions. Dust with flour which has been seasoned with salt, pepper and paprika. Fry in hot butter until golden brown.

You can also dice them and fry them with potato cubes. Some people like to season them with some spices and herbs such as tarragon, chervil or parsley.

On a deer, which is where venison comes from for those of you who don't know, the testicles are often larger than the brain. A lot of women say that this is also true in humans! At any rate, deer do have a very small quantity of brain matter, and it takes a couple of them to make a meal. You shouldn't be appalled. There are still restaurants that feature "brains and eggs" at hog-killing time, and Winn Dixie and other chain grocery stores offer them for sale, either fresh, frozen or canned in a milk gravy. Yankees often eat them without realizing it in a meat blend called "scrapple," which is pretty close to our "liver pudding."

Let me tell you what Jeff Eberbaugh has to say about mountain oysters in his *Road Kill Cooking, Volume II*. Of course, you realize this is purely satire!

Rocky Mountain Road Kill Oysters

Cut some oysters from a beef or a big bull moose
Or a white tail buck or a longneck goose
Any male road kill would do just fine
Get your oysters where you want, just don't bother mine
They're packed two in a bag and the meat's real sweet
Rocky mountain oysters are good to eat
Take em home and slice em and roll em in some flour
Add some garlic salt and pepper and fry em for an hour
The only way to serve em is hot from the grease
You should give your wife some and your kids a little piece
To give your wife some would be a wise choice
Or you could wake up with a high pitched voice.

It is weird because a big animal like a deer has such small brains, but each warm-blooded animal has enough tannic acid in its own brain to tan its hide. By contrast, hogs have a very large brain.

Brains and Eggs

¹/₄ cup onion, minced	**butter**
venison or other brains	**eggs, beaten**

Prepare the brains by soaking them in ice water for 3-4 hours, then removing membranes and clots. Drain well. Sauté the onion in butter and begin stirring the brains into the hot butter, stirring briskly. If you don't add anything else, they will firm up much like scrambled eggs, except a different color. At this point, either fold in the beaten eggs and continue cooking to scramble the eggs until done, or cook them separately and serve together. A lot of folks like to fix gravy in the pan to serve over the brains or brains and eggs.

Venison Tongue

1-2 venison tongues	**²/₃ cup salt**
¹/₃ cup brown sugar	**¹/₄ tsp. ground pepper**

Combine salt, pepper and brown sugar and rub thoroughly into tongue. Place in airtight container and store in refrigerator for 3 days. Turn daily. On the fourth day, remove tongue and rinse very well. Boil in water to cover about 2 hours or until tender. Cool 10 minutes and peel skin from tongue. Cool and slice. This is so good you can convince your guests it is expensive, imported lamb's tongue. Just drop a few hints or suggestions and don't out-and-out lie about it.

It is also amazing how many hunters throw away the liver and heart. Both are great grilled. Liver can be fixed in traditional ways with onions, chicken with no legs and wings or can be sliced into rings and fried. It is also very good cubed and used in a chili recipe.

Corned Venison Heart

1 heart, deer, elk or antelope	**water**
¹/₄ cup sugar	**3 tbsps. pickling spices**
¹/₂ cup apple cider vinegar	**1-2 beef bouillon cubes**

The bouillon cube provides the salt, so don't add any extra. Remove any fat and clots from heart, cleaning well. Place in a large pot, cover with water and add remaining ingredients. Cover, reduce heat and simmer 2 hours or until tender. Skim the surface as needed and add water when necessary. Slice thinly and serve hot or cold as main meat or in sandwiches.

Venison liver quickly turns gray when it is exposed to air, so don't let that put you off. It is tasty and nutritious. Just like beef liver, you want to make sure you don't overcook it.

Grilled Venison Liver

venison liver   **garlic salt**
Dale's Steak Seasoning Sauce

You can now find Dale's sauce in the grocery stores. It contains soy sauce, onion, garlic, ginger and paprika. If you can't find it, mix up your own. Get the charcoal grill ready so coals will be white when you start cooking. Slice cleaned liver into manageable pieces and soak in Dale's sauce or your own marinade while charcoal gets right. Drain and place on grill, cooking 4-6 minutes per side, being careful not to overcook.

Here's a good Scottish haggis recipe from Les Wilson.

Scottish Haggis
(White Tail)

1 deer paunch (stomach)   1 cup venison stock
1 deer heart   4 ounces beef fat
1 deer liver $^1/_2$ tsp. of the following spices: salt, black pepper,
1 set deer lungs   ground cloves, nutmeg, mustard, celery, thyme
1 set deer kidneys   basil, cayenne pepper, rosemary
1 lb. oatmeal   3 bay leaves
1 lb. onions $^1/_4$ cup Scotch whiskey
2 lb. venison stew meat, or hamburger

Empty and clean paunch. Boil and scrape out inside with dull knife. Paunch should now be much lighter color. Soak in salt water. Bring to boil heart, liver, lungs and kidneys in water and bay leaves. Simmer 1 hour. Roast oatmeal in oven, spread in a cake pan. Use food processor to chop up innards, beef fat, meat chunks and onions. Mix in stock, spices, Scotch and oatmeal. Put blended mixture into the drained paunch, leaving expansion space, and sew it closed. Prick with needle to prevent explosion. Boil in large pot for 1 to 2 hours, keeping enough water added at all times to cover paunch. Extra haggis can be baked in a covered bowl. Put bowl in pan of water and leave in oven at 350 degrees for 2 hours. Serve with a stiff Scotch drink. Serves eight hungry Scots.

This one is not for those faint of heart. Don't knock put this one until you have given it a try. Scotch whiskey goes well with this.

As hunting season approaches, many hunters will be looking for new recipes for previously uneaten cuts of meat. With our president begging for money to pay legal fees, a lot of us might stop asking, "You ain't really gonna eat that, are you?" and switch to a more polite, "Say, are you gonna eat that?"

At the beginning of this chapter, I mentioned eating earthworms and insects at the S.E.R.E. school. It wasn't so bad. To get the earthworms ready, I'd simply put them in a vegetable crisper on wet paper towels for three or four days to clean them out. Then with all the sand and grit out of them, they were like skinny hotdogs without all the preservatives!

Insects are a different matter. You have to be careful with them. Avoid any with strange smells, stingers, and pincers. As I mentioned before, Lauren Hutton once had her picture in a magazine eating beetle grubs in Africa. "After the first four or so, they started to taste like Brazil nuts," she said. You just get them out on a stick and toast them over a fire. They taste a lot like melted vanilla ice cream. They contain a lot of fat and make good winter survival food when you encounter them hiding deep in rotting logs. Be careful with them alive, though, because they have big pincers which you have to pop off. A friend of mine once swallowed one whole and it latched onto his throat about half way down. We finally dislodged it after a lot of pain when he swallowed half slices of bread to make it relax its grip. Took about a dozen slices. Insects are typically about 80% protein — about four times as much as our traditional meats.

There is a traditional Cherokee recipe that calls for making soup from the harmless larvae of yellow jackets which are found deep in the ground. Skunks and raccoons dig them out and eat them all the time.

Yellowjacket Soup

yellowjacket larvae
water

salt
bacon drippings

Gather the yellowjacket larvae on a cold or wet morning when the adults can't fly, or spray the nest with a CO₂ fire extinguisher like the ones college students use to cool down beer in an emergency. Toast the larvae in an open pan and then add boiling water seasoned with salt and drippings. Add vegetables if you like.

A lot of wild-food groups are serving insects, and cicadas frequently get chosen because they can often be collected in large numbers. You can use other insects like the soft, white crickets that are sold for bait. Remove the legs with the spurs on them. Go easy at first when eating insects. Some people have reported hallucinations. It may just be nerves, but you could get "swimmy-headed."

Cicada Tempura

cicadas
chopped fresh parsley
1 beaten egg

milk
flour
salt and pepper to taste

Kill the cicadas humanely by freezing them. Combine beaten egg and milk. Dip cicadas in this mixture and roll in flour seasoned with parsley, salt and pepper. Fry in hot oil until golden brown.

Cicadas are also good marinated overnight in teriyaki sauce and then added to stir-frys or browned in butter and garlic or even chopped and added to omelets with other ingredients. Cicadas are what we used to call "holler bugs" as children, because of the noise they make. Some people refer to them as 17-year locusts. Eating insects is no big deal. The Department of Agriculture allows a specified quantity of insects and insect parts in flour and prepared baked goods. Did you like them? Rich people delight in eating chocolate-covered ants. Ants, when added to food (on purpose or not), mysteriously add both a sugar and a salt flavor. There are lots of folks who don't think twice about sucking the "worm" out of a tequila bottle. That "worm" is actually (if it is the legitimate one and not a meal worm for commercial purposes) the larvae of a moth that feeds on the blue agave cactus and proves the tequila or mescal was made from the plant it was supposed to be. There is even a club for "Worm Eaters." Write the Monte Alban Golden Worm Club, PO Box 3994, Chicago, IL 60690 for an application or more information.

Food prejudices caused a lot of suffering among G.I.s in Vietnam, and they keep a lot of people from enjoying some delicious as well as nutritious dishes. During the time of the Seoul Olympics, Americans and Brits were appalled to find butcher shops near the stadium selling dogs and cats for consumption. An article by Susan Moffett appeared in *The New York Times* in which she interviewed an enterprising merchant named Lee Kyung Sam who was trying to stave off bad publicity by selling snails which the Americans and Europeans would readily eat. Not so the Koreans. "I think that Korea is the first country at this economic level to eat snails," Lee said. "It is in advanced countries that people eat snails." He conceded that "most Koreans' stomachs turn when they think of eating snails." His strategy was to call them not "talpenji" which means snail, but "wau," which is more akin to escargot.

At the Chungang Market, dogmeat merchant Huh Young Soo was more open-minded than most Koreans about eating snails. He said, "I have never heard of eating snails before, but if they taste good, why not?" That is the attitude of my brother-in-law Charles Crisp when he comes to visit. He says he doesn't really want to know what is in the pot. "As long as it smells good, I just eat it and don't ask any questions!"

The author's brother-in-law, Charles Crisp.

Wild Game Cookery From the "Sod Father"

When North Carolinians call Jim Graham the "Sod Father," they say it with love and admiration. Jim Graham, of course, is the Commissioner of Agriculture — has been for eight terms — and is probably the most outstanding challenge to the currently popular political maxim: "Don't re-elect anybody!" Commissioner Graham told me that he had wanted to hold that position since his father took him to see the Commissioner of Agriculture as a young child. Under his leadership, the Department of Agriculture is the only portion of state government that pays for itself, largely due to the

The Sod Father

success of the State Fair. Our State Fair is looked upon across the nation as a model of excellence. It promotes our agricultural heritage as well as providing young people a chance to show off their farming skills. It also represents one of the best entertainment values around. Each night of the fair, you can see a top-name entertainer in addition to all the other attractions as part of the admission price.

Commissioner Graham has long supported our sportsmen (and women), being a hunter and fisherman himself. He has kindly shared with me some of his favorite wild game recipes, and with hunting season rapidly approaching, you will want to clip and save these. Commissioner Graham says, "For many years, hunting of wild game has been a sport enjoyed across our great state. The problems came with what to do with the game after it was caught and butchered. Recipes are available in two categories: the gourmet, which is complicated both in locating ingredients and the procedure; and the generally vague instructions handed down from one hunter to another. The purpose of these recipes is to assist the people of our great state in utilizing wild game and increasing consumption of Tar Heel foods such as sweet potatoes, pickles and corn bread." All of these go well with any game dish or might even be among the ingredients.

Bear Roast

1 3- to 4-pound young bear roast	$^1/_4$ cup cooking oil
$^1/_3$ cup vinegar	$^1/_3$ cup water
2 tbsps. sugar	2 tsps. dry mustard
1/4 tsps. pepper	2 tsps. salt
1 garlic clove	1 onion, minced
2 bay leaves	1 tbsp. lemon juice
$^1/_2$ tsp. chili powder	$^1/_2$ tsp. cayenne pepper
$^1/_2$ cup catsup	$^1/_4$ cup soy sauce

Place roast in a skillet and add cooking oil. Braise roast on all sides using high heat. Add remaining ingredients and simmer the ingredients for 30 minutes. Place roast in an open pan, add sauce and cook for 3 to 4 hours at 350 degrees. Baste often. Roast should be served well done. Yields: 6 to 8 servings.

Catfish Gumbo

1 pound catfish cut into cubes
$^1/_2$ cup onion, chopped
$^1/_4$ cup butter
2 cups water
1 package frozen okra
1 tsp. cayenne pepper
2 bay leaves

$^1/_2$ cup celery, chopped
$^1/_2$ cup green pepper, chopped
2 beef bouillon cubes
1 can tomatoes
2 tsps. salt
$^1/_4$ tsp. thyme
1 tsp. parsley
2 cups cooked rice

Sauté celery, onion, and green peppers in butter until tender. Add bouillon cubes, water, tomatoes, okra and spices. Cook for approximately 30 minutes. Add catfish and rice and simmer 15 minutes or until fish is tender. Yields: 6 to 8 servings.

Catfish Steaks

2 pounds catfish steaks
$^1/_4$ tsp. white pepper
$1^1/_2$ tbsps. grated onion
$^1/_4$ cup butter

1 tsp. salt
$1^1/_2$ cups cooked rice
$^1/_2$ tsp. curry powder
1 lemon, sliced

Sprinkle steaks lightly with salt and pepper and place in a well-greased oven cooking dish. Mix rice, onion and curry powder well and pour over steaks. Dot with butter and lemon. Bake at 350 degrees for 25 to 30 minutes or until flaky-tender. Yields: 4 to 6 servings.

Southern Fried Catfish

4 skinned catfish
1 tsp. salt
1 cup cornmeal
1 tsp. paprika

8 bacon slices
$^1/_4$ tsp. white pepper
1 tbsp. flour
$^1/_2$ cup milk

Fry bacon until crisp and remove from pan. Mix salt, white pepper, cornmeal, flour and paprika. Dip catfish in milk and dredge in cornmeal mixture. Pan-fry fish in hot bacon fat for 4 to 5 minutes. Drain on paper towel. Garnish with bacon, lemon and tomato wedges.

Catfish Jubilee

2 pounds catfish fillet
$^1/_4$ tsp. white pepper
2 tbsps. lemon juice
3 tbsps. butter
1 lemon sliced

1 tsp. salt
$^3/_4$ cup green onions & tops, sliced
$^1/_2$ cup catsup
2 tbsps. white wine (opt.)

Cut fillets into serving pieces and place into a large oven baking dish. Season fish with salt and pepper. Combine remaining ingredients, pour over catfish and top with lemon slices. Yields: 4 to 6 servings.

Pan Braised Doves

6 doves
$^1/_2$ cup flour
$^1/_4$ tsp. pepper
$^2/_3$ cup water

$^1/_2$ cup milk
1 tsp. salt
$^1/_3$ cup shortening

Have doves picked, drawn and split open. Dip birds in milk and dredge in flour, mixed with salt and pepper. Heat shortening to about 350 degrees, place birds in frypan and cook until golden brown. Remove and drain on paper towel. Remove excess shortening. Add water and return birds to frypan. Simmer for 1 hour. Yields: 3 to 6 servings.

Dove Roast

8 doves
2 tsps. salt
$^1/_2$ tsp. pepper
$^1/_3$ cup green onion, chopped
$^1/_2$ cup sherry (opt.)

$^1/_2$ cup flour
$^1/_2$ tsp. salt
$^1/_2$ cup cooking oil
1 cup water

Split doves and dredge in flour, salt and pepper mixture. Heat cooking oil to 350 degrees and braise doves lightly. Place doves' excess cooking oil in roasting pan with cover and add chopped onion and water. Put in a 350 degree oven for 45 minutes or until tender. Baste often and add sherry during final minutes of cooking. Add parsley as a garnish. Yields: 4 to 6 servings.

Stuffed "Possum"

1 possum
$^1/_2$ tsp. pepper
$^1/_2$ cup cracker crumbs
1 tsp. vinegar
1 egg (raw)

1$^1/_2$ tsps. salt
$^1/_2$ cup onion, chopped
$^1/_2$ cup bread crumbs (toasted)
1 hard-boiled egg, chopped
1 quart water

Remove skin from possum and clean thoroughly. Soak possum in $^1/_4$ cup soda and 2 quarts water for 1 hour. Remove, dry, and salt and pepper lightly. Make stuffing by combining onion, cracker crumbs, vinegar and chopped egg. Toss ingredients and add raw egg to serve as a binder. Stuff interior cavity of possum, place in roasting pan and add water. Cook uncovered at 350 degrees for 2½ to 3 hours, basting occasionally. Serve with North Carolina yams. Yields: 6 servings.

Roasted Oysters

1 bushel of oysters
3 lemons, sliced

2 cups butter, melted
2 cups cocktail sauce

Build an outdoor fire and let burn until coals are very hot, approximately 1½ hours. Place a grill or metal plate over the fire. After rinsing oysters well, place about $^1/_4$ of the bushel of oysters on the heated metal plate. Cover oysters completely with wet burlap sacks. (The heat from the coals comes in contact with the wet burlap sacks and produces steam, thus cooking the oysters.) Cook oysters approximately 5 to 10 minutes. (The shells will start opening.) Remove oysters from fire and open shells. Repeat the procedure for the remaining oysters. Serve piping hot and with butter, lemon slices and cocktail sauce. Yields: 5 to 10 servings.

Oyster Stew

12 oysters
1 tbsp. onion, chopped
1 10 $^3/_4$-ounce can cream of
   mushroom soup
dash of pepper

$^2/_3$ cup celery, chopped
3 tbsps. butter
1 cup milk
1 tsp. salt
2 tsps. sherry (optional)

Remove oysters from shell. Sauté celery and onion in butter. Add oysters, mushroom soup, milk, salt and pepper. Cook over low heat for 15 to 20 minutes, stirring occasionally. Add sherry and garnish with paprika and parsley sprigs. Yields: 3 to 4 servings.

Sausage Stuffed Quail

4 quail
$^1/_2$ cup bread crumbs (toasted)
1 bay leaf
dash of pepper

$^3/_4$ pound country sausage
1 chicken bouillon cube
1 tsp. salt
1 cup water

Brown sausage slowly while adding bread crumbs, bouillon cube and bay leaf. Lightly salt and pepper quail and stuff with sausage mixture. Place quail breast-side up in an oblong casserole dish. Add water. Bake in 350 degree oven for 1½ hours. Serve on brown rice. Yields: 4 servings.

Country Broiled Quail

4 to 6 quail	1 tsp. salt
dash of pepper	$^1/_2$ cup butter
4 to 6 bacon strips	4 to 6 slices bread

Sprinkle salt and pepper over quail. Baste with melted butter and wrap each bird with a bacon strip. Place on broiler pan and put in broiler under low heat. Cook 15 to 20 minutes, turning frequently. Gravy: Add 2 tbsps. flour and 1 cup water to drippings. Place quail on toast points and pour gravy over each. Yields: 4 to 6 servings.

Bagged Quail

4 quail	1 cup flour
1 tsp. salt	dash of pepper
$^3/_4$ cup cooking oil	1 medium onion, sliced
1 3-ounce can of mushrooms	$^1/_2$ cup water

Combine flour, salt and pepper and use mixture to flour quail. Brown birds in cooking oil. Sauté onion and mushrooms until transparent; allow a few minutes to cool and add water. Place the quail, onion, mushrooms and water mixture into an oven cooking bag, place in pan and bake for 1 to $1^1/_2$ hours in 350 degree oven. Yields: 4 servings.

North Carolina Creamed Quail

6 quail	1 tsp. salt
$^1/_2$ tsp. pepper	2 sticks butter
2 cups heavy cream	$^1/_4$ tsp. oregano
$^1/_2$ cup bread crumbs, toasted	

Clean and split quail. Salt and pepper birds and simmer in butter in frypan until tender. Add cream and sprinkle oregano over birds, and continue to cook until done. Garnish with bread crumbs. Yields: 4 to 6 servings.

Roast Pheasant

1 pheasant	1 tsp. salt
$^1/_4$ tsp. pepper	1 bay leaf
3 lemon slices	3 stalks of celery
$^1/_3$ cup butter, melted	6 bacon slices
1 medium onion	1 3-ounce can mushrooms
1 chicken bouillon cube	

Sprinkle salt and pepper on pheasant. Put bay leaf, lemon slices and celery in bird's cavity. Place breast-side up in roasting pan. Dribble melted butter over breast and place bacon strips on top of bird. Mix onion, mushrooms and reconstituted chicken bouillon cube together and pour into bottom of roasting pan. Bake at 350 degrees 30 minutes per pound or until bird is tender. Serve with wild rice. Yields: 4 servings.

Pheasant In Cream Sauce

1 pheasant	1 tsp. salt
$^1/_2$ tsp. pepper	1 can cream of chicken soup
1 3-ounce can mushrooms	$^1/_2$ cup sour cream
$^1/_2$ cup white wine (opt.)	

Cut pheasant in serving-size pieces and sprinkle with salt and pepper. Place bird pieces skin-side up in a baking dish. Mix remaining ingredients, except wine, and pour over bird. Place in a 350 degree oven for $1^1/_2$ to 2 hours. Add wine if desired to the sauce the last 10 minutes of cooking time. Yields: 4 to 6 servings.

Rabbit Supreme

1 rabbit (cut up)
1 10 ¹/₂-ounce can cream of celery soup
1 tsp. Worcestershire sauce
1 2-ounce can of mushrooms

¹/₂ tsp. salt
dash of pepper
1 small onion, sliced
¹/₂ cup red wine (opt)

Sprinkle rabbit pieces with salt and pepper and place in an oblong casserole dish. Mix soup, onions, Worcestershire sauce, wine and mushrooms and pour mixture over rabbit. Cook in medium oven (350 degrees) for 1¹/₂ hours. Yields: 4 servings.

Pan Fried Rabbit

1 rabbit (cut up)
1 cup whole wheat flour
1 tsp. monosodium glutamate (MSG)
1 tsp. salt
1 cup cooking oil
3 cloves of garlic

Place whole wheat flour in a bag. Add rabbit, monosodium glutamate and salt and shake until each piece is covered with mixture. Heat cooking oil in a frypan and add garlic. Cook until garlic buds are brown, then remove from oil. Place floured rabbit in frypan and cover. Cook for 15 to 20 minutes or until golden brown. Remove from oil and drain on paper towel. Yields: 4 servings.

Rabbit Salad

2 cups cooked rabbit
³/₄ cup celery, chopped
¹/₂ cup mayonnaise
1 tsp. salt
¹/₄ cup pickles,chopped
2 hard-boiled eggs, chopped

The author and Big Bunny.

¹/₄ cup prepared mustard
¹/₂ tsp. pepper

Cook rabbit in boiling water until tender. Cut into cubes, and mix with pickles, celery, eggs, mayonnaise, mustard, salt and pepper. Serve on crisp lettuce leaf. Yields: 6 servings.

Rabbit In Fruit Sauce

2 rabbits (quartered)
2 quarts water
1¹/₂ tsps. salt
2 bay leaves
¹/₂ cup raisins
¹/₂ cup apricot nectar
¹/₄ cup water

³/₄ cup vinegar
¹/₂ cup vinegar
1 medium onion, sliced
³/₄ tsp. allspice
¹/₄ cup brown sugar
3 tbsps. flour

Parboil rabbit pieces in ³/₄ cup vinegar and 2 quarts of water for 10 minutes. Discard liquid mixture. Cover rabbit with ¹/₄ cup cool water and add ¹/₂ cup vinegar, salt, onion, bay leaves, allspice, raisins, brown sugar and apricot nectar. Cook for 1 hour or until tender. Remove rabbit. Make a paste of flour and water, add to broth to thicken. Return rabbit to mixture. Yield: 4 to 6 servings.

"Coon" With Yams

1 coon
1/2 tsp. cracked pepper
2 chicken bouillon cubes
2 apples, sliced
1 tsp. cinnamon
2 tbsps. butter

1 tsp. salt
2 bay leaves
1 medium onion, sliced
2 yams, sliced
1 tbsp. brown sugar
2 cups apple cider

Place coon in large cooking vessel, cover with water adding salt, pepper, bay leaves, bouillon cubes and onion. Allow mixture to boil for 45 minutes. Remove coon and place in roasting pan, adding sliced apples and yams. Sprinkle apples and yams with cinnamon and sugar, and dot with butter. Pour apple cider in bottom of pan. Cook for 30 minutes uncovered and 30 minutes covered. Baste occasionally. Coon should be served golden brown. Yields: 4 to 6 servings.

Roast Squab With Brown Rice

4 squabs
1 onion
1 cup brown rice
1/4 tsp. pepper

4 bacon slices
2/3 cup celery, chopped
1 tsp. salt

Cook bacon, remove, drain, and dice. Add onion and celery to drippings and sauté. Cook brown rice and mix with bacon, onions and celery. Stuff squabs and season with salt and pepper. Bake at 400 degrees for 25 minutes. Yields: 4 servings.

Pigeon Pie

4 squabs
3 tbsps. butter
2 1/2 cups broth
1 tsp. salt
1/2 cup bread crumbs

pastry
2 tbsps. flour
1 cup milk
1/4 tsp. pepper

Parboil squab, reserving broth, and brown in skillet. Place pastry in a casserole dish and add squab. Melt butter and blend with flour, broth, milk, salt and pepper. Pour mixture over squab. Sprinkle with bread crumbs and place in 400 degree oven for 20 minutes or until bread crumbs are crisp and brown. Yields: 4 servings.

Fried Squirrel

1 squirrel
1 tsp. salt
1/2 cup milk

3/4 cup flour
1/2 tsp. pepper
1 cup cooking oil or fat

Cut squirrel into serving portions. Mix flour, salt, and pepper. Dip each piece of meat in milk and dredge in flour. Heat cooking oil to 350 degrees (medium heat) and fry until golden brown. Yields: 3 to 4 servings.

Squirrel Stew

2 squirrels
2 carrots,sliced
1 green pepper, diced
2 tbsps. chili powder
1/2 tsp. cayenne pepper

2 medium onion, sliced
2 potatoes, diced
3 celery stalks, chopped
1 tsp. salt
1 cup cooked noodles or rice

Allow squirrels to parboil until tender. Remove meat from bones and put back into broth. Add all ingredients except noodles or rice. Simmer until vegetables are done. Add cooked rice or noodles. Yields: 4 to 6 servings.

Ground Venison

Grind venison that will not make cross-grain steak and use in ways similar to ground beef (meat loaves, deerburgers, meat sauces, etc.).

Venison Stew

1 to 2 pounds venison chunks
4 carrots, sliced
1 small onion, sliced
2 tbsps. butter

5 medium potatoes, cut in sections
$^1/_2$ cup celery, diced
1 8-ounce can tomato sauce
1 tsp. salt

Place all ingredients into an oven cooking bag and place in a 350 degree oven for 1½ hours. Serve piping hot. Yields: 4 to 6 servings.

Oriental Venison Ribs

4 to 6 pounds venison ribs
$^3/_4$ cup soy sauce
$^1/_2$ cup sherry (opt.)
$^1/_2$ cup water
3 tbsps. brown sugar
1 garlic clove, crushed
1 tsp. salt
dash of pepper

Place venison ribs in a large baking pan. Mix remaining ingredients well and pour over ribs. Cover pan with aluminum foil and place in oven at 350 degrees for 1 hour, basting occasionally. Yields: 4 to 5 servings.

Venison Meat Loaf

1$^1/_2$ pounds ground venison
$^1/_4$ cup onion, chopped
1 egg
dash of pepper

1 cup bread crumbs
1 can tomato soup
1 tsp. salt

Mix ingredients well and place in a lightly greased loaf pan. Place in a 350 degree oven for 1¼ hours. Garnish with catsup and parsley sprigs. Yields: 4 to 5 servings.

Venison Roast

3 to 4 pound venison roast
1 package dry onion soup mix
1 bacon strip
$^1/_2$ tsp. cracked pepper
2 cups water

3 tbsps. fat or shortening
1 can cream of mushroom soup
1$^1/_2$ tsps. salt
1 garlic clove

Place venison in large cooking utensil and brown quickly in fat on all sides. Put onion soup, mushroom soup, bacon strip, salt, pepper and garlic on top of venison. Add water, let cook for 2 hours or until it is tender. Yields: 10 servings.

Venison Stroganoff

1 pound venison, cut in strips	3 tbsps. butter
2 medium onions, sliced	1 8-ounce package cream cheese
$^1/_2$ cup milk	1 3-ounce can mushrooms

Melt butter in skillet and sauté venison strips and onions. Grate cream cheese directly into cooking utensil. Add milk and mushrooms. Reduce heat and simmer for 10 to 15 minutes. Serve with egg noodles or wild rice. Yields: 4 servings.

European Wild Boar

1 boar shoulder	1 quart water
$^1/_2$ cup salt	1 cup vinegar
1$^1/_2$ cups red wine	3 onions
$^1/_2$ head cabbage	3 carrots
4 stalks celery	1 bay leaf
2 tsps. butter	$^1/_4$ cup flour
1 cup cranberry sauce	

Parboil shoulder in heavily salted water (1 quart water and $^1/_2$ cup salt) for 1$^1/_2$ hours. Drain and add remaining ingredients except for cranberry sauce, butter and flour. Cover and cook until tender. Remove 2 cups broth for sauce, add butter and flour and blend in cranberry sauce. Slice meat and serve with sauce. Yields: 8 to 10 servings.

Wild Boar Ribs and Sauerkraut

2 pounds boar ribs	1$^1/_2$ cups sauerkraut
4 bacon strips, diced	2 apples, sliced
1$^1/_2$ tsp. salt	$^1/_2$ tsp. pepper
4 potatoes, quartered	

Place sauerkraut, bacon and apples in roasting pan. Season ribs with salt and pepper and place on top of kraut mixture. Place potatoes around the side of ribs and bake at 350 degrees for 1 to 1$^1/_2$ hours. Yields: 4 to 5 servings.

Wild Duck

Soak cleaned duck in cold water 12 hours with $^1/_2$ tsp. soda to each quart of water. Rinse bird and drain.

Barbecued Wild Duck

2 wild ducks	$^1/_2$ cup salad oil
$^1/_2$ cup vinegar	$^1/_4$ cup soy sauce
$^1/_4$ cup Worcestershire sauce	2 tbsps. brown sugar
1 tsp. salt	$^1/_4$ tsp. chili powder
$^1/_4$ cup catsup	$^1/_4$ cup chopped onion

Combine all ingredients except for ducks and simmer for 15 minutes. Split ducks in quarters and barbecue, turning often and basting with sauce until tender. Yields: 4 to 6 servings.

Roast Wild Duck

1 medium duck	1 apple, chopped
$^1/_2$ cup raisins	1$^1/_2$ tsps. salt
$^1/_2$ tsp. pepper	$^1/_2$ cup butter
4 bacon slices	2 tbsps. flour
$^1/_2$ cup sour cream (opt.)	

Fill cavity of duck with chopped apple and raisins. Salt and pepper skin of bird. Baste with melted butter and cover breast of duck with bacon slices. Put in roasting pan and place in hot oven at 450 to

500 degrees for 30 to 45 minutes. Baste every 5 minutes. Make a gravy from drippings, add flour to thicken. Add sour cream to gravy if desired. Yields: 2 to 4 servings.

Stuffed Wild Goose

1 medium wild goose	giblets from goose
4 cups bread crumbs	2 medium onions, chopped
2 apples, diced	$\frac{1}{4}$ tsp. sage
$\frac{1}{4}$ tsp. garlic powder	2 tsps. salt
$\frac{1}{2}$ tsp. pepper	2 tbsps. butter

Cook giblets until tender and reserve liquid. Chop giblets and add to bread crumbs, onions, apples and seasonings. Add liquid from giblets to moisten stuffing. Place goose in roasting pan and dot with butter. Put in 350 degree oven and baste often. Cook approximately 20 minutes per pound. Yields: 8 to 12 servings.

Outdoor Grilled Wild Turkey

1 wild turkey	2 tsps. salt
1 tsp. pepper	$\frac{1}{2}$ bunch of celery with leaves
2 onions	$\frac{1}{2}$ cup butter

Rub cavity of bird with salt and pepper. Place celery and onions inside cavity. Brush bird with melted butter. Place on outdoor grill and cook slowly for 3 to 4 hours. Continue to brush bird generously with butter. The last 30 minutes of cooking time, brush bird frequently with barbecue sauce.

Barbecue Sauce

$2\frac{1}{2}$ cups water	1 tbsp. sugar
3 tsps. black pepper	2 tbsps. butter
$\frac{1}{4}$ cup vinegar	3 tsps. salt
$\frac{1}{4}$ cup onion, chopped	1 garlic bud
1 tsp. red pepper	1 tsp. chili powder
2 tsps. mustard powder	3 tbsps. Worcestershire sauce

Combine all ingredients in saucepan and bring to a boil. Allow sauce to stand in overnight (if possible) to blend flavors. Warm sauce before using.

Stewed Woodchuck

1 woodchuck	$1\frac{1}{2}$ cups vinegar
$1\frac{1}{2}$ cups water	2 onions sliced
2 tsps. salt	$\frac{1}{4}$ tsp. pepper
$\frac{3}{4}$ cup celery, diced	5 whole cloves
$\frac{1}{4}$ cup flour	

Clean woodchuck and cut into serving pieces. Soak overnight in solution of $1\frac{1}{2}$ cups vinegar and $1\frac{1}{2}$ cups water. Rinse, drain and wipe dry. Parboil for 15 to 20 minutes, drain and cover with fresh water. Add onion, salt, pepper, celery and cloves. Cook 1 to $1\frac{1}{2}$ hours or until tender. Add flour the last 5 minutes of cooking time for gravy. Yields: 4 to 6 servings.

Frog Legs

12 frog legs	1 quart water
1 tsp. salt	$\frac{3}{4}$ cup lemon juice
$\frac{1}{2}$ tsp. pepper	1 egg, beaten
$\frac{1}{2}$ cup cracker crumbs	

Skin hind legs of frogs and place in boiling water, salt and lemon juice for two minutes. Drain and sprinkle with salt and pepper. Dip legs in egg mixture and dredge in cracker crumbs. Deep-fat fry quickly. Yields: 4 to 6 servings.

White Stew of Terrapin

1 terrapin (or cooter)
1 small onion, chopped
$^1/_4$ tsp. thyme
3 tbsps. butter
$^1/_4$ tsp. black pepper
$^3/_4$ cup heavy cream

2 quarts water
$^1/_2$ tsp. parsley
2 tbsps. flour
$1^1/_2$ tsps. salt
dash of red pepper
$^1/_4$ cup cooking wine

Remove terrapin head and soak terrapin in cold water for approximately 30 minutes to remove blood. Scald in boiling water and remove skin and nails. Discard liquid. Place terrapin in clean water, onion, parsley and thyme. Cook mixture until shell can be removed easily. Chop meat into small pieces and return to broth. Add flour, butter, salt and black and red pepper. Just before serving, add cream and wine. Yields: 8 servings.

Turtle Soup

2 cups cooked turtle meat,
   cut into sections
3 carrots, sliced
2 tbsps. butter
2 quarts beef stock
1 can tomato purée
5 whole cloves
1 lemon, sliced
salt to taste

$1^1/_2$ pounds beef bones
2 medium onions, sliced
3 celery stalks, sliced
$^1/_4$ cup flour
1 can tomatoes
$1^1/_2$ tsps. pepper
$^1/_2$ cup sherry (optional)
2 hard-boiled eggs, sliced

Braise beef bones, onions, carrots and celery in butter lightly until fork-tender. Add to mixture beef stock, tomatoes, tomato purée, salt, pepper and cloves. Cook for about 2 hours. Add sherry, if desired. Strain soup and add turtle meat, lemon and eggs. Bring to a boil, remove from heat and serve hot. Yields: 8 servings.

Fried Eel

3 to 4 eels
$^1/_4$ tsp. pepper
$^1/_4$ cup milk

1 tsp. salt
$^1/_2$ cup cornmeal

Skin and clean eels, remove heads and cut into 3 inch strips. Parboil for approximately 10 minutes. Drain. Sprinkle with salt and pepper, dip into milk and dredge in cornmeal. Pan-fry and drain on paper towels. Yields: 3 to 4 servings.

The author, daughter Jessica and Commissioner Jim Graham.

Once while having lunch with Commissioner Graham, I interviewed him for an article I was doing about where people do their best thinking. He said that he was flattered "that anyone thought that he ever did any thinking!" and that he did his best thinking on his old farm up in Rowan County where there is no television. Like me, Jim Graham will eat just about anything. I saw him once going to the head of the line as was his privilege at the Ramp Festival in Waynesville, North Carolina. A ramp, in case you don't know, is a wild leek, a relative of the onion and the most powerful-tasting and -smelling one you can find. They make your breath smell so bad, we used to eat them on the way to school in order to be sent out of the classroom!

Probably Mr. Graham's most famous and widely enjoyed recipe is his Brunswick stew. I wrote about it once just before the State Fair opened, and a couple of booth owners cut the recipe out, fixed it and gave it out in little cups!

Jim Graham's Tar Heel Brunswick Stew

1 large stewing chicken
2 large potatoes, diced
1 large onion, diced
4 cups lima beans
salt
pepper
Worcestershire sauce

1 pound veal, beef, goat or squirrel
4 cups fresh or canned corn
2 8-ounce cans tomato sauce or canned tomatoes
Tabasco sauce
butter

Stew chicken and other meat until chicken is ready to fall from bones. Cool and shred chicken and other meat with fingers, discarding skin and fat. Put meat back in broth, skim off excess fat and continue to simmer. Cook potatoes with onion, corn, lima beans and tomato sauce. When potatoes are tender, combine with chicken. The mixture will be thin like soup. Simmer for several hours to thicken. Season to taste with salt, pepper, hot pepper sauce, Worcestershire sauce and butter. Yields: 10 to 12 servings. Note: Can also be frozen.

I know that we have a variety of hot pepper sauces made right here in North Carolina, but I have to stick with Tabasco sauce in spite of Commissioner Graham's "Goodness Grows In North Carolina" campaign. Tabasco is so good that all the Green Berets I know used to pack a bottle of Tabasco and a roll of toilet paper into their rucksack before anything else. So did a lot of other troops. Finally the Army got smart enough to come up with little individual bottles to pack in their MRE's (Meals Refused by Ethiopians!).

Natural Spices in the Kitchen

With all the cold weather and snow lately, I'll bet there have been many pots of soup made, and some of us may be needing to restock our spices.

We don't have to rush down to the grocery store to do it, either, because we can find many of our herbs and spices growing wild. The herb and spice substitutes can be a great deal less expensive than their counterparts in the stores, and they are certainly fresher and probably healthier for us.

How do you prepare soups, stews, and Italian dishes calling for bay leaves when you don't have any? True bay leaves, *Laurus nobilis*, come from the area around Turkey and the Mediterranean and were so renowned in ancient Rome that a wreath of them was used to crown the heads of scholars, nobles and heroes. There is a tree around here we have come to call the Carolina Bay. Many botantists aren't sure if it is native laurel or if it escaped cultivation long ago. It is, however, easily recognized because of the bay-leaf odor which comes from the glossy evergreen leaves when crushed. This distinguishes it from other laurels, some of which may be poisonous. These leaves retain much of the color and scent and are popular in herbal wreaths at Christmas time and in potpourris.

If the leaves have the supermarket bay-leaf scent, use them in the same manner, and if not, leave them alone.

The author and his daughter Jessica admire their
home-grown fennel in the Squier family herb garden.

Another member of the laurel family that is common around here and the natural source of a popular spice is the Sassafras, *Sassafras albidum*. Besides using the roots to make tea, we dry and grind the leaves to produce the filé powder so essential to Cajun cooking and used both as a soup thickener and for its distinctive flavor. It is a must in gumbo and fairly costly in the stores.

One of the things that make botany both confusing and interesting is the way common names are used. We get our juniper berries from the eastern red cedar, *Juniperus virginiana*, or its relative the common juniper, *Juniperus communis*, though they come from other members of the cypress family in other parts of the world.

McCormick and Company spice company says theirs are imported from Yugoslavia. They should be very special at about $3.25 per ounce, but they taste the same as our wild ones.

These berries are essential in the game recipes of Europe and the British use them to flavor gin. If you know anybody who makes their own liquor, the addition of a handful of juniper berries to each bottle will give it a flavor to rival Tanqueray!

Along many of our streams and around old homesteads wild mints, *Mentha* species, abound, and they often remain green all winter here or jump at the first hint of warm weather. Mint leaves are used in Middle Eastern cooking and in making jelly to accompany lamb and goat dishes. Some people are horrified at the idea of eating goats, mint or not, but love the taste of "Cabrito" in the restaurants. Guess what!

We can make our own mustard by locating some wild mustard and there is plenty of it around. Wild mustards, *Brassica* species, are recognized by their yellow, white, or occasionally pale blue flowers which have their four petals in the shape of a cross. That's why they are sometimes referred to as "crucifers." They also have the distinctive mustard smell and taste. The leaves and flowers add a tang to salads and cooked greens. The roots of some are grated when big enough and called wild horseradish and used in the same way. The seed pods can be ground and added to water, vinegar, or oil to make our own mustard spread. That is basically the way commerical mustards are made, except that they may have added herbs, or food coloring and preservatives. Making your own is healthier!

Need some lemon flavor to add to your tea or for making a big pitcher of lemonade? The red, oily berries of the nonpoisonous sumacs, *Rhus* species, are perfect for the job and they actually contain vitamin C. They are differentiated from their poisonous cousins because the poison ones have smooth leaves and white berries and grow in wet spots. The safe ones have red berries and rough-edged leaves and grow in drier locations. Take the berries off the stem when making lemonade to avoid the pithy taste of wood. It makes a very nice pink lemonade.

Gingerbread and gingersnaps were part of growing up for many of us. I'm still "in progress" as they say. Nowadays we use ginger for cooking in oriental, Latin American, and Indian (like Gunga Din's India) dishes. True ginger comes from tropical areas and is not related to our little ground-hugging, evergreen wild ginger *(Asarum canadense)* that grows around here with its heart-shaped leaves. Though unrelated, they have the same flavor and scent in the roots. Once you locate a clump of wild ginger and pull it out of the ground, the uses are the same — wild spice, candied as a confection, and in natural medicines. The smell gives it away and makes it easy to recognize. Wild ginger will impart the same flavor to your stir-frys, baked goods and desserts, and makes a nice warming and mildly stimulating tea. To candy the roots in the way of the settlers, simply boil the roots in a sugar syrup until transparent and tender. Dry them in the air and roll in dry sugar for a coating.

Dr. Jim Duke, whom I've mentioned elsewhere, and another friend, Jim Meuninck, have co-authored a videotape called *Edible Wild Plants,* which lists about 100 useful wild herbs. In the tape Jim discusses the many applications for the wild onion, and he says "how fortunate one is to find the 'elusive' wild garlic" when foraging. Jim Meuninck is from Michigan where there aren't as many as we have, I guess. He would be in hog heaven here, where you can literally find acres of these "elusive" plants.

Wild onions are a major pest around here in some people's lawns, and a nemesis to dairy farmers because most people don't like onion-flavored milk after the cows graze in the pasture where they grow. But they are an excellent addition to the wild-foods forager's diet, the spice rack, or the herbal medicine chest. They contain the same medicinal properties as garden-grown onions and garlic. Their high organic sulfur content makes them effective as an antibacterial, insect repellant, and as a condiment. A great deal of research is taking place now concerning the anti-cancer and anti-cholesterol qualities of the garlic, onions, and chives. The entire plant is useable and excellent as long as it has a characteristic onion or garlic odor. Beware though, because these wild lilies have some poisonous relatives with no scent. Wild onions can be braided just like garlic and used as needed. These cold-loving plants disappear from our lawns and roadsides during the hot summer months while the bulbs are resting under the surface.

An excellent substitute for onion rings is made by stripping the outer skin from the wild onions, cutting off the green part (save the chives) and deep frying the bulbs until tender. It is up to you if you batter them or not, but they turn out surprisingly sweet.

If you would like some nice anise flavor for cooking or as a tea, you can use the leaves and flowers of sweet goldenrod, *Solidago odora*. They work fresh or dried.

As you can see, there are plenty of wild substitutes for our favorite herbs and spices in the kitchen. Most of our spices were discovered accidentally anyhow, as people were experimenting with wild plants as food or medicine.

I guess we still need to mention our basics — salt, pepper and sugar. If you are near the ocean, you can dehydrate sea water and use the resulting sea salt, or you can dry and grind seaweeds for salt substitutes. Seaweeds also contain many trace elements and minerals that make them very nutritious. If you aren't near the sea, you can get a salt flavor in the manner of the early settlers by scraping and powdering the bark of hickory trees, *Carya* species. Use the nut shells and hulls as well as the wood to smoke your foods on the grill.

There are many peppery-tasting plants, including the leaves of the wild mustard when cooked with other foods, and their pods and mature roots. One common wild plant, *Lepidium virginicum,* is known as "Poor Man's Pepper," because its seeds look like the seeds inside a bell pepper and it has a definite pepper taste. The seeds can be used fresh or dried in place of pepper and peppercorns.

Of course, the best and most appetizing source of natural sweetening around here is honey. In other places sweetness can be obtained from sugar beets, sugar cane and the sap of various trees. The sap can be used as is or it can be converted to syrup like they do in maple-sugar country. It takes 35-40 gallons of sap to make 1 gallon of syrup. That is why your pure maple syrup may cost $16 a quart in the stores. A less-appealing source of sugar is available, especially in a survival situation. Those big black ants contain a chemical called formic acid that makes their bites painful, but it tastes sweet when they are eaten fresh or dried. So you might want to save those little pests instead of spraying them!

There are many other wild or escaped herbs and spices we can use. Italian and Chinese recipes call for pine nuts in their preparation. Although our long-leaf pines have relatively small seeds and they are not easy to get out of the unopened cones, they make an equally good tasting substitute for pignoli or Chinese pine nuts. In the west, piñon pines have large nuts which the Utes and other Native Americans gather as they fall. These aren't really nuts, but seeds we commonly refer to as nuts. In this area the Native Americans would gather green pine cones and when they wanted the nuts would place them in the ashes of a fire to open them just the way Mother Nature does with wildfires.

We can't cook without oil either, but nuts such as walnuts and hickories have so much oil that it can be squeezed out and used for cooking and making a mock butter.

The common roadside pineapple weed, *Matricaria matricariodes,*has the scent and flavor of pineapple and makes a delicious tea. When we need some little finishing touch for punches or desserts we can add the blossoms of violets or the Eastern redbud. To make our baked goods a beautiful golden color and to boost their nutrition we can add the pollen from cattails, using the male flowerheads in the spring. Some people have used the highly abundant pollen from our pine trees.

I know when it comes to cooking, someone is going to ask about mushrooms, and there is no reason to pay expensive prices for imported porcini because that is just the Italian name for our common boletes, *Boletus edulis* and other species. If you get them in the store, you will think it is the Italian word for expensive. Other well-known marketed mushrooms are equally available, but you must know what you are doing more so with mushrooms than most other wild plants.

The videotape I mentioned called *Edible Wild Plants* is available from Media Methods, 24097 North Shore Drive, Edwardsburg, MI 49112. It retails for $29.95 plus $1.50 postage.

Lilies' Extensive Family Extends Into The Kitchen

If Euell Gibbons were still alive he would probably still be autographing copies of his most famous and popular book, *Stalking the Wild Asparagus*. Or he might be out looking for it — the wild asparagus!

Each spring at nearby Fort Bragg, hordes of Oriental ladies descend on the back roads of the reservation armed with sharp knives and grocery bags to pick blossoms of daylilies. At another part of the post, a soldier on a survival training exercise grubs out the edible tubers of the same plant. In one of the gourmet restaurants in Pinehurst, a chef delicately seasons his *pièce de résistance* with chives and shallots, while an Italian housewife nearby seasons her spaghetti sauce with just the right touch of garlic. An Indian in the desert is happily gathering the ripe fruits of the yucca plant and the roots of other yuccas nearby. Out among the pines at Weymouth Woods Nature Preserve, a fox squirrel carefully digs up the roots of Solomon's seal for his dinner.

What do all these people — and the squirrel — have in common? Why, they are eating lilies, of course! At least botanically speaking, because all of the plants we mentioned and many others we couldn't begin to suspect as being related to each other are all members of the family of lilies. This large family also includes the tiger lily, one of our most beautiful wild flowers; the shade-loving plantain lily, better known to most of us as the hosta; and hyacinths, trout lilies, and all the onions. Another member of the family is the autumn crocus, which by now you know isn't a crocus at all but just as surely a lily as asparagus, yuccas, fritillaries, and the sweet-scented lily of the valley.

For many years we have been told in legends and more recently on television that garlic will ward off vampires, witches and demons. Well, I don't know about that one, but intensive studies are being conducted to determine what there is in garlic and other members of the Allium genus that gives it antibacterial properties and possibly the ability to destroy cancer cells. There have been many experiments that have proved garlic's ability to reduce cholesterol in blood vessels and lower blood pressure. Unfortunately, sulfur-containing compounds in garlic oil give it a very strong odor, and cooking destroys their effectiveness somewhat. So, if you are taking raw garlic oil for your cholesterol levels and blood pressure, it won't be a secret!

In herbal medicine, garlic is probably more of a panacea than ginseng, with at least 125 ailments mentioned as being treated by it. The greatest claim to fame, though, for garlic, *Allium sativa*, is as a kitchen herb. In Gilroy, California, the "Garlic Capital of the World," there is an annual Garlic Festival held in its honor with garlic candy, wine, and ice cream included among the more traditional uses. There has even been a club formed to promote its virtues called "Lovers of the Stinking Rose." They can be reached at 1621 Fifth St., Berkeley, CA 94710.

It is said that daylilies, *Hemerocallis fulva*, were originally grown as a food in the gardens of China, carried to England by traders as an ornamental garden flower, and then carried to the colonies (the United States) by British colonists where it escaped to become a common roadside wild flower. Many color variations have been developed and some can be quite expensive. The fact remains, however, that they form delicious underground tubers which when eaten raw are crunchy like water chestnuts, but when boiled and buttered taste like sweet corn. They also produce beautiful flowers that are delicious raw in salads or stuffed with cream cheese, sautéed or added to stir-frys, battered and frittered, or dried and added to soups as a thickener and spice.

Asparagus certainly doesn't look like a lily, but it is. In spring when it is commonly "stalked" it is a single green spear whose leaves look like scales. Later it will be tall and feathery and will look more like a five-foot-tall fern. The asparagus fern, which really is a fern, was so named because of its similarity to asparagus. In the dead of winter the gray-white stalks with their load of red berries look like caricatures of Christmas trees. This plant is a very popular lily in the kitchen, and in January these green spears known to botanists as *Asparagus officinalis*, are going for $4.29 a pound in the grocery stores.

Yuccas are generally thought of as desert plants from the arid lands of the Southwest, but they do well here, too. One, beargrass or *Yucca filamentosa*, is native to this area. I have seen yuccas growing as far north as New York and New Jersey. They do well here in the Sandhills with very little care. You will find them in the landscape in many shopping centers. There are many varieties, and they take on various shapes and sizes. Many have edible roots, though the roots of one type produce a natural shampoo rich in lather when crushed and beaten in water. Amole shampoos are made from this yucca. The yuccas have white, waxy blossoms which are delicious fried, steamed with butter or chopped raw and added to salads. The green, purple or red fruits are also edible. They are eaten as a vegetable while they are fresh and green, and as a fruit when they darken and turn soft and sweet as they ripen.

Well, with a family this extensive we could go on and on. Instead, here are a few recipes for what you may or may not have thought of as lilies or as edible before you knew they were lilies.

Daylily Buds Almondine

3 cups daylily buds	1$\frac{1}{2}$ cups fresh mushrooms, sliced
1 tbsp. soy sauce	3 tbsps. real butter
$\frac{3}{4}$ cup slivered almonds	

Boil the fresh daylily buds in salted water one minute and drain. Melt the butter in a sauce pan. Add mushrooms and daylily buds and sauté about five minutes or until tender. Add the almonds and soy sauce, mixing well. Serve at once.

Daylily Fritters

2$\frac{1}{2}$-3 dozen daylily blooms	$\frac{1}{2}$ tsp. salt
2 cups cooking oil	1 egg, beaten
1 cup milk	$\frac{1}{8}$ tsp. pepper
confectioner's sugar (opt.)	flour as needed

Combine egg, milk, flour and salt and pepper and mix to form a thick batter. Heat oil to about 375 degrees. When ready a drop of batter will turn golden brown. Dip flowers in batter and fry to a golden brown. Drain. Sprinkle with sugar if desired.

Garlic Ice Cream

1-2 tsps. gelatin	2 cups milk
$\frac{1}{8}$ tsp. salt	2 cloves garlic, minced (4, if using wild garlic)
$\frac{1}{4}$ cup cold water	1 cup sugar
2 tbsps. lemon juice	2 cups whipping cream

Soak the gelatin in cold water. Bring the milk, sugar, and salt to a boil and remove from heat. Dissolve the gelatin in the hot milk and cool. Add lemon juice and garlic when cool. Whip the cream and fold into mixture. Freeze in molds or in an ice cream freezer. Good after a spaghetti dinner.

Marinated Asparagus (Wild is Best)

1 pound asparagus
$^1/_2$ tsp. fresh basil
1 garlic clove, crushed
1 tbsp. rosemary vinegar

$^1/_2$ cup dry white wine
$^1/_4$ tsp. fresh oregano
1 cup Italian salad dressing
2 cups dandelion leaves

Cook asparagus about 7 minutes until tender in small amount of water. Drain. Combine all ingredients except dandelion leaves. Shake well. Pour over the asparagus in a dish and marinate overnight, chilled. Drain and serve on a bed of dandelion leaves.

Our Native Plants
Make it Tea Time, Naturally

Euell Gibbons said that "American history is steeped in tea. We might be a nation of great tea drinkers if the Revolution had not intervened. Tea played such a large part in our fight for independence that this struggle has been called the tea war."

Being mainly of British heritage at the time of the Revolution, the daily teatime was strongly ingrained in the colonists, and many of the other settlers were accustomed to using tea as a healing medicinal beverage, making it from various wild and cultivated plants. England's decision to tax the tea sent to "the Colonies in the New World" was the straw that broke the camel's back. The colonists were here to escape the oppression of the British government, and when a tax was levied against the tea, they refused to pay it. Attempts to collect it by force led to the Boston Tea Party and other armed battles which opened the Revolution and paved the way for independence.

It also led to the "discovery" of many wild teas that the Native Americans were using, including sassafras, which was so popular in England that it became the first cash crop exported from here. Our familiar Chinese tea in its various forms comes from a relative of the camellias that grace our winter gardens, known to botanists as *Camellia sinensis*. After the Revolution, the gutsy Americans harvested a "weed" called the goldenrod and exported it to China as "Blue Mountain Tea" where it soon became a popular item of trade.

Last week I got a letter from Mom Laudenslager, and in part this is what she had to say: "I wanted to tell you when we were down at your brother Chuck's he gave us some sassafras roots and I made some tea with them. Delicious — Dad Laudenslager used to get sassafras to burn in the smoke-house when they butchered. He said it was the best wood for this purpose. I really enjoyed the tea. Did you do a column on tea? Often Paul and I would go on walks and pick peppermint tea and pennyroyal tea. We would hang it upside down and dry it to store for the winter. The best (or worst) of it was called 'boneset' and was gathered by my grandmother in the spring. We had to take some every spring to clean out our system. Doctors laugh at some of these old remedies, but were they so bad?" Many of our old spring tonics were used to purge the system of poisons built up in the blood after a sluggish winter life and were composed of some really bad-tasting herbs and referred to as "bitters." As a child I always heard the elders saying medicine wasn't good for you if it didn't burn or taste bad! The letter ended like this: "If you have done a column on tea, I would like a copy. If you have not — do so. I am very interested in all the things we can use to make tea."

Other people have also asked me about wild and herbal teas, and again this is one of those subjects there are entire books about, but here are some of the common plants we can find around here or grow in our gardens which make excellent "teas."

Whether a tea is used as a beverage or medicine depends on its strength. There are many herbal teas on the market, and often these have some medicinal value, but it is limited by the fact that generally there is only about one-fifteenth of an ounce of the herb in each tea bag. Medicinal doses recommended by the herbalists usually have an ounce or two of the dried herb boiled in a pint of water.

When gathering plants for tea, it is just as essential to be absolutely positive of the plant's identity as when gathering wild plants to eat. In these days, especially, don't take the easy way and gather your plants right along the road where they absorb all the chemicals from exhaust emissions. Plants gathered for tea should be picked in the early morning after the dew has dried, and hung upside down in a dark place until completely moisture-free, then crushed and placed in dark containers. Gather berries such as sumac as soon as they are mature and root in winter after the sap goes down. They are stronger then.

The Blue Mountain Tea mentioned earlier is made from the sweet goldenrod, *Solidago odora*, which when crushed gives the sweet scent of anise. This plant is a good one for the wildflower gardens here in the Sandhills because it produces large stands of yellow flowers from its perennial rootstocks when established and is drought-hardy. The tea is good just because of its anise or licorice flavor, but the other benefits attributed by herbalists include calming the stomach, easing gas pains, and helping to dissolve stones. There are about 80 species of goldenrods, but the ones we're seeking smell like anise when crushed between the fingers. It can be used fresh or dried, but properly dried herbs are usually stronger than fresh ones.

We can hardly neglect one of our commonest trees, especially after mentioning Euell Gibbons, who is often mocked as people ask, "Did you know that many parts of a pine tree are edible?" Actually, a nice tea can be made from green pine needles. It has a pleasant taste if not made too strong, and contains a good amount of vitamin C.

Lots of our plants are gone now for the winter, but our little wild and garden strawberries are making their presence known by turning a brilliant red color. All through the winter they provide a tea which is high in vitamin C and naturally sweet. As with other leaf teas, cover about three teaspoons of fresh leaves or one teaspoon dried, chopped leaves with boiling water and steep. Euell Gibbons found these leaves averaged 229 milligrams of vitamin C per 100 grams of leaves when he had them tested by Penn State University. This is so high that they then picked their own leaves because they thought the test leaves were altered somehow. Native Americans used this tea for anemia, lack of appetite, and diarrhea.

Gibbons says that for sheer luxury there is no tea that equals the sweet, fragrant tea made of basswood blossoms. This tree is also known as the linden or lime tree. I found the tea being sold in Central America under the name "tilo." The tea made from basswood, *Tilia cordata*, is recommended by herbalists for sore throats. Several of these trees grow around the old homesites in the Carthage, NC area. The small brown seeds are used later in a chocolate-flavored drink when they are dried. The flowers produce a sweet, aromatic honey. The tea produces a gentle sweat which some say will nip a cold in the bud.

The mints, *Mentha* species, are easily recognized by their square stems and blue flowers shaped like lips, giving them the family name *Labiatae* in Latin. There are many species of mints, both wild and in the garden. They don't all smell like peppermint and some don't even smell good. Others may smell like lemon or pineapple. The chemical menthol or mint oil is one constituent that makes them a carminative to herbalists. That means simply that they are good for upset stomachs while horehound mint is supposedly good for coughs and fevers and its bitter taste is familiar to many of us as the candy throat remedy — the horehound drops of our youth. Pennyroyal is another mint that we grow in our gardens, often as a form of insect repellent. American pennyroyal, *Hedeoma pulegioides*, makes a somewhat bitter tea that has a flavor that may last for many hours and is said to promote sweating, calm stomach spasms and induce menstrual flow. It is not recommended for pregnant women. The sweet smell of peppermint is often most obvious when mowing the grass in areas where it has escaped into the lawn.

The boneset tea is made from the plant known as Joe-Pye Weed, named after a Native American medicine man who used it for many ailments, including a typhus epidemic. Boneset, *Eupatorium purpureum* and others, was once listed in the *U.S. Pharmacopoeia* as a stimulant, febrifuge, and laxative — a spring tonic. It grows in wet meadows and puts up tall stalks of pinkish flowers.

One of the most famous teas associated with our history is sassafras. It is mentioned in all the herb books, seen on television programs, and even found in grocery stores in raw root, teabag, and liquid concentrate forms. Some like this tea hot with milk and sugar, while others prefer it cold, sweetened or not. Gibbons said, "Personally, I take it anyway I can get it."

The last wild tea that space will allow us to talk about is the tart, red tea made from several members of the sumac family. These trees produce red, often velvety berries as opposed to the white berries of poison sumac, which is smooth of leaf and stem. Not all the hard berries (seeds) of the sumac, *Rhus glabara,* are hairy, but they are all covered with an acid coating having a citrus taste and high vitamin C content. The earlier after maturity they are gathered, the stronger they will be, but they can be used all winter until the migrating flocks of songbirds have eaten them. This tree has been called wild lemonade or Indian lemonade, and makes a delicious hot or cold drink. Sometimes the lemon taste has to be tamed with sugar, it is so strong. Either soak the berry stalks in cold water until the water turns red or strip the berries off the stalks to avoid the "pithy" taste when you boil them.

These are just a few of the plants that can be used for tea and are easy to recognize. Many others including the weed dandelion in our yards are used to make healthful tonic teas and they don't taste bitter like boneset. Others such as rosehips and hawthornes are used just because they taste good and have some medicinal value, too. Some of the old remedies really work. My son recently woke up sick in the middle of the night, so the first thing I did was get out the KRK prescribed by Doctor Peter Goth of Wilderness Medical Associates. The KRK or "Karmic Repair Kit" consists of just plain sympathy and TLC — always a good combination to begin treatment of childhood ailments. Actually, it is essential in the treatment of all ailments! Then I gave him some nice peppermint tea to calm his stomach and nerves and he slept like a baby the rest of the night. He even said "Thanks!" Now where would a teenager pick up such language?

To the Author:

"He's a lot smaller than you, but I can see how you and your brother Chuck favor each other." — R.W. Parks

Explanation:

"All my kids look alike. I never went to any of those picnics!" — Mom Laudenslager

How I Almost Did In Lewis Grizzard

This is just a little story I want to share with my friends. Lewis Grizzard didn't have to live off the land. He made enough money that he could eat what he wanted and not have to worry about it. He was just so good at writing about earthy things that he got rich at it. He was a helluva story teller and an incredibly clever writer. It was my distinct great fortune to get to know him before he died.

Courtesy David Barbour, Carolina Cartoons.

Beatrice Barfield writes a column for the *Spring Lake* (NC) *News,* and it is usually as interesting as its title — "So You Think Life Is Boring." She wrote about how she would miss reading Lewis' columns right after he passed on. She wrote, "I liked his books and I liked his newspaper columns...Replace Lewis Grizzard? It can't be done. Goodbye Lewis..." What follows is a column I did for the *Spring Lake News* on April 6, 1994. It was called:

"How I Almost Did In Lewis Grizzard"

Bea Barfield's column stirred my own memories of Lewis Grizzard. He was smart and he was funny. He made it okay to be Southern. He could have been rich if he hadn't been married so many times. He might have been anyway. Despite all his successes, Lewis Grizzard never got a swelled head. He never "got above his raisin'!" Lewis Grizzard was a helluva nice person. We need more like him.

I was Lewis' guest at his Celebrity Golf Tournament in Pinehurst last year, and it was special. Lewis introduced me to his fiancée Dedra and her daughter: "This is the guy who wrote the book we were reading last night." He had gotten out of the hospital and was still a little bit woosie. Still had an I.V. hookup so he could take his antibiotics. Lewis plays golf; I don't. Naturally, though, a golf question had to come up in our conversation.

"What is your handicap?" Lewis asked me. I leaned on my cane and smart-alecked back, "I

LEWIS GRIZZARD

CELEBRITY GOLF TOURNAMENT

DAY PASS
LEGACY GOLF LINKS
JULY 31, 1993
WEAR AT ALL TIMES FOR
IDENTIFICATION ON THE COURSE

ADMIT ONE $5.00

broke my neck in a parachute jump." I thought Lewis would lose his breath for good, coughing and laughing at the same time. It is rewarding making jokes when somebody has a quick wit and can figure out what you're saying. We settled down again and started wandering around the pro shop. "You're going the wrong way, Lewis," one of the tournament officials advised. "We are supposed to be outside now."

"You know what they say about mad dogs," Lewis responded. "You let 'em go where they want!"

Lewis stayed funny and down-to-earth until the end. One of his final columns was about Tonya Harding and he used it to talk about a fading treasure — the good ol' girl!

"Tonya Harding strikes me as something that has been lost in this world of feminism and 32 other -isms that are always getting in the way of just living life as it ought to be. That something is the good ol' girl. I used to know a lot of them. Yeah, they smoked. They would drink a beer with you right out of the can and could curse a blue streak. God bless 'em for it. They were never homecoming queens or skating princesses, but they were always there when you needed a friend or somebody to help you change the spark plugs on your car."

A lot of people are going to miss you, Lewis. You may be gone, but you won't be forgotten!

The author and Lewis Grizzard.

I Like That Filipino Cooking!

Filipino - Oriental
Cuisine

One of the advantages of being the "acting editor" of the *Spring Lake News* when Pat Wilson goes on vacation is that I can put whatever I want to in the paper. Another is that I can eat at a different place for lunch every day — if I want to! I have found a favorite restaurant called Manila Fast Food, and the owners Carlos and Susie Bamberger work hard to offer a wide variety of freshly prepared vegetable and meat dishes on the buffet. I have "foundered" myself there on more than one occasion. The food is authentic, fresh and delicious. There is a Chinese restaurant nearby that features chocolate pudding and hushpuppies on their buffet. Give me a break!

Renelvis

Anyway, I really got to liking this Filipino cooking, when like destiny I made a great friend through the *John Boy and Billy Big Show*. One of their other guests is Renée Escarcha — better known as Renelvis. He is a Filipino who speaks 10 languages and sings in all of them as well. He is best known as an Elvis impersonator and songwriter, though. Renée will be the first to admit that he doesn't look like Elvis. He is too short to be confused with the King, but does have some excellent jumpsuits just like the real Elvis wore. When Renée talks, he has a slight accent, but when he sings he sounds so much like Elvis that a hush comes over the crowd. He even was permitted to record three of Elvis' songs on his own album, so that should tell you how good he is.

Renée has a fan club of his own, too. The address is Renelvis Fan Club, P.O. Box 561531, Charlotte, NC 28256. I asked him if he could give me some Filipino recipes for an article and I just changed the ingredients. As you would expect, they eat a lot of fish, chicken and pork there. I just changed the main ingredient to wild stuff we have here.

Roasted Small Game Filipino Style

1 cleaned armadillo, raccoon,
   beaver or other small game
coarse rock or sea salt
4-6 garlic cloves, crushed
butter
6 ripe plantain bananas

$^1/_2$ cup brown sugar
1 cup dark soy sauce
freshly ground black pepper
$^1/_2$ cup vegetable oil
lime or lemon
2 pounds sweet potatoes

Wash the animal thoroughly after cleaning and pat it dry. Rub the meat thoroughly with crushed garlic and salt and pepper. Dissolve the brown sugar in the soy sauce and rub it on the meat, inside and out, saving half of it. Allow 3-4 hours for flavor to soak in. Preheat oven to 450 degrees. Place meat in a deep pan in a position with front feet pointed forward and back legs bent. Mix remaining soy mixture with oil and spread over the meat. Roast 15 minutes at 450 degrees and then reduce heat to 325 degrees and bake for 3$^1/_2$ to 4 hours, basting frequently. To check for thorough cooking, pierce with fork and it is done when juices run clear. Peel the plantain and sweet potatoes and cut into 2-inch chunks. Boil until tender, but not mushy, and drain well. Drizzle with lemon or lime juice and butter and place in pan for last 15-20 minutes of cooking.

Island Shrimp (or Crawfish)

1 pound large shrimp or crawfish
salt and pepper to taste
1 cup onion, minced

taro leaves (or collard leaves)
1 cup coconut cream

Preheat oven to 350 degrees. Boil, peel, and de-vein shrimps and set aside. Place taro or collard leaves on six aluminum foil squares, about 8 x 10 inches. Chop 2 or 3 extra leaves like slaw and combine with shrimp, onion, and salt and pepper. Spoon mixture onto collard or taro leaves and drizzle with coconut cream. Fold leaves over and then wrap aluminum foil securely. Bake for 1 hour.

Filipino Style Stuffed Meat Rolls

1 pound thin venison steak
1 cup olive oil
1 garlic clove, minced
$^1/_4$ pound ham, ground
$^1/_2$ pound ground sausage
1 onion, chopped
2 celery stalks, diced
stuffed olives

1 tsp. salt
$^1/_4$ cup vinegar
dash of ground pepper
2 hard-boiled eggs, sliced
$^1/_4$ cup sweet pickle relish
1 cup tomato, chopped
salt and pepper to taste
parsley

Cut venison into strips 1 inch wide and 6 inches long. Marinate in salt, olive oil, vinegar, garlic and pepper for 1 hour or more. Drain and spread with paste made from ground ham, sausage and egg slices. Roll each strip and skewer with toothpick. Save olives and parsley for garnish and combine remaining ingredients. Place mixture in pot and put meat rolls on top. Cover and simmer for 1$^1/_2$ hours or until meat is tender. Add a little water to pot if needed.

-- FILIPINO FAVORITES --

SHISH KEBAB - BBQ Pork On A Stick
PANSIT CANTON - Wheat Noodles
LUMPIA - Eggrolls (Beef/Vegetables)
PANSIT BIJON - Rice Noodles
ADOBO - Chicken/Pork/Beef In Brown Sauce
LECHON - Roast Pork With Sauce
CHICKEN TINOLA - Ginger Casserole Soup
CHICKEN CURRY - Chicken In Curry Powder w/Coconut Milk
BEEF KARE - Kare - Beef In Peanut Butter Sauce
AMPALAYA CON KARNE - Bitter Melon With Beef (Seasonal)
BAKARETTA - Pork/Beef Stew
PORK SINIGANG - Pork Knuckles In Guava Broth
PINAKBIT - Mixed Vegetables In Shrimp Paste
CRISPY PATA - Fried Pork Ham Hock
BEEF ASADO - Beef With Onions
DINUGUAN - Pork In Brown Sauce & Beef Blood
FRIED FISH - Marinated Fried
HUMBA - Pork Ham Hock In Brown Sauce
MONGO BEANS - With Spinach (Pork/Beef)
TORTANG TALONG - Eggplant Omelette
SOTANGHON - Rice noodle Soup

What Do You Do with a Dead Guinea?

Well, there it was. Right there in the middle of the road. A car had just zoomed past us in the opposite direction and there were still feathers floating in the air — guinea feathers. Their black and white polka-dotted pattern was unmistakable — an easy clue to follow. Besides, right there as we rounded the curve was the guinea. Immediately, that old song came to mind: "There's a dead skunk in the middle of the road, dead skunk in the middle of the road..." Remember it from back in the '60s? I pulled over and stopped and brother Chuck sauntered over and recovered the bird. We knew it was fresh because the "guilty" car had just flown by us. It was still dry in a misting rain, further confirming its freshness. Examination showed it to be undamaged, and when the feathers were cleared away there was only a small bruise where its neck was broken.

Chuck recovering the guinea.

Well, this wasn't a skunk, but rather one of those natural alarm clocks that some people keep around instead of watch dogs. You can't sneak up on a flock of guineas in a tree without them making a lot of noise, believe me. They are also the best non-poisonous weed killers around. Guineas make interesting birds to try to raise. They must be the cats of the bird world. They are so independent. You can keep them in a cage, like a cat in the house, but once they get out, it is *adios, sayonara*... see ya when I get back. They usually do come back, like a cat, but they go where they want to during the day.

Guineas are really called guinea fowl and come from Africa. They roost together in the trees at night if you will let them roam free. They also have communal nests. If you can ever find them, you will discover huge bowl-shaped nests with very hard-shelled little ping-pong-ball-shaped eggs — lots of them — all in one nest. If you have a dozen guineas, you might have a hundred eggs in one nest and the hens all take turns sitting on them. The feathers are treasured by fishermen for tying flies for trout and other fish. This one was destined for the pot — well, the oven, actually.

Stuffed Baked Guinea

1 guinea, cleaned	**stuffing mix**
Tropicana Twister juice concentrate	**salt and pepper to taste**
honey	

Rub cleaned guinea inside and out with salt and pepper to taste. Stuff with your choice of stuffing mix. Coat outside with honey and then with Tropicana Twister juice concentrate, undiluted. I usually use orange juice concentrate, but this time I went wild with orange-peach and it was tremendous. Bake covered in a 350 degree oven for 1 hour, basting once or twice. Remove cover and bake at 350 degrees 30-40 more minutes until done. Raise oven temperature to 400 for 10 minutes or so to brown the honey and juice on top of the meat.

Roasted guinea.

If you want, you can turn the bird once while it is baking to ensure complete cooking and browning. The guinea was a young one and very tasty. Guineas get *real* tough as they get old, suitable only for stew. Young ones are tender and delicate like all dark-meat chicken. We cooked this one with two cornish hens fixed the same way to make sure there was enough and in case the kids didn't want to eat it. They did, however.

The whole thing was a learning experience for the kids — you know: "Waste not; want not!" Also, when Chuck makes stuffing he has his daughter tear up the bread, getting her involved in the cooking process. When stuffing is being made, P.J. automatically assumes this duty.

Chuck's Stuffing Blend

bread, torn in chunks	**butter**
2 eggs, beaten	**2 onions, chopped**
salt and pepper to taste	**6-8 mushrooms, sliced**

Sauté the onion until tender in butter, lots of butter, and add the mushrooms. Put the bread chunks in a bowl and cover with the well-beaten eggs, the butter and onion mixture and mix well after you wash your hands. Stuff into both cavities of the bird and secure. Proceed with the baking or roasting.

Actually, this time I had some leftover rice — brown and wild mixed — and convinced Chuck to add it to the stuffing, with good results.

Giblet Gravy

giblets	**water to cover**
mushrooms, chopped	**flour**
salt and pepper to taste	**garlic salt to taste**

Boil the giblets — heart, liver, gizzard and neck — in water to cover until the meat is ready to come off the neck. Add mushrooms (and $\frac{1}{2}$ cup or so chopped onion) while boiling. Season to taste. Cool and pick neck meat off bones and discard the bones. Chop the liver and gizzard. When ready to make gravy, dissolve a half cup of flour in an equal amount of *cold* water, stirring to remove lumps. Pour into simmering giblet water and continue cooking until thick. You may add more water or flour and water as necessary.

A couple of days later we finished off the rest of the guinea in this recipe for cleaning out the refrigerator and making a delicious stew. Obviously, quantities and ingredients are flexible!

Pam Laudenslager's One-of-a-Kind Stew

guinea meat	Cornish game hen meat
frog leg meat	bear meat
pork and beef rib meat	chopped pork barbecue
bacon	Salisbury steaks, chunked
celery and onion	carrots and parsnips
green beans	broccoli
potatoes	oyster and chanterelle mushrooms
rice (3 kinds)	tomato sauce
horse mushrooms	

Chop the vegetables into suitable-sized portions and remove all the bones from the meat. Season with: fennel seed, chervil, basil, parsley, gumbo filé (sassafras leaves), wild-game seasoning blend and salt and pepper to taste. Use whatever spices (and other ingredients) you have on hand. Combine all ingredients in a large canning pot, adding water if necessary and slowly bring to a simmer. Allow to simmer slowly, cooking all day.

The stew was absolutely delicious and about three gallons disappeared in two meals!

The Real Roadkill Chapter

The first edition of my wild-foods cookbook became a runaway seller when a writer from the *Wall Street Journal* decided to use a single statement as his "hook" for getting readers to read the front page story he wrote about me, "The Screech of Tires Means a Tasty Meal For This Rural Chef." The statement was from my first book's introduction and said: "I am realistic, however, and many times the bottom line has been 'If I can't save them (animals injured in the road), I am going to sauté them!' I believe in that old Indian saying 'Waste not; want not,' and I think it is more ridiculous to waste free meat than to eat it. Yes, I eat roadkills, at times!"

P.J. and D.D. Laudenslager inspect roadkilled raccoon for ectoparasites.

I went on all sorts of television and radio programs, from religious programs in Iowa to CNN and all the local television stations, even Chevy Chase's syndicated talk show. So, when I was talking about a revision of the book with my editor at Loompanics, he insisted on a real roadkill chapter. After all, I had found out that there is a lot of interest out there in roadkills.

While working on the revised edition I was attending a class at Saint Andrews Presbyterian College called "Human Choices in Global Issues." My professor was Dr. Dennis McCracken, a biologist and environmentalist. He was also known to be a tough grader, and as looking for new ideas for research papers and presentations. Our senior paper had to deal in some way with the environment and be unique enough to get his attention if we wanted a good grade. I did, and came up with an idea that I thought was unique to me. After all, there can really only be one "Road Kill King." And because I am concerned about the environment, it was a challenge I was looking forward to.

Dr. McCracken had a beard, an ever-present smile that would have been labeled mischievous in a child, and there was always a twinkle in his eye as if he was thinking of some private joke. Overall, he gave the appearance of being, perhaps, the world's largest leprechaun! Getting a good grade would be easy. What follows is my paper as I submitted it. I got an A on the paper, an A for the presentation and an A in the course. So, like they say in the Army, "If it ain't broke — don't fix it!" Here is my paper. At the end I will go into a little more depth about identifying a good roadkill and making best use of it. In keeping with academic preferences, I wrote the paper from a third-person point of view.

MISSION IMPOSSIBLE:
Use the Roadkill Phenomenon to Defend the Environment

Many of us can remember the popular old television series *Mission Impossible* in which government agents with special skills were given assignments which were considered to be nearly impossible for these highly trained and motivated agents and absolutely impossible for normal humans, soldiers and civilians alike. They always started with a scenario of the crisis and then a mission statement. "Your mission, should you decide to accept it, is..."

Picture this: First a little theme music. *Dehn dehn de de dehn dehn...*

"The situation is this. The earth is being fast destroyed by the people who live on it. The skies are being polluted, the waters poisoned and the land laid barren or burned up with chemical compounds. Who knows what effects they have on our health as individual humans and as the human race, or what effect they will have on the health of our planet? Entire plant and animal communities and species are being threatened and destroyed. Animals are disappearing because there is no place for them to live and raise their young, no food to eat and no safe water. The problem is real, very real!

"To make matters worse, there is so much hype out there that the seriousness of the issue is being diminished by all the 'dog and pony show' doomsayers and publicity seekers. People are as tired of hearing about the environment as they are about abortion, smoking and gun control. They don't know what to believe, where to turn or what to do next.

"Your mission, should you decide to accept it, is to get people, the average citizen, to listen to an environmental message, to become earth stewards. It won't be easy. Too many cries of 'WOLF!' have already been heard. John Q. Public has been so bombarded with conflicting 'facts' that when the word 'environment' is spoken, the mind's switch goes to the 'off' position. Your message must be real, must be honest and must be subtle. To get their attention, you will have to become... the Roadkill King!"

All the while the mission statement is being given, video clips of environmental calamities are shown on a screen while a thin ribbon of tape turns between the reels of a tape player. That tape now flashes into smoke and self-destructs as we hear the music once more. *Dehn dehn de de dehn dehn...*

The scenario above is, of course, contrived. It could, however, have come "from today's news headlines" as all the made-for-television movies lifted from real life start out these days. There seems, for some reason, to be a roadkill phenomenon "out there." Roadkills as food are talked about on such prominent television shows as *Married With Children* and *Roseanne. The Beverly Hillbillies* movie made such a point of eating roadkilled squirrel that the segment was used in promoting the movie!

Jeff Eberbaugh wrote two *Road Kill Cooking* cookbooks, but they were simply spoofs — mostly in the form of poems.

Road Kill Nutrition

**The reason why hillbillies are so strong and stout
Is they know what road kill nutrition's about...
From the liver of the critters there's a lot of iron and steel
There's all kinds of goodies in a roadkill meal
Ya can't balance out your diet eatin' french fried frog
Ya need to eat some stir fry and scalded dog
If ya follow these instructions you'll be healthy all the time
But don't forget the whiskey and the muskydine wine."
(Eberbaugh, 1991)**

Jeff is a nurse and wrote the books as a lark. They aren't intended to be taken seriously and he tells us so in volume II. The foreword warns us: "When you look at this book, you will know it's not true. Nobody could eat what this book says they (Rednecks) do. It's really all fiction, but please take a look. I just wrote it all down and made it a book." (Eberbaugh, 1992) Jeff admits to writing the books purely in jest, but points out on the back cover of volume II: "Automobiles are responsible for the death of millions of wild and domestic animals on American highways each year. However, without road kills, there would be a great over-population of these animals, possibly resulting in starvation."

The Roadkill Gourmet.

Perhaps people have gotten more interested in roadkills because so many collisions are occurring between vehicles and deer. The *Moore County Citizen News-Record* of November 23, 1994, carried a story about two separate incidents in which cars were overturned trying to avoid collisions with deer. North Carolina Highway Patrol spokesperson, Vickie Mims, was quoted as saying: "We had 18 deer wrecks last week. They're doing megabucks in damage." (Wilson, 1994) That same day, an unattributed article in the *Pilot* of Southern Pines reported that 20 deer were killed by cars and said that "hunters are taking a back seat to motorists when it comes to decimating the deer population this year...In most of the accidents the deer were either killed or severely injured." (*Pilot*, 1994)

Across the country, gift shops sell what is purported to be canned roadkilled animal parts — mostly, 'possum or armadillo. One can from "Armadillo Recyclers" of Texas tells us that the armadillo was "killed on a highway near North Zulch, Texas, by an 18-wheeler" and that we can trust it to be "not more than 10% gravel and shell." From Mark Makers of Nashville we find a "Tennessee Road Kill Crew, Brown Bag Lunch offering a Moon Pie, an RC Cola and a can of Flynn's Cove Possum Stew." The can advises that "these beautiful critters thrive in the great state of Tennessee, but fortunately for us they are so dumb they get run over. This natural process makes the possum meats tender and delicious." 'Possums are apparently tougher than armadillos as far as the meat is concerned, because although the animal is "pure-mountain grown possum killed by an 18-wheeler on I-40," it is also "tenderized by at least 10 cars." We are told to "watch for our gourmet brand guaranteed to be run over by a late-model Cadillac." This may come into play later as the media attempts to change Tom Squier's image from "Road Kill King" to "Road Kill Gourmet!"

It can be seen that the majority of products on the market attempt to make a joke of roadkill eating and are not to be taken seriously. Jeff Eberbaugh, the poet laureate of roadkills, offers a cooking apron which states that "ROAD KILLS" are "Not Just For Breakfast Anymore" and depicts a 'possum in the road, behind which appears a sign bearing the words "Dead End." Gag Foods, Incorporated markets a box of pasta noodles called "Roadkill Helper" which spoofs the "Hamburger Helper" products on the market, popular with cooks in a hurry or with little culinary skills.

They say the product is "Made For Laughs, *Not For Consumption,*" and refer to it as "Macaroni and Sleaze Sauce." Their box does warn, tongue-in-cheek, that "there are no guarantees this time around." Road Kill Cafe T-shirts and hats of various designs abound, although there is no real eating establishment of that name. One fire department in Vermont does raise money each year with its Annual Roadkill Supper, but for the most part the market is a gag market when roadkills are involved.

One entrepreneur offers a "Road Kill Bingo" game in which the object is to put your marker on various dead animals until you fill the spaces in a traditional diagonal or straight-line bingo win. *Flattened Fauna* is a pseudo-scientific guide although its subtitle calls it *A Field Guide to Common Animals of Roads, Streets, and Highways*. The author, Roger M. Knutson, tells us "This book is about animals that, like the Wicked Witch of the West in *The Wizard of Oz*, are not merely dead, but really most sincerely dead... Dead and flattened animals on the road are a part of the common experience of all Americans, from the family on a drive in the country to the daily commuter travelling the same route 250 days each year, or from the bike rider on the quiet park road to the professional truck driver who spends hundreds of hours per month on our major highways... With *Flattened Fauna* in hand, a Sunday drive can become a safari into a new habitat populated with animals unlike those you have seen before." (Knutson, 1987) In the manner of other field guides the author shows photos of the silhouettes of dead animals along with biological "facts" about their "habits and abundance" and their "field marks and range." It is entertaining, if not scientific.

The author and daughter Jessica admire a roadkill (porcupine) in Maine.

There is also a special "Glove Compartment Edition" of *Road Kill "Goremet Cooking"* on the market which bears a sandwich-board sign like those on which cafes advertise their specials. However, this one hawks, "Meals From Under Wheels." Author Richard Marcou tells us that "All over North America, the world for that matter, hundreds of thousands of families are finding it ever more difficult to make ends meet; the highest single cost after the monthly commitment for a roof over one's head is the monthly food bill. At the very same time, hundreds of thousands of animals are killing themselves by coming into contact with moving vehicles on national highways, residential streets, country back roads and lanes. Approximately 193 million pounds of meat go unclaimed, not to mention the considerable amount of protein going to waste." (Marcou, 1987) It doesn't take a rocket scientist to put two and two together, but for our benefit the author concludes: "We would strongly suggest it's time hungry families and those wanting to increase their disposable incomes be shown how to benefit from the carnage on our highways. We feel the lack of available information on the subject has been the reason the two remain apart. This void has now been finally filled with the exciting publication of *How to Cook Roadkill 'Goremet Cooking.'*" Marcou is probably more excited about sharing his "*gore*-met" recipes like, "18-Wheelers Delight — Hub Cap-O-Soup," than readers will be about trying them!

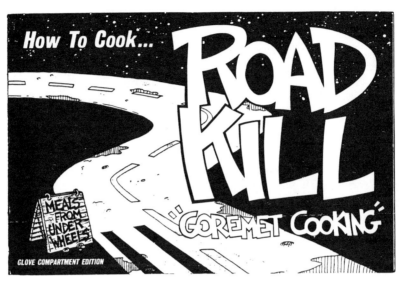

Tom Squier wrote what he called a "legitimate" wild-foods cookbook in 1992. He called it the *Living Off The Land Wild Foods Cookbook*. It was a collection of recipes for game and fish, wild fruits and berries. It was reviewed by Pat Robertson of the statewide South Carolina newspaper *The State* in an article titled "Book Helps Find Feasts In Places Others Overlook," and was a good synopsis of the book. "The average cook," Robertson wrote, "might not find much use for Squier's book, but the game cook will find it fascinating, and many of the recipes are downright mouth-watering." (Robertson, 1993)

In the book, Squier wrote about his work in the Army's SERE (Survival, Evasion, Resistance, Escape) School where he taught military and State Department personnel how to both avoid and survive the rigors of becoming a POW (Prisoner of War). He told about his classes, stating "it was ridiculous to waste free meat," and clarifying that statement with, "Yes, I eat roadkills, at times." (Squier, 1992)

It wasn't the first time he had made that declaration in print. A 1988 interview with John Meyers, editor of the *Moore County Citizen News-Record* ran under the headline, "Surviving In the Sandhills No Problem For Expert." Meyers featured Squier and his classes at the survival school, as well as his background. One of the classes, "Preparation of Fish and Game," taught soldiers how to fix animals into food once they had captured or killed them. It wasn't a lecture class, but what the Army calls "performance-oriented training." First you see it at normal speed; then after you see it done step-by-step, you do it on your own. In this case, the "grade" was ending up with an edible product to make into a meal. Students got a goat or two for the class, occasionally a deer, and chickens or rabbits individually. "One of my (SERE) classes had a special sign made up for my car. It says, 'Caution. I Brake For Roadkills.' That's what I feed my classes," Squier told Meyers. It pretty much went unnoticed. (Meyers, 1988)

The remark in the cookbook went unnoticed for a while, too. Eventually, articles and regular reviews led to a little sporadic attention. A feature story on Squier appeared in the magazine *Men's Health*. It was titled "Walk the Wild Life," and author Mark Canter actually came and spent some time in the woods with Squier. He wrote: "Meeting Tom Squier is like returning to an age when men called the forests home. Flying low over eight lanes of rush-hour Atlanta traffic on the way back home, it's good to know that wildmen like Thomas Squier still carry on a tradition of self-reliance." (Canter, 1991) After the book came out, it was read by a columnist named Robert Tomsho, staff writer for *The Wall Street Journal*. With all the recipes, anecdotes and nature lore to focus on, that one line, "Yes, I eat roadkills, at times!" caught his eye. It was the hook that Tomsho used in his front-page *Wall Street Journal* article. He called it "The Screech of Tires Means a Tasty Meal For This Rural Chef." (Tomsho, 1993) Instantly, Tom Squier became the Road Kill King! He appeared on CNN, the Canadian Broadcasting System and on countless local television shows as well as some 50 radio broadcasts, some via phone and some live in the studios. John Boy and Billy brought him to Charlotte, North Carolina and their syndicated show, along with his television appearances and many newspaper stories ("So many I can't count them all!" Squier said.) helped make the book a best-seller. It seemed like the name Road Kill King was going to stick, and it has to a large degree. But Chevy Chase tried to change that when he asked Squier to come on his show and cook a roadkilled rattlesnake. Squier did, with Chase's assistance, in a moment to remember. Chevy Chase gave him an autographed photo which read, "Thanks, Tom, You Were Great!" and quipped, "You don't think people will take that wrong, do you?" Chase and *T.V. Guide* billed Squier as a "Road Kill Gourmet." In the *Pilot*, Claudia Madeley wrote: "The ex-Green Beret serves on the Moore County Environmental Quality Advisory Board and is the recipient of numerous awards and honors." (Madeley, 1992)

There it is — the link between the "Road Kill King" and the environment. Squier has been an environmentalist all his life, and was recognized by the Governor of North Carolina as the state's "Conservationist" in 1983 and by the Woodmen of the World as Conservationist of the Year in 1984. Being an earth steward was nothing new. Squier is in *Who's Who of the South* and *Who's Who of the World* as an "environmentalist and educator." (Marquis, 1994) Now, with all this attention, Squier could tell others how to protect and care for the earth he loves so much. All sorts of groups military and civic, church and scout groups, garden clubs and service agencies asked him to come and talk about being the Road Kill King, and Squier did. The talk always got around, however, to what people could do for the environment.

John Boy, the author, and Billy give roadkill a "thumbs-up."

I'm Chevy Chase... and you're not!

Word spread and Squier was asked to do a 90-second spot for the PBS station, WUNC to promote Earth Day 1994. It was produced by reporter Beth Hardee, who spent the afternoon with Squier at his home, and when it aired on April 21, it turned out to be nearly 15 minutes long. Shown on WUNC's *North Carolina Now* news program, the segment was introduced by the show's co-host Audrey Bailey. She said, "Tomorrow is Earth Day, one day set aside to create environmental awareness. Since 1970, conservationists have been celebrating this day." Her partner, John Bason added, "Tonight Elizabeth Hardee introduces

The author and Beth Hardee.

us to Tom Squer, an environmentalist from Aberdeen who celebrates the earth every day. Squier doesn't believe in wasting anything, including dead animals along the road."

Reporter Elizabeth Hardee introduced Squier saying, "Some people claim to be environmentalists, eager to conserve and preserve. Then there's Tom Squier. This earth steward believes it's a crime to waste anything. Squier picks up trash and yes, even *roadkills!*" The segment continued with the two looking in Squier's freezer at frozen, dead animals, squirrels and rattlesnakes. They toured Squier's property looking at plants and animals and then went for a ride and walk in some woods not far away. Squier laughed because Hardee didn't recognize juniper berries as the flavoring for gin. "Well, good for you," he said. Laughing, he noted, "A lot of the old soldiers say, 'Yeah I know that flavor'." Later, Hardee talked about eating roadkills again, and mused, "Is there anything he won't eat? Well, Squier isn't crazy about sea gulls, hot dogs or 'possum!"

"I believe people should have the right to hunt," Squier told Hardee, "as long as they do it in an ethical and conservative manner." This story was about Earth Day, though, so she steered the conversation back to that topic, saying "The dangers, according to Squier, are that many people don't realize that nature's resources are limited and that individuals really can create change."

Squier points out, "Some people think, 'Well why waste your time? What difference does it make, because everybody else is destroying the earth? What difference are you gonna make?' You can really go out and do some good for the world — one person can do something."

"Recycled tires and plastic buckets decorate Squier's yard," explained Hardee. "Squirrels and birds have made them their home."

"I think if people would just go and lie in the yard on their stomachs," Squier said, "forget about the fax machines and the computers, and smell the dirt — some people have no idea what dirt smells like, what a real carrot smells like — I think if they get closer to the earth, that they'll be more concerned about the earth because it'll mean more to them."

The King of roadkill displays his spoils.

As the segment continued, Hardee stood over a dead raccoon she found along the side of the road. If it was fresh, Squier would have eaten it, as his recipe for Crockpot Coon Stew attests, but Hardee commented: "You may be saying, 'Sure, I'm willing to do my part to help save the earth, but there is no way I'm going to eat weeds or look for my dinner along the side of the road.' But don't worry. Remember, there are other alternatives that we all could do to help preserve the environment." Squier talked about some of those alternatives, proving this may not be such a mission impossible as the story continued.

"Recycle and use recycled goods. Compost your waste rather than throw it away. Find a way to do that. Don't throw things on the landscape. Maybe get involved actively in the program to 'Adopt-A-Highway,' and go out with your church group, school group or business. Tell kids *why* you're doing things for the earth, explain the importance to them and get them involved. Maybe get your children involved with planting a tree. And grow something. Start a little garden, even if it's just a couple of tomato plants in a pot on the back porch. Plant something you can nurture and be closer to nature, even if it's containerized. The more you do to get closer to nature, the more you'll do to try to take care of it.

"We have to protect the earth better so that we're not...(long pause)...oxygen thieves. That's a phrase they use in the Army to describe useless people. We can't be oxygen thieves. We have to be productive, caring people and nurture the earth."

Beth Hardee concluded, "The challenge goes out across the state," but it really goes out across the world. We can all do something, together and one at a time.

Audrey Bailey closed the segment, saying: "When you first hear Tom's ways, you may be slightly taken aback by his methods, but there's a very serious message to his madness!"

Eating yucca blossoms for CNN.

In the CNN broadcasts, edited by Brian Cabell, Squier was interviewed by reporter Rick Ricks. Squier told Ricks, "When I see a dead deer on the side of the road, or a rabbit, and I'm not talking about a squashed one, but a basically whole animal that just happened to die on a bumper or the side of a vehicle, I think it's a sin to throw that food away. That's basically what people are doing." So how can you tell if it is fresh or safe enough to eat?

In the *Wall Street Journal* piece by Rob Tomsho, Squier advised that roadkills "keep longer in the winter, and the freshest ones are those found on a stretch of highway passed... earlier." When you go to town and don't see any animals on the road on the way in, but they are there on the way home, they haven't been there very long. Hunters, farmers and even kids with 4-H animal projects are familiar with what a freshly dead animal looks like. If you see it get hit, or if you are the one who actually has the deer-truck collision, you *know* it is fresh, maybe *too* damned fresh!

You can use the same general guidelines for checking roadkills as you do for checking the freshness of fish in the store. According to *Sea Food Cookery* by Lily Haxworth Wallace, "Be sure that it is absolutely fresh; this means that it will be free from strong odor, with red gills, clear bright eyes, and firm elastic flesh." (Wallace, 1964) Naturally, roadkills don't have gills, but the eyes and nose of a roadkilled animal can tell you a great deal about its condition. They should be full and clear. The moister they are, the fresher your meat, because in hot weather the eyes and nose dry quickly. In cold weather they will freeze. In very cold weather, the eyes will turn white as they freeze. When you cut into freshly-killed roadkill flesh, it bleeds freely and with a bright color, except of course where bruises result from impact.

A lifelong environmental ethic as well as a habit of eating roadkills will make the mission of educating the public about caring for the earth by being the Road Kill King very possible and a lot of fun.

[End of paper.]

Everybody in class stood up and clapped after my presentation and it made me feel proud to be "The Roadkill King." I showed clips of some of the news broadcasts to give my presentation a kind of multimedia approach. One of my favorites comes from the CNN broadcast. They had stopped in Fayetteville to interview Thomas Pope, who is a sports writer for the *Fayetteville Observer Times*. He was the person I submitted my columns to for three or four years. Thomas had this to say: "He'll eat anything. He says there's some things he won't eat, but I'm not so sure about that!"

I am not going to give you a bunch of recipes here because you can use any recipe with a roadkill that you can use with any other meat. One reporter, Don Ross from Durham's WTVD, asked if the meat's flavor isn't changed by the rubber in the tire. Later he jokingly quipped for the camera, when eating some roadkilled squirrel which we'd barbecued, that he could "taste Goodyear with just a hint of diesel fuel." If there are tire marks destroying the meat, we don't fool with it. Like I already stated — no "road pizzas!" It is important to note, however, that with a large animal like a deer or moose, there is almost always some good meat in the large rear hams and along the backbone where the tenderloin is found, even if the animal looks destroyed at first sight.

Roadkilled meat can be better for you than store-bought meat; there is definite proof of that. It is mostly game, although I once salvaged two pigs that had fallen off a truck and been run over by the car behind it. Game and wild meat tends to be higher in protein and leaner, so it is less fatty and lower in cholesterol in most cases. It definitely lacks the steroids, growth hormones and antibiotics that some store-bought beef and other meats contain, isn't filled with preservatives, and doesn't float around in a vat of chicken dookie for hours like we have seen on some of those news shows.

You have to use common sense when using roadkilled animals for food. You need to know when it was killed, if possible, and how badly it is damaged (if it is damaged at all.) In the summertime and in the southern states where it is hot, an animal will spoil more quickly than where it is cold. In the winters up north, an animal may last for days or weeks if the temperature doesn't get above freezing. The meat freezes so hard that you have to partially thaw it in a shed or kitchen to even skin it. In Montana, I have encountered antelope and elk that were killed by trains and frozen so hard they could be stood up on their icy legs!

You have to use all your senses, too. Look at some freshly killed animals and see what their blood looks like, their eyes and their mouth. Freshly dead warm-blooded animals have limbs that are flexible, protruding eyes, moist eyes and noses and "lifelike"-looking fur or feathers. An animal can be killed during or after a storm, and its fur will stay natural-looking for a few hours. An animal that was already dead when it started raining will end up looking like the proverbial "drowned rat." A deer killed on a very cold night will be stiff in the morning when it gets light enough to see it on the side of the road, but in hot weather, stiff limbs — rigor mortis — means you probably can only use the animal for dog food and perhaps save its fur.

With practice it is a very easy thing to determine the freshness of a roadkilled carcass. Let's face it, times are getting tougher, and with the economy like it is, roadkilled meat can be a blessing. As the largest and most common predator in the food chain across most of our country, we need to make wise use of these FORD animals.

No Connection Between Squire's Pub and Squier's Grub

People have asked me several times since the restaurant called The Squire's Pub opened its doors on Highway 1 in Southern Pines if I had anything to do with the place. It never occurred to me that people might be asking the people at the restaurant the same question until I had a chat with the owner and manager recently. Scott Dawson was very nice about the way he stated it, but I got the impression that some people might be a little hesitant about eating there if they thought I might be supplying the meat. I stopped there to start with because they had a big sign out front which invited patrons to try their Harvest Specials including roasted quail and venison stew.

The author eats here... but he doesn't provide the food!

We don't even spell our names the same way, although some of my father's cousins and uncles (mine, too, I guess) spell their name the traditional way like you see it at The Squire's Pub. We, in my family line, spell with the "e" before the "r" rather than after. Makes for some funny pronunciations.

I wanted to see if they would share their recipes for game dishes with me, since we are in the middle of the harvest month and this is an area with a lot of hunters. Scott Dawson didn't insist that I disassociate myself from the Pub, but he did insist that I be certain to tell you that all the game he uses comes from government-inspected purveyors of farm-raised game animals — just like the meat in the grocery stores. He wanted to be sure there would be no misunderstanding that people were perhaps selling meat that hadn't been inspected or was killed and prepared under less-than-sanitary conditions. He must have seen some of our hunters dragging their meat into the kitchen covered with leaves, or heard about it from their wives!

Here is the recipe that The Squire's Pub uses to prepare their version of venison stew, which feeds more than 40 people and would be perfect for church socials and hunt club suppers at the end of the season.

Venison Stew

1 lb. margarine	1 lb. bacon, diced
4 bay leaves	20 pounds venison stew meat
$\frac{1}{2}$ cup garlic, chopped	3 large onions, julienne cut
1$\frac{1}{2}$ tbsps. thyme leaves	1 tbsp. rosemary leaves
2 cups sifted flour	2 cans condensed chicken consommé
3 (consommé) cans water	4 cups Irish Stout (beer/ale)
1 cup parsley, chopped	2 lbs. carrots, sliced
1 lb. celery, diced	4 lbs. red bliss potatoes, diced
2 lbs. mushrooms, sliced	2 lbs. field peas
1 tbsp. beef soup base	2 tbsps. black pepper

Marinate the venison stew meat overnight with the Irish Stout. Prior to preparation drain the stout from the meat and save the liquid for later use. Heat a large rondo kettle over high heat for 3 or 4 minutes. Using the hot rondo kettle will make browning of the following ingredients easy. Add the margarine and bacon and cook until a light golden brown, *do not burn*. Add the meat and brown completely over high heat, *stirring frequently to prevent sticking or burning*. Add the julienned onions and cook until clear. Reduce the heat. Add garlic, rosemary, thyme, bay leaves and flour and stir in well. Cook for about 8 minutes and then add the chicken consommé, water and Irish Stout reserved from above. Bring to a low simmer for about 30 minutes. Once the mixture begins to thicken, add the remaining ingredients and simmer on low heat for about 1 hour or until tender. Adjust consistency with water if needed. Adjust salt and pepper as needed. Stir often to prevent sticking.

Scott Dawson said that normally when searching for a perfect recipe, they will check three or four cookbooks for recipes for the same dish, cook them all, and then have them taste-tested by him and his wife and the employees. If necessary, they will adjust and modify a recipe to their own needs, like the venison stew recipe. What a great idea. Some recipes are used straight out of the book they find them in, like this one.

Jugged Hare

4-5 pound hare, jointed	3 tbsps. flour
3 tbsps. bacon drippings	2 onions, sliced
$\frac{1}{2}$ cup bacon, diced	2$\frac{1}{2}$ cups light game stock
4 tbsps. mixed sweet herbs	$\frac{1}{2}$ tsp. mace
1 tbsp. cloves	

Flour the pieces of hare (rabbit) and brown them in the bottom of a Dutch oven or deep fireproof jug, in the bacon drippings; remove the pieces when browned, add the onions and brown them, and then add the bacon. Replace the hare and add the stock, cloves, mixed herbs and mace. Bring to a boil, then reduce the heat and simmer gently for 2-3 hours, or until tender.

That recipe comes straight from one of Mr. Dawson's favorite cookbooks — *Seven Hundred Years of English Cooking* by Maxime McKendry. Another he likes a lot for the harvest special recipes is the *L.L. Bean Game and Fish Cookbook* by Angus Cameron and Judith Jones.

The recipe for the roasted quail is one that he devised himself through trial and error, and sounds good. You marinate and baste the quail in a lemon juice and honey combination, and before roasting, dust them with a mixture of rosemary, onion powder, thyme, paprika, and white pepper.

A lot of people are eating game these days, and seeing it on the menu in a quality restaurant elevates its status as "real" food, not just for country people and the poor.

If you aren't inclined to hunt for your own quail, venison or hare, you can order them through the mail these days by calling Dale's Exotic Foods at 1-800-BUY-WILD and telling them what you want. Not only do they have venison, quail and rabbit, they offer rattlesnake, alligator, buffalo and other exotics such as ostrich and bear. If "escargot" or snails is as fancy or gourmet as you want to go, you can order them through Ralph Tucker and the Snail Club of America at 4849 North Seventy Street, #R, Fresno, CA 93726 or 1-209-224-7728.

Afterword

As the book draws to a conclusion, I have drawn some conclusions of my own — a lot of people are eating roadkills, many more are fascinated by the idea and virtually everybody is at least mildly curious, even if repulsed by the idea of "finding my dinner by the side of the road," as reporter Beth Hardee remarked. You *can* eat roadkilled animals if you just apply a little common sense. Heck, with practice, you can get good at it. You can feed it to other people without their knowledge and they won't know the difference. While working on this closing chapter, my wife asked for some "tamale pie." I made it with roadkilled venison which I ground in the kitchen. She said it was good. It's simple to make — layers of cheese, ground meat, salsa, onions and mushrooms and a crust of either crushed corn chips or corn bread.

I have a friend in West Virginia, named Maxine. She's another alumni of *The John Boy and Billy Show*, only uses one name and answers all the mail she gets. When it's Christmas time, send her a card to add to her collection. One year she got around 1,200 — and sent that many back. Maxine writes backwards, speaks a West Virginia dialect she invented that rearranges the syllables in words, and is an immigration officer — even though she's in her seventies, according to reports. Send a Christmas card to: Maxine, 812 Summers Street, Hinton, WV 29591. Here is her Christmas poem from 1994. If you hold it to the mirror you can read it. Note the last two lines apply to any hungry person — roadkill eater or not. "All I wish for is a set of teeth, so I can eat me a X'mas dinner."

Please Wish Me A Merry X'Mas
By Maxine

Would someone wish me a Merry X'Mas,
I ain't got no friends "a-tall".
My one and only car friend, just fell dead in the hall.
My mom and pop are gone, my sisters have moved away,
My hair is long and shaggy and I shave every other day.
My socks are full of holes, my jacket has worn thin,
I can tell I'm losing weight, 'cause I see I end where I begin.
My pants are worn & ragged from wrestlin' with the pup,
I look like I'm sitting down, when actually I'm standing up.
I don't care if I got no clothes, and am slowly getting thinner,
All I wish for is a set of teeth, so I can eat a X'Mas dinner.

Love y'all - Maxine

In one of her letters, Maxine wrote "what a nice surprise hearing from the roadkill guy." She enclosed one of her favorite roadkill poems, "Road Toad Ala Mode," which comes from one of Jeff Eberbaugh's books. Thanks Maxine.

ROAD TOAD - ALA MODE
TAKE A BUCKET FULL OF TOADS FROM A NEARBY STREET
GREEN TOADS ARE BETTER CAUSE THEY HAVE BETTER MEAT
MAKE UP A PIE SHELL OR BUY IT AT THE STORE
YOU CAN MAKE YOURSELF ONE OR EVEN THREE OR FOUR
LET EM COOK IN THE OVEN AND SIT BACK AND DROOL
PUT EM ON THE WINDOW SILL AND LET THE PIES COOL
ADD SOME HOMEMADE ICE CREAM - VANILLA OR PEACH
TOAD PIE GROWS ON YA LIKE A BLOOD SUCKIN LEECH.

"I ain't very pretty, but I am stylish."

Hopefully, this book will make others aware of the wonders, visual and culinary, that nature has to offer. I hope that we will all do something about taking care of our earth for our children and theirs.

Two of the greatest gifts I ever received were related to learning. My grandfather instilled in my soul a yearning to know all I could about the world around me that has maybe saved my life a time or two. You can never stop learning. I know I don't, and I'm an *expert* — the government says so! When I was a small child, two of my grandfather's friends were retired missionaries, Mr. Henry and Miss Elizabeth Bottomly. They were the kindest souls I ever met, and they loved the printed word. They had books everywhere, and taught me to read when I was only four. Later I skipped a grade in school. Books have always been my friends. We need to get our own kids in the book habit and away from the Nintendo machines.

ST. ANDREWS COLLEGE

Pembroke
State
University

OF THE UNIVERSITY OF NORTH CAROLINA

We all need all the education we can get. There is nothing wrong with "book learning" as long as you aren't "educated beyond your intelligence," like we used to say about lieutenants.

If you really want to know about living off the land, if you really want to be close to nature and comfortable in the woods, you have to put in what Tom Brown, the Tracker, calls "dirt time." You'll be a better person for it.

The author digging up wild onions in his backyard.

"TOM'S KITCHEN."

References and Recommended Reading

Ausband, Terry, *Cooking With Just Herbs,* Just Herbs, 185 Big Creek Road, Marshall, NC 28753, 1991.

Brown, Tom, Jr., *Tom Brown's Field Guide to Edible and Medicinal Wild Plants,* Berkley Books, NY, 1985.

Eberbaugh, Jeff, *Road Kill Cooking Gourmet Style, Road Kill Cooking Redneck Style,* Unique Publications, P.O. Box 13592, Sissonville, WV 25360. $9.95 each postpaid.

Gail, Peter, *The Dandelion Celebration,* Goosefoot Acres Press, P.O. Box 18016, Cleveland, OH 44118-0016, 1994.

McDermott, Mike, *Venison Processing: A Meatcutter's Way,* (video) Ryebrook Productions, 7461 Ryebrook, Rockford, IL, 61111.

Meyer, Paul, *Nature Guide to the Carolina Coast,* Avian-Cetacean Press, P.O. Box 4532, Wilmington, NC 28406, $15.95 postpaid, 1991.

New York Conservation Officers Cookbook, NY Conservation Officers Assn., P.O. Box 698, Stony Brook, NY 11790-0698. $9 postpaid.

Newman, Paul, *Newman's Own Cookbook,* compiled by Ursula Hotchner & Nell Newman, Contemporary Books, Inc., Chicago, 1985.

Nugent, Ted, *Blood Trails: The Truth About Bowhunting,* Ted Nugent World Bowhunters, Jackson, MI 1991.

Peterson, Lee Allen, *A Field Guide to Edible Wild Plants,* Houghton Mifflin Co., Boston, 1977.

Phillips, John E., *Masters' Secrets of Catfishing,* Nighthawk Publishing Company, P.O. Drawer 375, Fairfield, AL 35064, $11.95 postpaid, 1993.

Reppert, Bertha, *A Heritage of Herbs,* Remembrance Press, 120 So. Market St., Mechanicsburg, PA 17055, 1990 printing.

Rosso, Julee, *Great Good Food,* Crown Publishers, Inc., New York, 1993.

Shufer, Vickie, editor, *The Wild Foods Forum,* P.O. Box 61413, Virginia Beach, VA 32462.

Slick, Rosemary Gladstar, *The Science and Art of Herbology,* (correspondence or residence course) SAGE, P.O. Box 420, E. Barre, VT 05649.

Stark, Debra, *Round-The-World Cooking at the Natural Gourmet.* Keats Publishing, Inc., New Canaan, CT 1994.

Troy, Jim, editor, *Coltsfoot,* Box 313A, Shipman, VA 22971.

Composition of Foods, USDA, Agricultural Handbook #8, Washington, DC, 1975.

Van Atta, Marian, editor, *Living Off The Land: A Subtropical Newsletter,* P.O. Box 2131, Melbourne, FL 32902-2131.

Willoughby, Jim and Sue, *Cactus Country,* Golden West Publishers, 4113 N. Longview Avenue, Phoenix, AZ 85014, 1993.

Wilson, Justin, *Justin Wilson's Homegrown Louisiana Cookin'*, MacMillan Publishing Co., NY, 1990.

Wood, Edelene, *A Taste of the Wild*, Allegheny Press, Elgin, PA 16413, 1990.

Index

Venison *continued*
    Venison Stroganoff, 242
    Venison Tongue, 230
    Western-style Game Omelet, 6
Vitamins,
    A, 1
    B, 1
    C, 1
    E, 1

W

Walnuts, 47, 200
Weed soup, 10
Weeds,
    sheep sorrel, 31
Wild Onion Soup, 221
Wine
    Dandelion Wine, 66
    Dock Wine, 180
    Jack Van Atta's Cactus Pear Wine,
      42
Woodchuck,
    Stewed Woodchuck, 243

Y

Yams,
    "'Coon" With Yams, 240
    Roasted Yams with Maple Sauce,
      203
Yellowjacket Soup, 232

Z

Zucchini, 91

YOU WILL ALSO WANT TO READ:

"Yes, there are book about the skills of apocalypse —spying, surveillance, fraud, wiretapping, smuggling, self-defense, lockpicking, gunmanship, eavesdropping, car chasing, civil warfare, surviving jail, and dropping out of sight. Apparently writing books is the way mercenaries bring in spare cash between wars. The books are useful, and it's good the information is freely available (and they definitely inspire interesting dreams), but their advice should be taken with a salt shaker or two and all your wits. A few of these volumes are truly scary. Loompanics is the best of the Libertarian suppliers who carry them. Though full of 'you'll-wish-you'd-read-these-when-it's-too-late' rhetoric, their catalog is genuinely informative."
— **The Next Whole Earth Catalog**

THE BEST BOOK CATALOG IN THE WORLD!!!

We offer hard-to-find books on the world's most unusual subjects. Here are a few of the topics covered IN-DEPTH in our exciting new catalog:

- *Hiding/Concealment of physical objects! A complete section of the best books ever written on hiding things.*
- *Fake ID/Alternate Identities! The most comprehensive selection of books on this little-known subject ever offered for sale! You have to see it to believe it!*
- *Investigative/Undercover methods and techniques! Professional secrets known only to a few, now revealed to you to use! Actual police manuals on shadowing and surveillance!*
- *And much, much more, including Locks and Locksmithing, Self-Defense, Intelligence Increase, Life Extension, Money-Making Opportunities, Human Oddities, Exotic Weapons, Sex, Drugs, Anarchism, and more!*

Our book catalog is 290 pages, 8½ x 11, packed with over 800 of the most controversial and unusual books ever printed! You can order every book listed! Periodic supplements keep you posted on the LATEST titles available!!! Our catalog is $5.00, including shipping and handling.

Our book catalog is truly THE BEST BOOK CATALOG IN THE WORLD! Order yours today. You will be very pleased, we know.

LOOMPANICS UNLIMITED
PO BOX 1197
PORT TOWNSEND, WA 98368
USA

Now accepting Visa and MasterCard. For credit card orders *only*, call 1-800-380-2230 between 9am and 4pm, PST, Monday thru Friday.

Tom Squier's

LIVING OFF THE LAND

Classes

• Herbology • Children's Nature Study •
• Edible, Medicinal and Poisonous Plants •
• Environmental Awareness • Survival •

4925 Ashmont Road, Aberdeen, NC 28315 (910) 281-4732